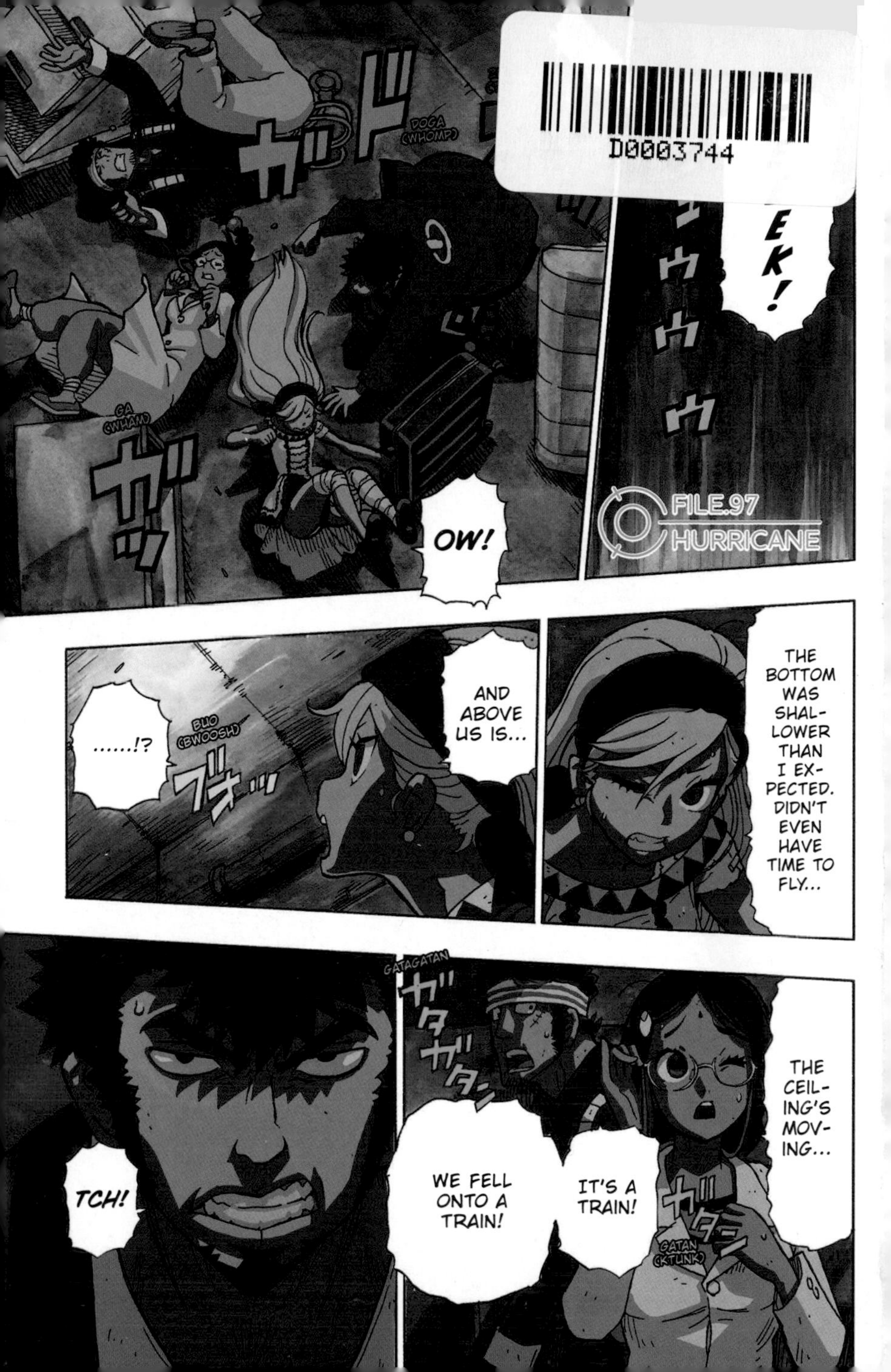
EK!
FILE.97
HURRICANE
DOGA (WHOMP)
GA (WHAM)
OW!
THE BOTTOM WAS SHALLOWER THAN I EXPECTED. DIDN'T EVEN HAVE TIME TO FLY...
AND ABOVE US IS...
BUO (BWOOSH)
......!?
THE CEILING'S MOVING...
GATAN (KTUNK)
IT'S A TRAIN!
WE FELL ONTO A TRAIN!
GATAGATAN
TCH!

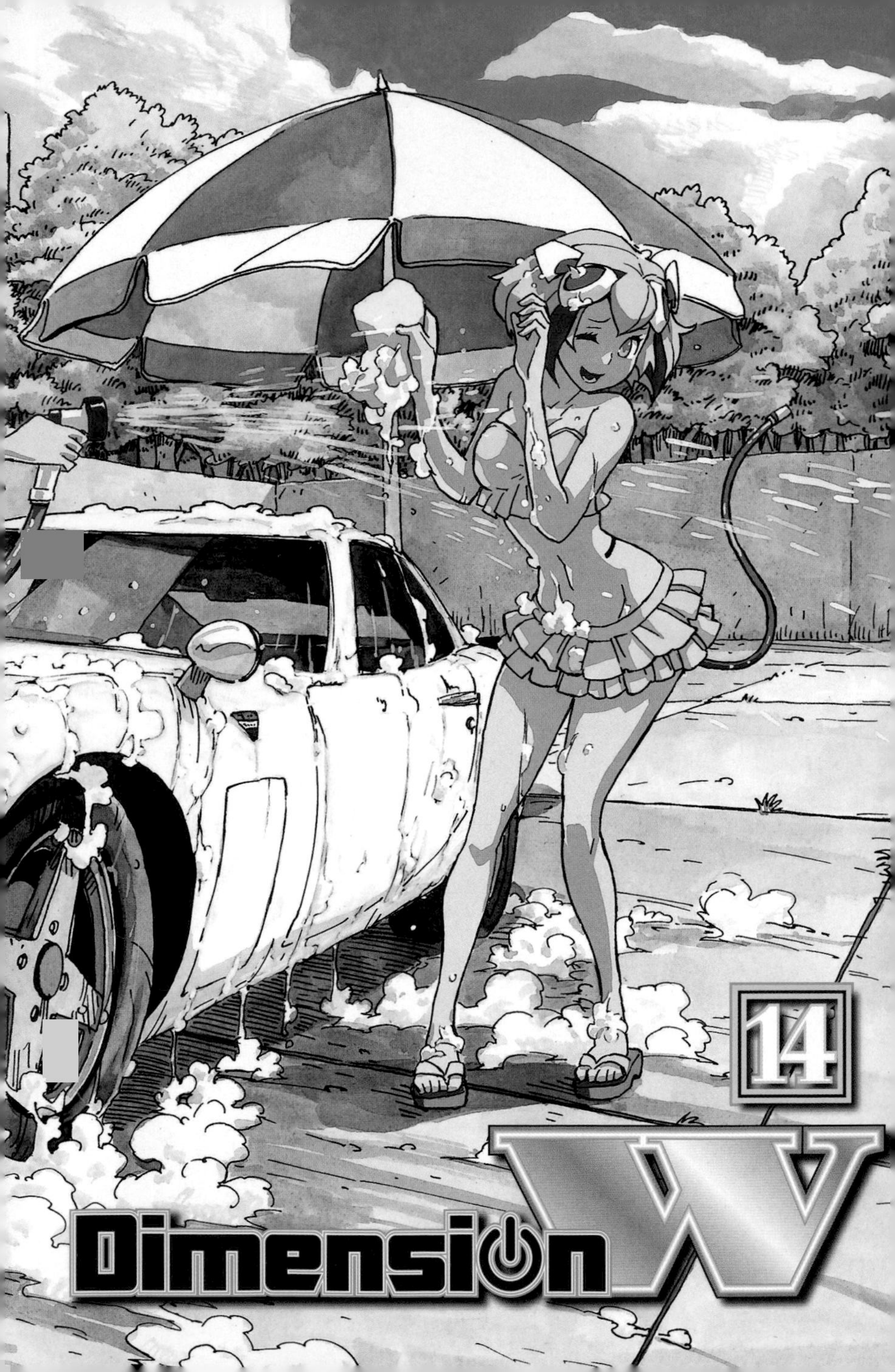
14
Dimension W

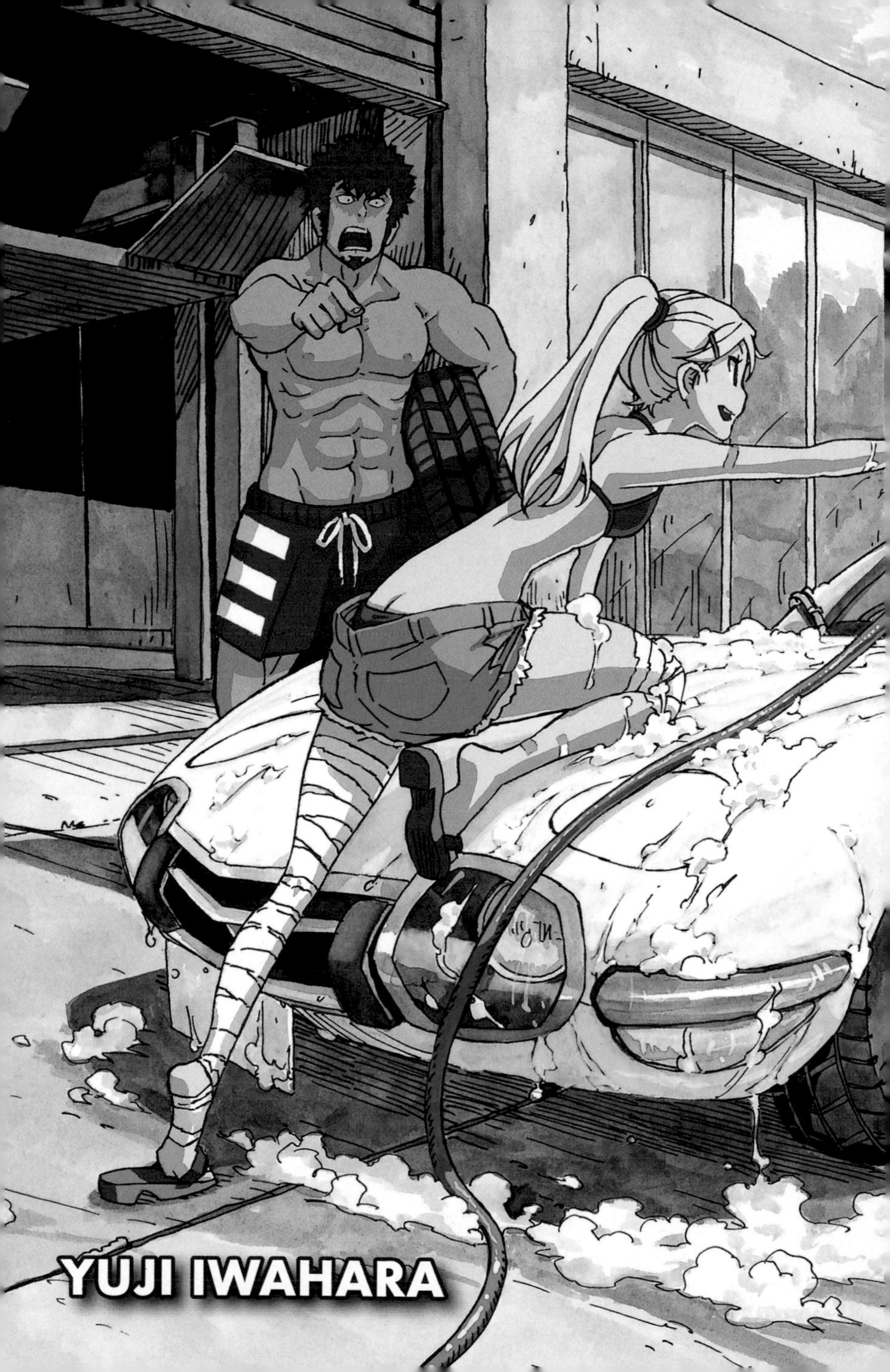
YUJI IWAHARA

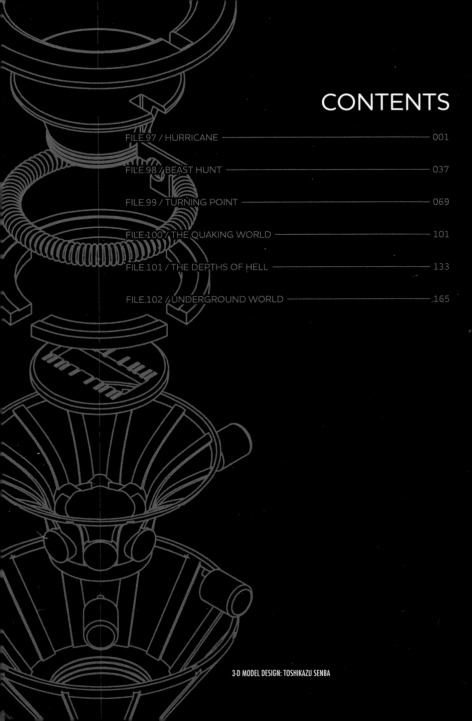

CONTENTS

3-D MODEL DESIGN: TOSHIKAZU SENBA

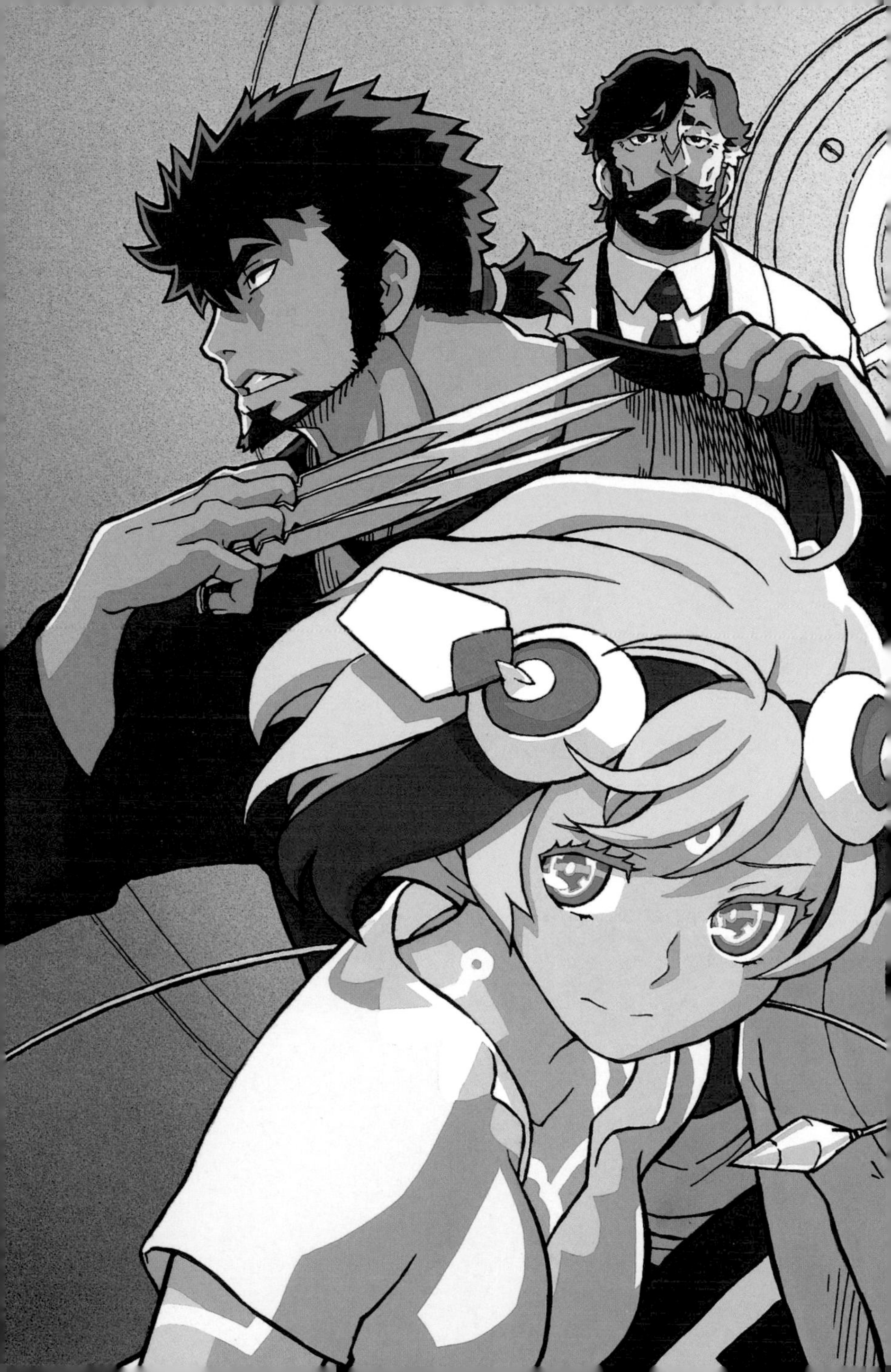

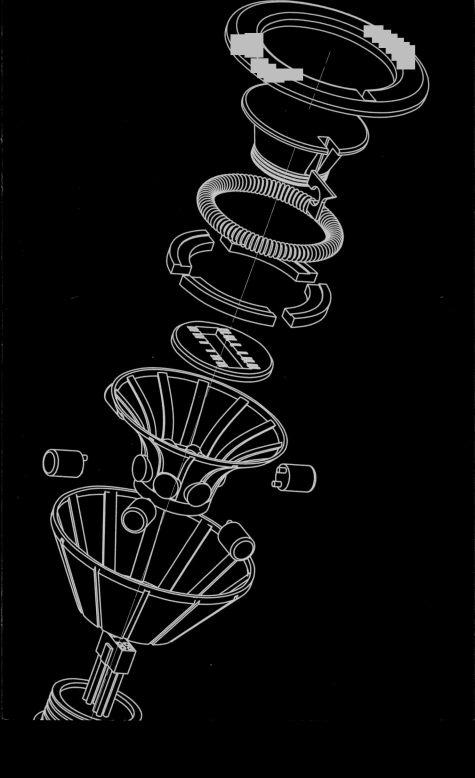

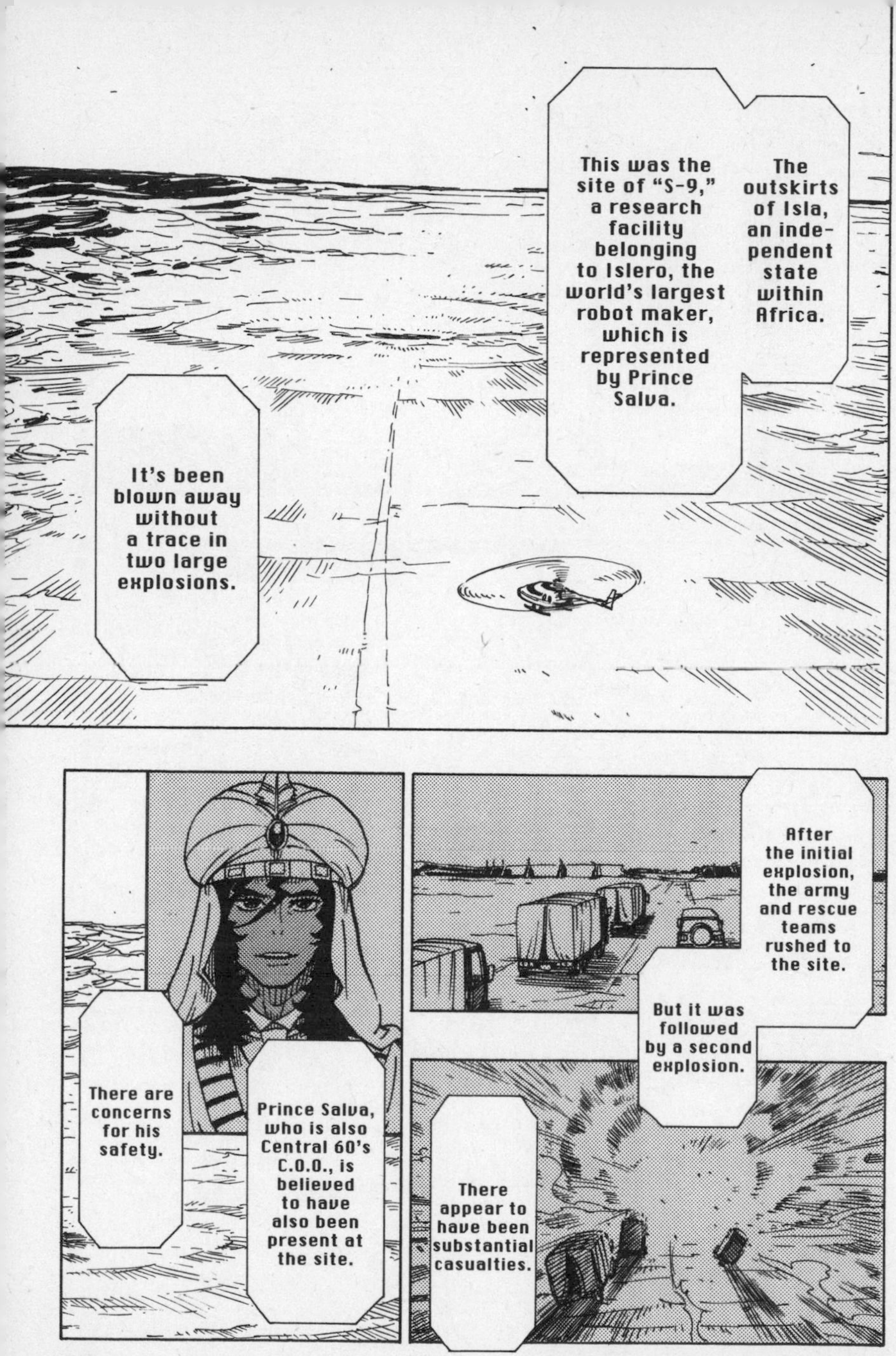
The outskirts of Isla, an independent state within Africa.
This was the site of "S-9," a research facility belonging to Islero, the world's largest robot maker, which is represented by Prince Salva.
It's been blown away without a trace in two large explosions.
After the initial explosion, the army and rescue teams rushed to the site.
But it was followed by a second explosion.
There appear to have been substantial casualties.
Prince Salva, who is also Central 60's C.O.O., is believed to have also been present at the site.
There are concerns for his safety.

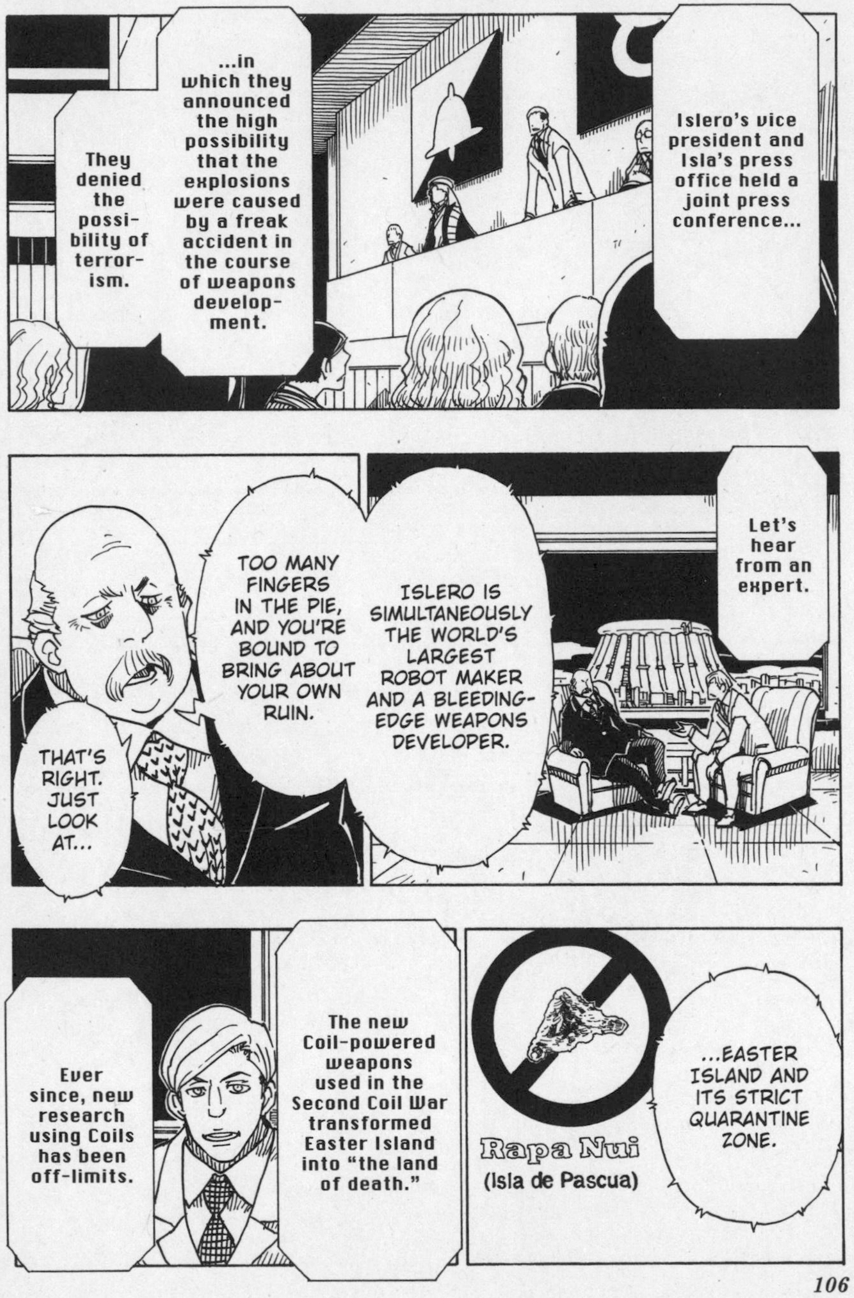
Islero's vice president and Isla's press office held a joint press conference...
...in which they announced the high possibility that the explosions were caused by a freak accident in the course of weapons development.
They denied the possibility of terrorism.
Let's hear from an expert.
ISLERO IS SIMULTANEOUSLY THE WORLD'S LARGEST ROBOT MAKER AND A BLEEDING-EDGE WEAPONS DEVELOPER.
TOO MANY FINGERS IN THE PIE, AND YOU'RE BOUND TO BRING ABOUT YOUR OWN RUIN.
THAT'S RIGHT. JUST LOOK AT...
...EASTER ISLAND AND ITS STRICT QUARANTINE ZONE.
Rapa Nui
(Isla de Pascua)
The new Coil-powered weapons used in the Second Coil War transformed Easter Island into "the land of death."
Ever since, new research using Coils has been off-limits.

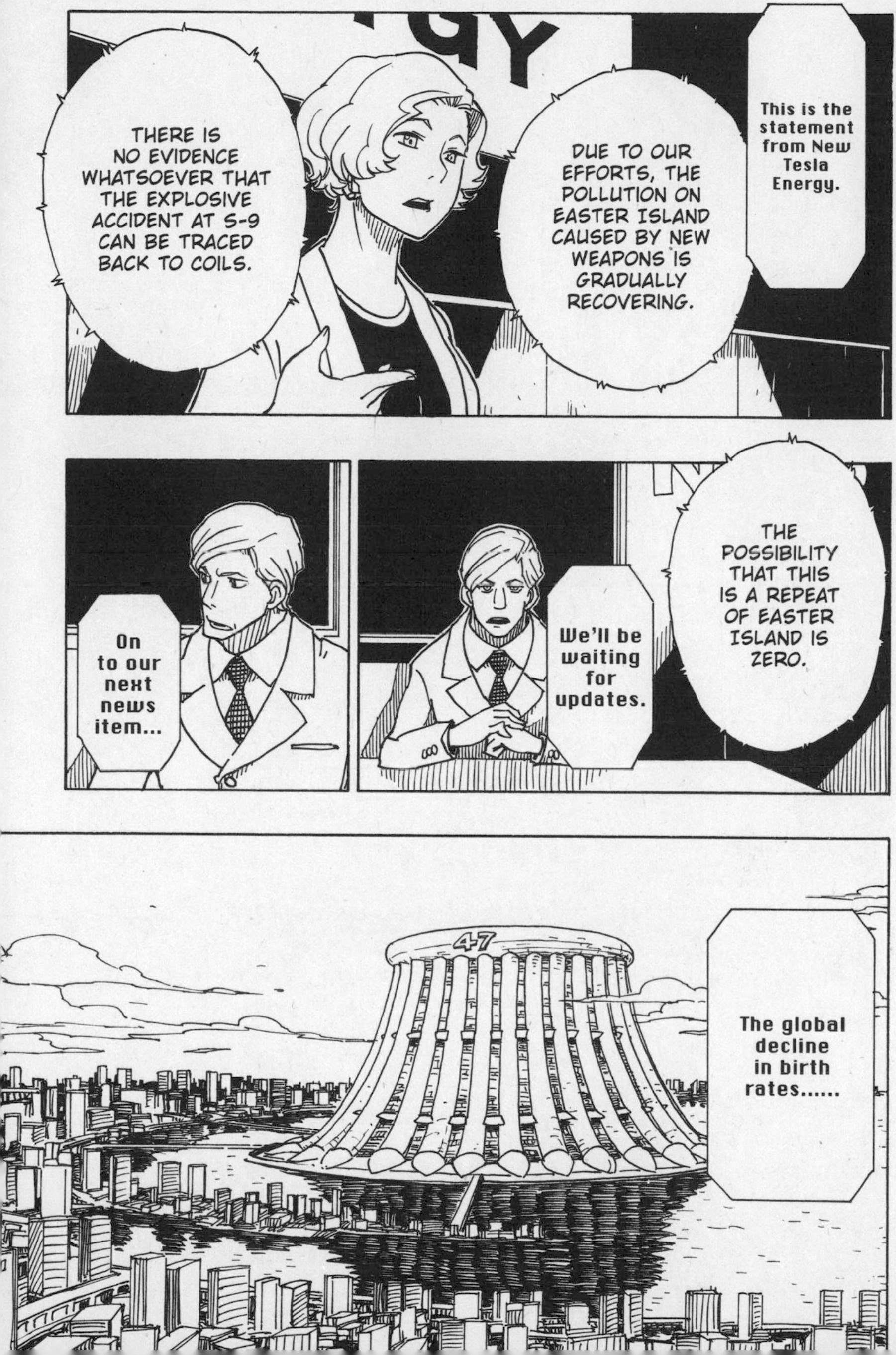
This is the statement from New Tesla Energy.
DUE TO OUR EFFORTS, THE POLLUTION ON EASTER ISLAND CAUSED BY NEW WEAPONS IS GRADUALLY RECOVERING.
THERE IS NO EVIDENCE WHATSOEVER THAT THE EXPLOSIVE ACCIDENT AT S-9 CAN BE TRACED BACK TO COILS.
THE POSSIBILITY THAT THIS IS A REPEAT OF EASTER ISLAND IS ZERO.
We'll be waiting for updates.
On to our next news item...
47
The global decline in birth rates......

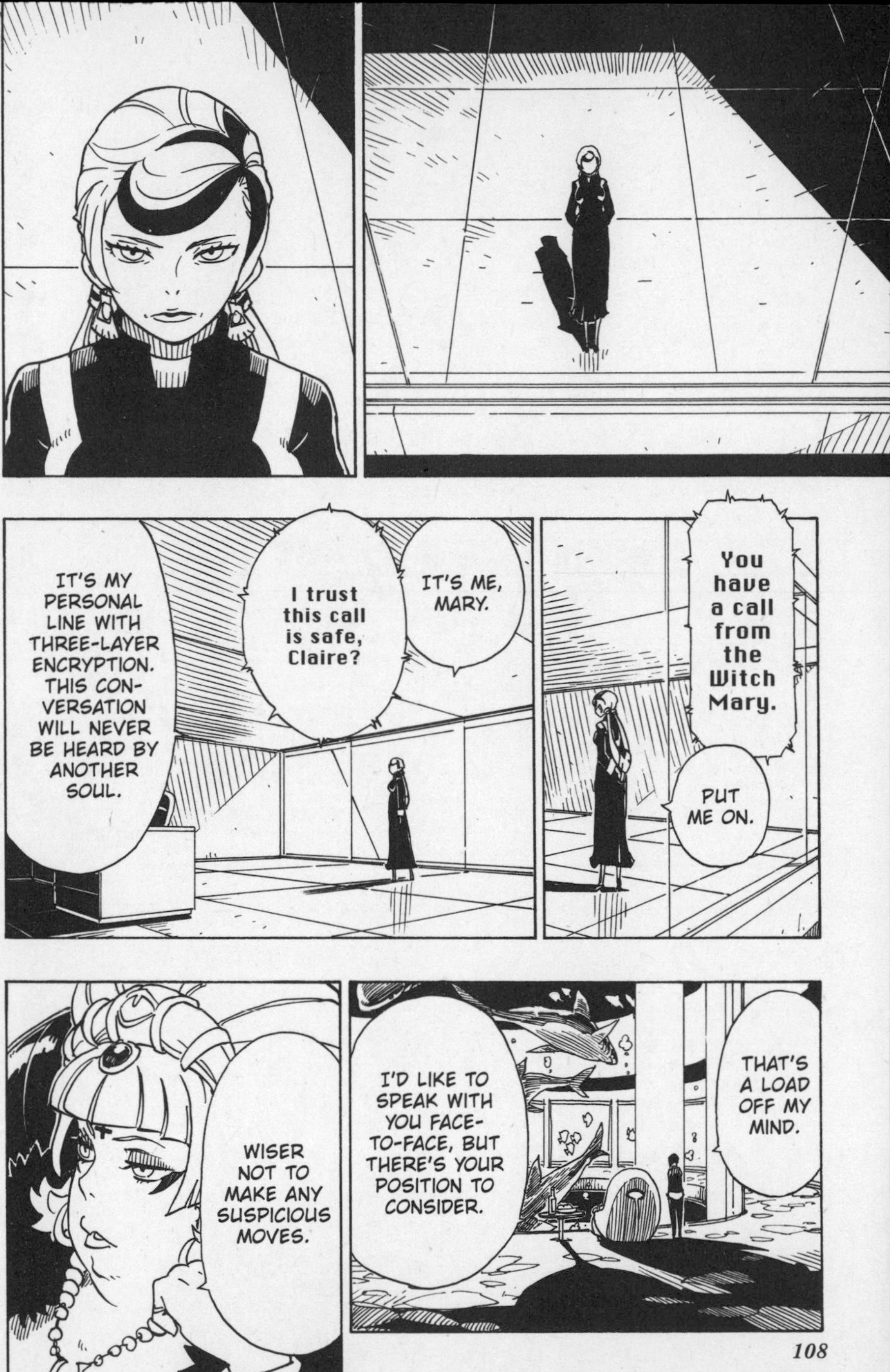
You have a call from the Witch Mary.
PUT ME ON.
IT'S ME, MARY.
I trust this call is safe, Claire?
IT'S MY PERSONAL LINE WITH THREE-LAYER ENCRYPTION. THIS CONVERSATION WILL NEVER BE HEARD BY ANOTHER SOUL.
THAT'S A LOAD OFF MY MIND.
I'D LIKE TO SPEAK WITH YOU FACE-TO-FACE, BUT THERE'S YOUR POSITION TO CONSIDER.
WISER NOT TO MAKE ANY SUSPICIOUS MOVES.

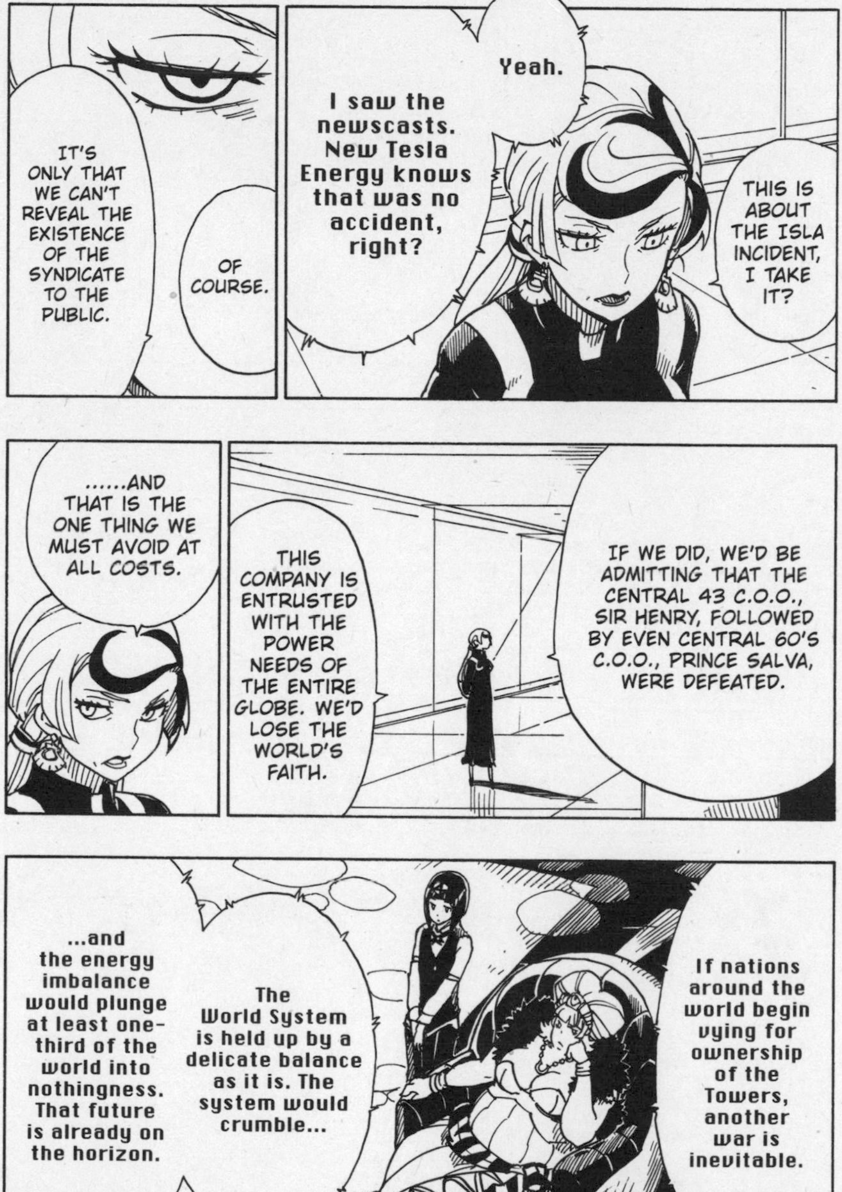
THIS IS ABOUT THE ISLA INCIDENT, I TAKE IT?
Yeah.
I saw the newscasts. New Tesla Energy knows that was no accident, right?
OF COURSE.
IT'S ONLY THAT WE CAN'T REVEAL THE EXISTENCE OF THE SYNDICATE TO THE PUBLIC.
IF WE DID, WE'D BE ADMITTING THAT THE CENTRAL 43 C.O.O., SIR HENRY, FOLLOWED BY EVEN CENTRAL 60'S C.O.O., PRINCE SALVA, WERE DEFEATED.
THIS COMPANY IS ENTRUSTED WITH THE POWER NEEDS OF THE ENTIRE GLOBE. WE'D LOSE THE WORLD'S FAITH.
......AND THAT IS THE ONE THING WE MUST AVOID AT ALL COSTS.
If nations around the world begin vying for ownership of the Towers, another war is inevitable.
The World System is held up by a delicate balance as it is. The system would crumble...
...and the energy imbalance would plunge at least one-third of the world into nothingness. That future is already on the horizon.

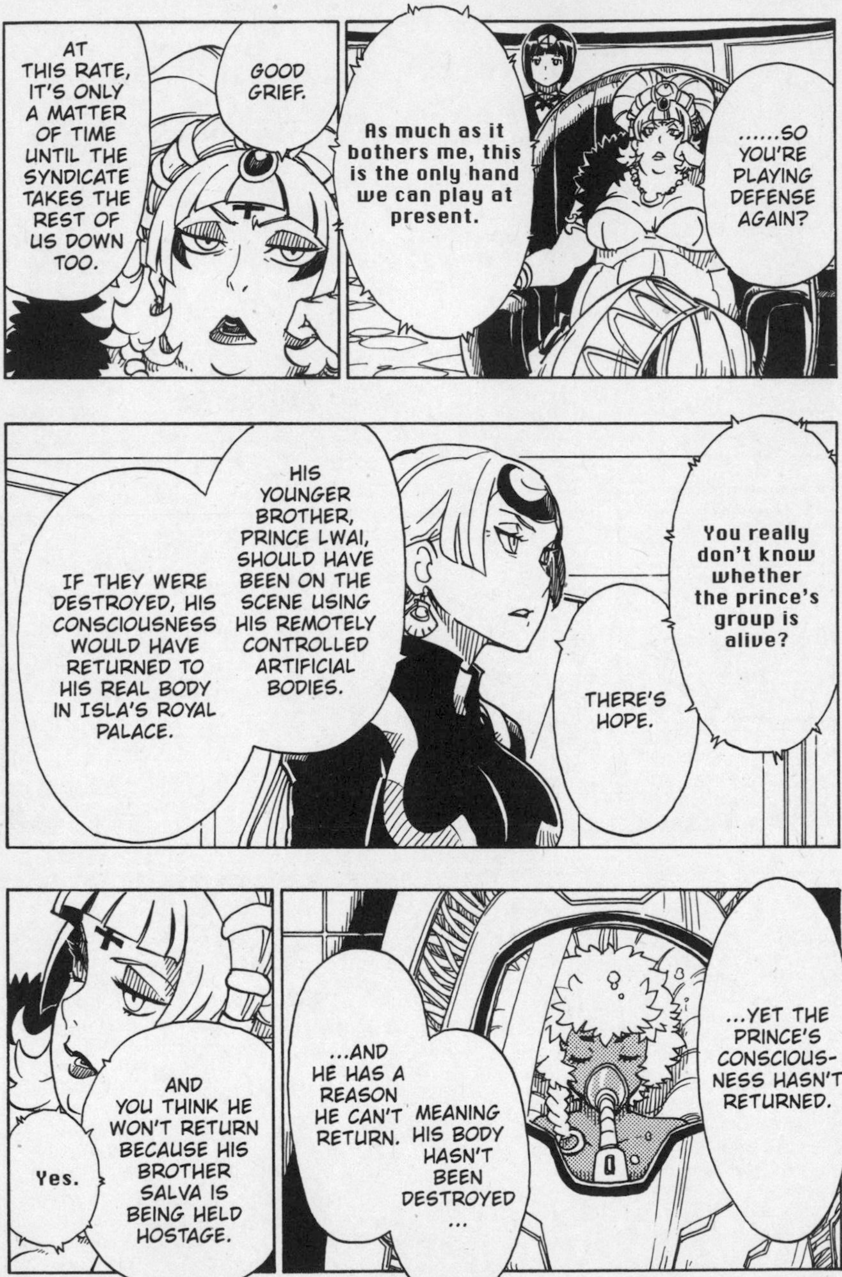
......SO YOU'RE PLAYING DEFENSE AGAIN?
As much as it bothers me, this is the only hand we can play at present.
GOOD GRIEF.
AT THIS RATE, IT'S ONLY A MATTER OF TIME UNTIL THE SYNDICATE TAKES THE REST OF US DOWN TOO.
You really don't know whether the prince's group is alive?
THERE'S HOPE.
HIS YOUNGER BROTHER, PRINCE LWAI, SHOULD HAVE BEEN ON THE SCENE USING HIS REMOTELY CONTROLLED ARTIFICIAL BODIES.
IF THEY WERE DESTROYED, HIS CONSCIOUSNESS WOULD HAVE RETURNED TO HIS REAL BODY IN ISLA'S ROYAL PALACE.
...YET THE PRINCE'S CONSCIOUSNESS HASN'T RETURNED.
MEANING HIS BODY HASN'T BEEN DESTROYED...
...AND HE HAS A REASON HE CAN'T RETURN.
AND YOU THINK HE WON'T RETURN BECAUSE HIS BROTHER SALVA IS BEING HELD HOSTAGE.
Yes.

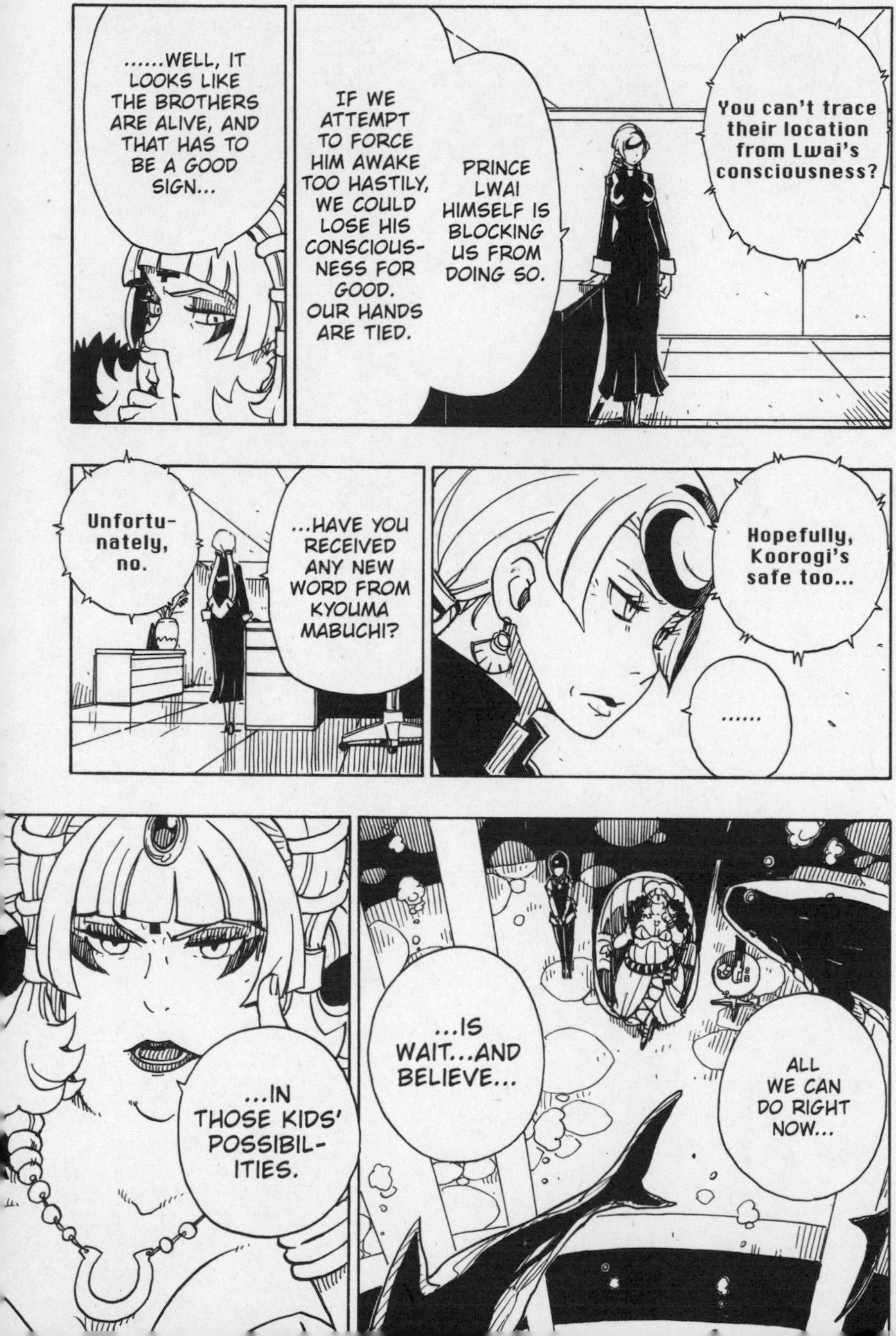
You can't trace their location from Lwai's consciousness?
PRINCE LWAI HIMSELF IS BLOCKING US FROM DOING SO.
IF WE ATTEMPT TO FORCE HIM AWAKE TOO HASTILY, WE COULD LOSE HIS CONSCIOUSNESS FOR GOOD. OUR HANDS ARE TIED.
......WELL, IT LOOKS LIKE THE BROTHERS ARE ALIVE, AND THAT HAS TO BE A GOOD SIGN...
Hopefully, Koorogi's safe too...
......
...HAVE YOU RECEIVED ANY NEW WORD FROM KYOUMA MABUCHI?
Unfortunately, no.
ALL WE CAN DO RIGHT NOW...
...IS WAIT...AND BELIEVE...
...IN THOSE KIDS' POSSIBILITIES.

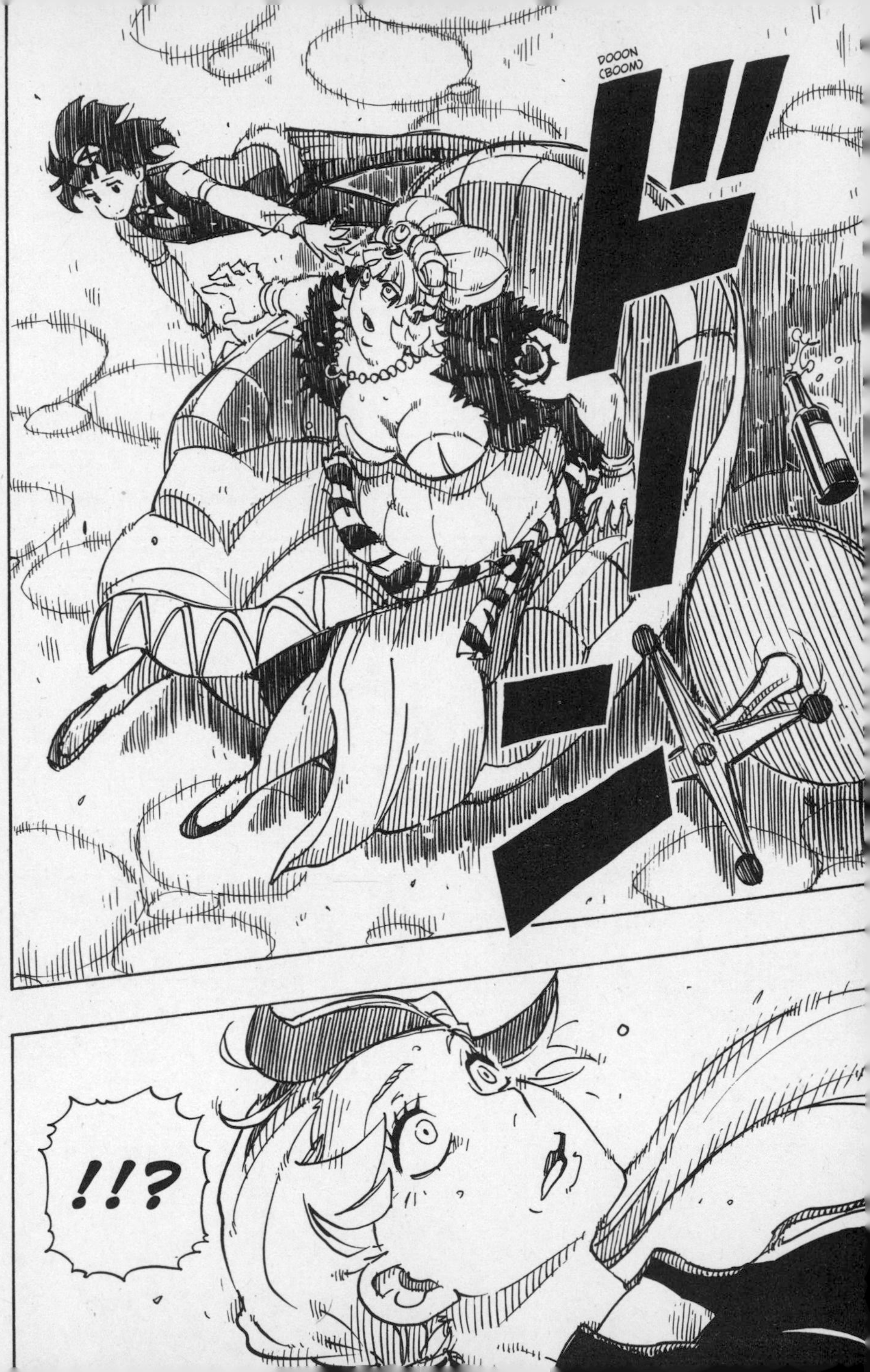
DOOON
(BOOM)
!!?

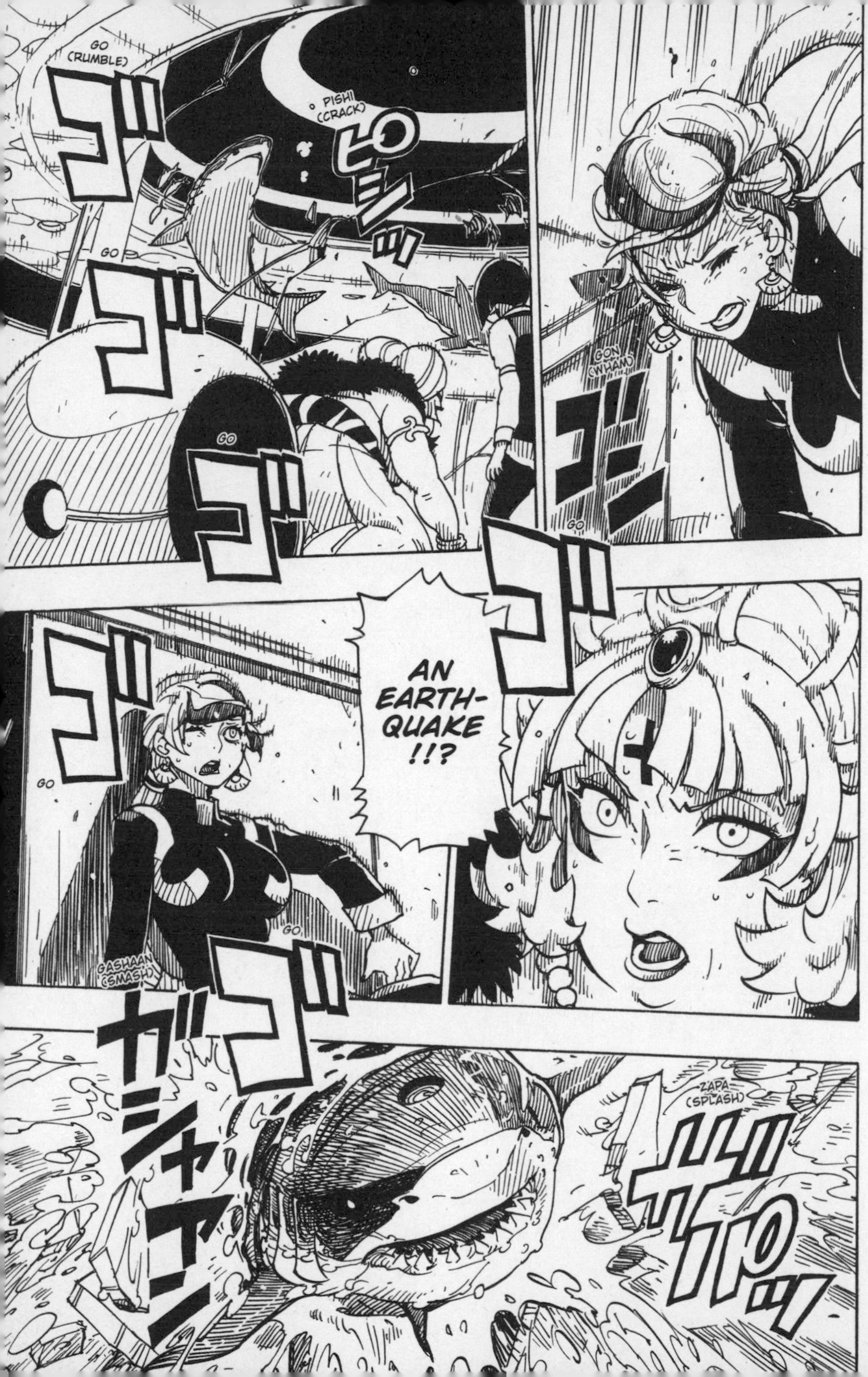
GON (WHAM)
GO
PISHI (CRACK)
GO (RUMBLE)
GO
GO
AN EARTH-QUAKE!!?
GO
GO
GASHAAN (SMASH)
ZAPA (SPLASH)

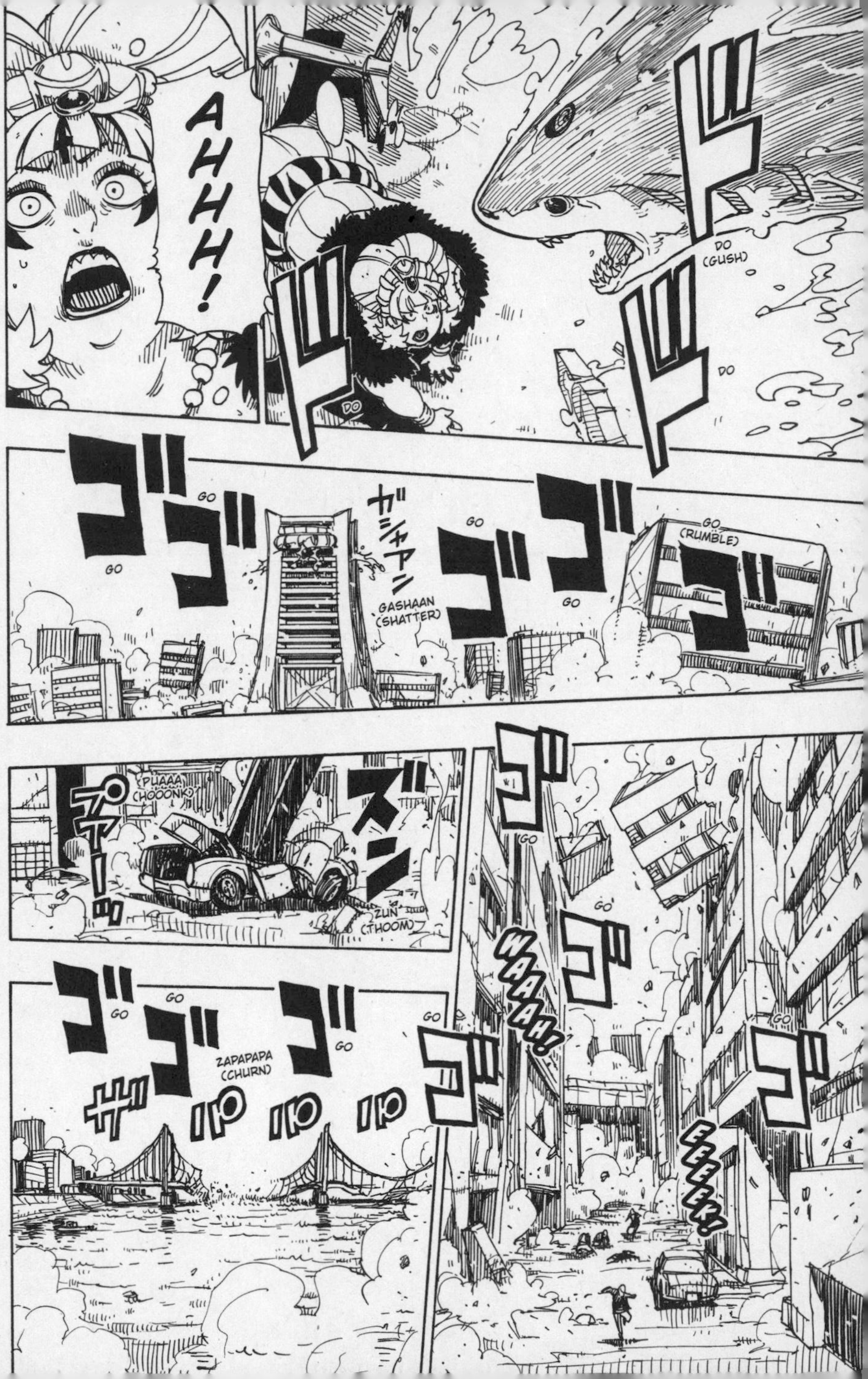
DO (GUSH)
DO
DO
AHHH!
GO (RUMBLE)
GO
GO
GASHAAN (SHATTER)
GO
GO
GO
GO
WAAAH!
GO
EEEEK!
PUAAA (HOOONK)
ZUN (THOOM)
GO
GO
GO
ZAPAPAPA (CHURN)
GO

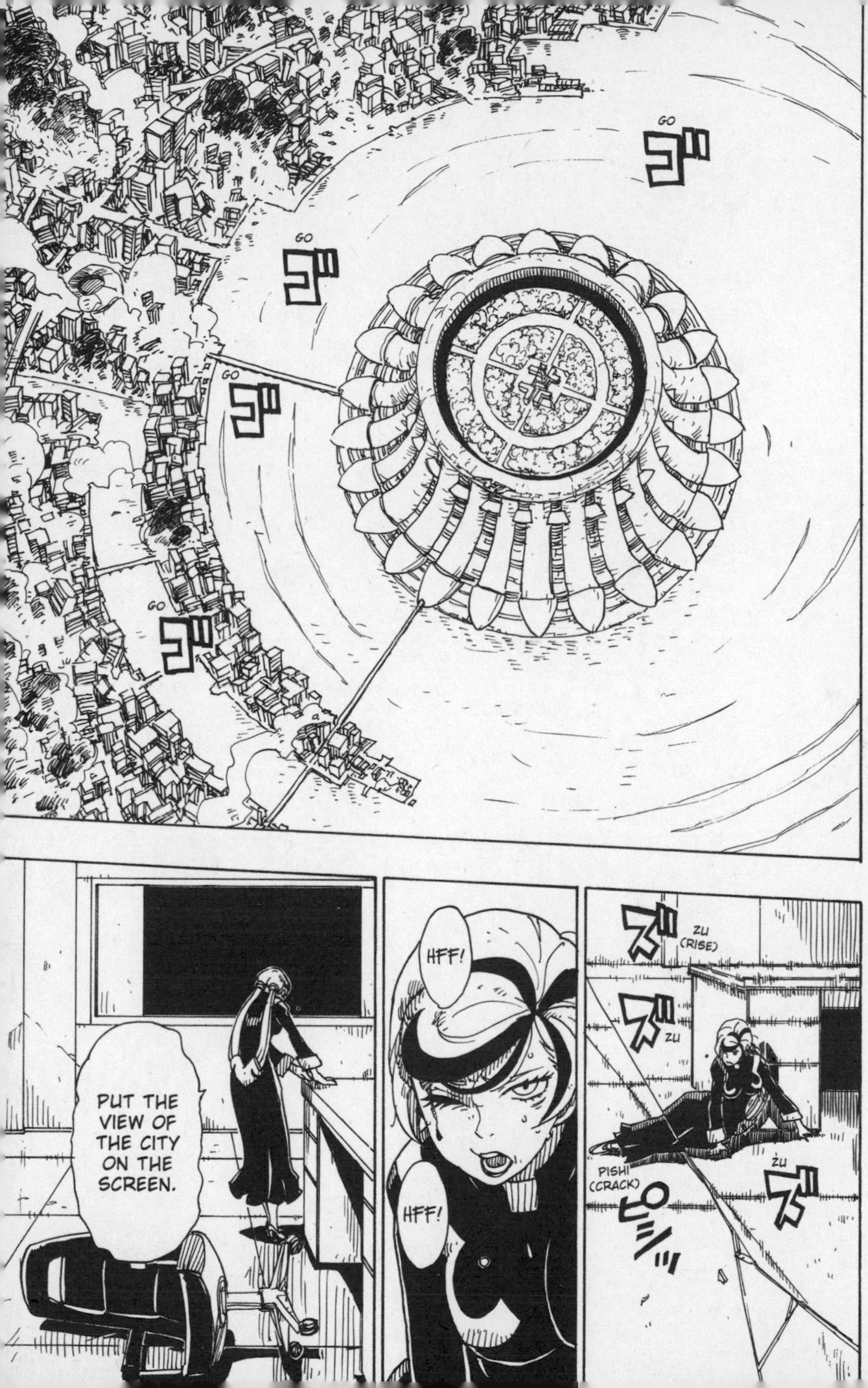
GO
GO
GO
GO
ZU
(RISE)
ZU
ZU
PISHI
(CRACK)
HFF!
HFF!
PUT THE VIEW OF THE CITY ON THE SCREEN.

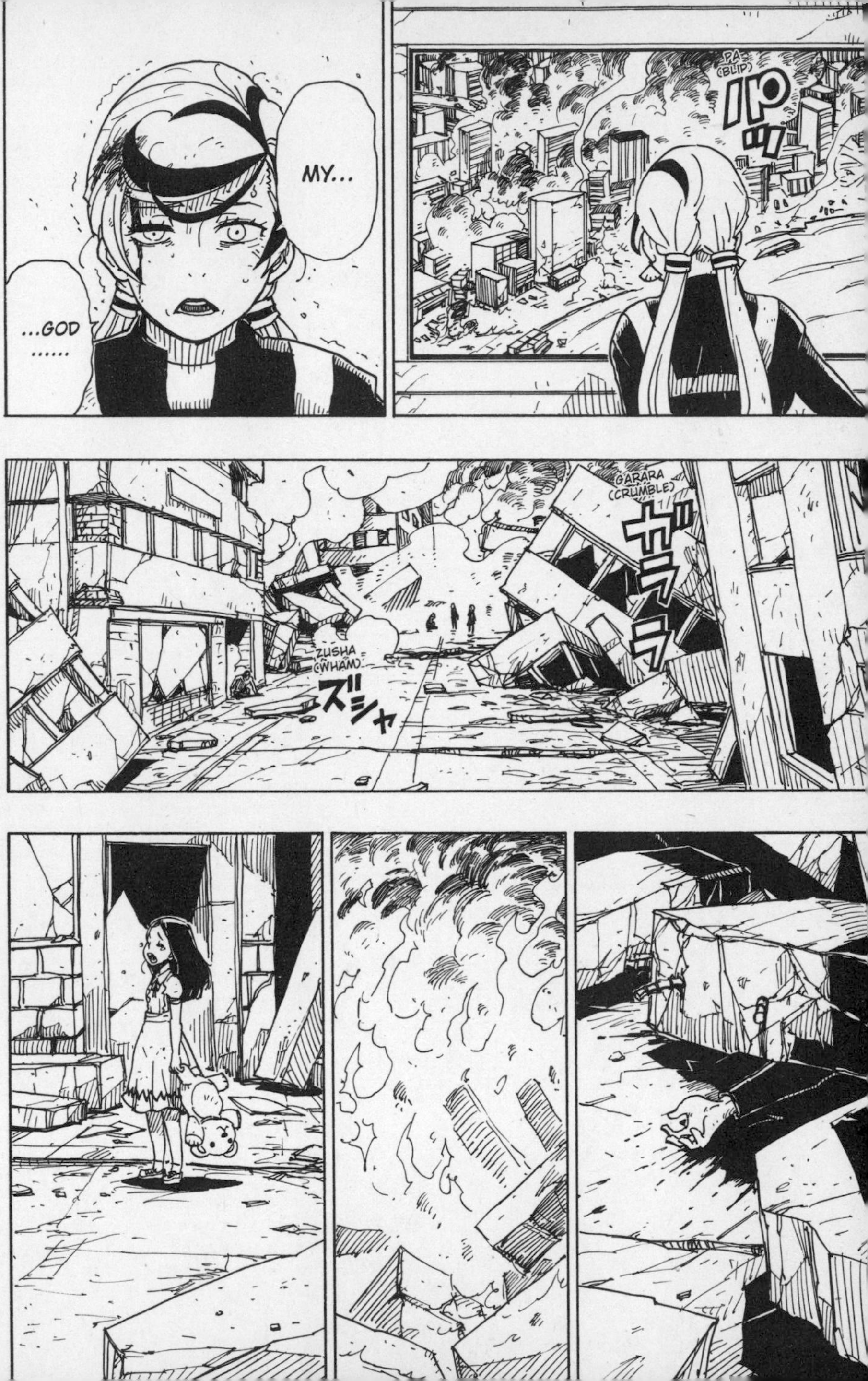
PA (BLIP)
パッ
MY...
...GOD ......
GARARA (CRUMBLE)
ガララ
ZUSHA (WHAM)
ズシャ

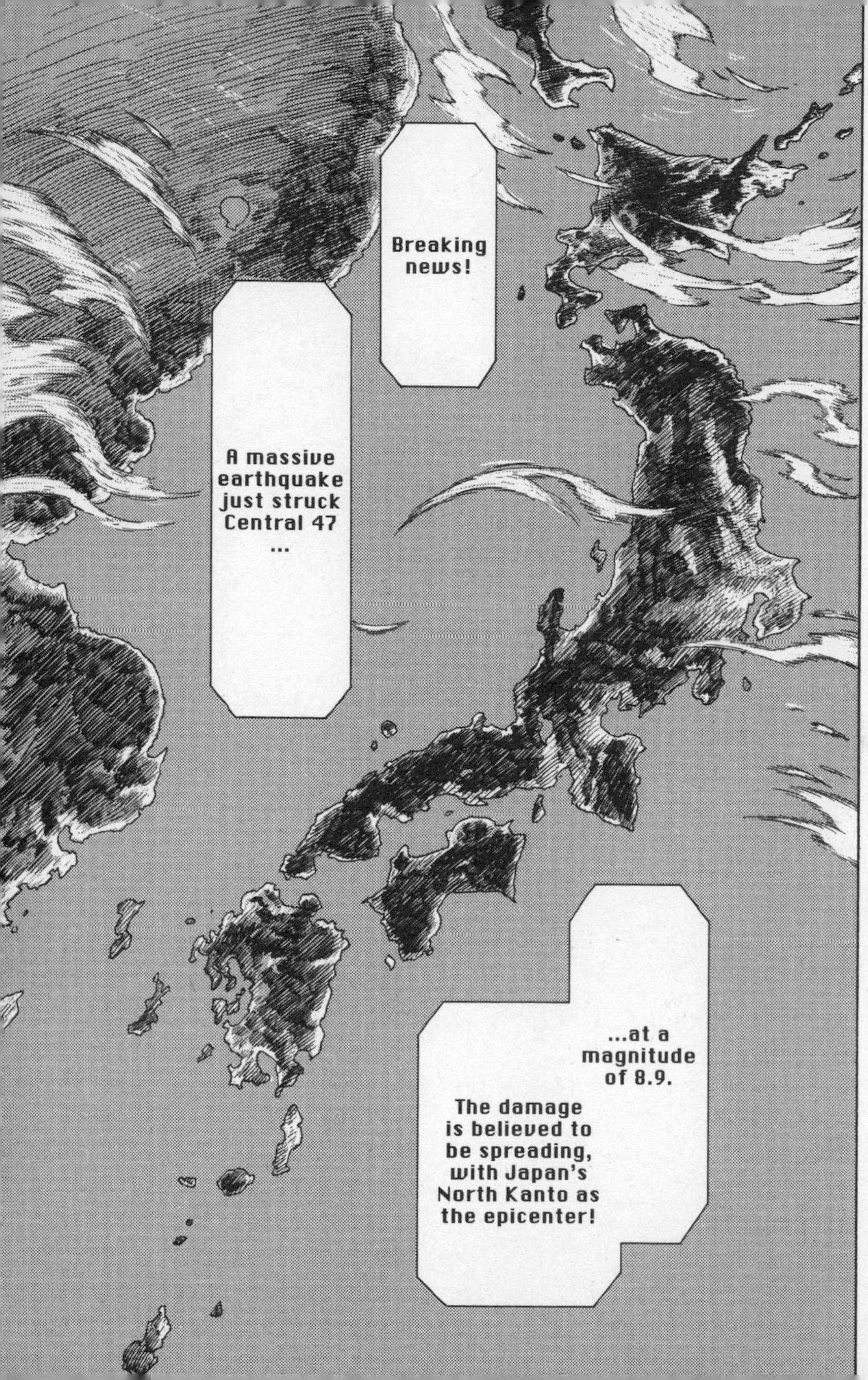

Breaking news!
A massive earthquake just struck Central 47 ...
...at a magnitude of 8.9.
The damage is believed to be spreading, with Japan's North Kanto as the epicenter!

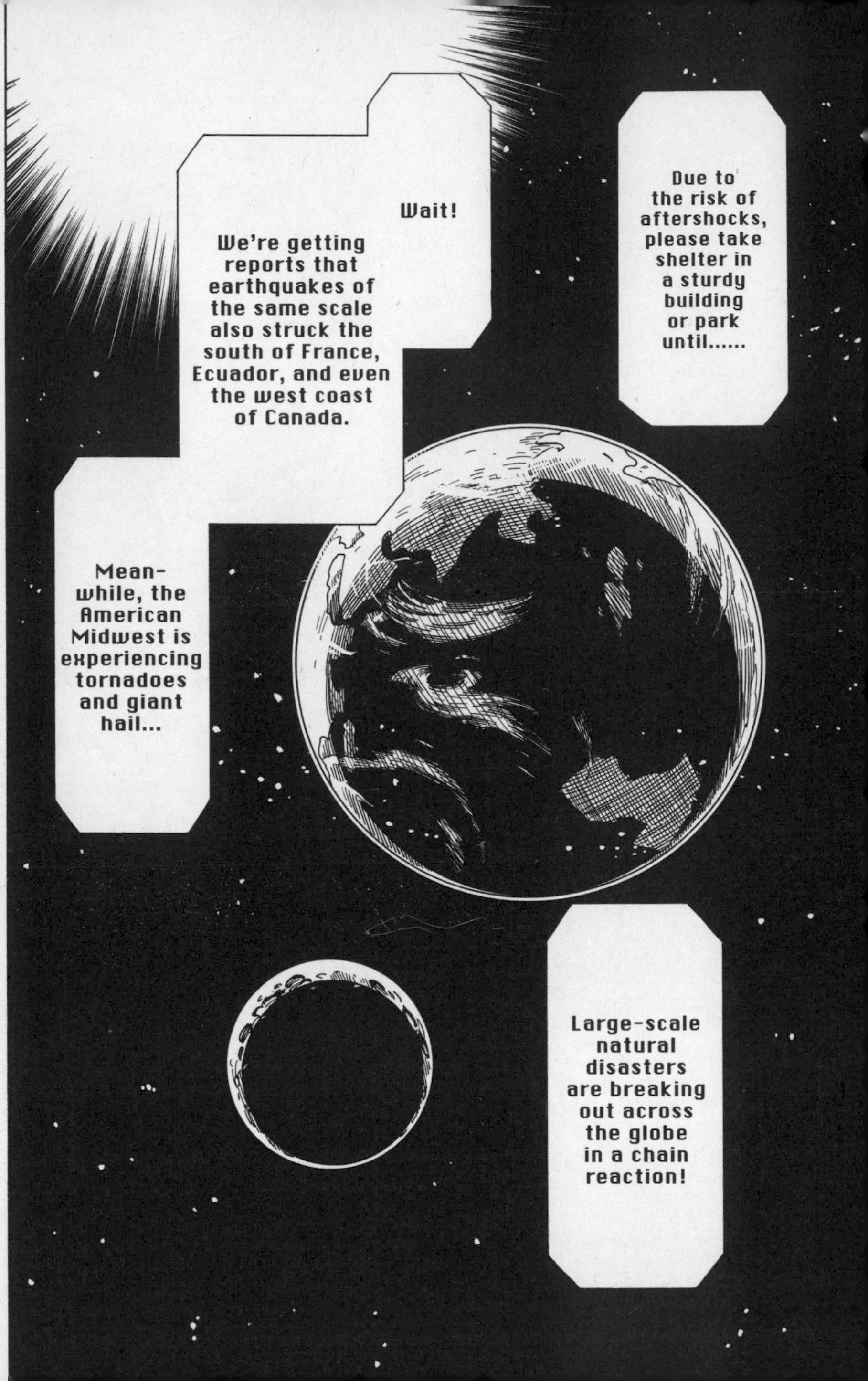

Due to the risk of aftershocks, please take shelter in a sturdy building or park until......
Wait!
We're getting reports that earthquakes of the same scale also struck the south of France, Ecuador, and even the west coast of Canada.
Mean-while, the American Midwest is experiencing tornadoes and giant hail...
Large-scale natural disasters are breaking out across the globe in a chain reaction!

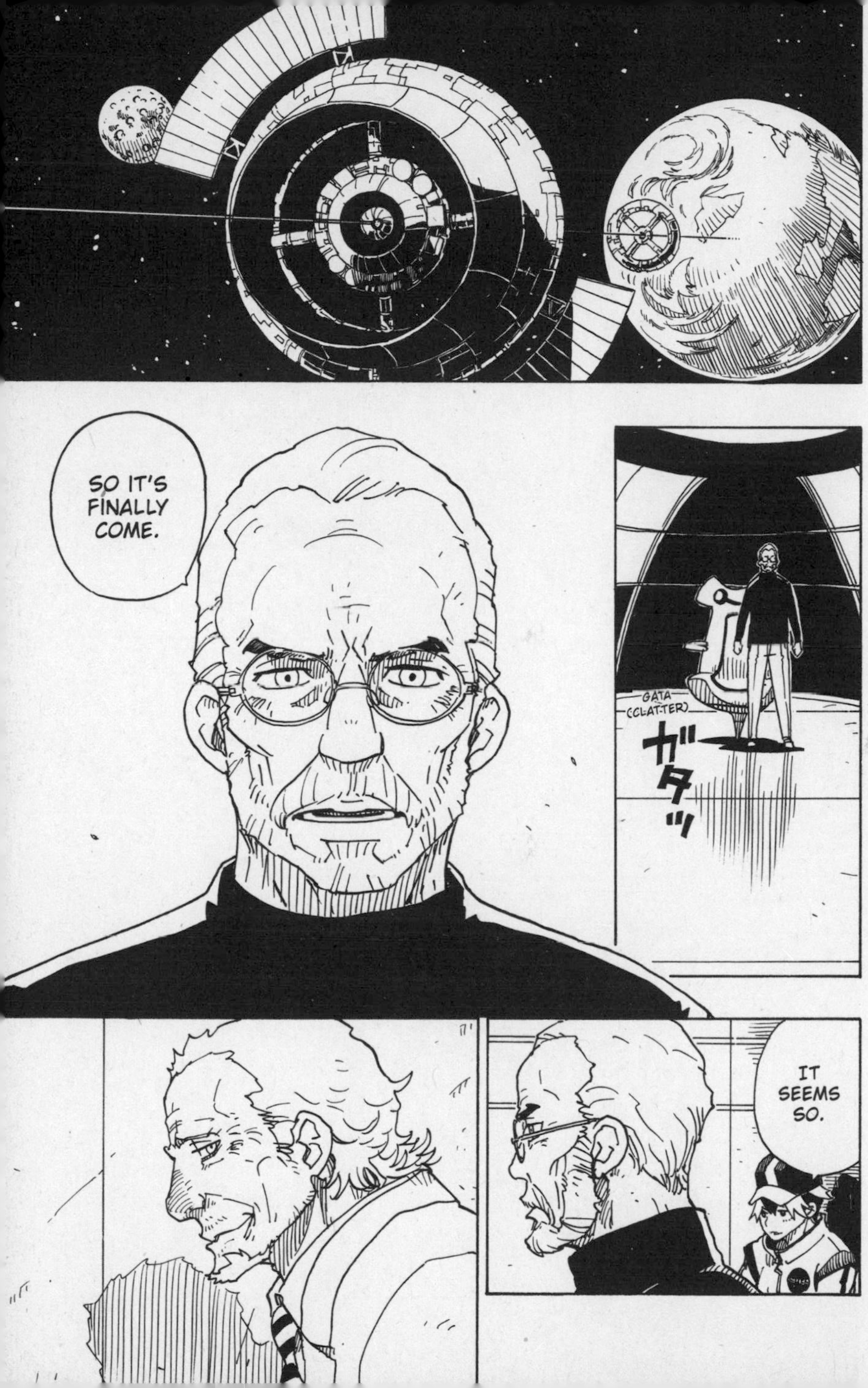
GATA
(CLAT-TER)
ガタッ
SO IT'S FINALLY COME.
IT SEEMS SO.

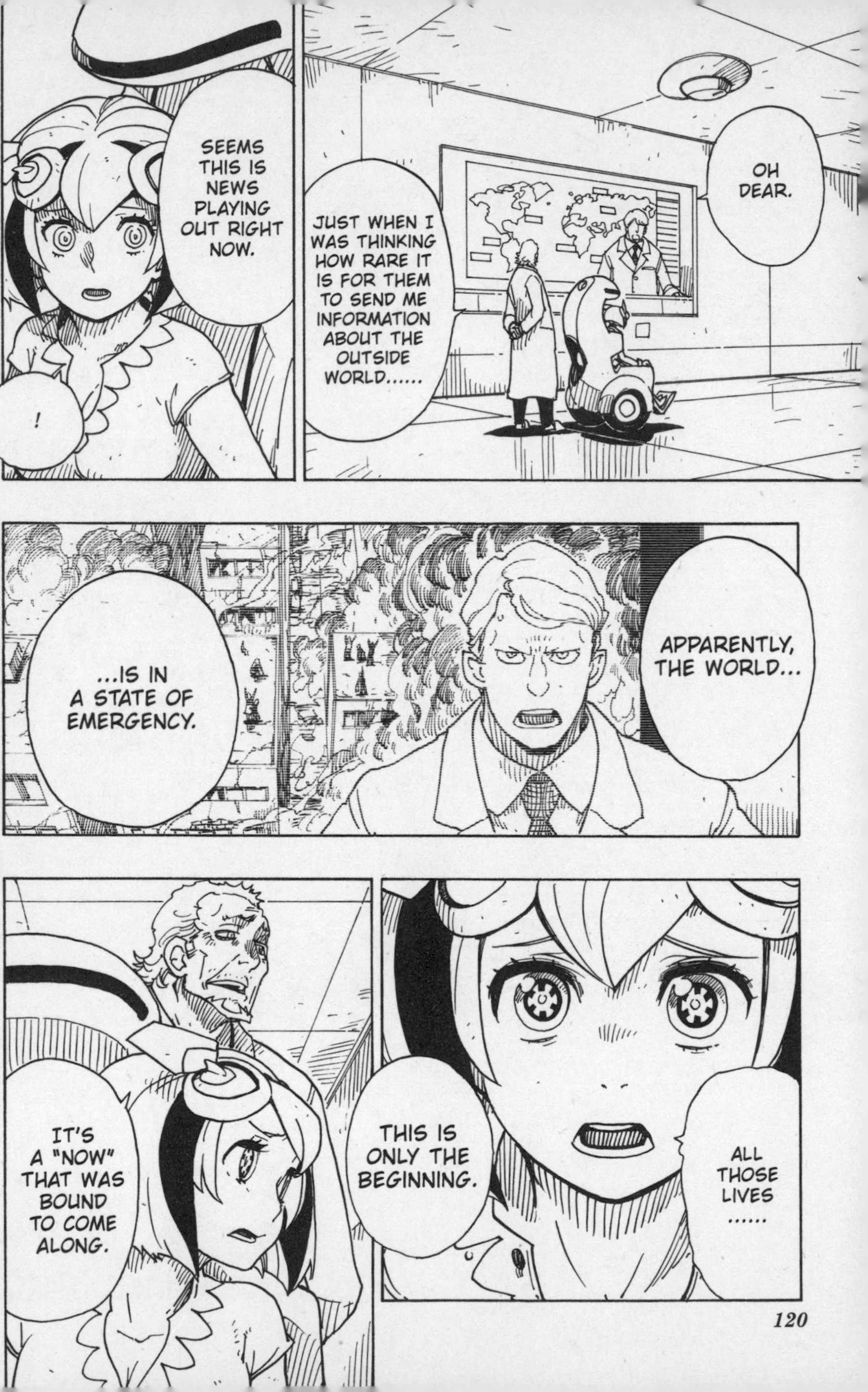
OH DEAR.
JUST WHEN I WAS THINKING HOW RARE IT IS FOR THEM TO SEND ME INFORMATION ABOUT THE OUTSIDE WORLD......
SEEMS THIS IS NEWS PLAYING OUT RIGHT NOW.
!
APPARENTLY, THE WORLD...
...IS IN A STATE OF EMERGENCY.
ALL THOSE LIVES ......
THIS IS ONLY THE BEGINNING.
IT'S A "NOW" THAT WAS BOUND TO COME ALONG.

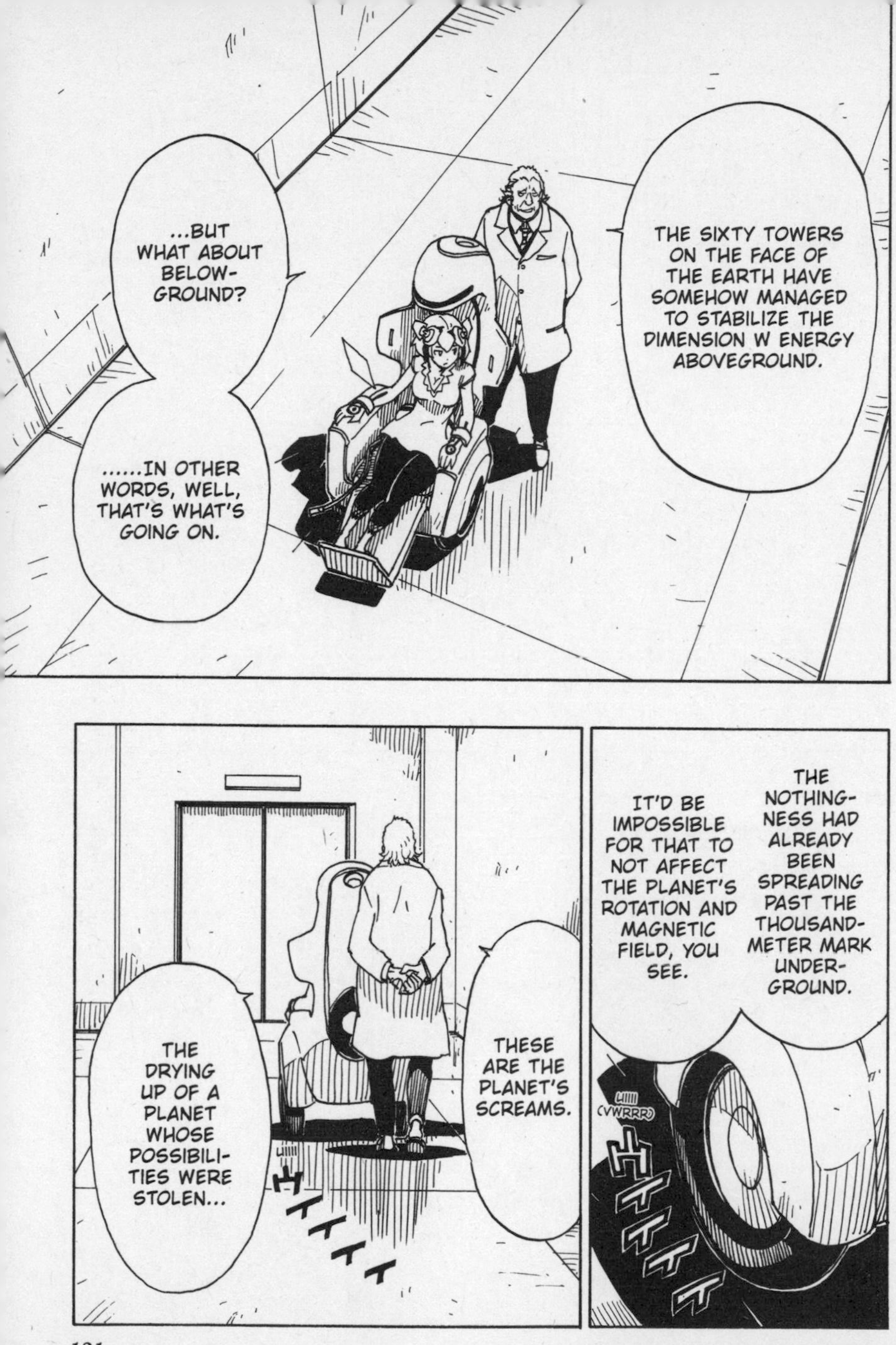
THE SIXTY TOWERS ON THE FACE OF THE EARTH HAVE SOMEHOW MANAGED TO STABILIZE THE DIMENSION W ENERGY ABOVEGROUND.
...BUT WHAT ABOUT BELOW-GROUND?
......IN OTHER WORDS, WELL, THAT'S WHAT'S GOING ON.
THE NOTHING-NESS HAD ALREADY BEEN SPREADING PAST THE THOUSAND-METER MARK UNDER-GROUND.
IT'D BE IMPOSSIBLE FOR THAT TO NOT AFFECT THE PLANET'S ROTATION AND MAGNETIC FIELD, YOU SEE.
(VWRRR)
THESE ARE THE PLANET'S SCREAMS.
THE DRYING UP OF A PLANET WHOSE POSSIBILI-TIES WERE STOLEN...

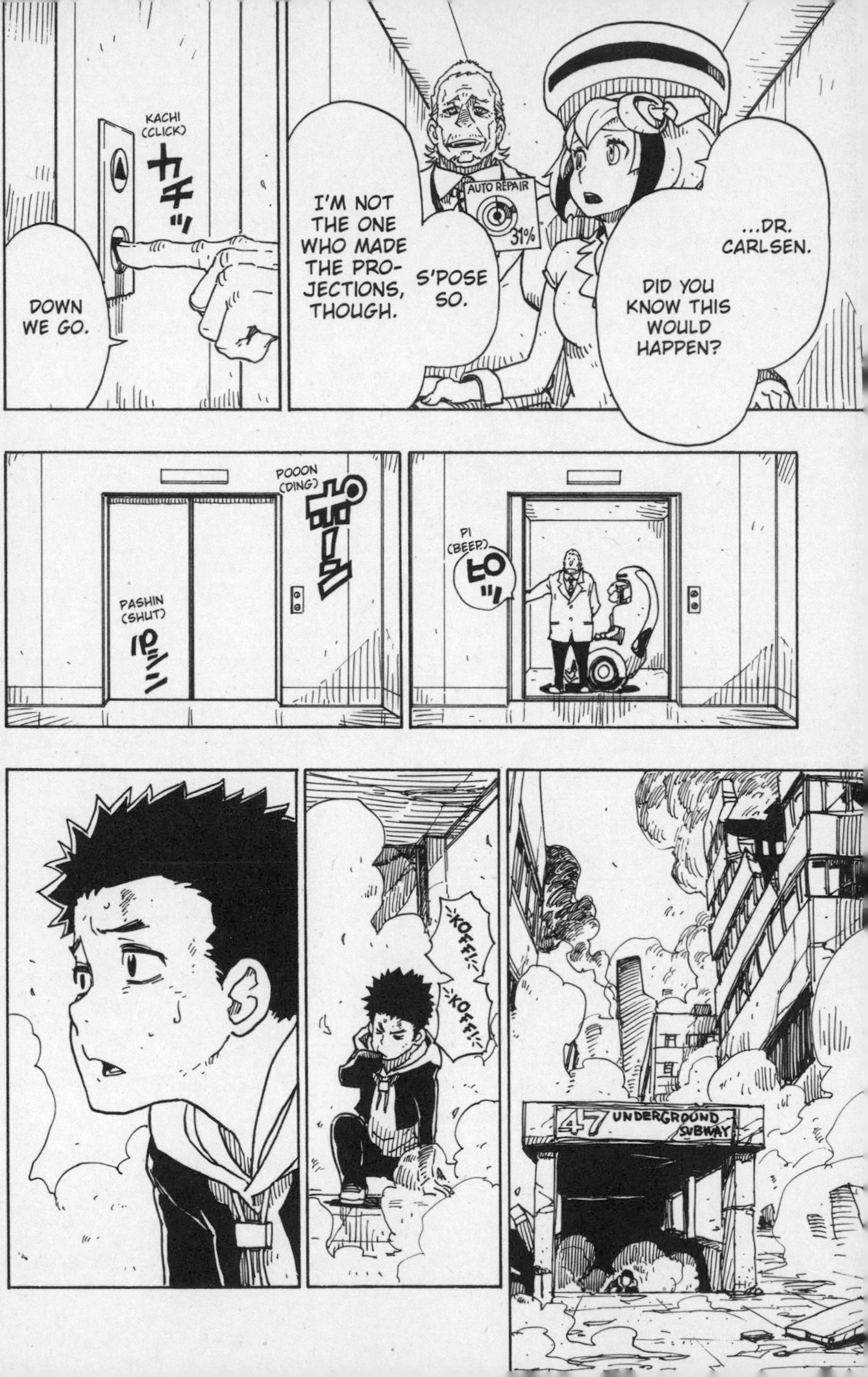

...DR. CARLSEN.
DID YOU KNOW THIS WOULD HAPPEN?
AUTO REPAIR
31%
S'POSE SO.
I'M NOT THE ONE WHO MADE THE PRO-JECTIONS, THOUGH.
KACHI (CLICK)
カチッ
DOWN WE GO.
PI (BEEP)
ピッ
POOON (DING)
ポーン
PASHIN (SHUT)
パシン
47 UNDERGROUND SUBWAY
KOFF!
KOFF!

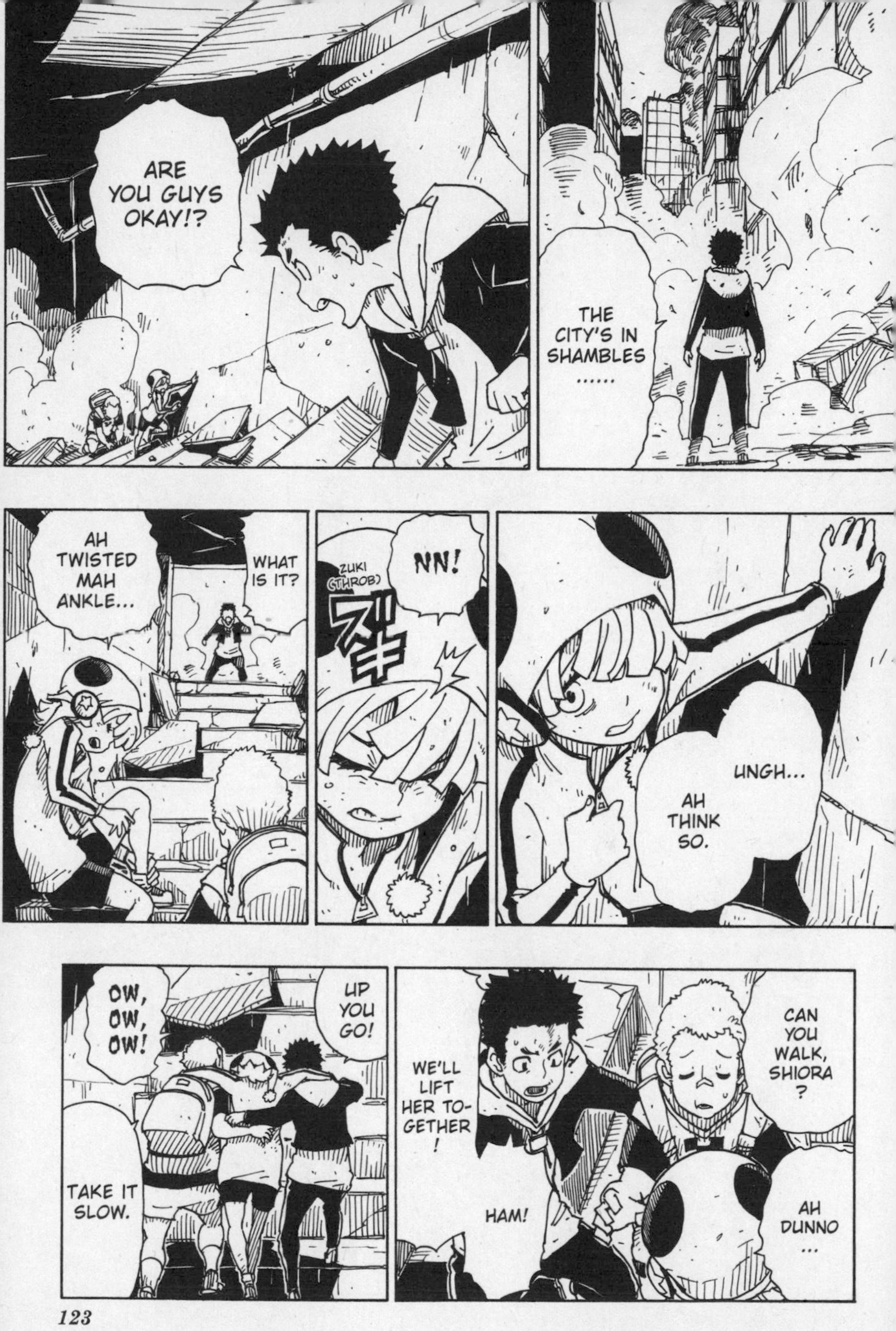
THE CITY'S IN SHAMBLES ......
ARE YOU GUYS OKAY!?
UNGH...
AH THINK SO.
NN!
ズキ
ZUKI (THROB)
WHAT IS IT?
AH TWISTED MAH ANKLE...
CAN YOU WALK, SHIORA?
AH DUNNO ...
WE'LL LIFT HER TO-GETHER!
HAM!
UP YOU GO!
OW, OW, OW!
TAKE IT SLOW.

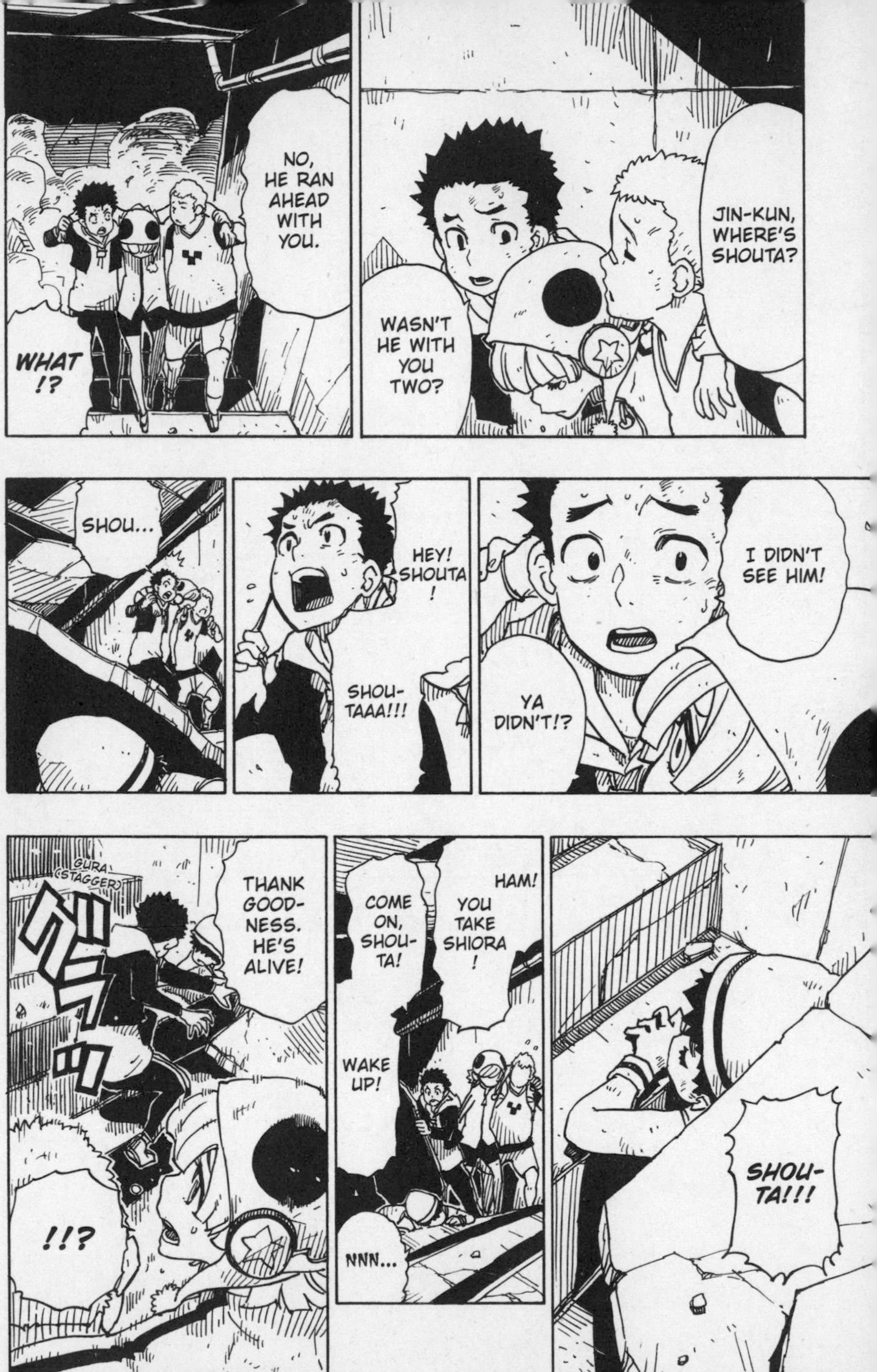
JIN-KUN, WHERE'S SHOUTA?
WASN'T HE WITH YOU TWO?
NO, HE RAN AHEAD WITH YOU.
WHAT!?
I DIDN'T SEE HIM!
YA DIDN'T!?
HEY! SHOUTA!
SHOU-TAAA!!!
SHOU...
SHOU-TA!!!
HAM! YOU TAKE SHIORA!
COME ON, SHOU-TA!
WAKE UP!
NNN...
THANK GOODNESS. HE'S ALIVE!
GURA (STAGGER)
!!?

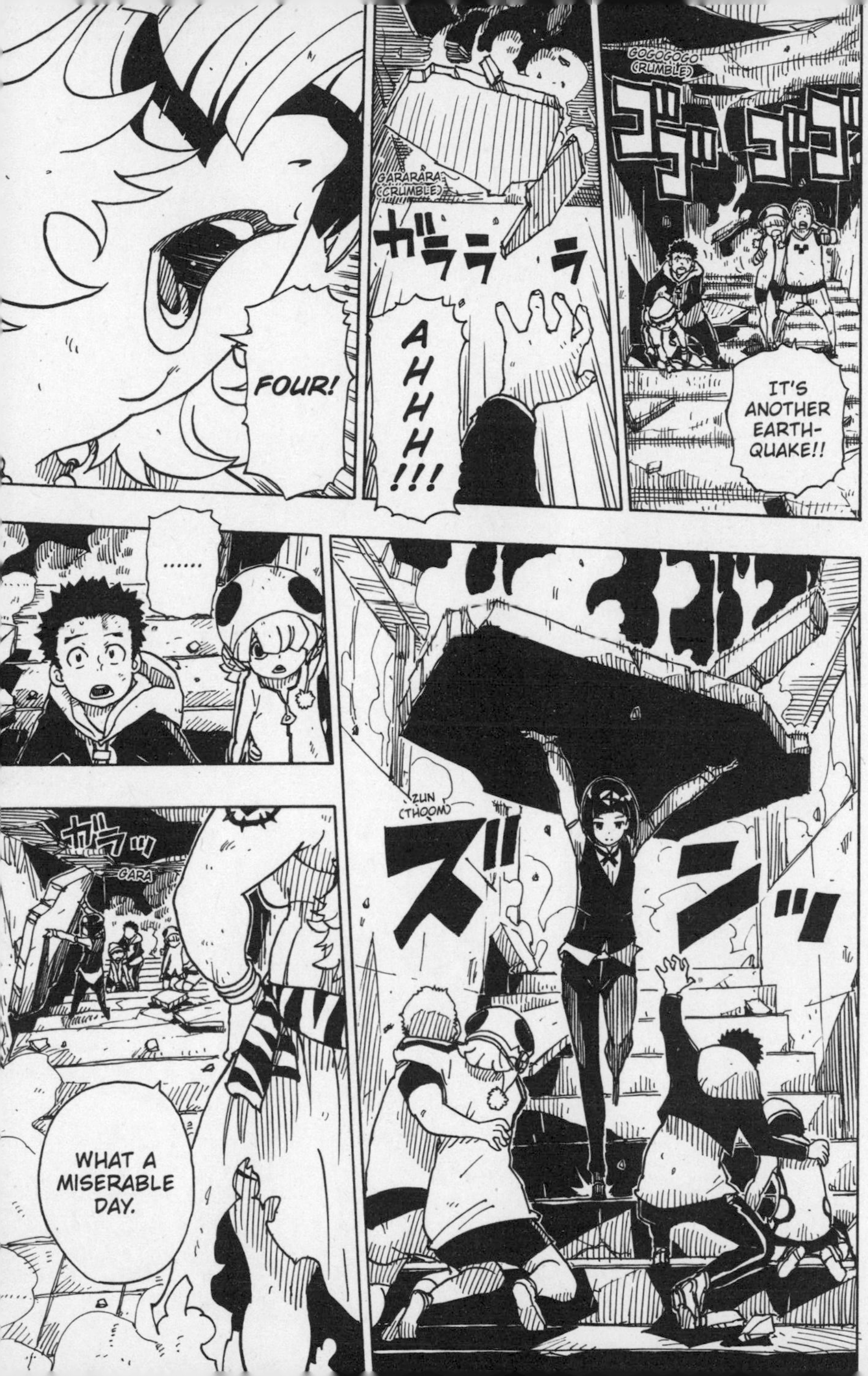
GOGOGOGO (RUMBLE)
IT'S ANOTHER EARTHQUAKE!!
GARARARA (CRUMBLE)
AHHHH!!!
FOUR!
ZUN (THOOM)
......
GARA
WHAT A MISERABLE DAY.

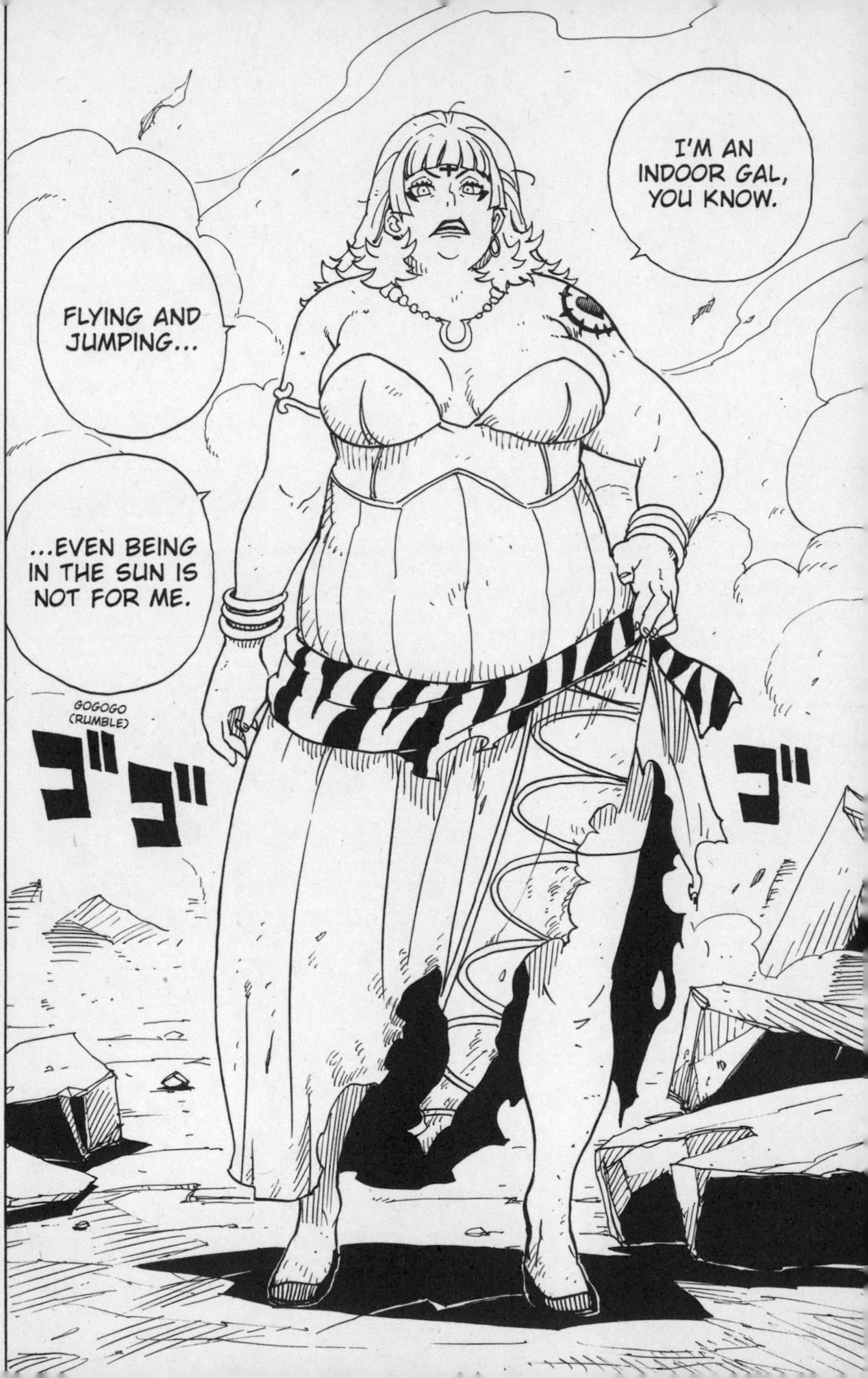
I'M AN INDOOR GAL, YOU KNOW.
FLYING AND JUMPING...
...EVEN BEING IN THE SUN IS NOT FOR ME.
GOGOGO (RUMBLE)

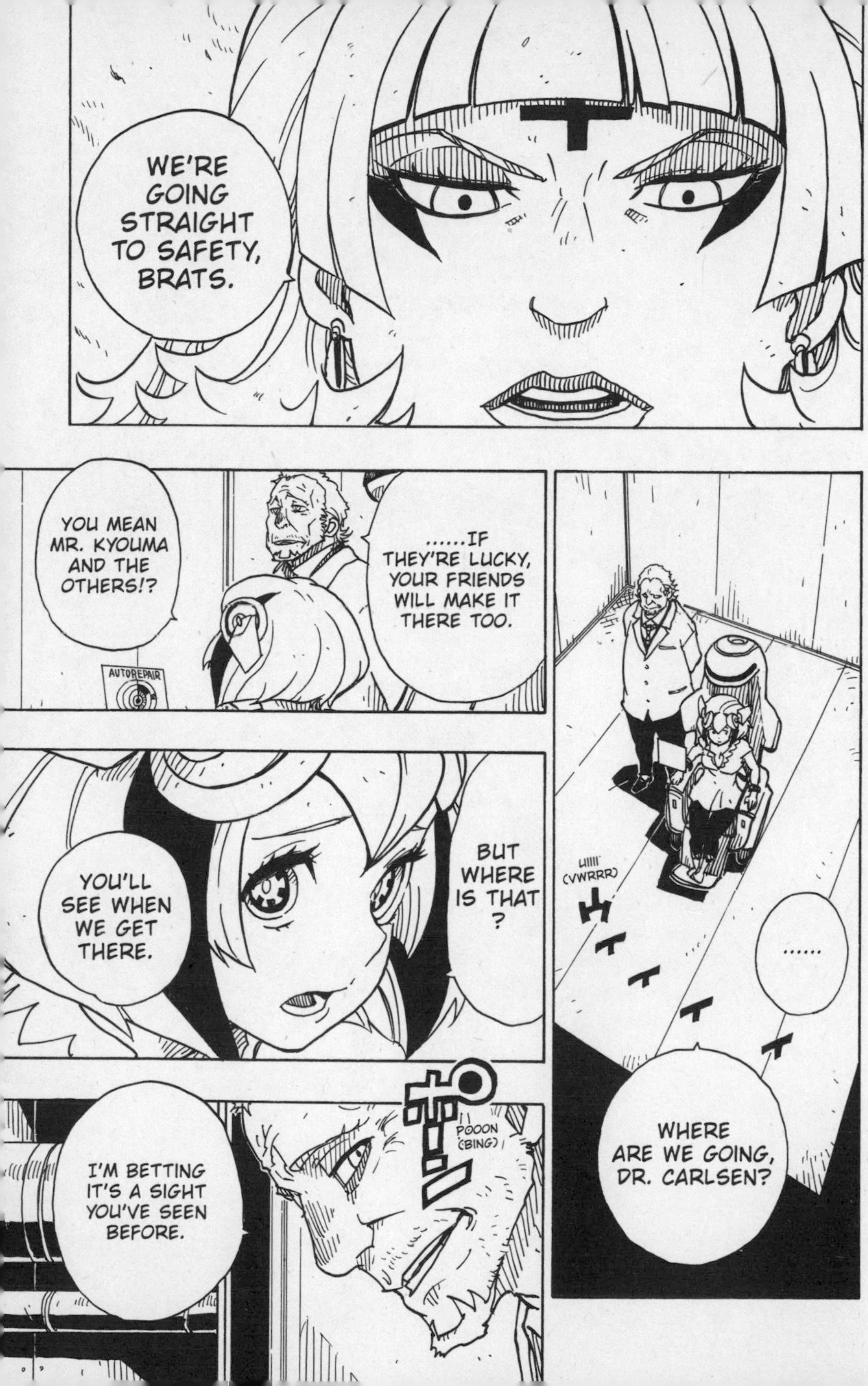
WE'RE GOING STRAIGHT TO SAFETY, BRATS.
......
WHERE ARE WE GOING, DR. CARLSEN?
(VWRRR)
YOU MEAN MR. KYOUMA AND THE OTHERS!?
......IF THEY'RE LUCKY, YOUR FRIENDS WILL MAKE IT THERE TOO.
AUTOREPAIR
BUT WHERE IS THAT ?
YOU'LL SEE WHEN WE GET THERE.
POOON (BING)
I'M BETTING IT'S A SIGHT YOU'VE SEEN BEFORE.

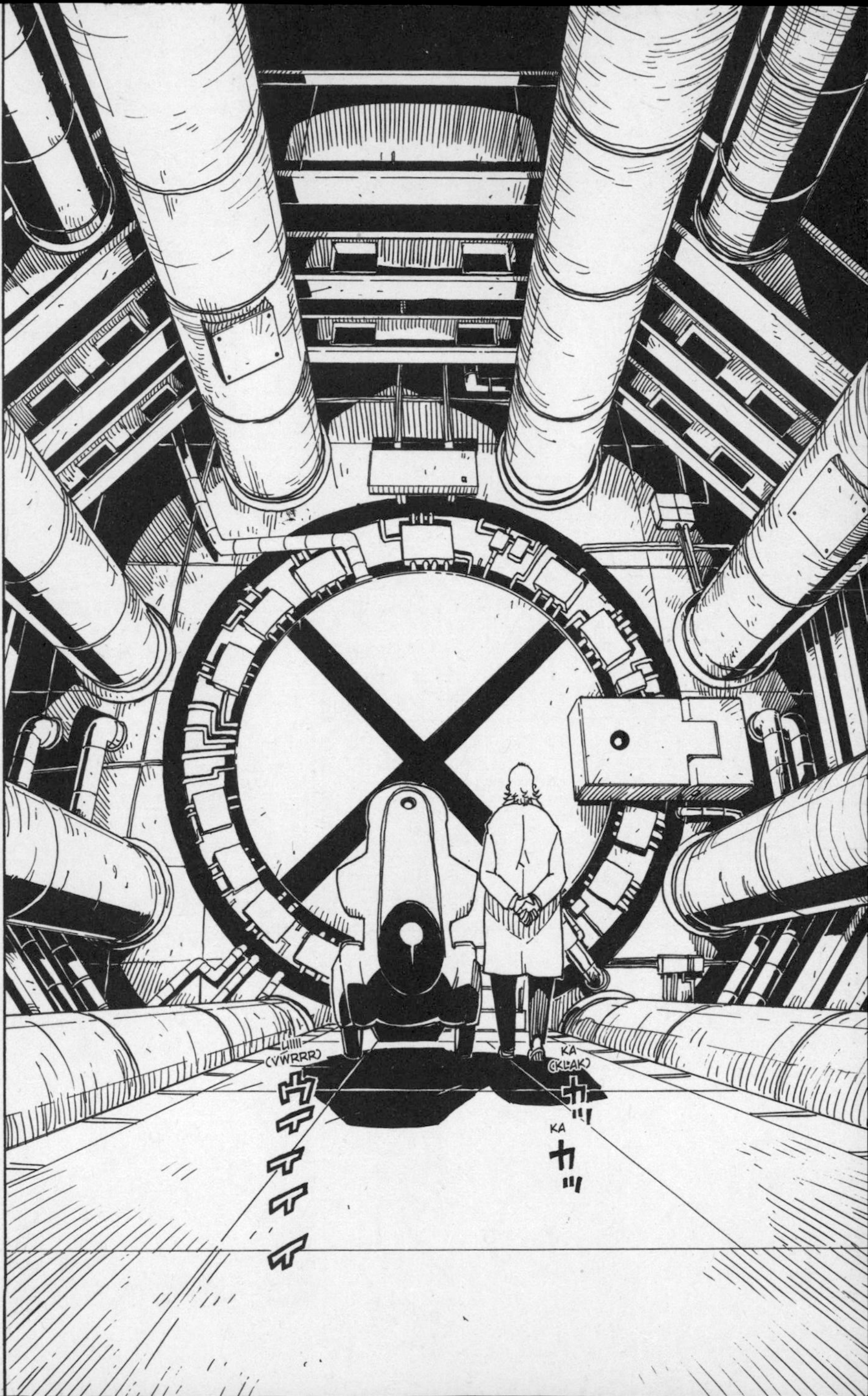

KA
(KLAK)
カッ
KA
カッ
U
(VWRRR)
ウィィィィ

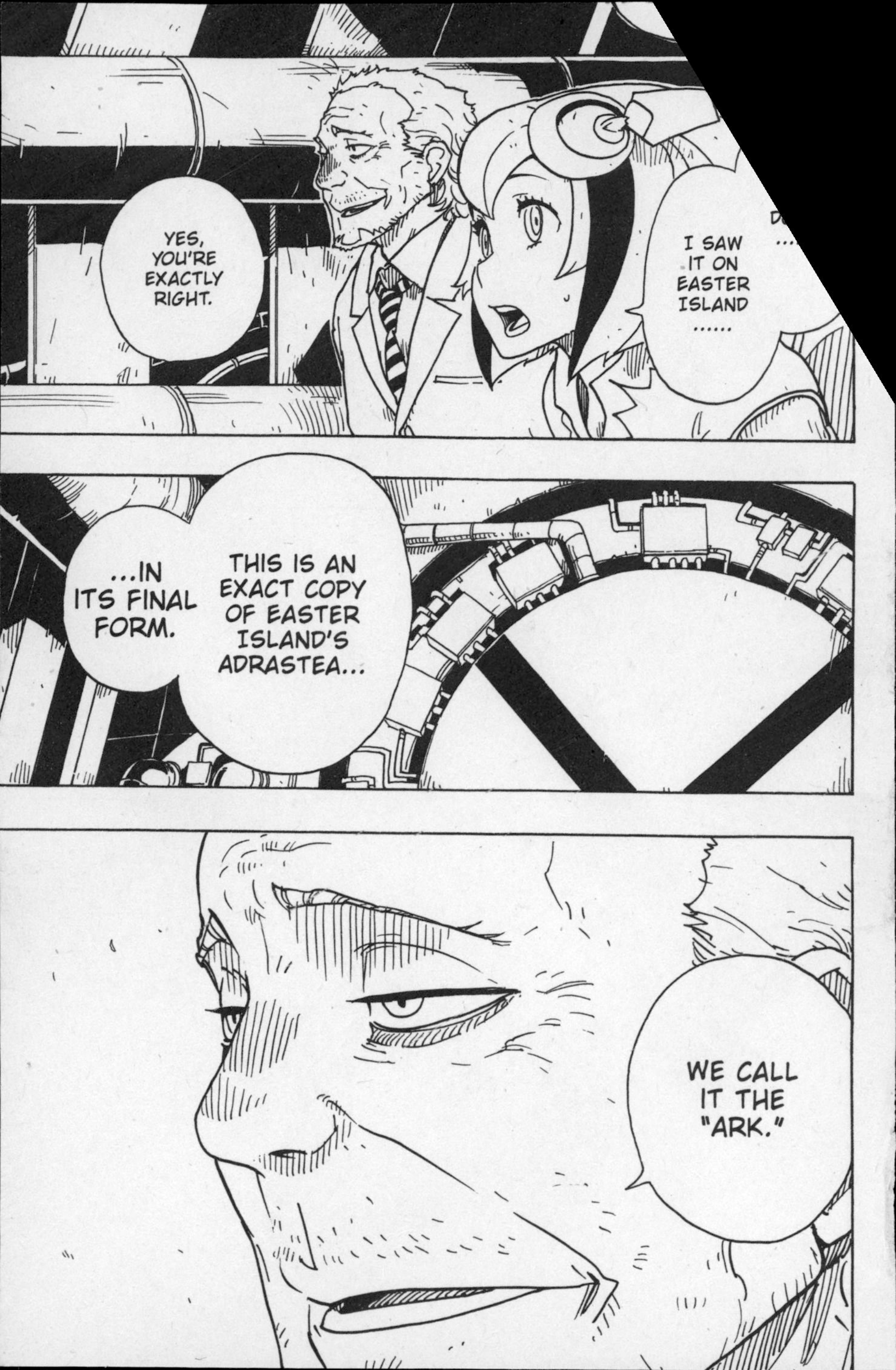
I SAW IT ON EASTER ISLAND ......
YES, YOU'RE EXACTLY RIGHT.
THIS IS AN EXACT COPY OF EASTER ISLAND'S ADRASTEA...
...IN ITS FINAL FORM.
WE CALL IT THE "ARK."

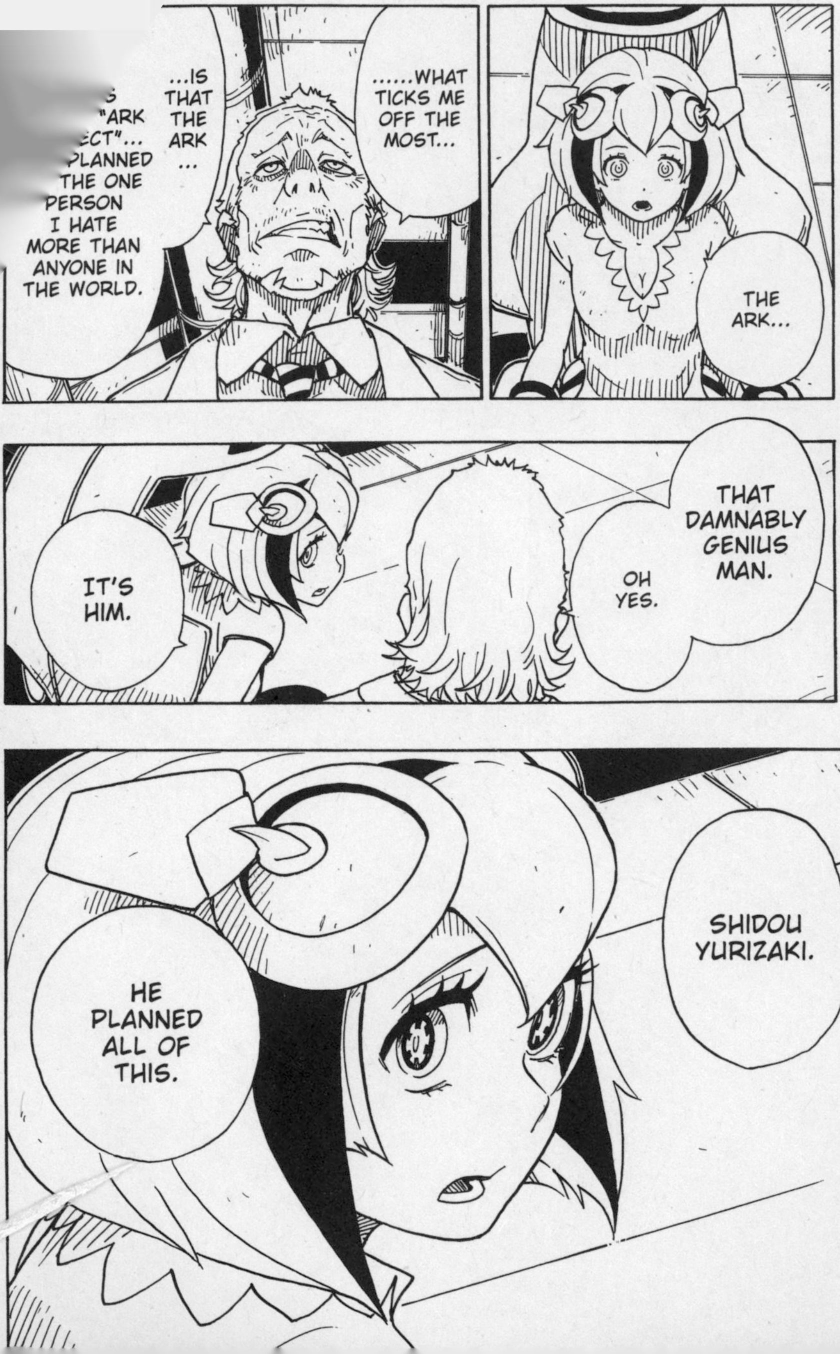
THE ARK...
......WHAT TICKS ME OFF THE MOST...
...IS THAT THE ARK ...
S "ARK ECT"... PLANNED THE ONE PERSON I HATE MORE THAN ANYONE IN THE WORLD.
THAT DAMNABLY GENIUS MAN.
OH YES.
IT'S HIM.
SHIDOU YURIZAKI.
HE PLANNED ALL OF THIS.

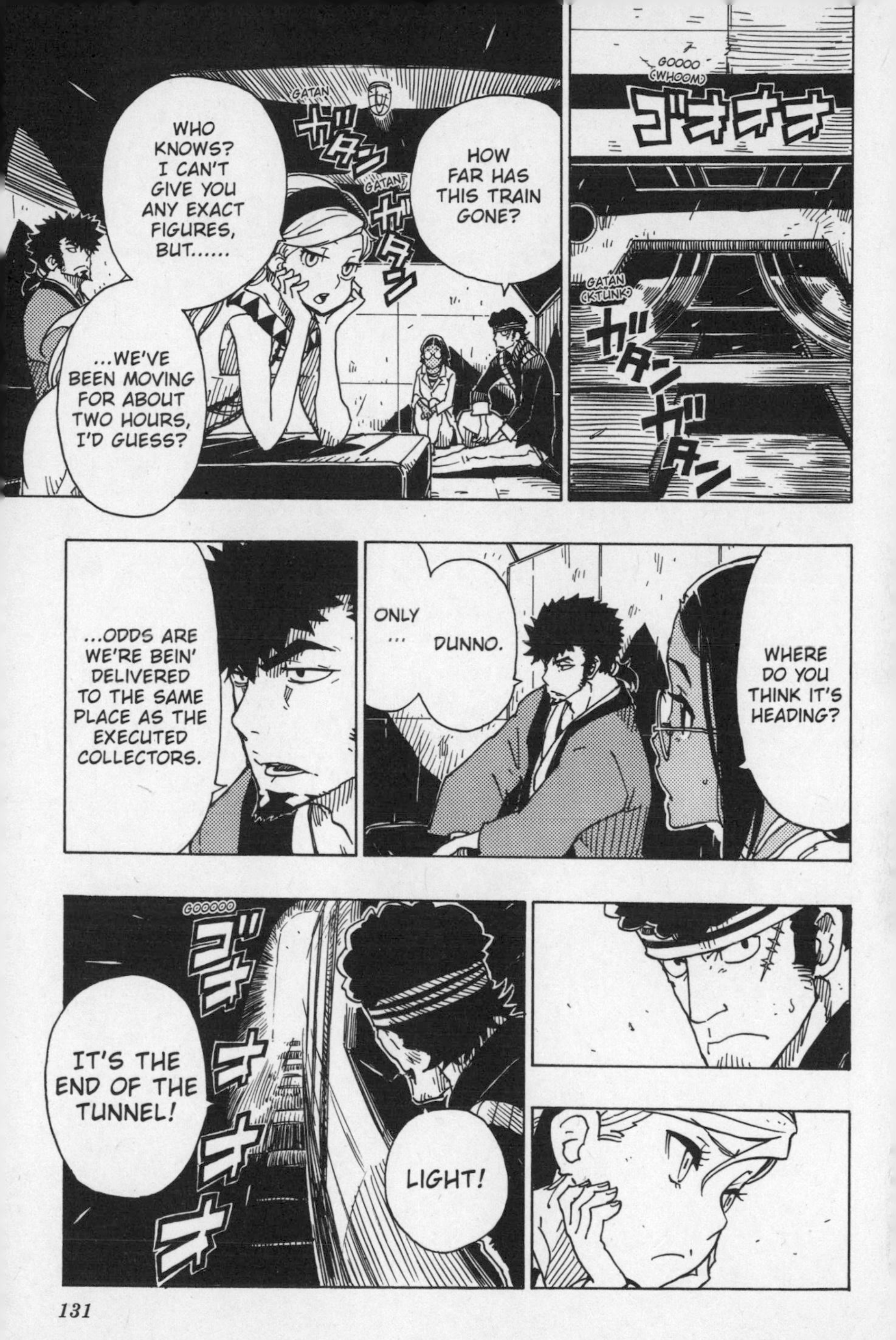
GOOOO (WHOOM)
ゴオオオ
GATAN (KTUNK)
ガタン
ガタン
HOW FAR HAS THIS TRAIN GONE?
GATAN
ガタン
GATAN
ガタン
WHO KNOWS? I CAN'T GIVE YOU ANY EXACT FIGURES, BUT......
...WE'VE BEEN MOVING FOR ABOUT TWO HOURS, I'D GUESS?
WHERE DO YOU THINK IT'S HEADING?
DUNNO.
ONLY ...
...ODDS ARE WE'RE BEIN' DELIVERED TO THE SAME PLACE AS THE EXECUTED COLLECTORS.
GOOOOO
ゴオオオオ
LIGHT!
IT'S THE END OF THE TUNNEL!

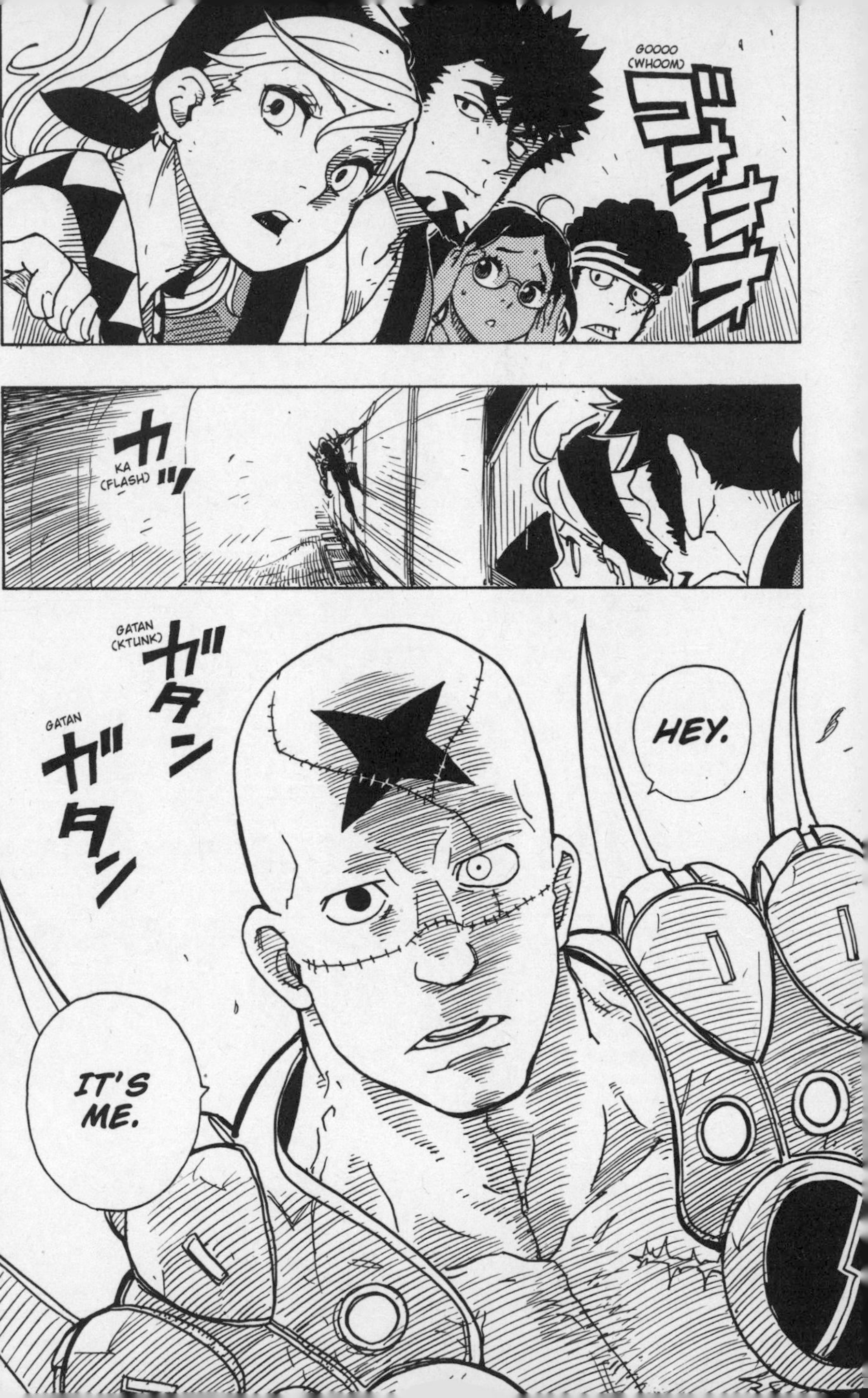
GOOOO (WHOOM)
ゴオオオ
KA (FLASH)
カッ
GATAN (KTUNK)
ガタン
GATAN
ガタン
HEY.
IT'S ME.

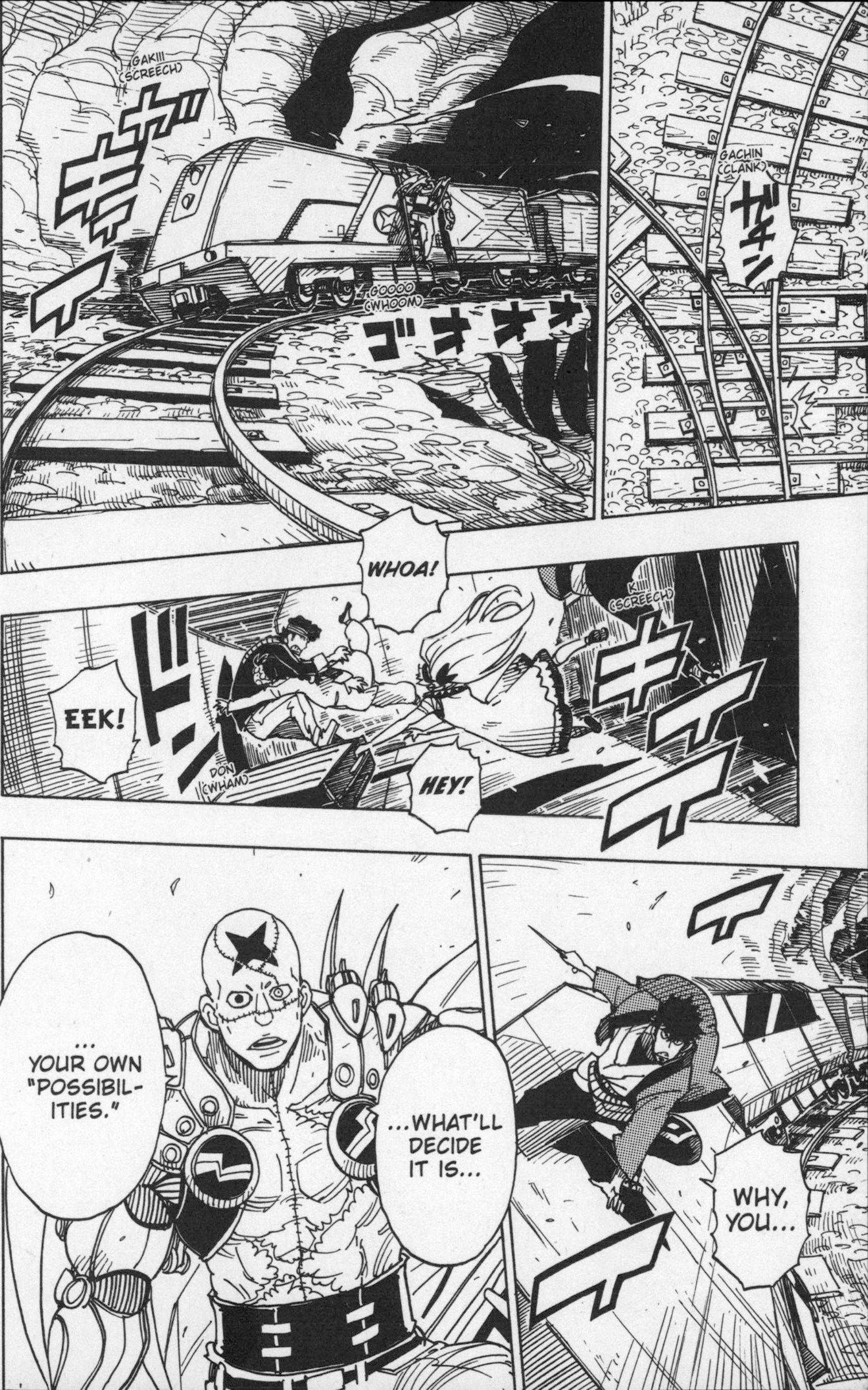
GACHIN (CLANK)
GAKIII (SCREECH)
GOOOO (WHOOM)
KII (SCREECH)
WHOA!
HEY!
EEK!
DON (WHAM)
WHY, YOU...
...WHAT'LL DECIDE IT IS...
... YOUR OWN "POSSIBIL-ITIES."

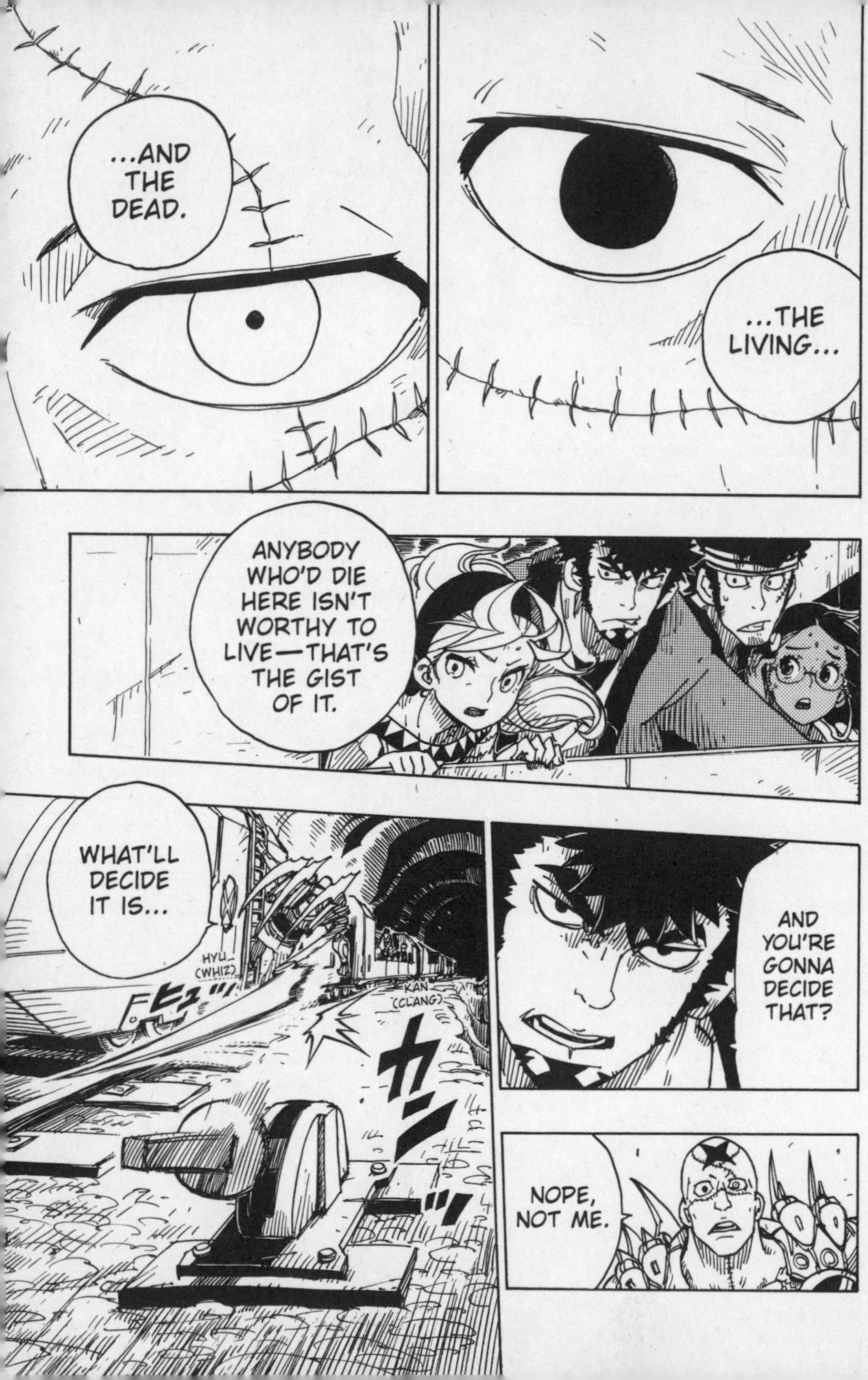
...THE LIVING...
...AND THE DEAD.
ANYBODY WHO'D DIE HERE ISN'T WORTHY TO LIVE—THAT'S THE GIST OF IT.
AND YOU'RE GONNA DECIDE THAT?
NOPE, NOT ME.
WHAT'LL DECIDE IT IS...
HYU (WHIZ)
KAN (CLANG)

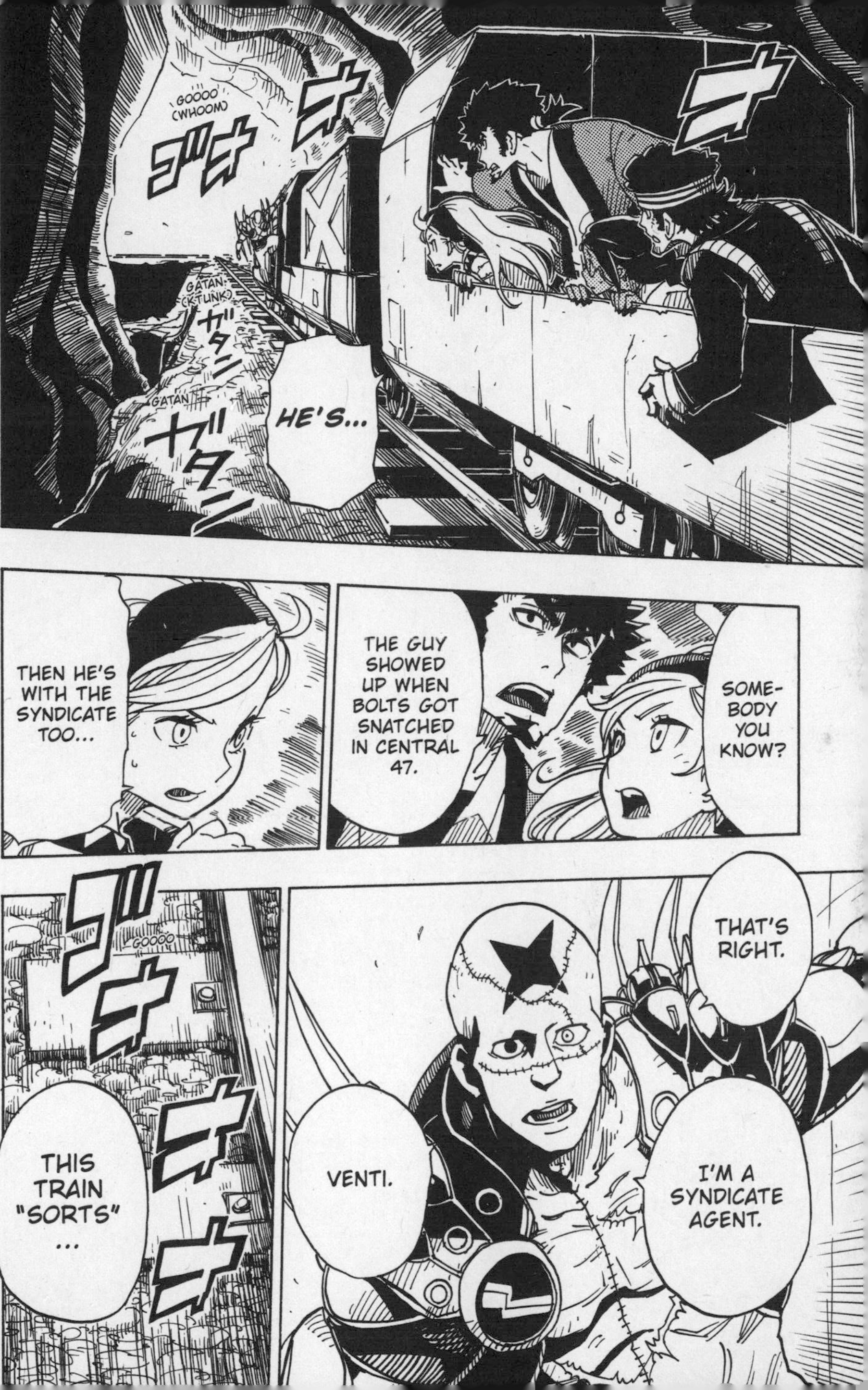
GOOOO (WHOOM)
GATAN (K-TUNK)
ガタン
GATAN
ガタン
HE'S...
SOMEBODY YOU KNOW?
THE GUY SHOWED UP WHEN BOLTS GOT SNATCHED IN CENTRAL 47.
THEN HE'S WITH THE SYNDICATE TOO...
THAT'S RIGHT.
I'M A SYNDICATE AGENT.
VENTI.
GOOOO
THIS TRAIN "SORTS" ...

FILE.101 THE DEPTHS OF HELL

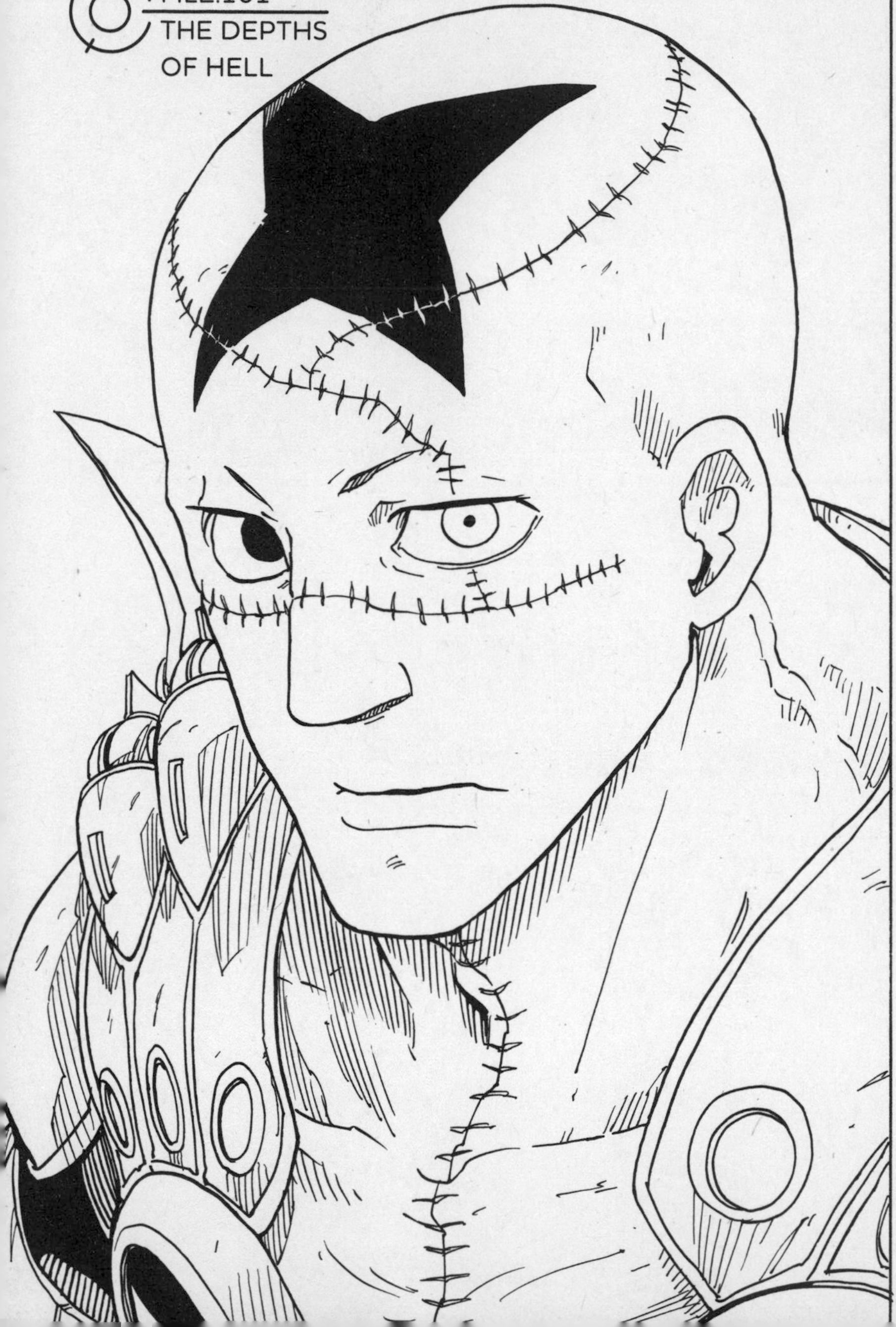

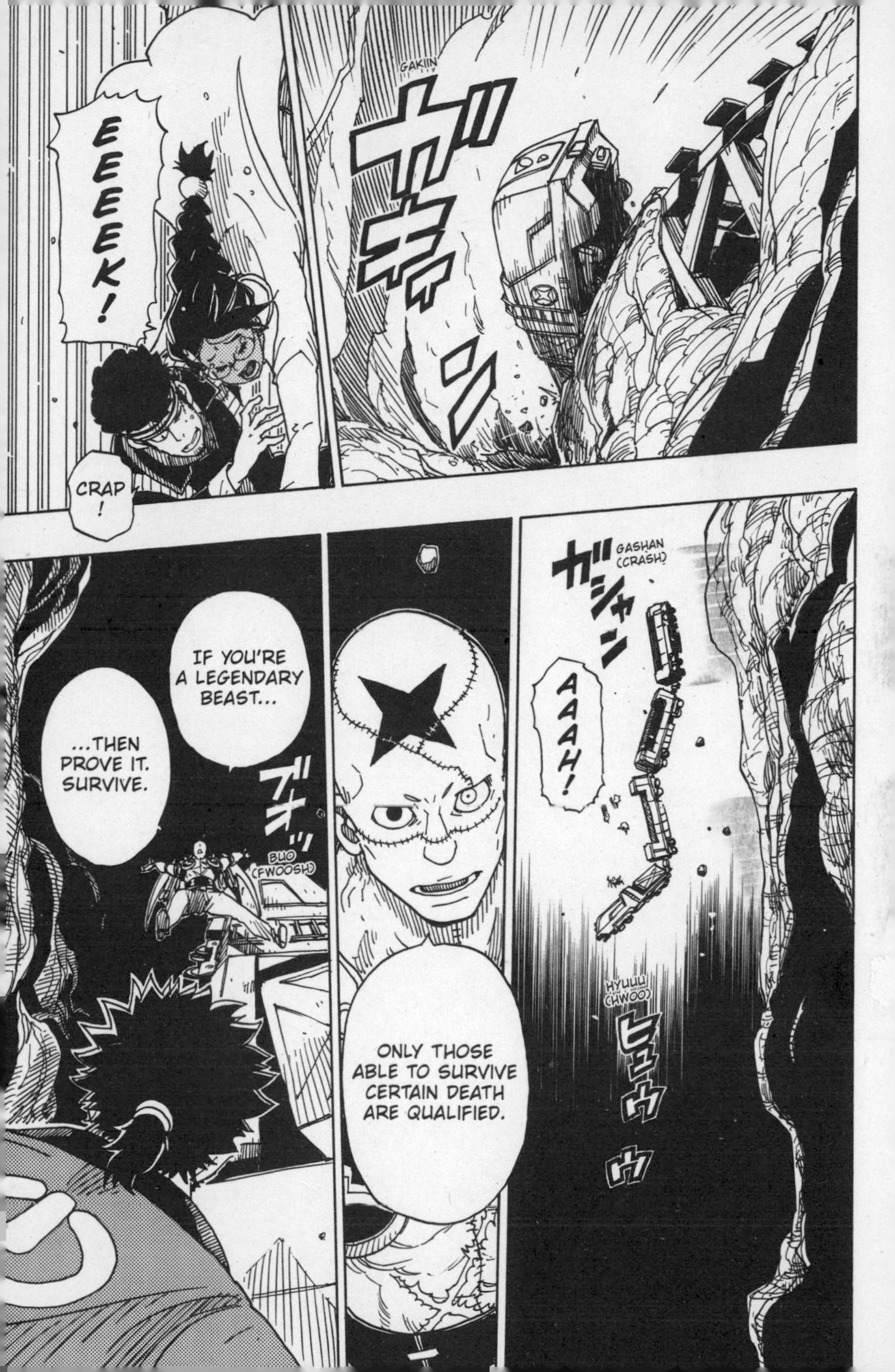
GAKIIN
EEEEEK!
CRAP!
GASHAN (CRASH)
AAAH!
HYUUU (HWOO)
ONLY THOSE ABLE TO SURVIVE CERTAIN DEATH ARE QUALIFIED.
IF YOU'RE A LEGENDARY BEAST...
...THEN PROVE IT. SURVIVE.
BUO (FWOOSH)

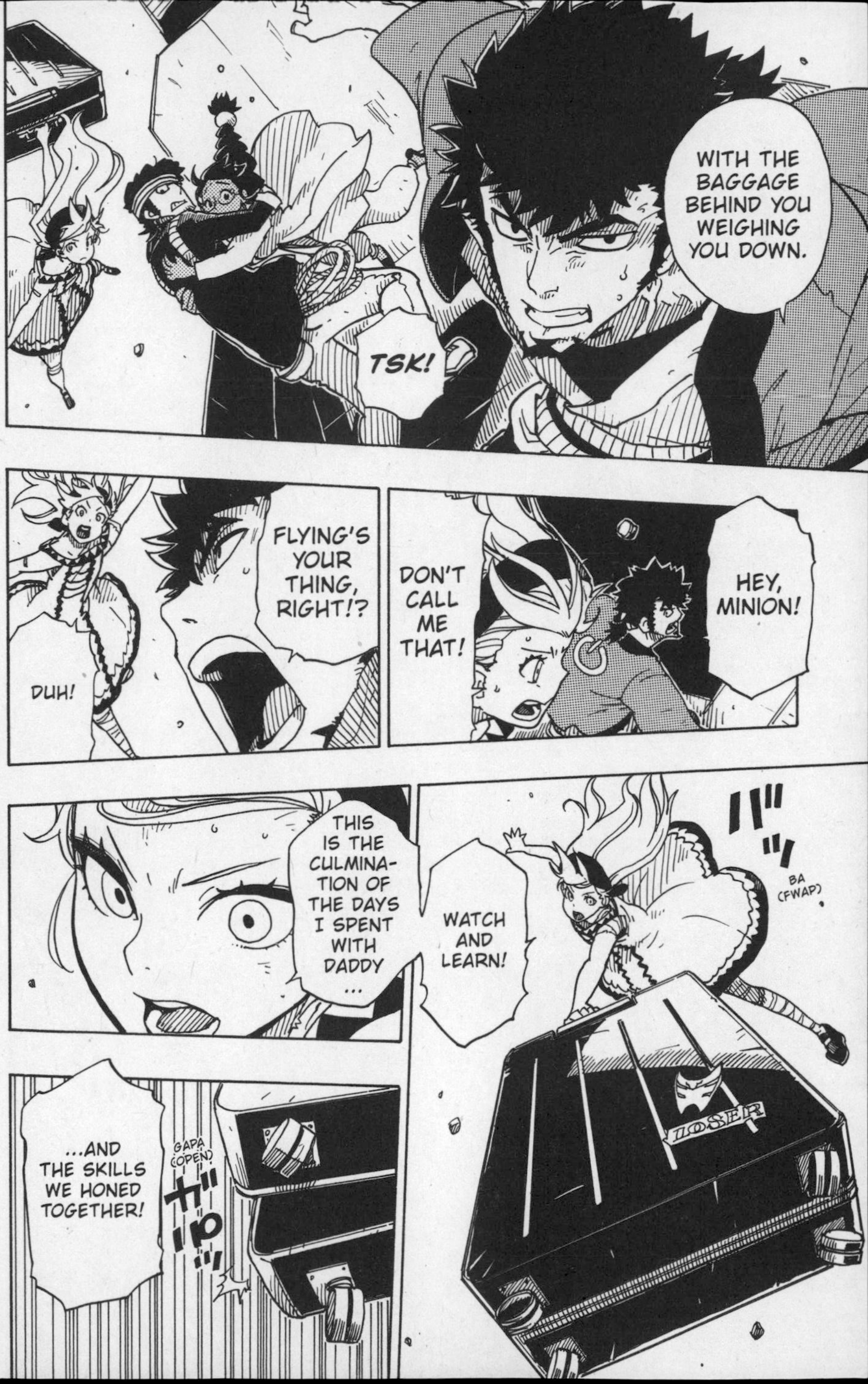
WITH THE BAGGAGE BEHIND YOU WEIGHING YOU DOWN.
TSK!
HEY, MINION!
DON'T CALL ME THAT!
FLYING'S YOUR THING, RIGHT!?
DUH!
BA (FWAP)
WATCH AND LEARN!
LOSER
THIS IS THE CULMINATION OF THE DAYS I SPENT WITH DADDY ...
...AND THE SKILLS WE HONED TOGETHER!
GAPA (OPEN)

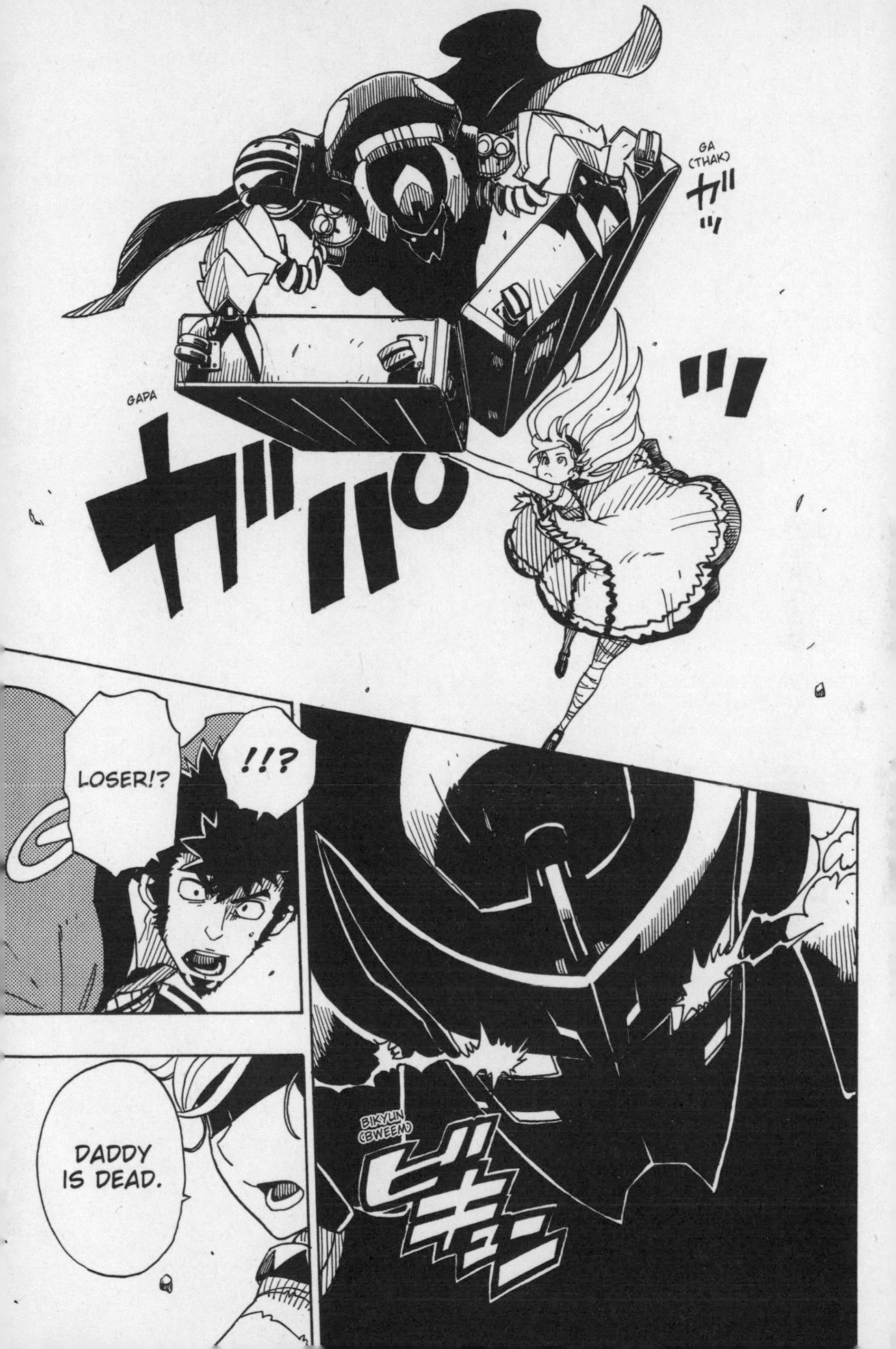
GA (THAK)
ガッ
GAPA
ガパッ
BIKYUN (BWEEM)
ビキュン
!!?
LOSER!?
DADDY IS DEAD.

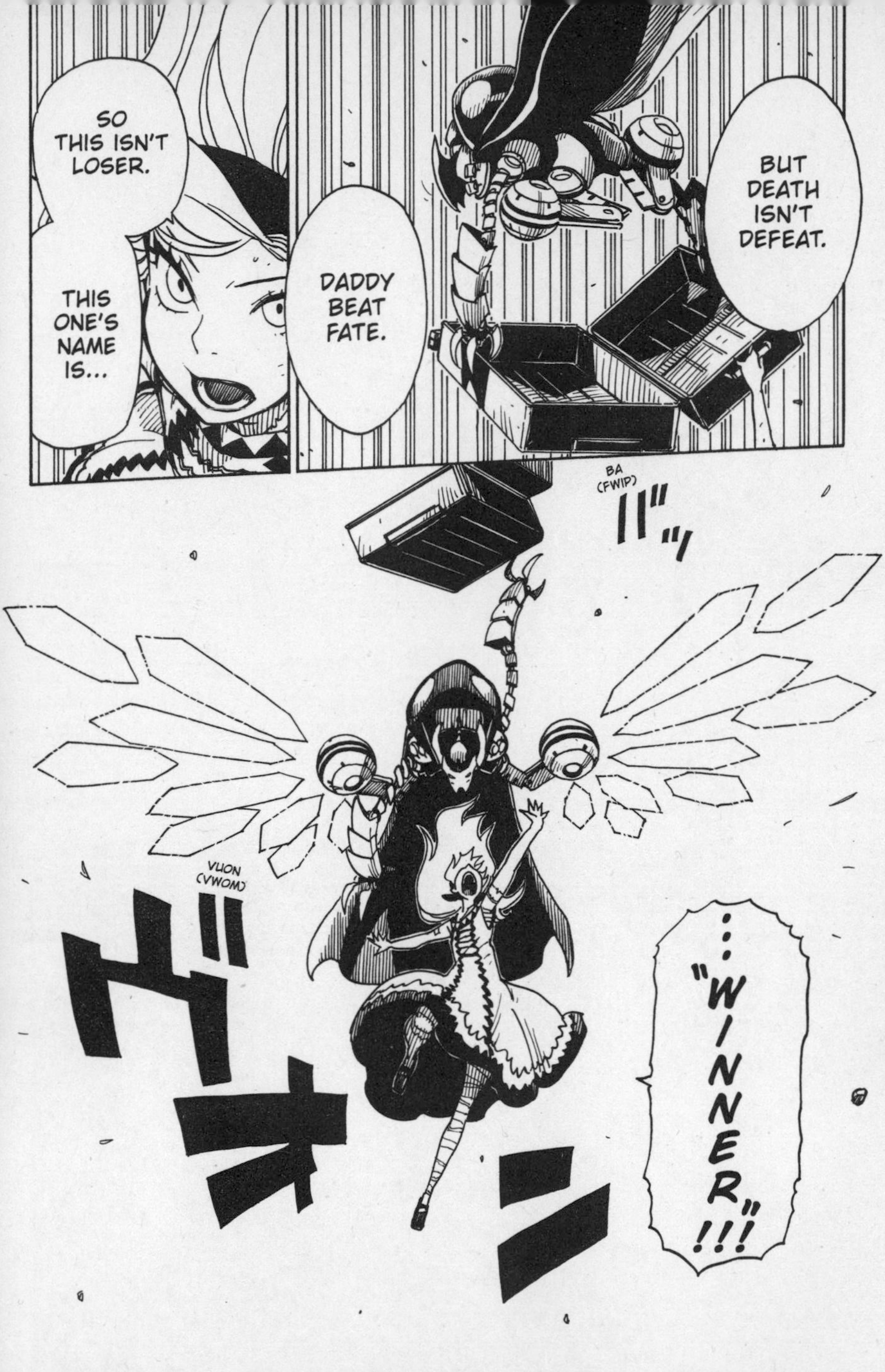
BUT DEATH ISN'T DEFEAT.
DADDY BEAT FATE.
SO THIS ISN'T LOSER.
THIS ONE'S NAME IS...
BA (FWIP)
..."WINNER"!!!
VUON (VWOM)

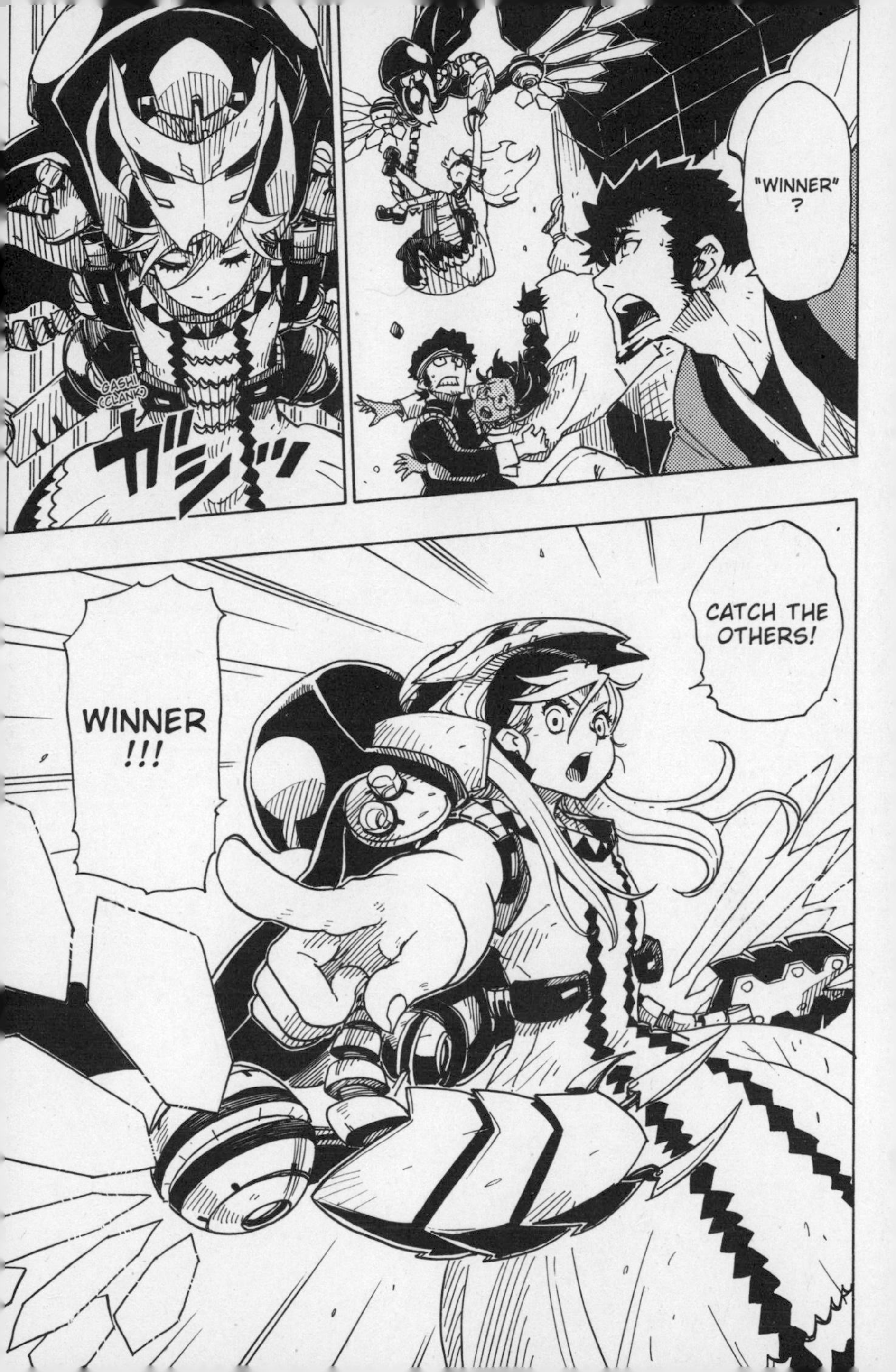
"WINNER"
?
GASHI
(CLANK)
ガシッ
CATCH THE
OTHERS!
WINNER
!!!

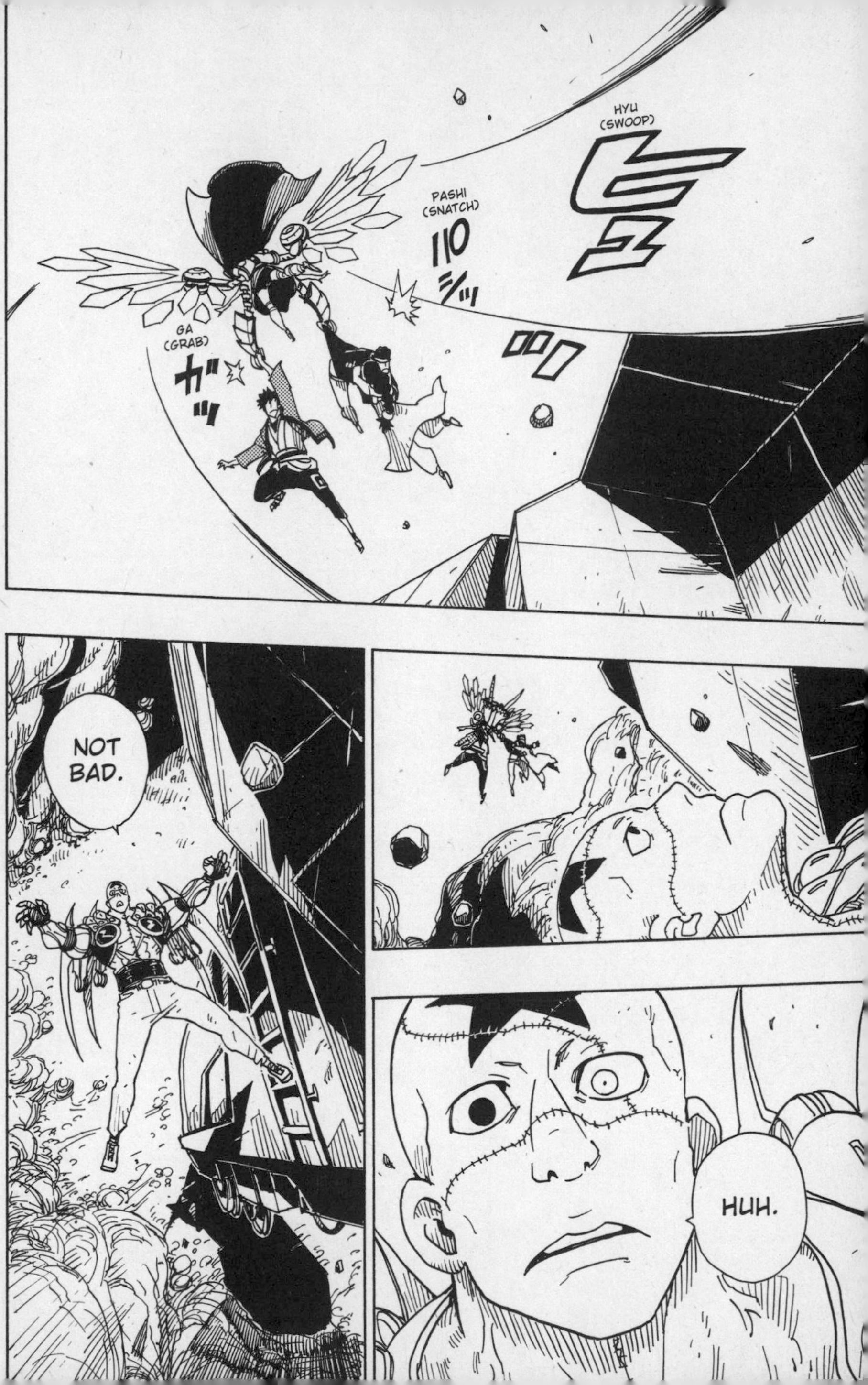
HYU (SWOOP)
PASHI (SNATCH)
GA (GRAB)
HUH.
NOT BAD.

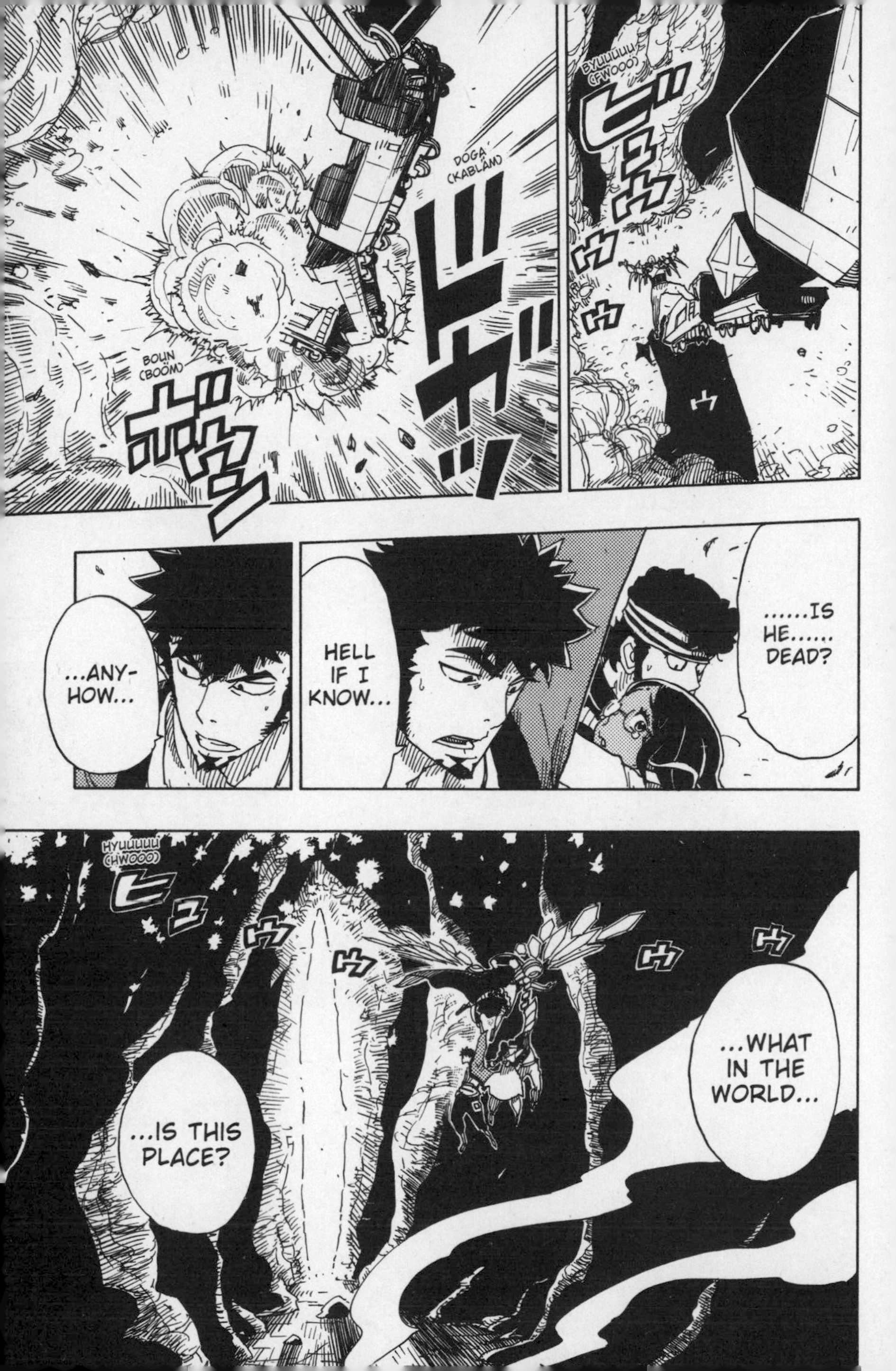

BYUUUUUU (FWOOO)
DOGA (KABLAM)
BOUN (BOÖM)
......IS HE...... DEAD?
HELL IF I KNOW...
...ANY-HOW...
HYUUUUUU (HWOOO)
...WHAT IN THE WORLD...
...IS THIS PLACE?

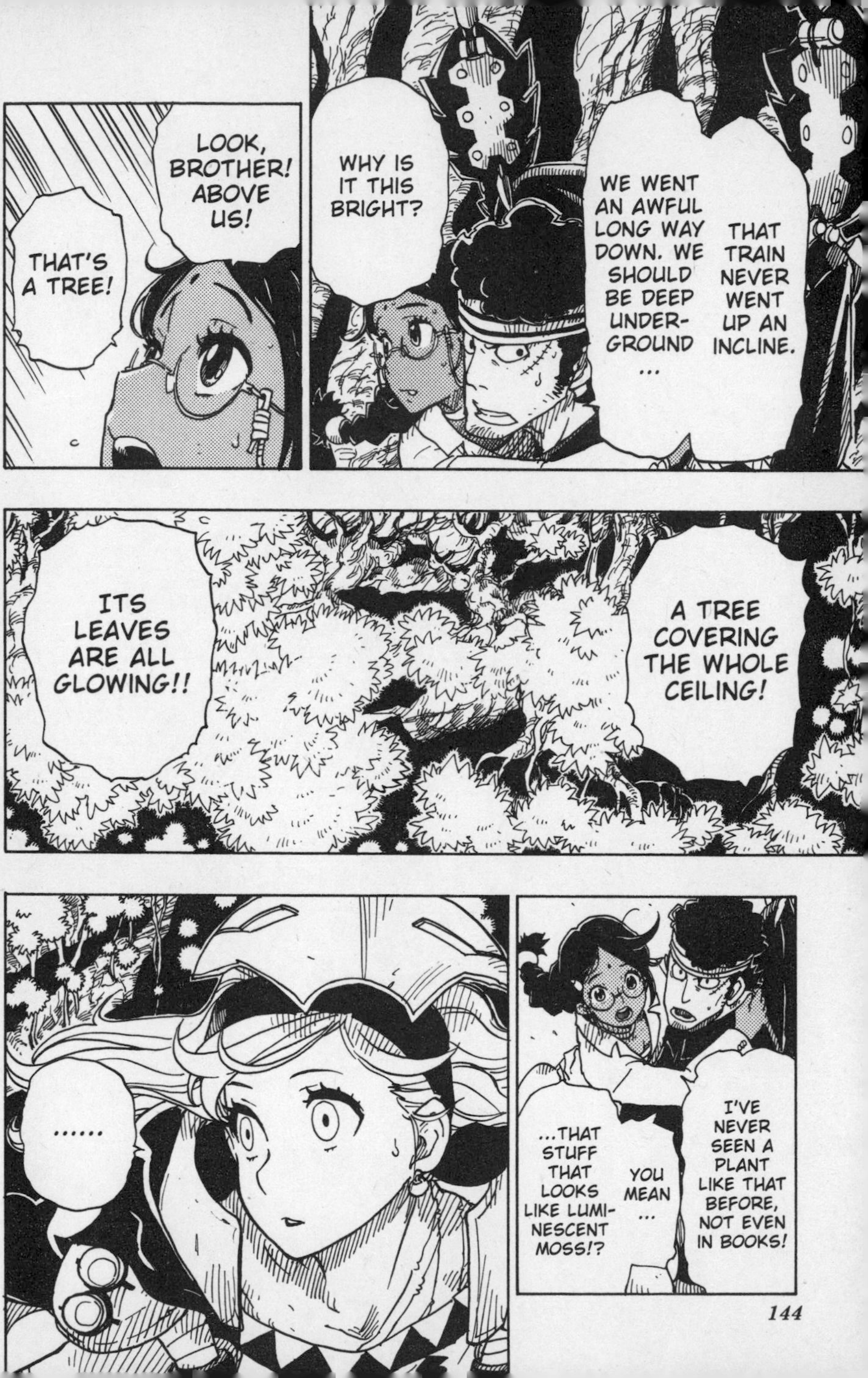
THAT TRAIN NEVER WENT UP AN INCLINE.
WE WENT AN AWFUL LONG WAY DOWN. WE SHOULD BE DEEP UNDER-GROUND ...
WHY IS IT THIS BRIGHT?
LOOK, BROTHER! ABOVE US!
THAT'S A TREE!
A TREE COVERING THE WHOLE CEILING!
ITS LEAVES ARE ALL GLOWING!!
I'VE NEVER SEEN A PLANT LIKE THAT BEFORE, NOT EVEN IN BOOKS!
YOU MEAN ...
...THAT STUFF THAT LOOKS LIKE LUMI-NESCENT MOSS!?
......

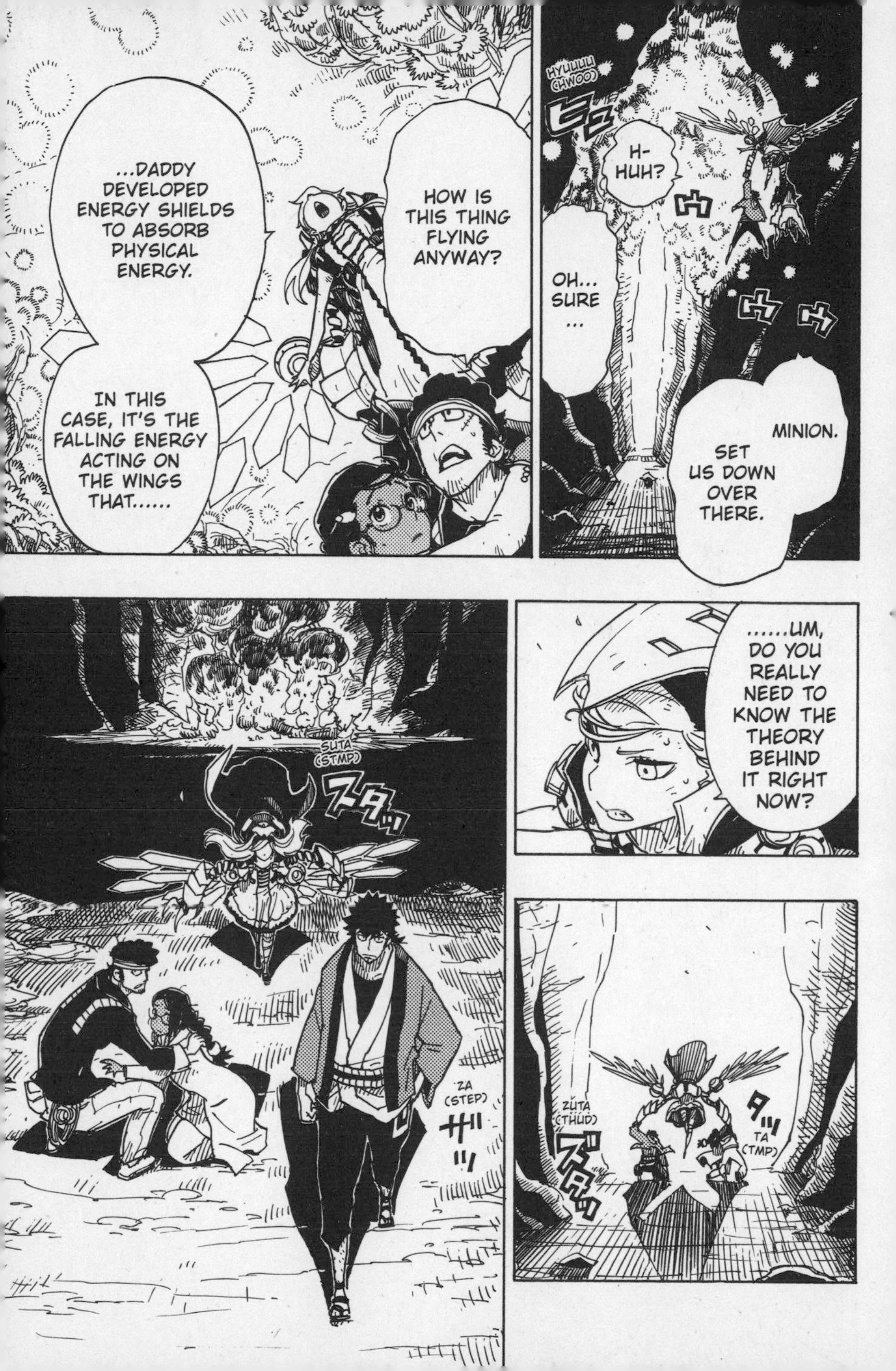
HYULULU (HWOO)
H-HUH?
OH... SURE ...
MINION. SET US DOWN OVER THERE.
HOW IS THIS THING FLYING ANYWAY?
...DADDY DEVELOPED ENERGY SHIELDS TO ABSORB PHYSICAL ENERGY.
IN THIS CASE, IT'S THE FALLING ENERGY ACTING ON THE WINGS THAT......
......UM, DO YOU REALLY NEED TO KNOW THE THEORY BEHIND IT RIGHT NOW?
TA (TMP)
ZUTA (THUD)
SUTA (STMP)
ZA (STEP)

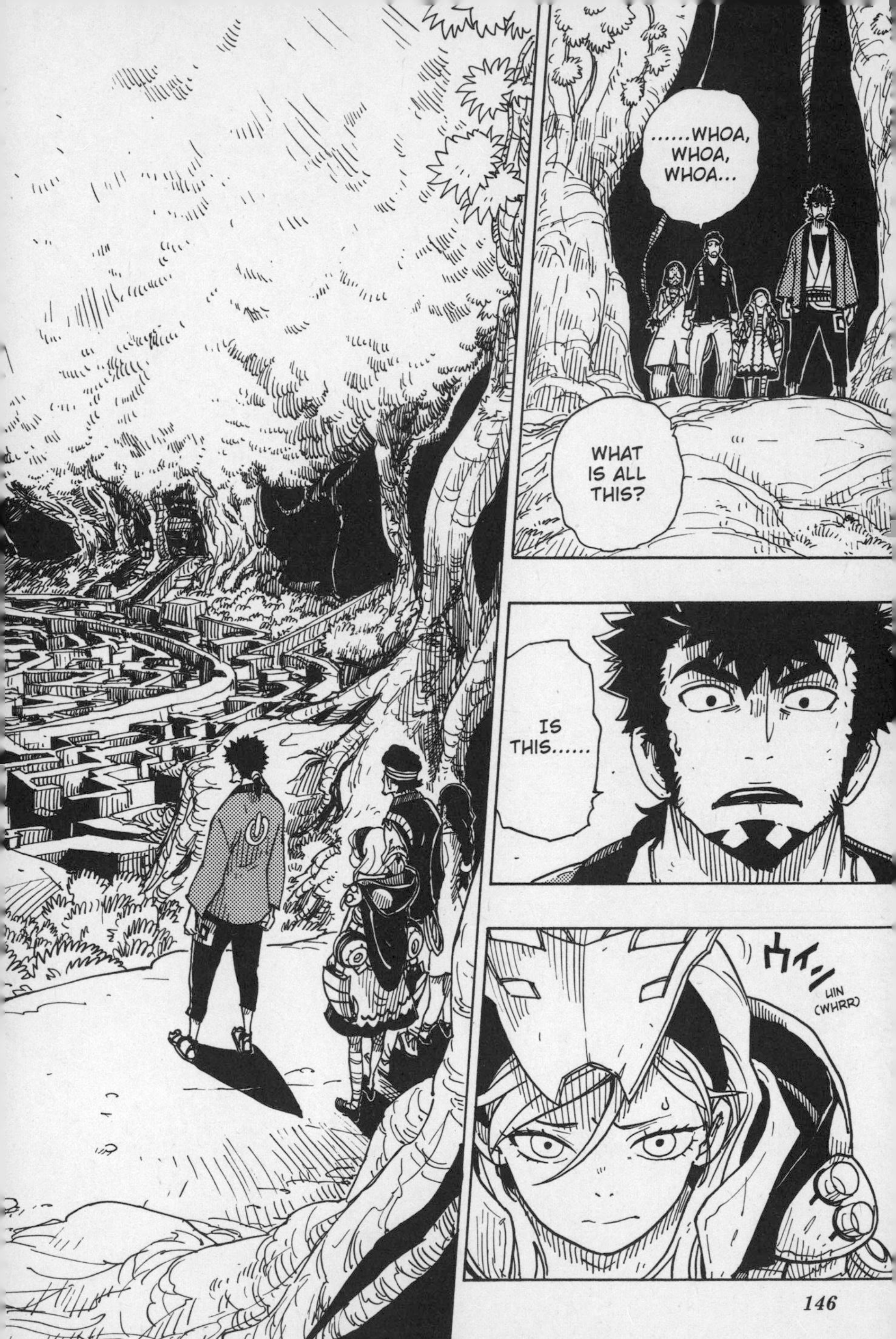
......WHOA, WHOA, WHOA...
WHAT IS ALL THIS?
IS THIS......
UIN (WHRR)

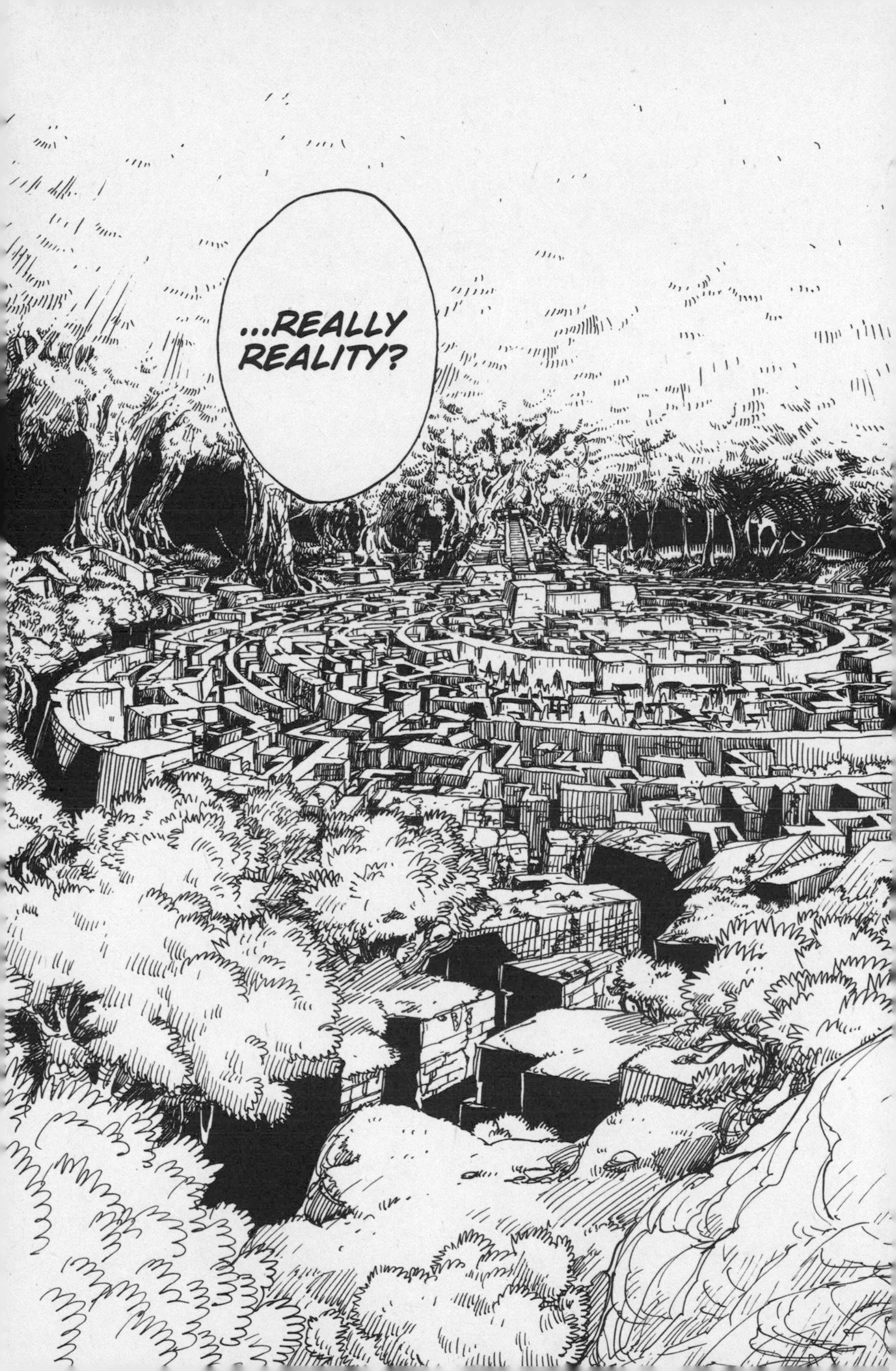
...REALLY REALITY?

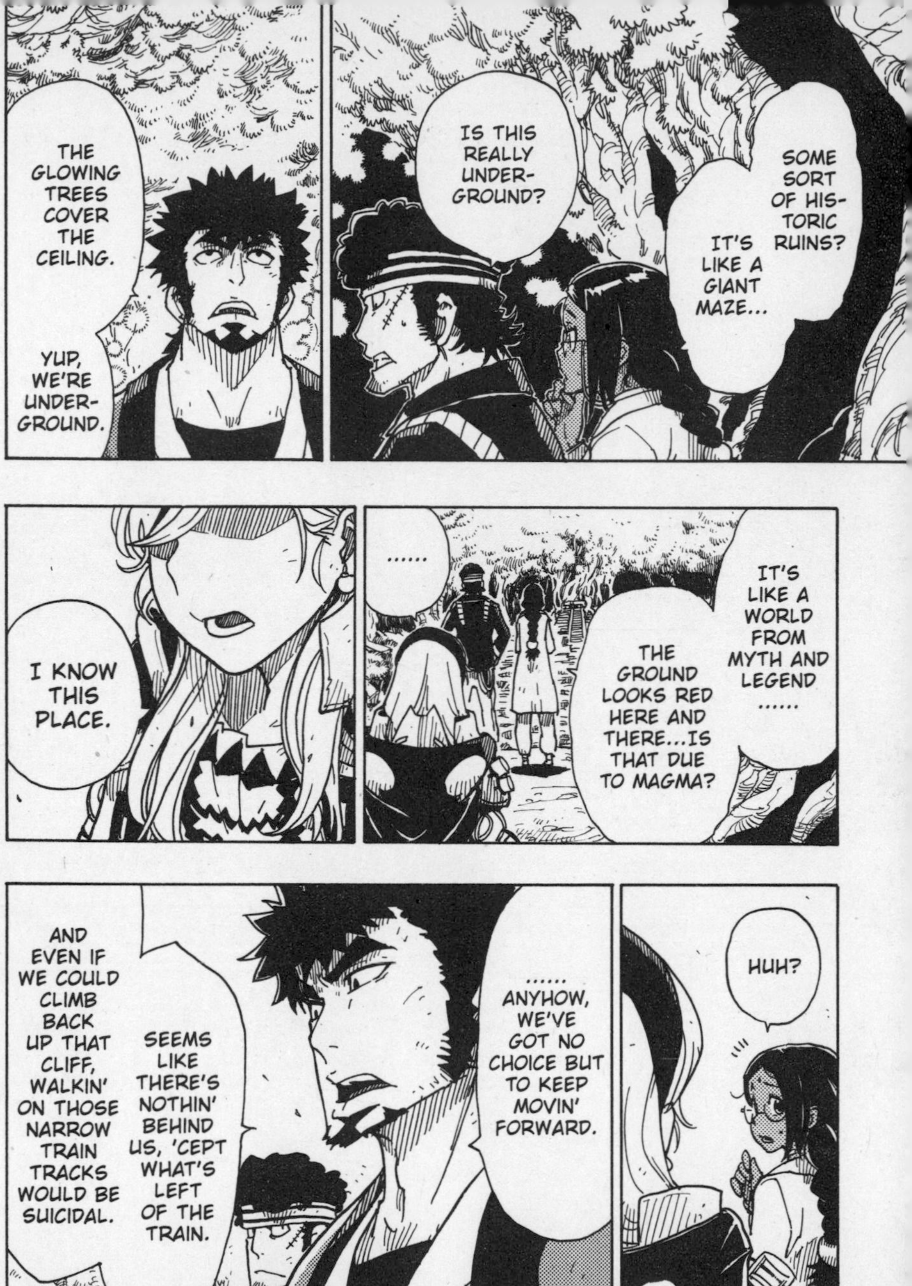
SOME SORT OF HISTORIC RUINS? IT'S LIKE A GIANT MAZE...
IS THIS REALLY UNDERGROUND?
THE GLOWING TREES COVER THE CEILING.
YUP, WE'RE UNDERGROUND.
IT'S LIKE A WORLD FROM MYTH AND LEGEND ......
THE GROUND LOOKS RED HERE AND THERE...IS THAT DUE TO MAGMA?
......
I KNOW THIS PLACE.
HUH?
...... ANYHOW, WE'VE GOT NO CHOICE BUT TO KEEP MOVIN' FORWARD.
SEEMS LIKE THERE'S NOTHIN' BEHIND US, 'CEPT WHAT'S LEFT OF THE TRAIN.
AND EVEN IF WE COULD CLIMB BACK UP THAT CLIFF, WALKIN' ON THOSE NARROW TRAIN TRACKS WOULD BE SUICIDAL.

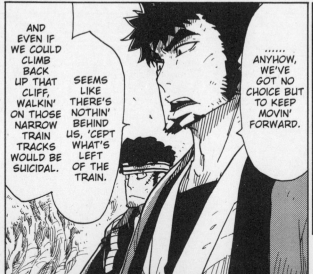

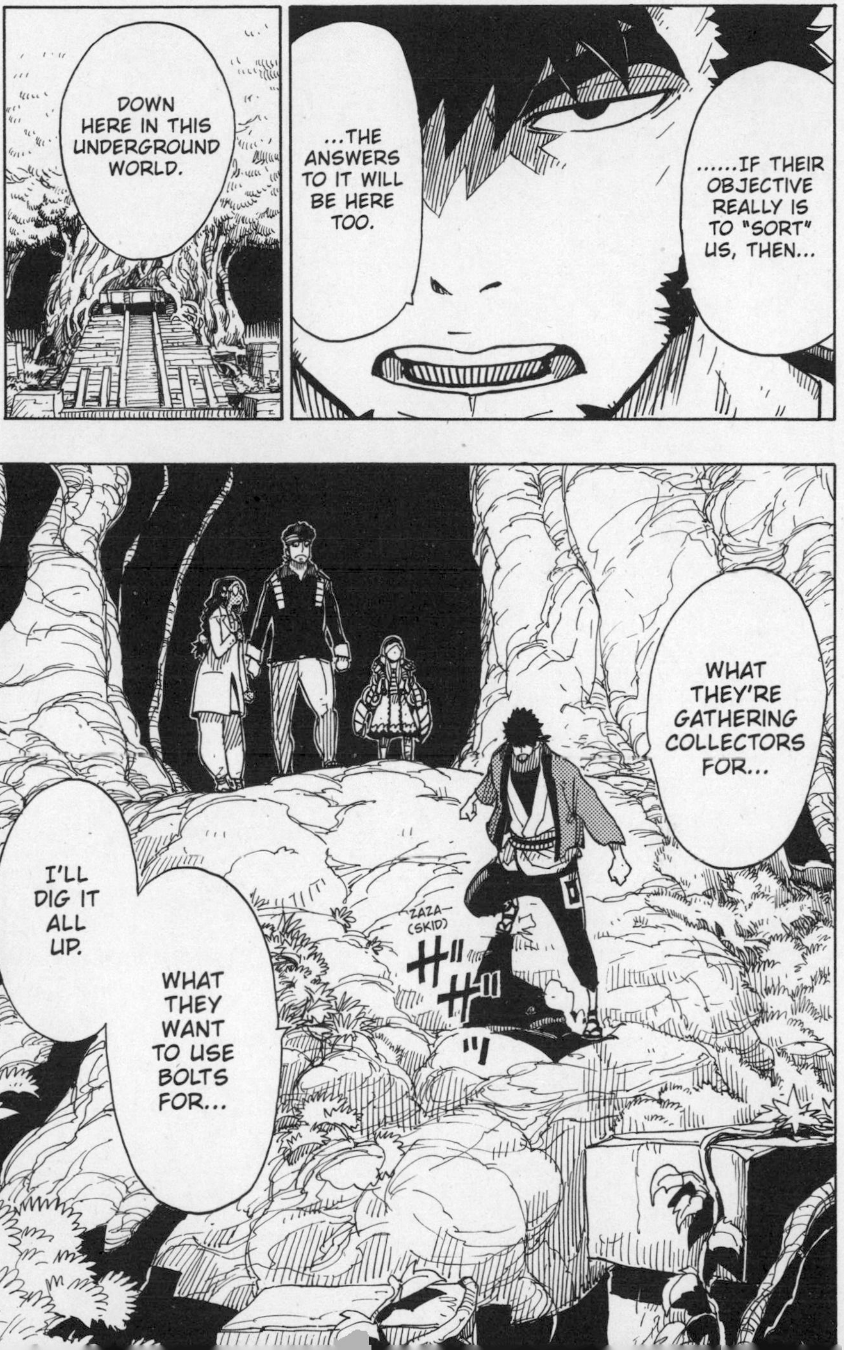
......IF THEIR OBJECTIVE REALLY IS TO "SORT" US, THEN...
...THE ANSWERS TO IT WILL BE HERE TOO.
DOWN HERE IN THIS UNDERGROUND WORLD.
WHAT THEY'RE GATHERING COLLECTORS FOR...
ZAZA (SKID)
WHAT THEY WANT TO USE BOLTS FOR...
I'LL DIG IT ALL UP.

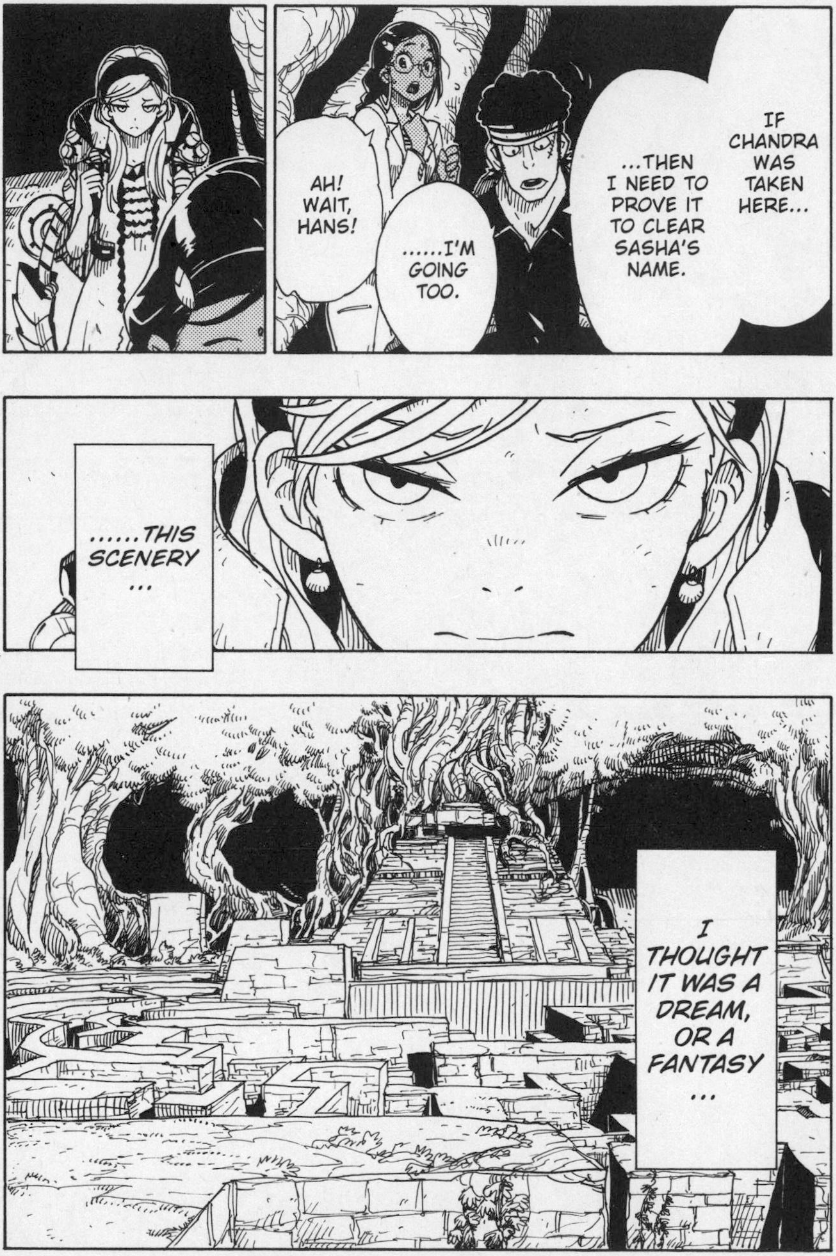
IF CHANDRA WAS TAKEN HERE...
...THEN I NEED TO PROVE IT TO CLEAR SASHA'S NAME.
......I'M GOING TOO.
AH! WAIT, HANS!
......THIS SCENERY ...
I THOUGHT IT WAS A DREAM, OR A FANTASY ...

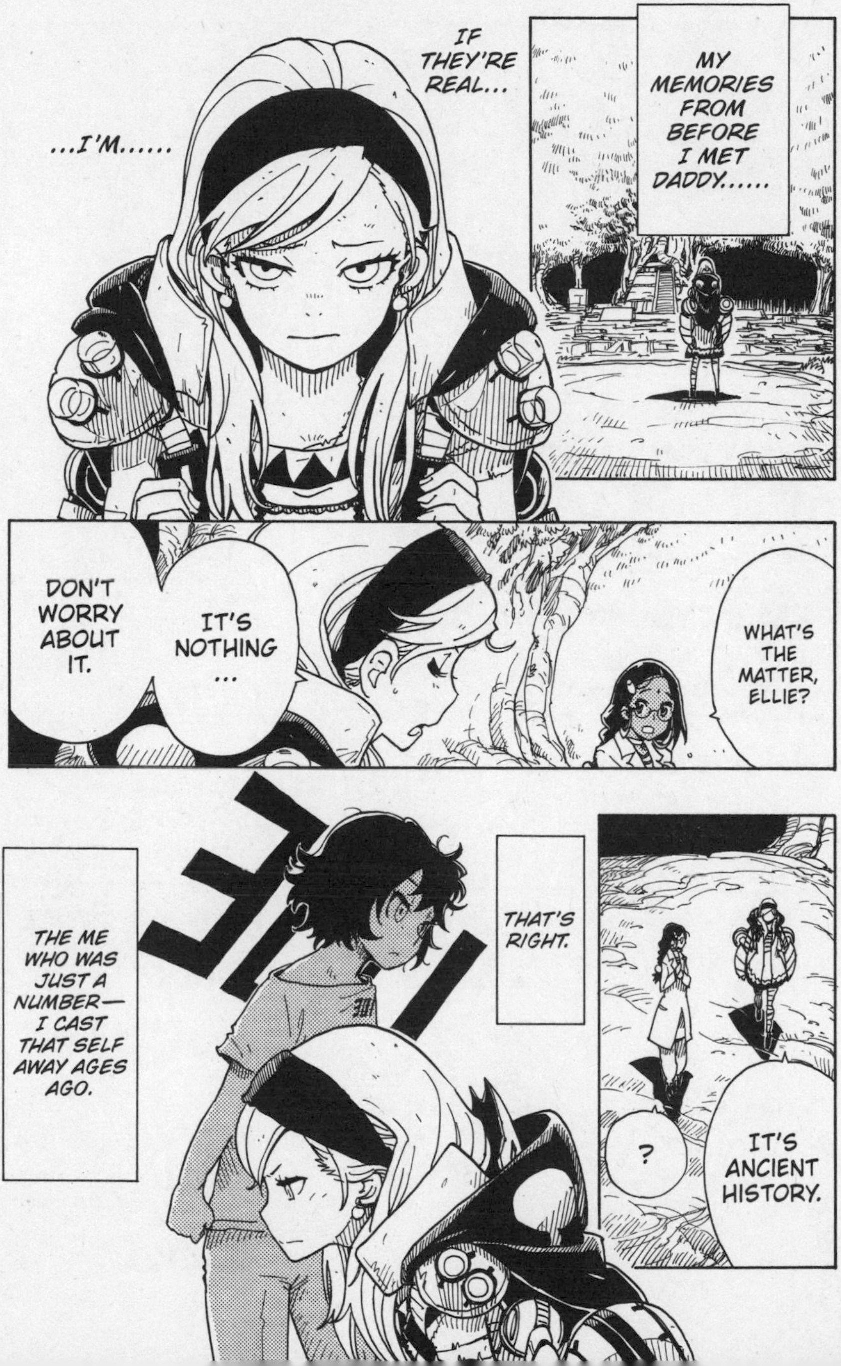
MY MEMORIES FROM BEFORE I MET DADDY.....
IF THEY'RE REAL...
...I'M......
WHAT'S THE MATTER, ELLIE?
IT'S NOTHING ...
DON'T WORRY ABOUT IT.
IT'S ANCIENT HISTORY.
?
THAT'S RIGHT.
THE ME WHO WAS JUST A NUMBER— I CAST THAT SELF AWAY AGES AGO.

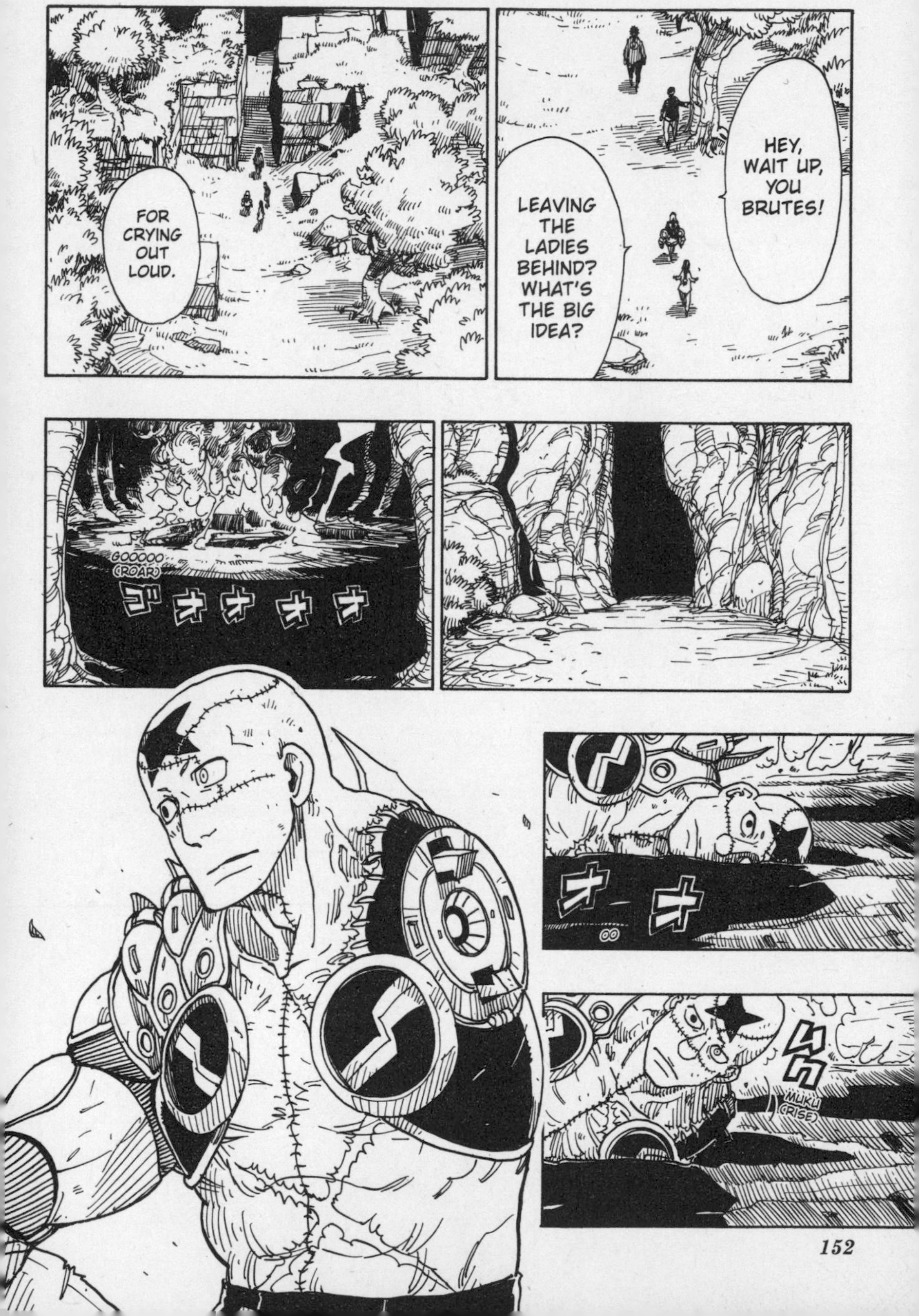
HEY, WAIT UP, YOU BRUTES!
LEAVING THE LADIES BEHIND? WHAT'S THE BIG IDEA?
FOR CRYING OUT LOUD.
GOOOOO (ROAR)
ゴオオオオ
オオ
ムク
MUKU (RISE)

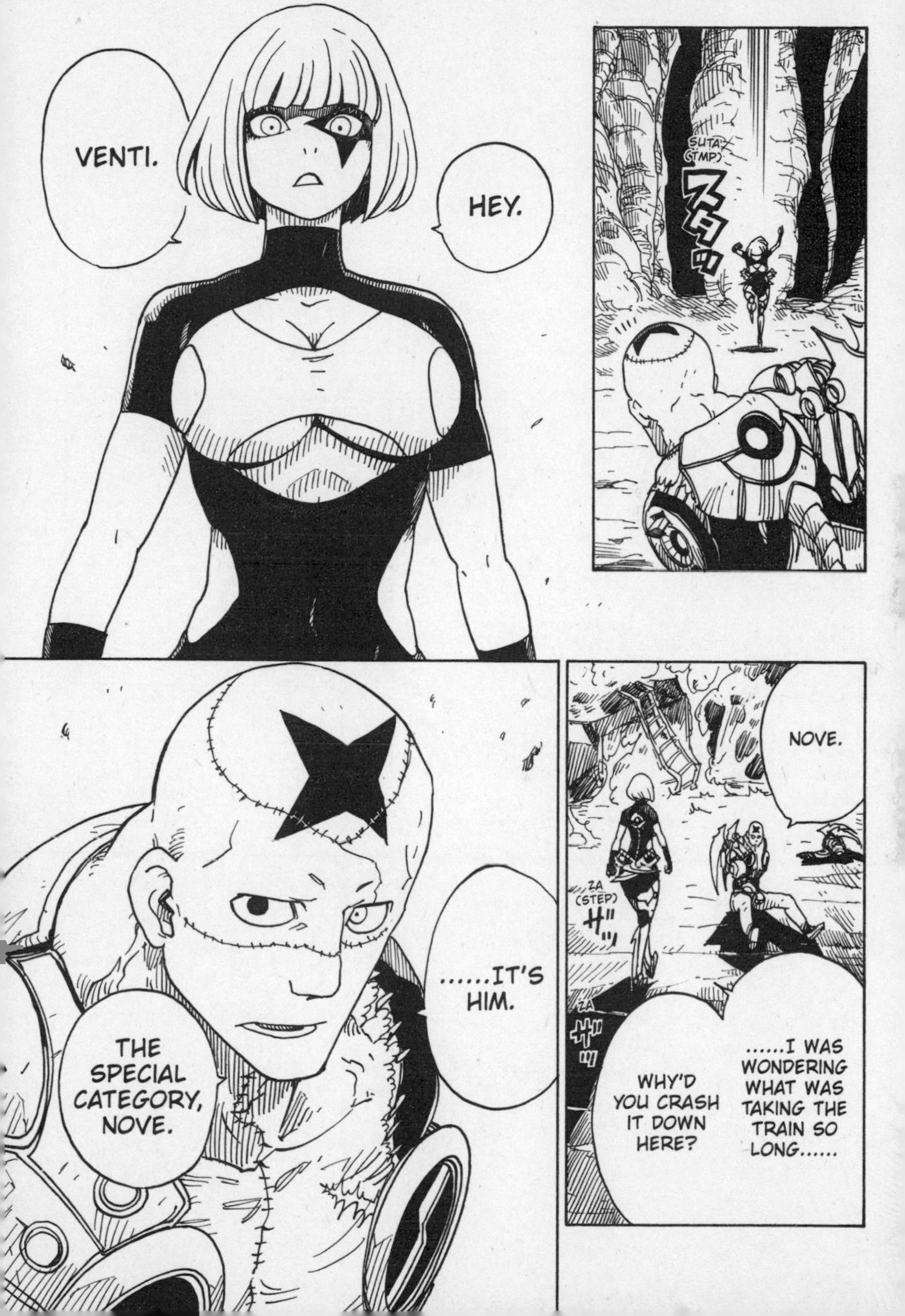
SUTA (TMP)
スタッ
HEY.
VENTI.
NOVE.
ZA (STEP)
ザッ
ZA
ザッ
......I WAS WONDERING WHAT WAS TAKING THE TRAIN SO LONG......
WHY'D YOU CRASH IT DOWN HERE?
......IT'S HIM.
THE SPECIAL CATEGORY, NOVE.

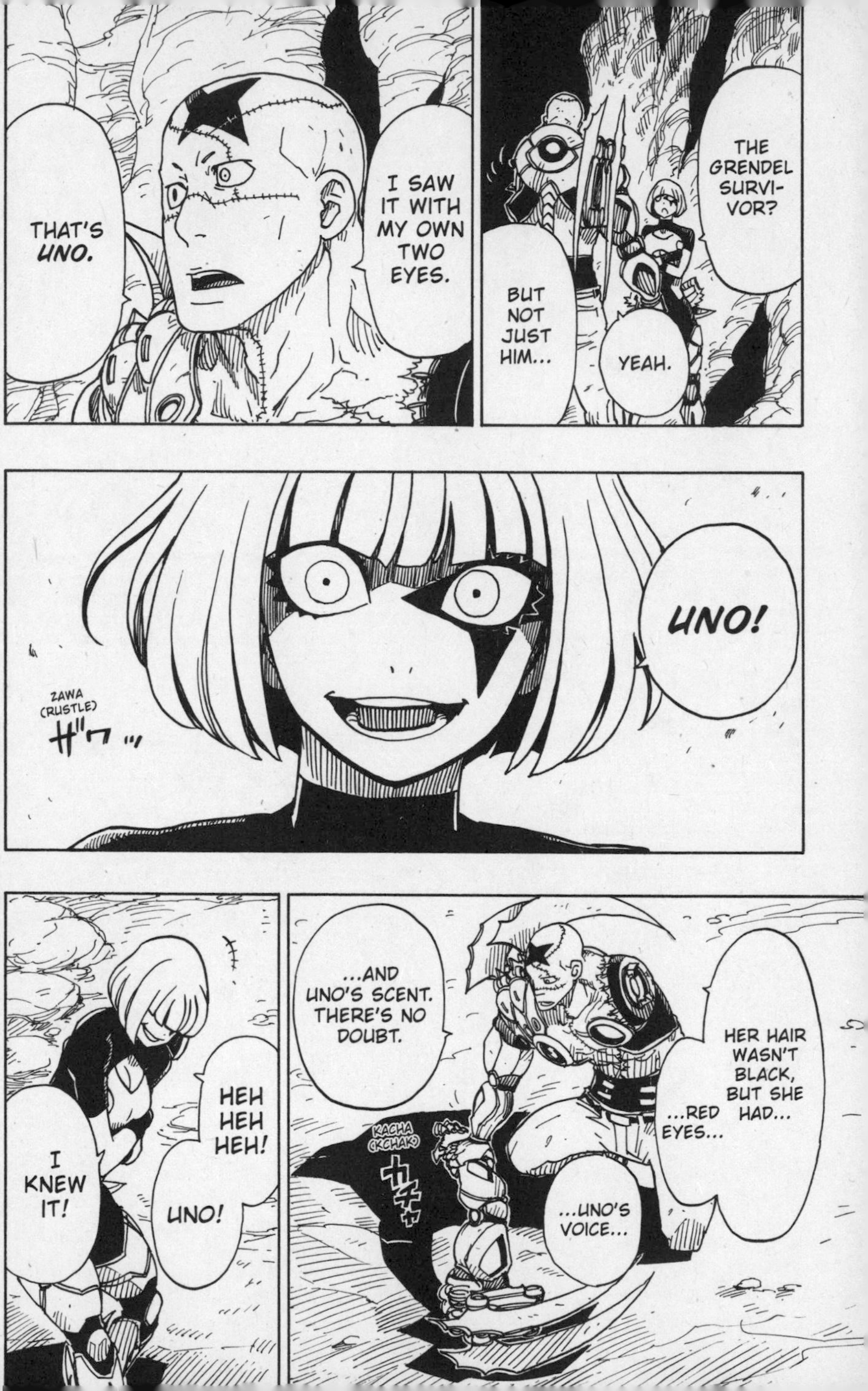
THE GRENDEL SURVIVOR?
YEAH.
BUT NOT JUST HIM...
I SAW IT WITH MY OWN TWO EYES.
THAT'S *UNO.*
UNO!
ZAWA (RUSTLE)
ザワッ
HER HAIR WASN'T BLACK, BUT SHE HAD...
...RED EYES...
...UNO'S VOICE...
...AND UNO'S SCENT. THERE'S NO DOUBT.
KACHA (KCHAK)
カチャ
HEH HEH HEH!
UNO!
I KNEW IT!

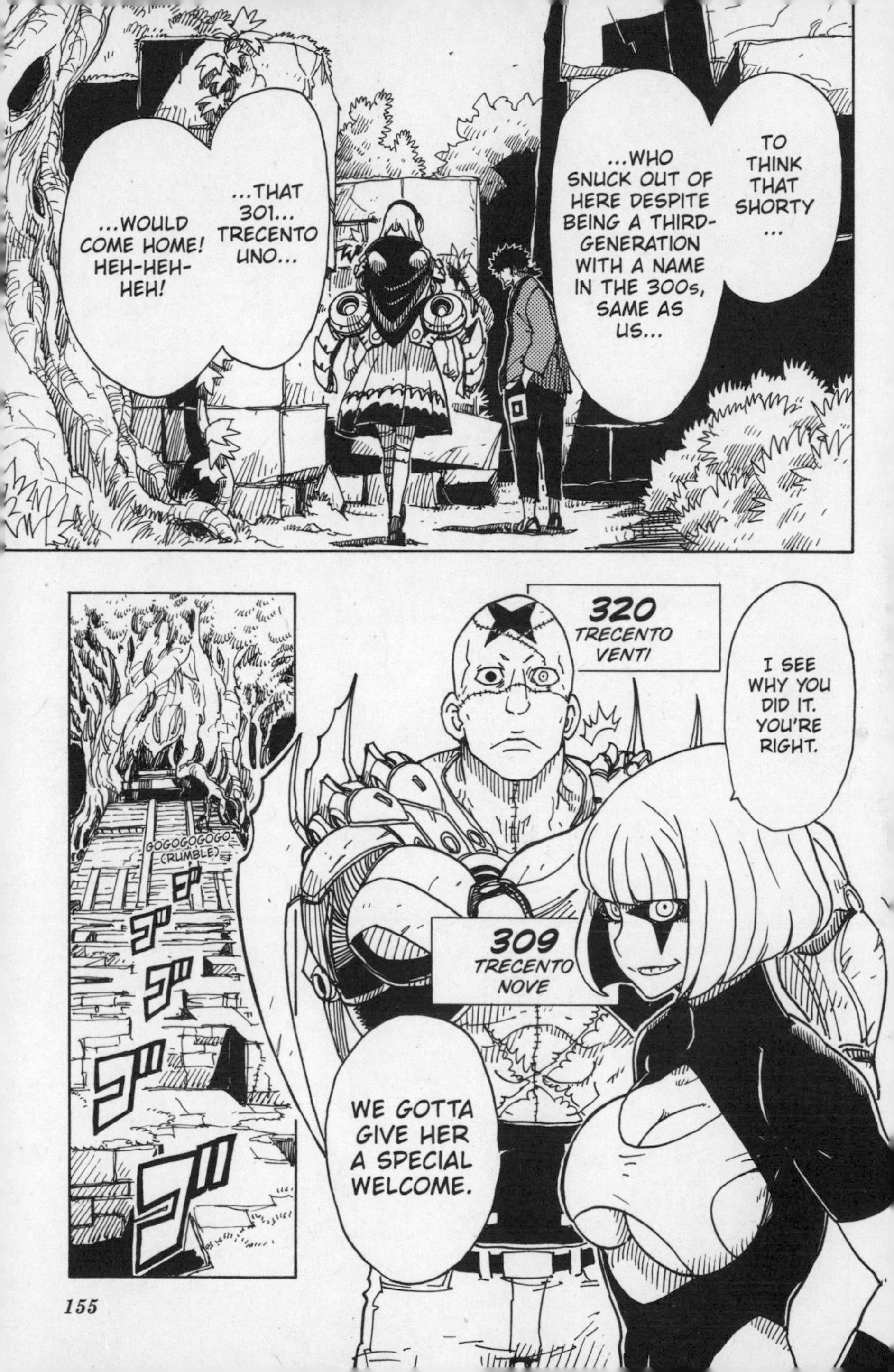
TO THINK THAT SHORTY ...
...WHO SNUCK OUT OF HERE DESPITE BEING A THIRD-GENERATION WITH A NAME IN THE 300s, SAME AS US...
...THAT 301... TRECENTO UNO...
...WOULD COME HOME! HEH-HEH-HEH!
I SEE WHY YOU DID IT. YOU'RE RIGHT.
320 TRECENTO VENTI
309 TRECENTO NOVE
WE GOTTA GIVE HER A SPECIAL WELCOME.
GOGOGOGOGO (RUMBLE)

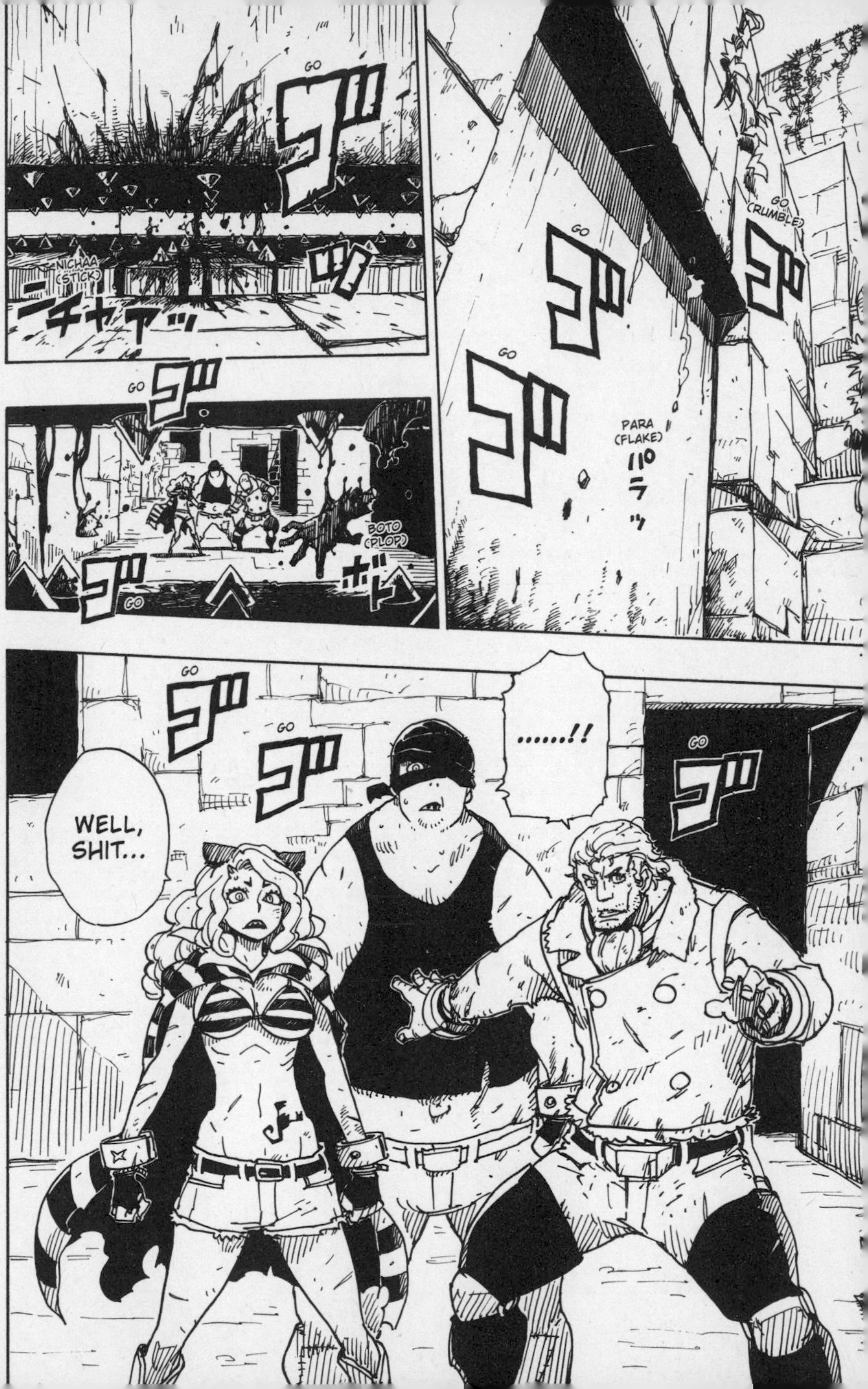
GO (RUMBLE)
ゴ
GO
ゴ
PARA (FLAKE)
パラッ
GO
ゴ
GO
ゴ
NICHAA (STICK)
ニチャアッ
GO
ゴ
BOTO (PLOP)
ボト
GO
ゴ
GO
ゴ
......!!
GO
ゴ
GO
ゴ
WELL, SHIT...

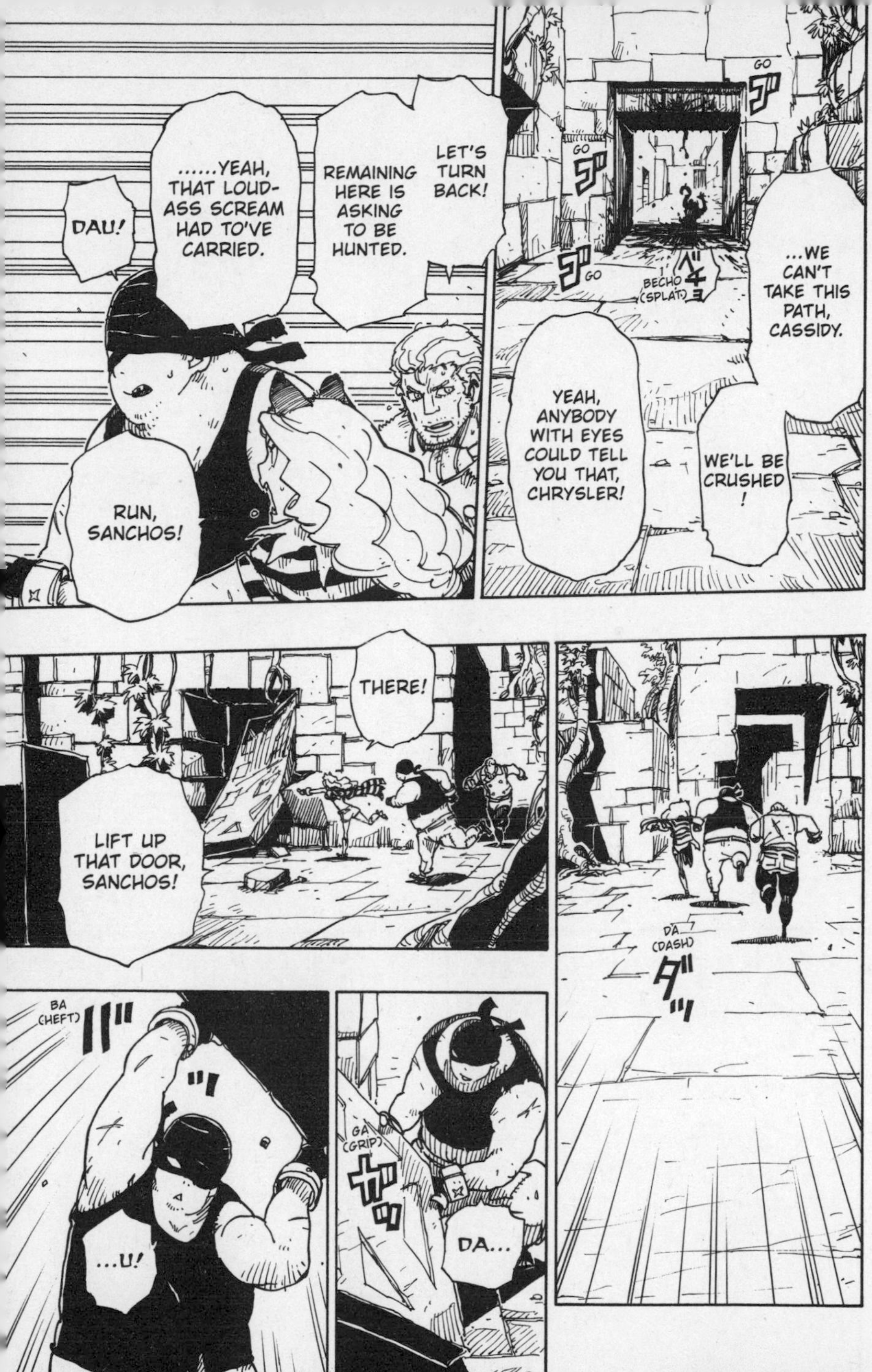
GO
GO
GO
BECHO (SPLAT)
...WE CAN'T TAKE THIS PATH, CASSIDY.
WE'LL BE CRUSHED!
YEAH, ANYBODY WITH EYES COULD TELL YOU THAT, CHRYSLER!
LET'S TURN BACK!
REMAINING HERE IS ASKING TO BE HUNTED.
......YEAH, THAT LOUD-ASS SCREAM HAD TO'VE CARRIED.
DAU!
RUN, SANCHOS!
DA (DASH)
THERE!
LIFT UP THAT DOOR, SANCHOS!
GA (GRIP)
DA...
BA (HEFT)
...U!

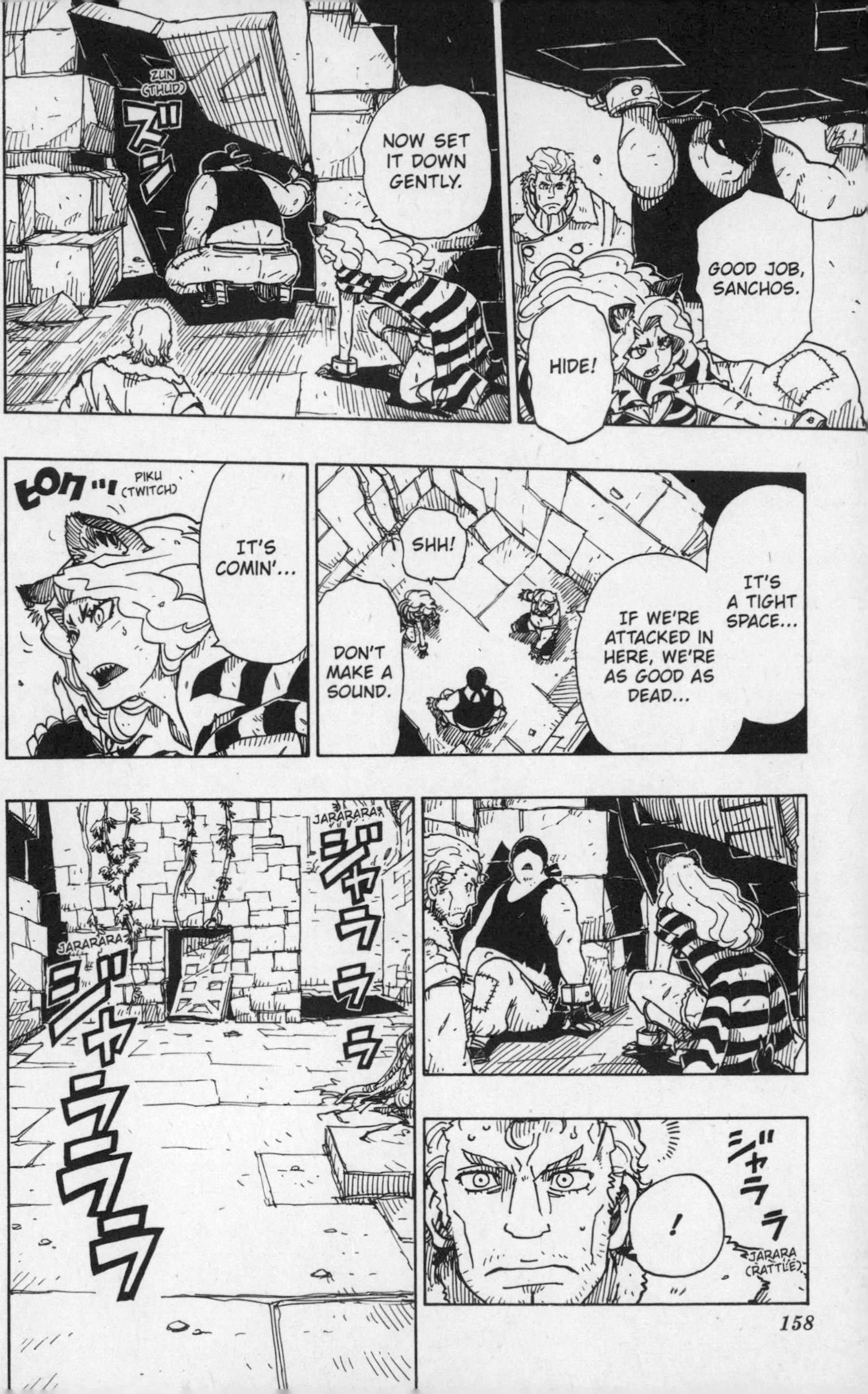
GOOD JOB, SANCHOS.
HIDE!
ZUN (THUD)
NOW SET IT DOWN GENTLY.
IT'S A TIGHT SPACE...
IF WE'RE ATTACKED IN HERE, WE'RE AS GOOD AS DEAD...
SHH!
DON'T MAKE A SOUND.
PIKU (TWITCH)
IT'S COMIN'...
JARARA (RATTLE)
!
JARARARA
JARARARA

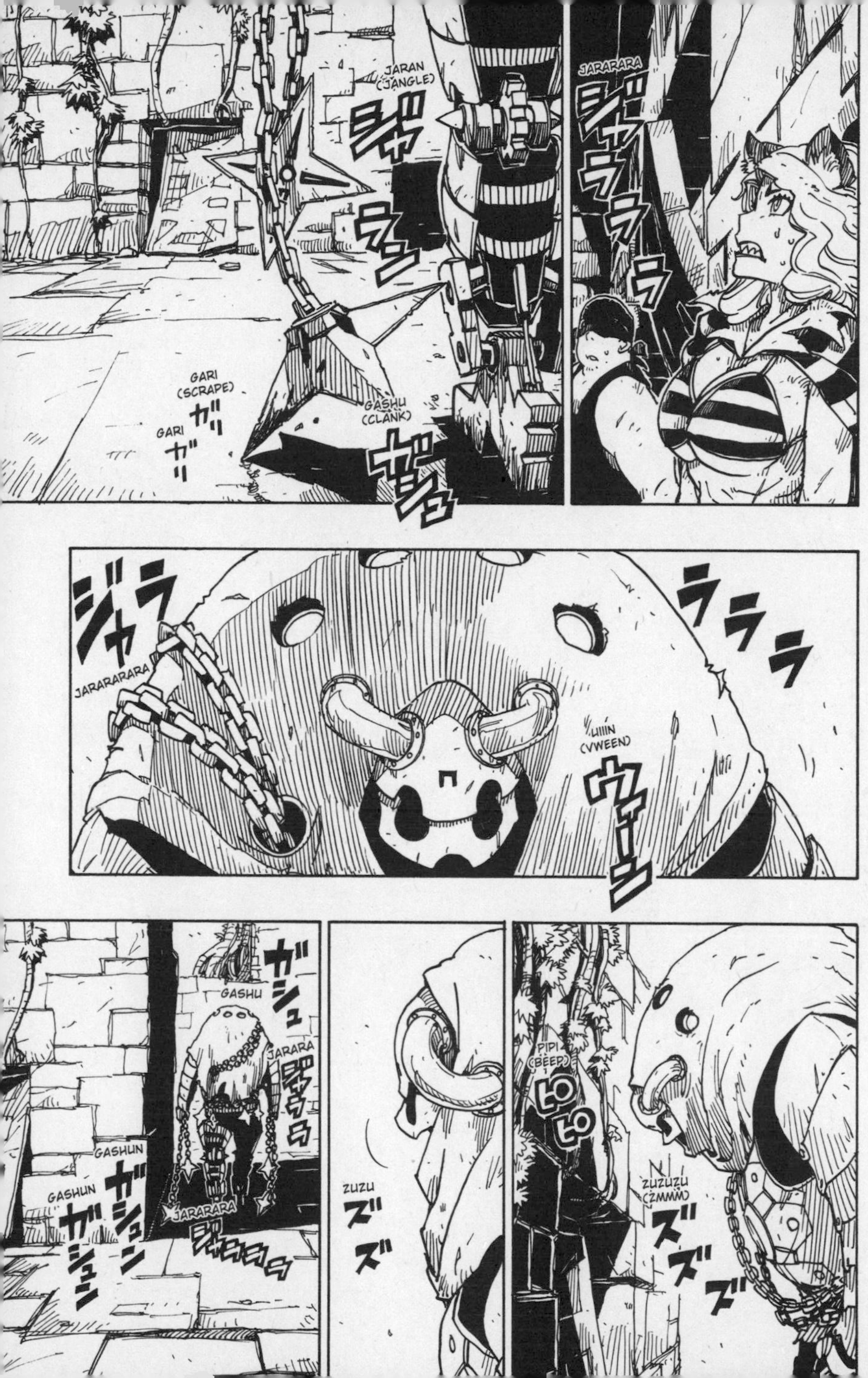
JARARARA
ジャララララ
JARAN (JANGLE)
ジャラン
GASHU (CLANK)
GARI (SCRAPE)
ガリ
GARI
ガリ
ジャラ
ラララ
JARARARARA
UIIIN (VWEEN)
ウィーン
PIPI (BEEP)
ピピ
ZUZUZU (ZMMM)
ズズズ
ZUZU
ズズ
ガシュ
GASHU
JARARA
ジャララ
GASHUN
ガシュン
GASHUN
ガシュン
JARARARA
ジャラララ

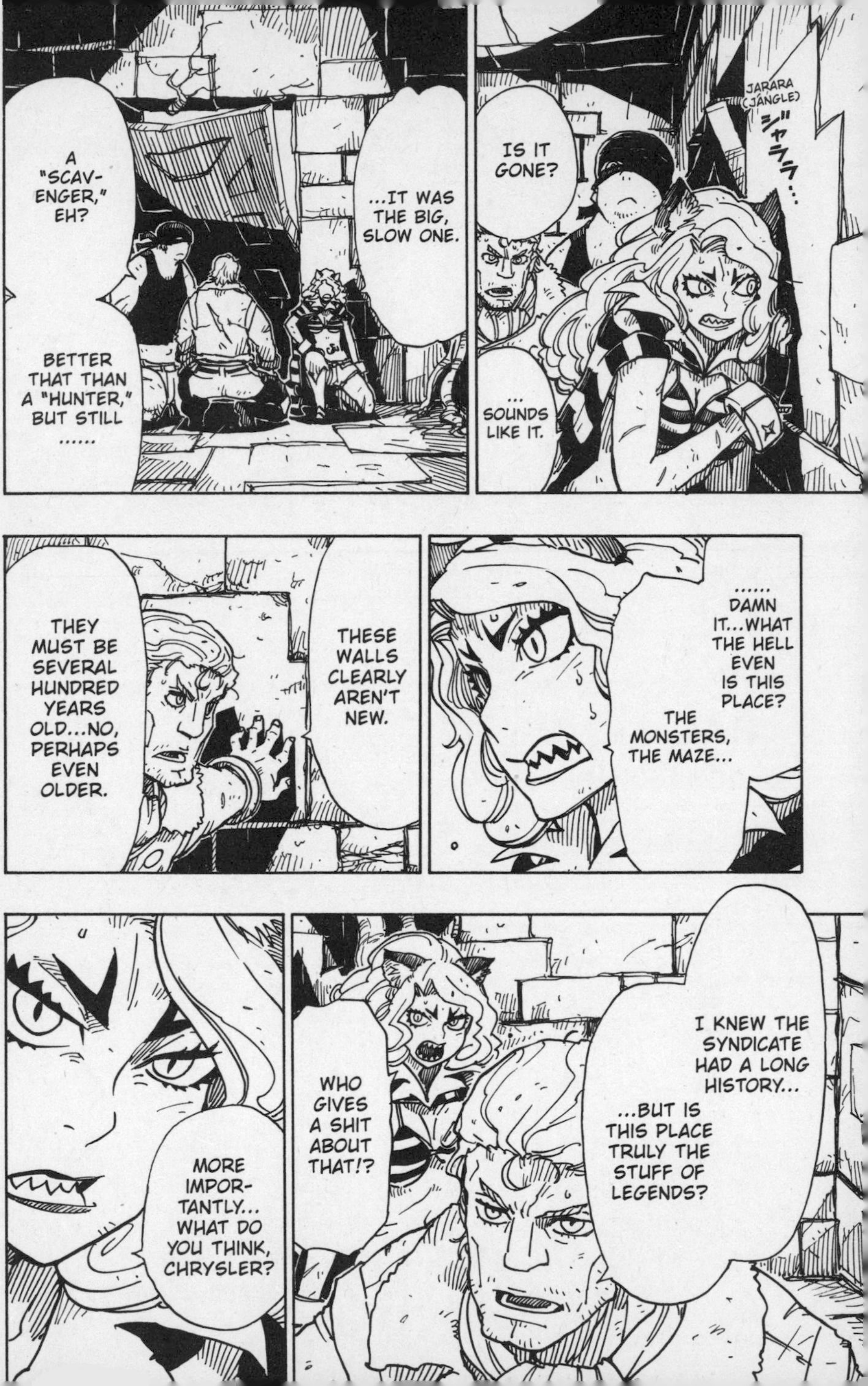
JARARA (JANGLE)
ジャラララ…
IS IT GONE?
... SOUNDS LIKE IT.
...IT WAS THE BIG, SLOW ONE.
A "SCAVENGER," EH?
BETTER THAT THAN A "HUNTER," BUT STILL ......
...... DAMN IT...WHAT THE HELL EVEN IS THIS PLACE?
THE MONSTERS, THE MAZE...
THESE WALLS CLEARLY AREN'T NEW.
THEY MUST BE SEVERAL HUNDRED YEARS OLD...NO, PERHAPS EVEN OLDER.
I KNEW THE SYNDICATE HAD A LONG HISTORY...
...BUT IS THIS PLACE TRULY THE STUFF OF LEGENDS?
WHO GIVES A SHIT ABOUT THAT!?
MORE IMPORTANTLY... WHAT DO YOU THINK, CHRYSLER?

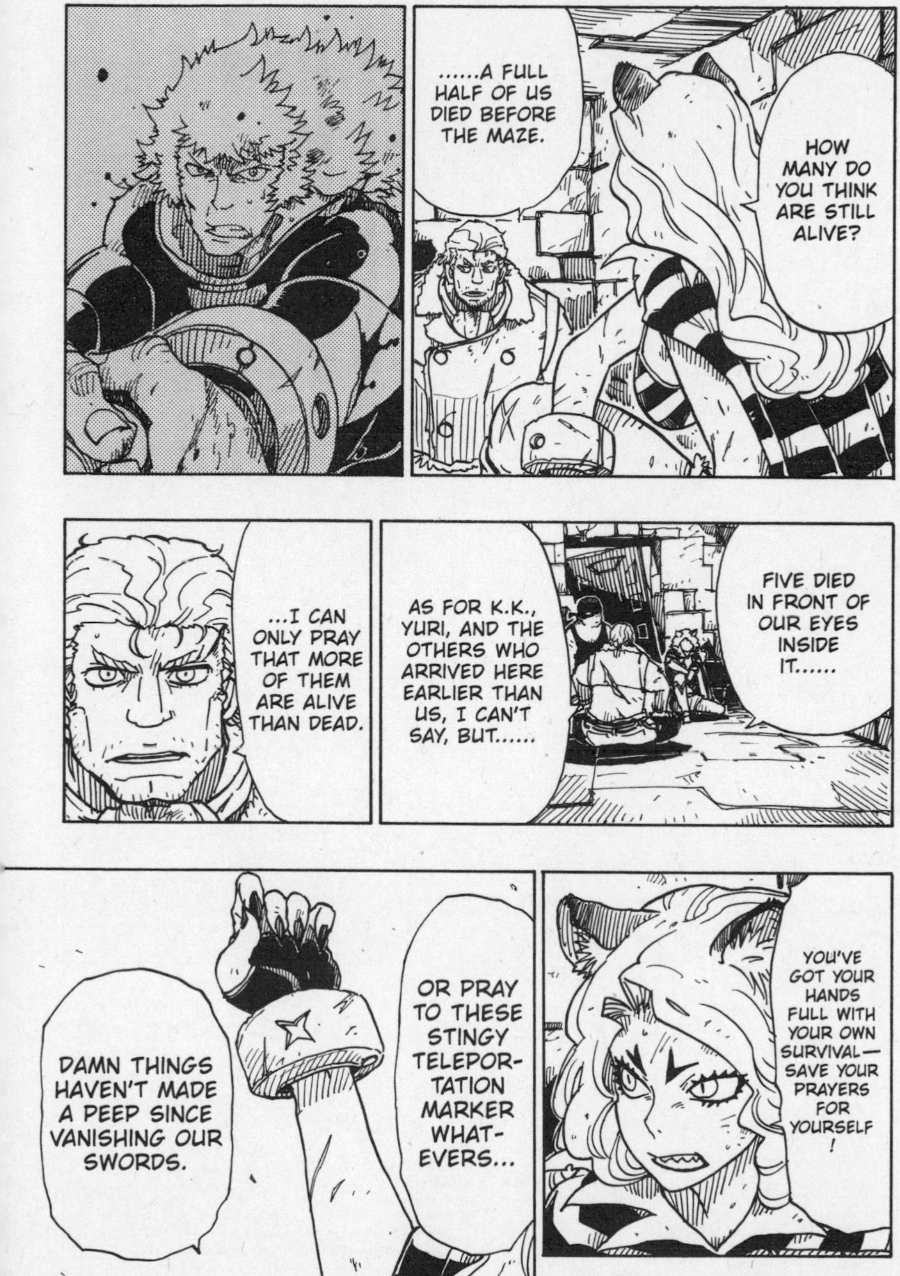
HOW MANY DO YOU THINK ARE STILL ALIVE?
......A FULL HALF OF US DIED BEFORE THE MAZE.
FIVE DIED IN FRONT OF OUR EYES INSIDE IT......
AS FOR K.K., YURI, AND THE OTHERS WHO ARRIVED HERE EARLIER THAN US, I CAN'T SAY, BUT......
...I CAN ONLY PRAY THAT MORE OF THEM ARE ALIVE THAN DEAD.
YOU'VE GOT YOUR HANDS FULL WITH YOUR OWN SURVIVAL—SAVE YOUR PRAYERS FOR YOURSELF!
OR PRAY TO THESE STINGY TELEPOR-TATION MARKER WHAT-EVERS...
DAMN THINGS HAVEN'T MADE A PEEP SINCE VANISHING OUR SWORDS.

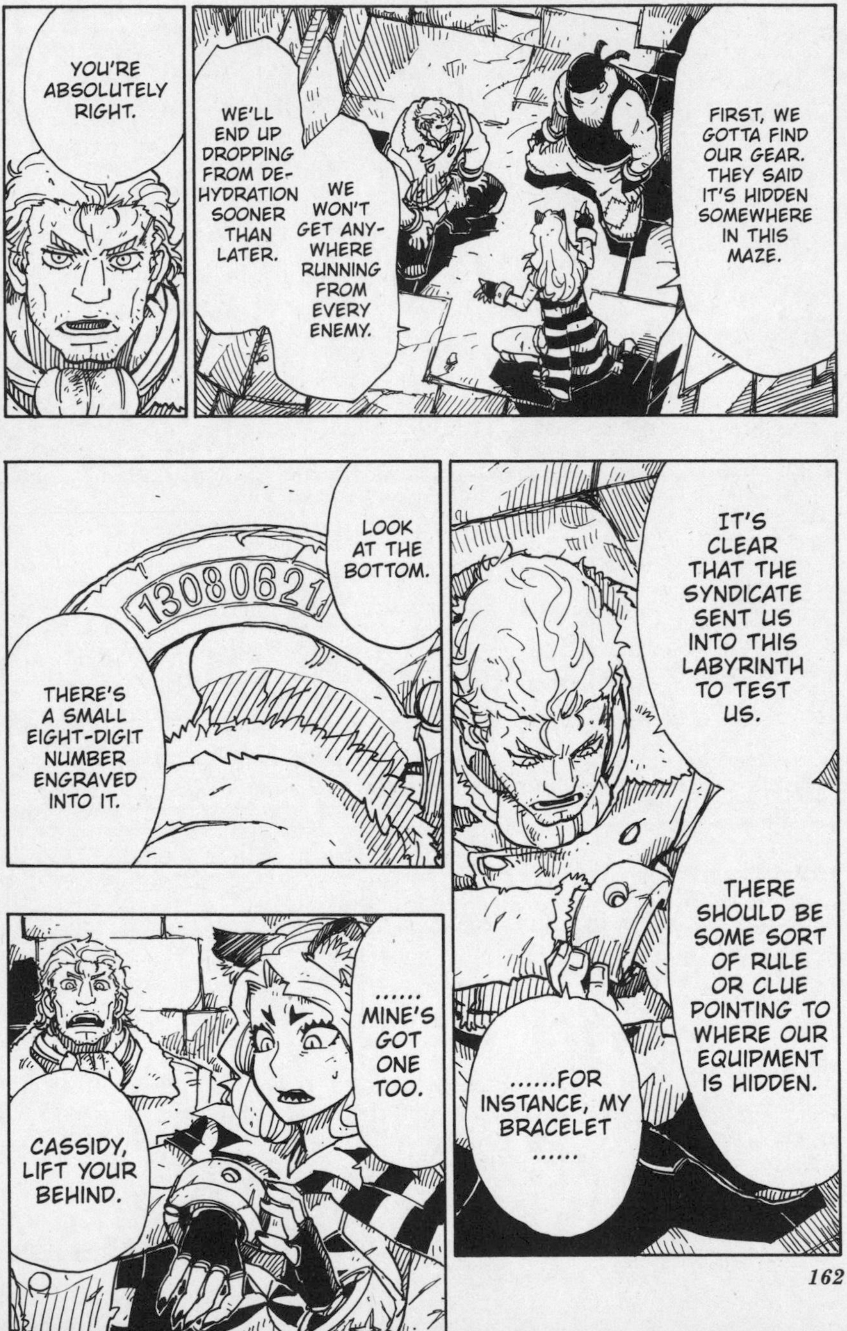
FIRST, WE GOTTA FIND OUR GEAR. THEY SAID IT'S HIDDEN SOMEWHERE IN THIS MAZE.
WE WON'T GET ANY-WHERE RUNNING FROM EVERY ENEMY.
WE'LL END UP DROPPING FROM DE-HYDRATION SOONER THAN LATER.
YOU'RE ABSOLUTELY RIGHT.
IT'S CLEAR THAT THE SYNDICATE SENT US INTO THIS LABYRINTH TO TEST US.
THERE SHOULD BE SOME SORT OF RULE OR CLUE POINTING TO WHERE OUR EQUIPMENT IS HIDDEN.
......FOR INSTANCE, MY BRACELET ......
LOOK AT THE BOTTOM.
13080621
THERE'S A SMALL EIGHT-DIGIT NUMBER ENGRAVED INTO IT.
......MINE'S GOT ONE TOO.
CASSIDY, LIFT YOUR BEHIND.

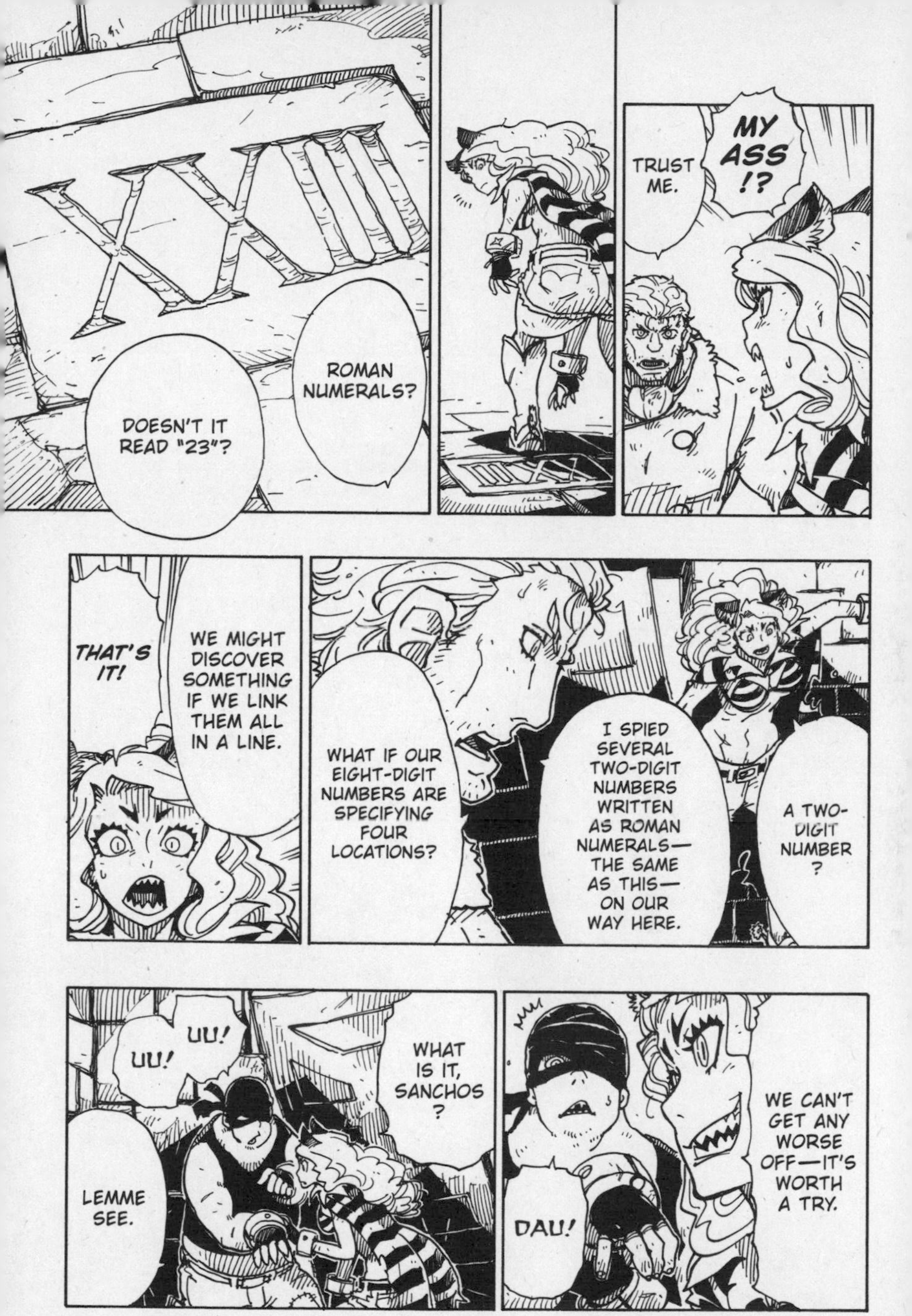
TRUST ME.
MY ASS!?
ROMAN NUMERALS?
DOESN'T IT READ "23"?
A TWO-DIGIT NUMBER?
I SPIED SEVERAL TWO-DIGIT NUMBERS WRITTEN AS ROMAN NUMERALS—THE SAME AS THIS—ON OUR WAY HERE.
WHAT IF OUR EIGHT-DIGIT NUMBERS ARE SPECIFYING FOUR LOCATIONS?
WE MIGHT DISCOVER SOMETHING IF WE LINK THEM ALL IN A LINE.
THAT'S IT!
WE CAN'T GET ANY WORSE OFF—IT'S WORTH A TRY.
DAU!
UU!
UU!
WHAT IS IT, SANCHOS?
LEMME SEE.

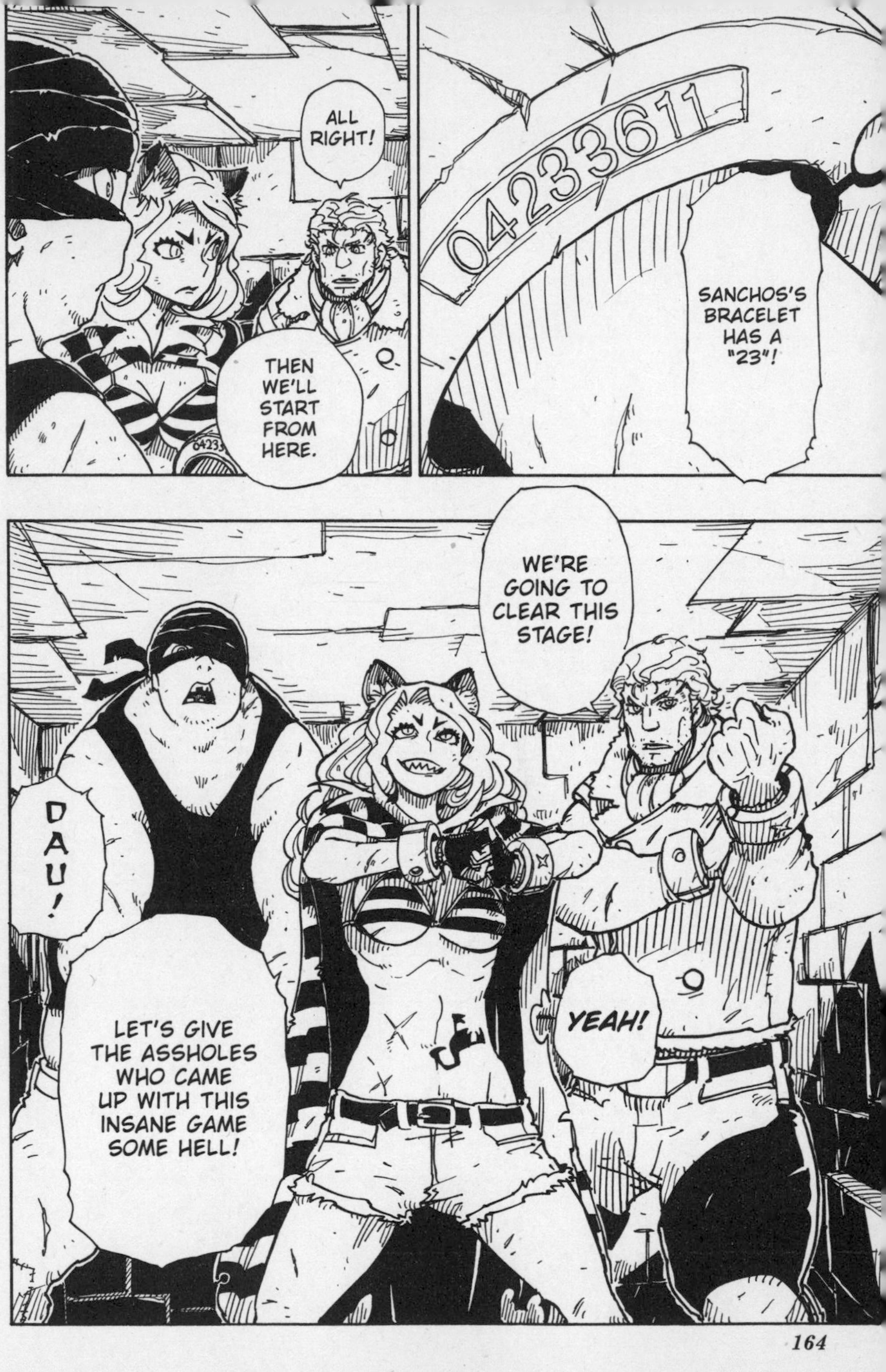
04233611
SANCHOS'S BRACELET HAS A "23"!
ALL RIGHT!
THEN WE'LL START FROM HERE.
WE'RE GOING TO CLEAR THIS STAGE!
DAU!
YEAH!
LET'S GIVE THE ASSHOLES WHO CAME UP WITH THIS INSANE GAME SOME HELL!

FILE.102
UNDERGROUND WORLD

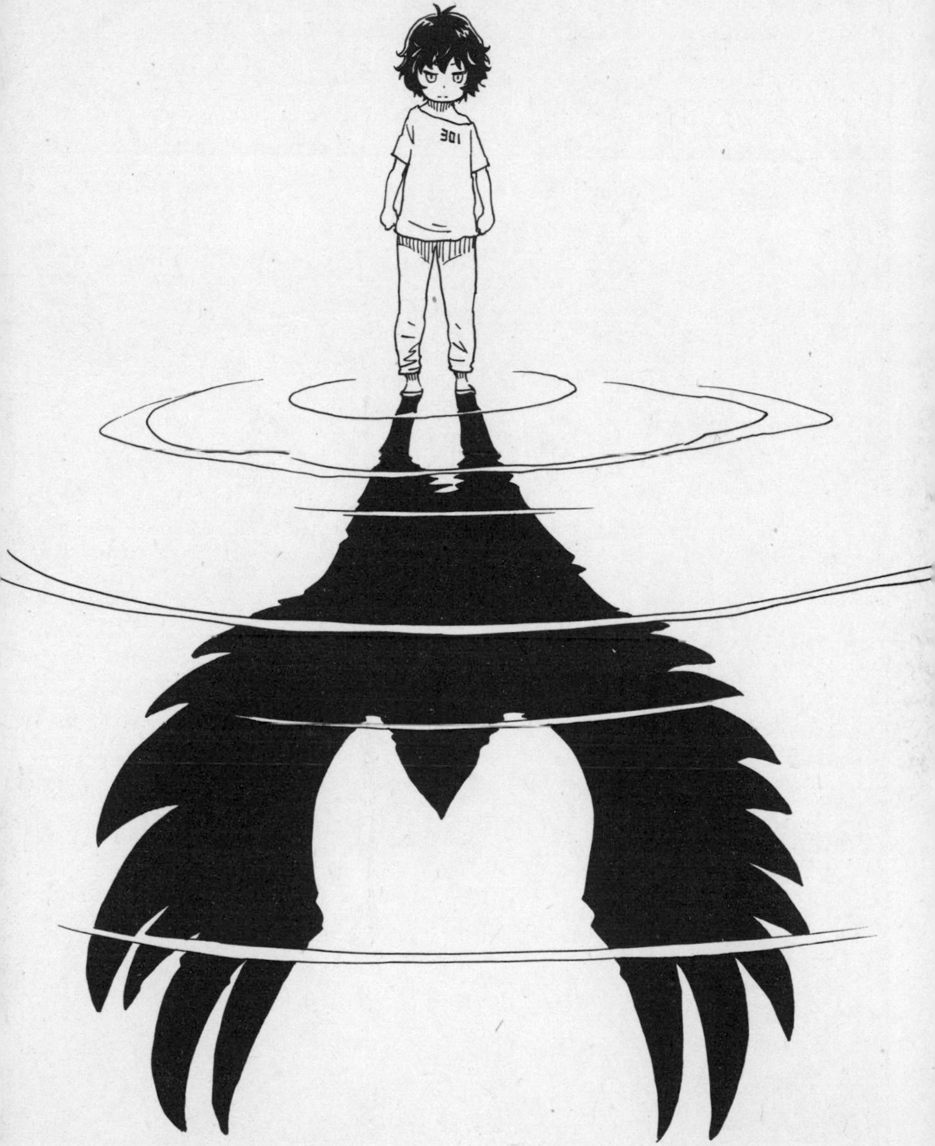
301

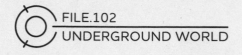

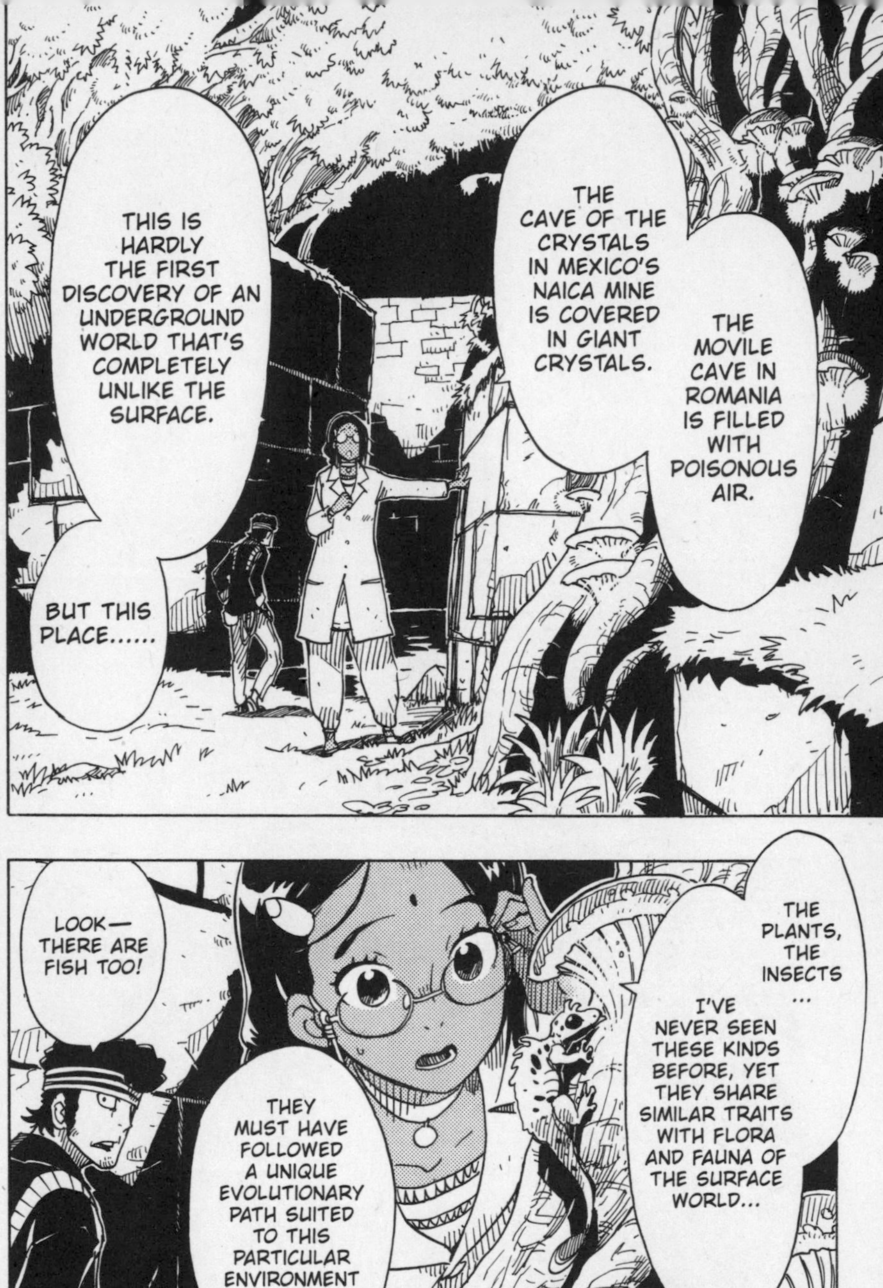
THIS IS HARDLY THE FIRST DISCOVERY OF AN UNDERGROUND WORLD THAT'S COMPLETELY UNLIKE THE SURFACE.
THE CAVE OF THE CRYSTALS IN MEXICO'S NAICA MINE IS COVERED IN GIANT CRYSTALS.
THE MOVILE CAVE IN ROMANIA IS FILLED WITH POISONOUS AIR.
BUT THIS PLACE......
THE PLANTS, THE INSECTS...
I'VE NEVER SEEN THESE KINDS BEFORE, YET THEY SHARE SIMILAR TRAITS WITH FLORA AND FAUNA OF THE SURFACE WORLD...
THEY MUST HAVE FOLLOWED A UNIQUE EVOLUTIONARY PATH SUITED TO THIS PARTICULAR ENVIRONMENT......
LOOK—THERE ARE FISH TOO!

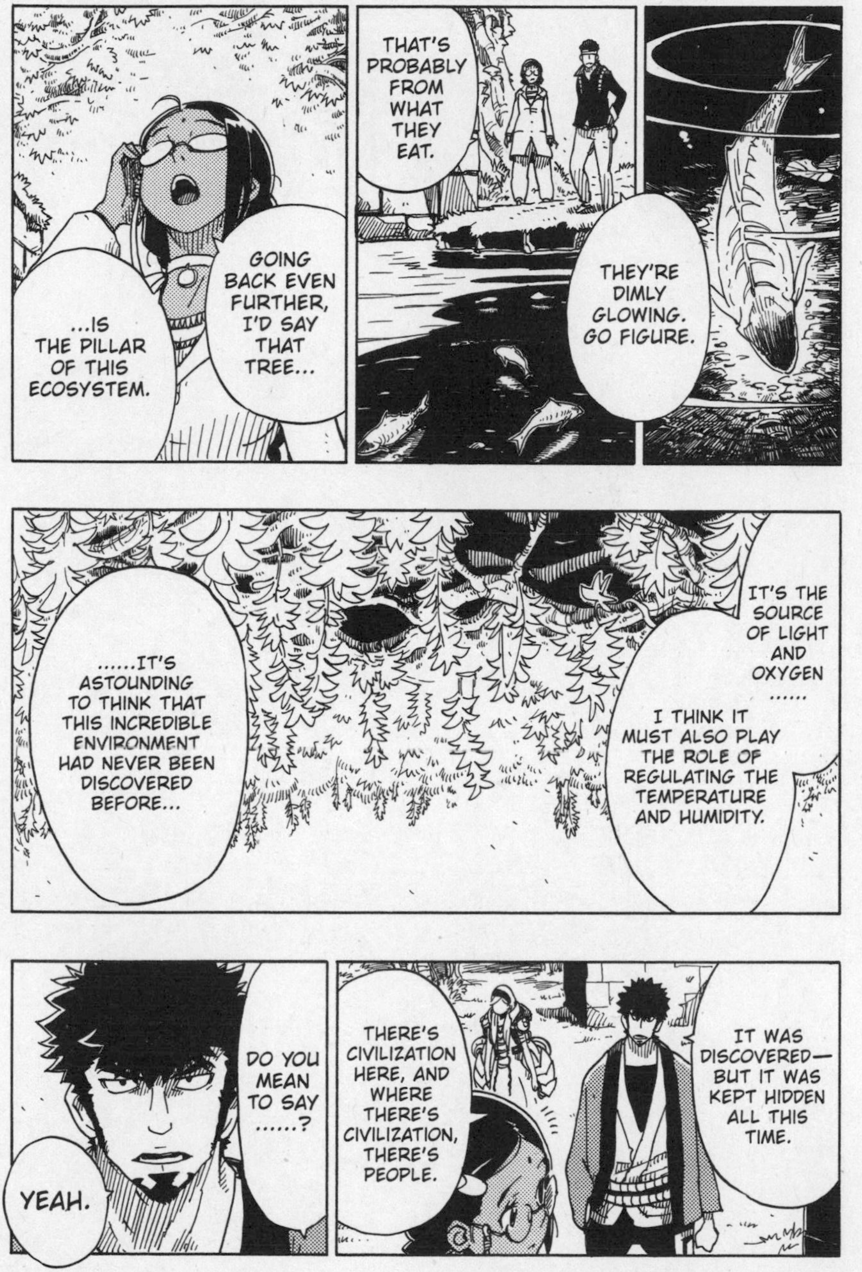
THEY'RE DIMLY GLOWING. GO FIGURE.
THAT'S PROBABLY FROM WHAT THEY EAT.
GOING BACK EVEN FURTHER, I'D SAY THAT TREE...
...IS THE PILLAR OF THIS ECOSYSTEM.
IT'S THE SOURCE OF LIGHT AND OXYGEN ......
I THINK IT MUST ALSO PLAY THE ROLE OF REGULATING THE TEMPERATURE AND HUMIDITY.
......IT'S ASTOUNDING TO THINK THAT THIS INCREDIBLE ENVIRONMENT HAD NEVER BEEN DISCOVERED BEFORE...
IT WAS DISCOVERED— BUT IT WAS KEPT HIDDEN ALL THIS TIME.
THERE'S CIVILIZATION HERE, AND WHERE THERE'S CIVILIZATION, THERE'S PEOPLE.
DO YOU MEAN TO SAY ......?
YEAH.

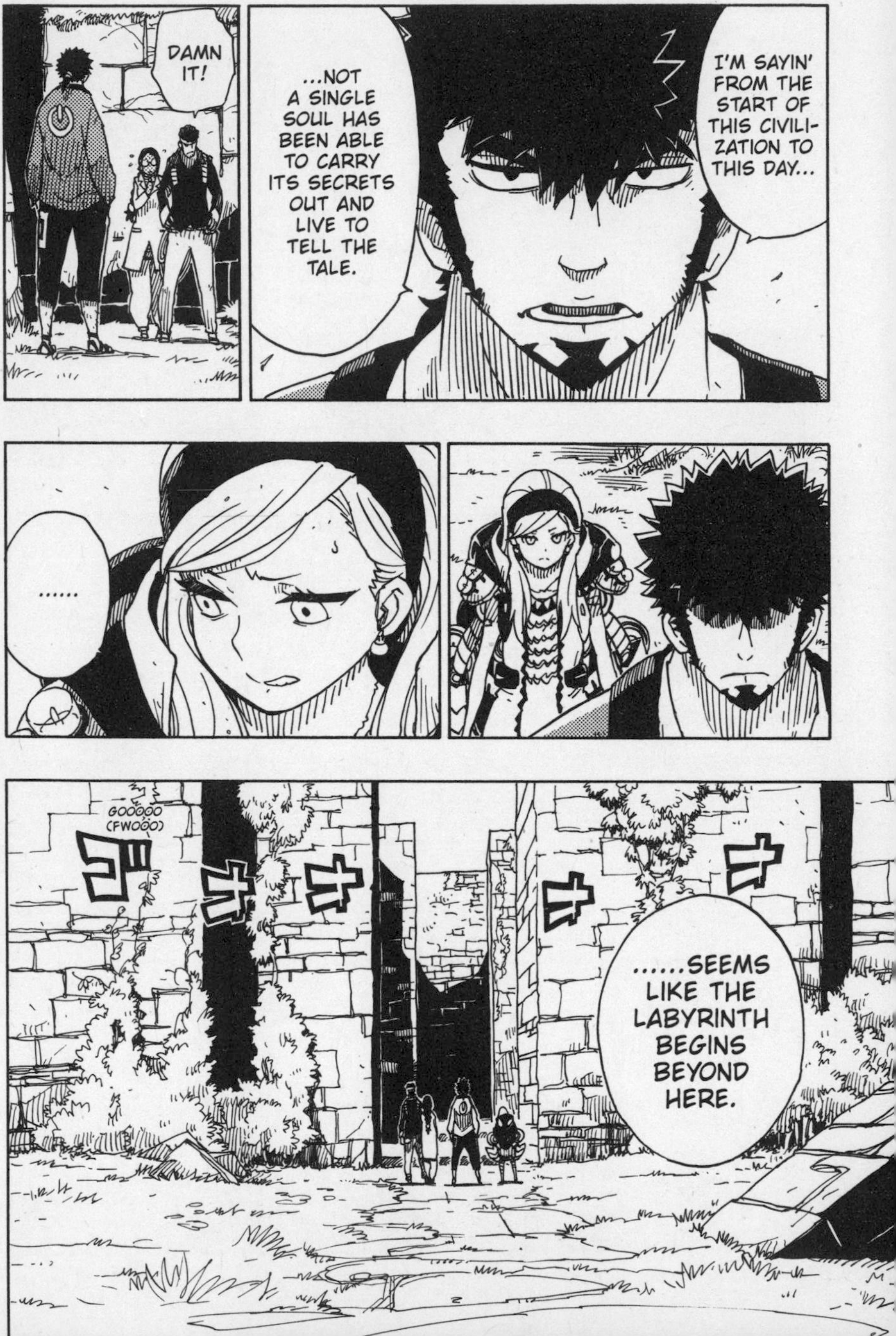
I'M SAYIN' FROM THE START OF THIS CIVILI-ZATION TO THIS DAY...
...NOT A SINGLE SOUL HAS BEEN ABLE TO CARRY ITS SECRETS OUT AND LIVE TO TELL THE TALE.
DAMN IT!
......
......SEEMS LIKE THE LABYRINTH BEGINS BEYOND HERE.
GOOOOO (FWOOO)

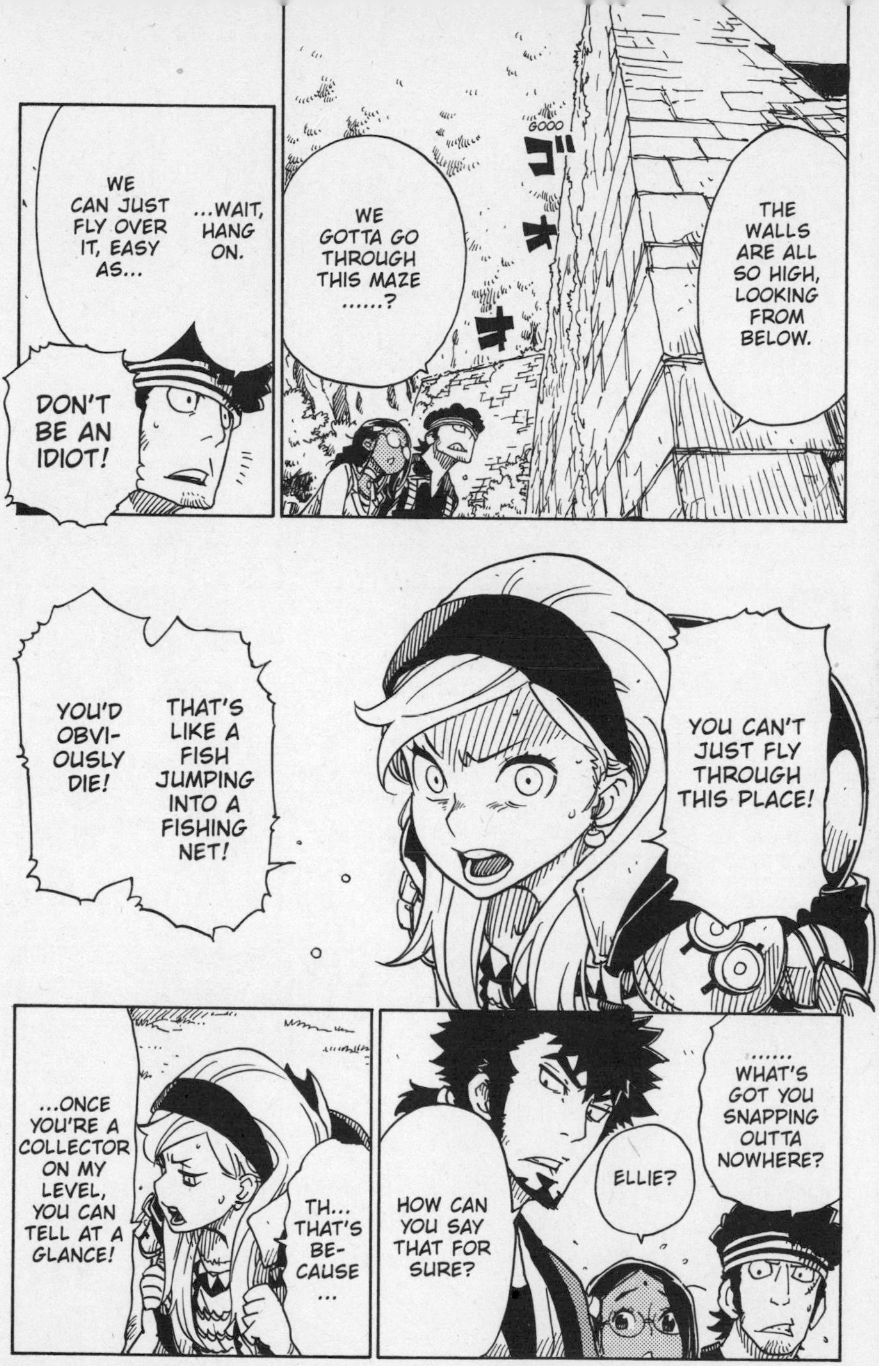
THE WALLS ARE ALL SO HIGH, LOOKING FROM BELOW.
GOOO
ゴオオ
WE GOTTA GO THROUGH THIS MAZE ......?
WE CAN JUST FLY OVER IT, EASY AS... ...WAIT, HANG ON.
DON'T BE AN IDIOT!
YOU CAN'T JUST FLY THROUGH THIS PLACE!
YOU'D OBVIOUSLY DIE! THAT'S LIKE A FISH JUMPING INTO A FISHING NET!
...... WHAT'S GOT YOU SNAPPING OUTTA NOWHERE?
ELLIE?
HOW CAN YOU SAY THAT FOR SURE?
TH... THAT'S BE-CAUSE ...
...ONCE YOU'RE A COLLECTOR ON MY LEVEL, YOU CAN TELL AT A GLANCE!

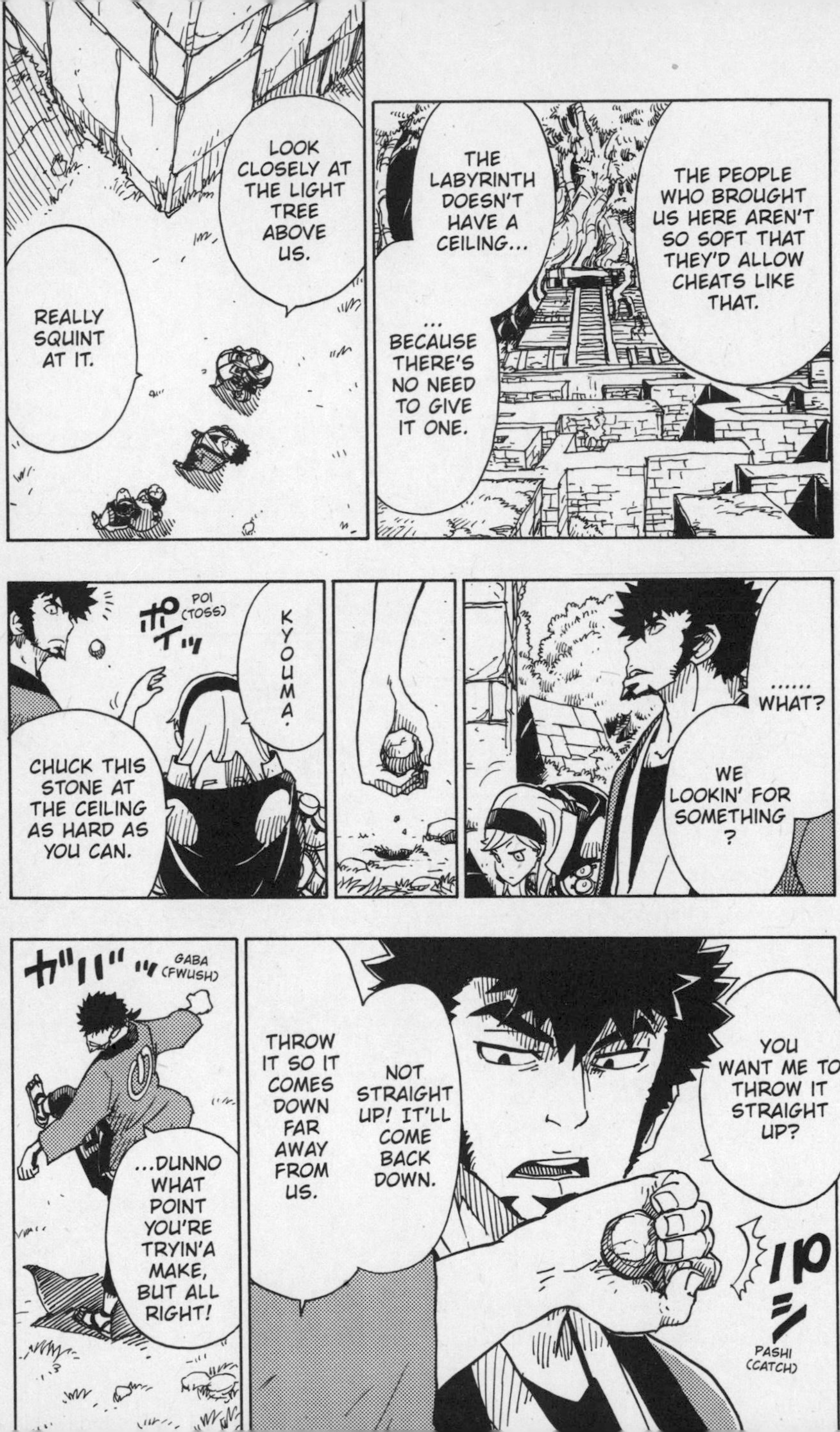
THE PEOPLE WHO BROUGHT US HERE AREN'T SO SOFT THAT THEY'D ALLOW CHEATS LIKE THAT.
THE LABYRINTH DOESN'T HAVE A CEILING...
...BECAUSE THERE'S NO NEED TO GIVE IT ONE.
LOOK CLOSELY AT THE LIGHT TREE ABOVE US.
REALLY SQUINT AT IT.
......WHAT?
WE LOOKIN' FOR SOMETHING?
KYOUMA.
POI (TOSS)
CHUCK THIS STONE AT THE CEILING AS HARD AS YOU CAN.
YOU WANT ME TO THROW IT STRAIGHT UP?
PASHI (CATCH)
NOT STRAIGHT UP! IT'LL COME BACK DOWN.
THROW IT SO IT COMES DOWN FAR AWAY FROM US.
GABA (FWUSH)
...DUNNO WHAT POINT YOU'RE TRYIN'A MAKE, BUT ALL RIGHT!

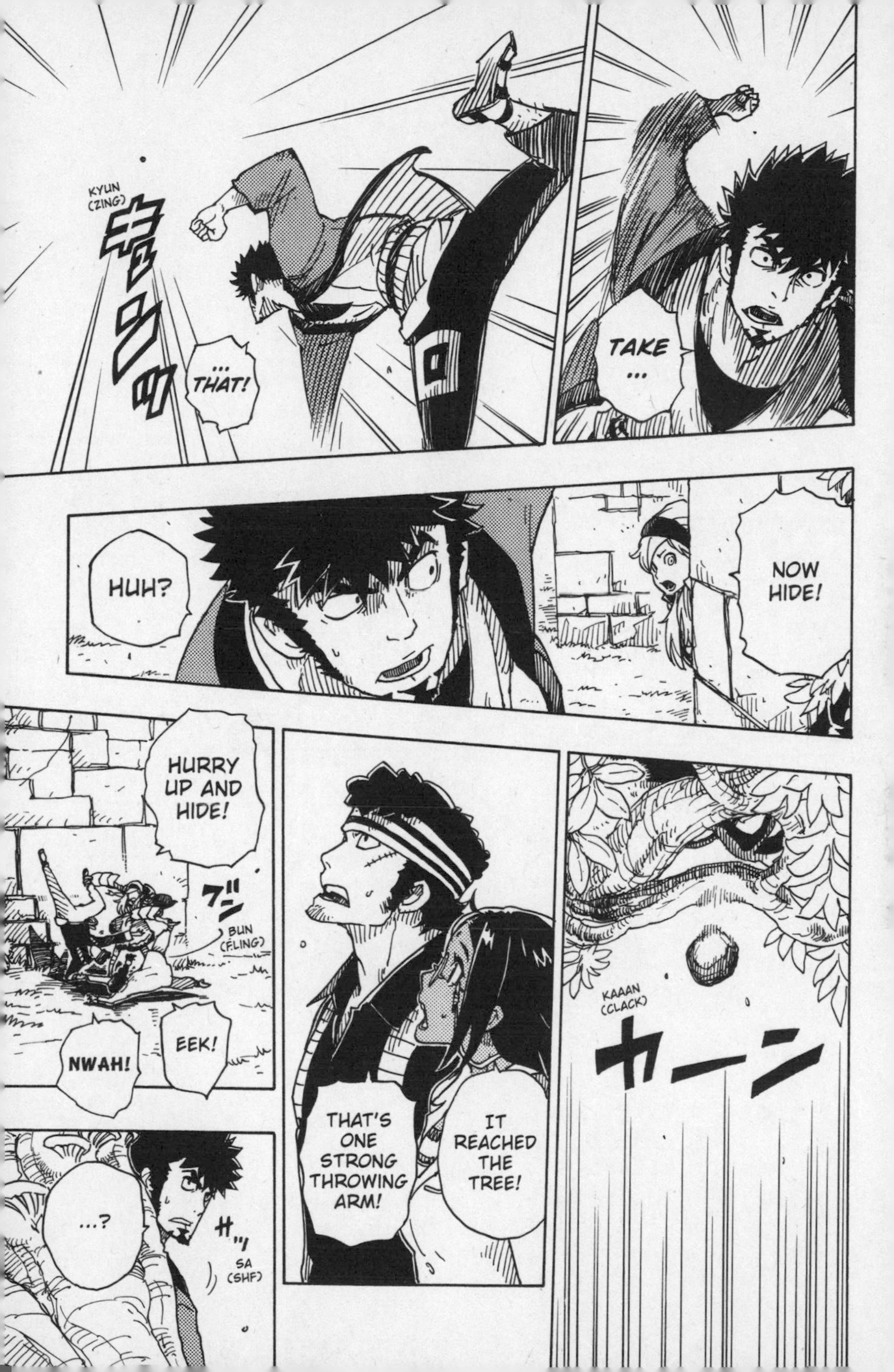
TAKE ...
KYUN (ZING)
... THAT!
NOW HIDE!
HUH?
KAAAN (CLACK)
IT REACHED THE TREE!
THAT'S ONE STRONG THROWING ARM!
HURRY UP AND HIDE!
BUN (FLING)
EEK!
NWAH!
...?
SA (SHF)

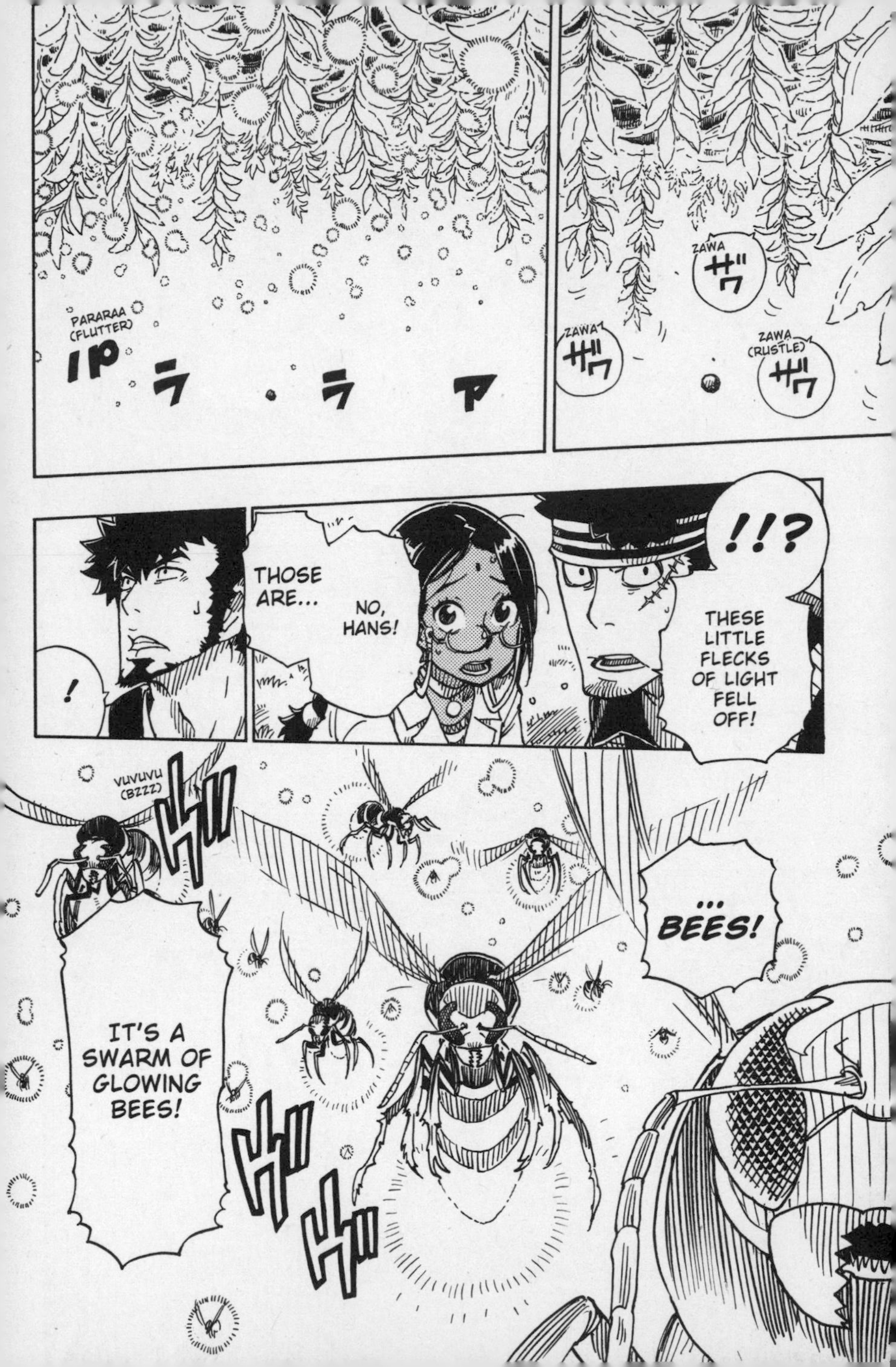

ZAWA
ザワ
ZAWA (RUSTLE)
ザワ
ZAWA
ザワ
PARARAA (FLUTTER)
パラ・ラア
!!?
THESE LITTLE FLECKS OF LIGHT FELL OFF!
NO, HANS!
THOSE ARE...
!
...BEES!
VUVUVU (BZZZ)
IT'S A SWARM OF GLOWING BEES!

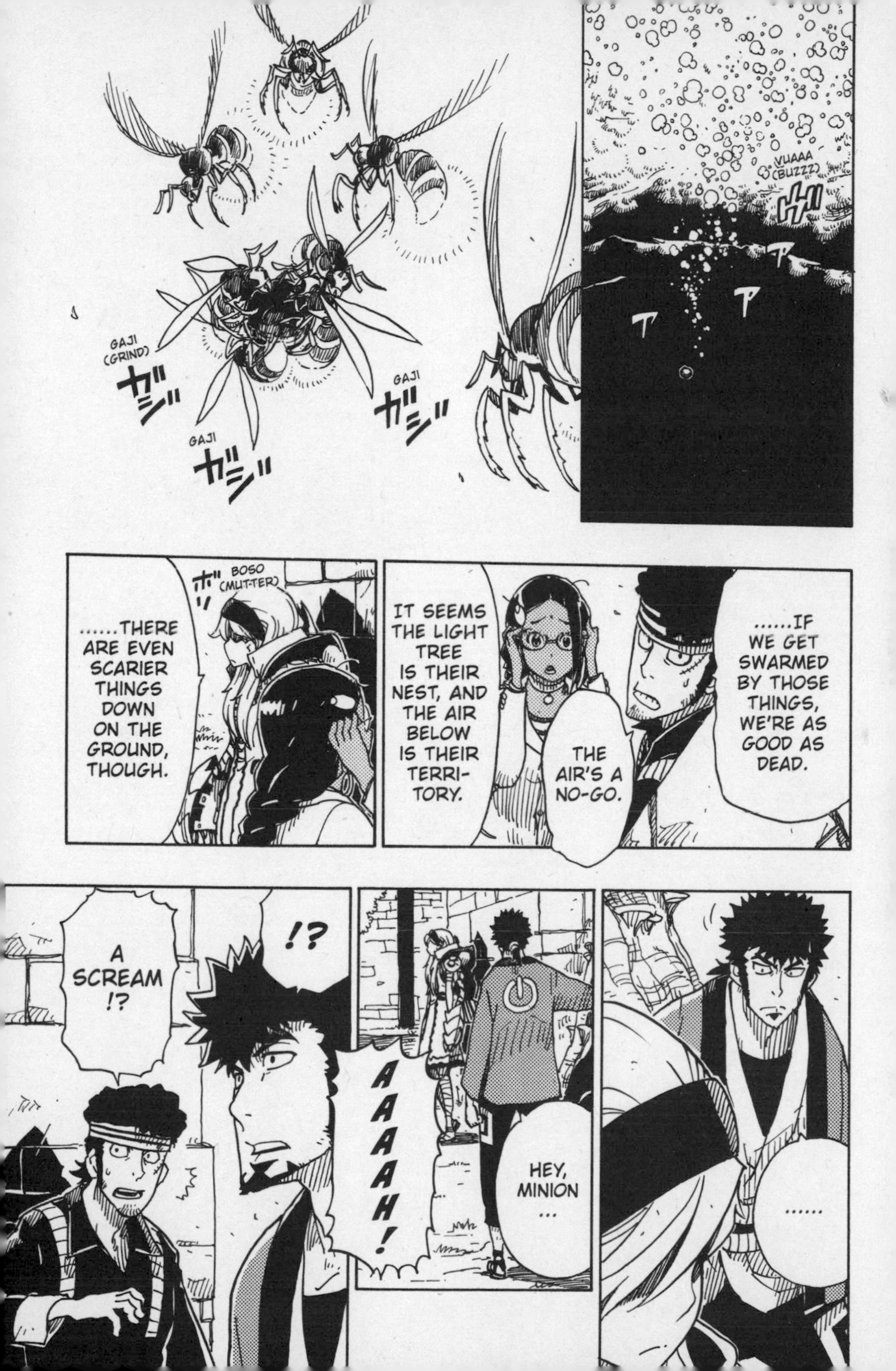
VUAAA (BUZZZ)
GAJI (GRIND)
ガジ
GAJI
ガジ
GAJI
ガジ
......IF WE GET SWARMED BY THOSE THINGS, WE'RE AS GOOD AS DEAD.
THE AIR'S A NO-GO.
IT SEEMS THE LIGHT TREE IS THEIR NEST, AND THE AIR BELOW IS THEIR TERRITORY.
BOSO (MUTTER)
......THERE ARE EVEN SCARIER THINGS DOWN ON THE GROUND, THOUGH.
......
HEY, MINION ...
AAAAAH!
!?
A SCREAM !?

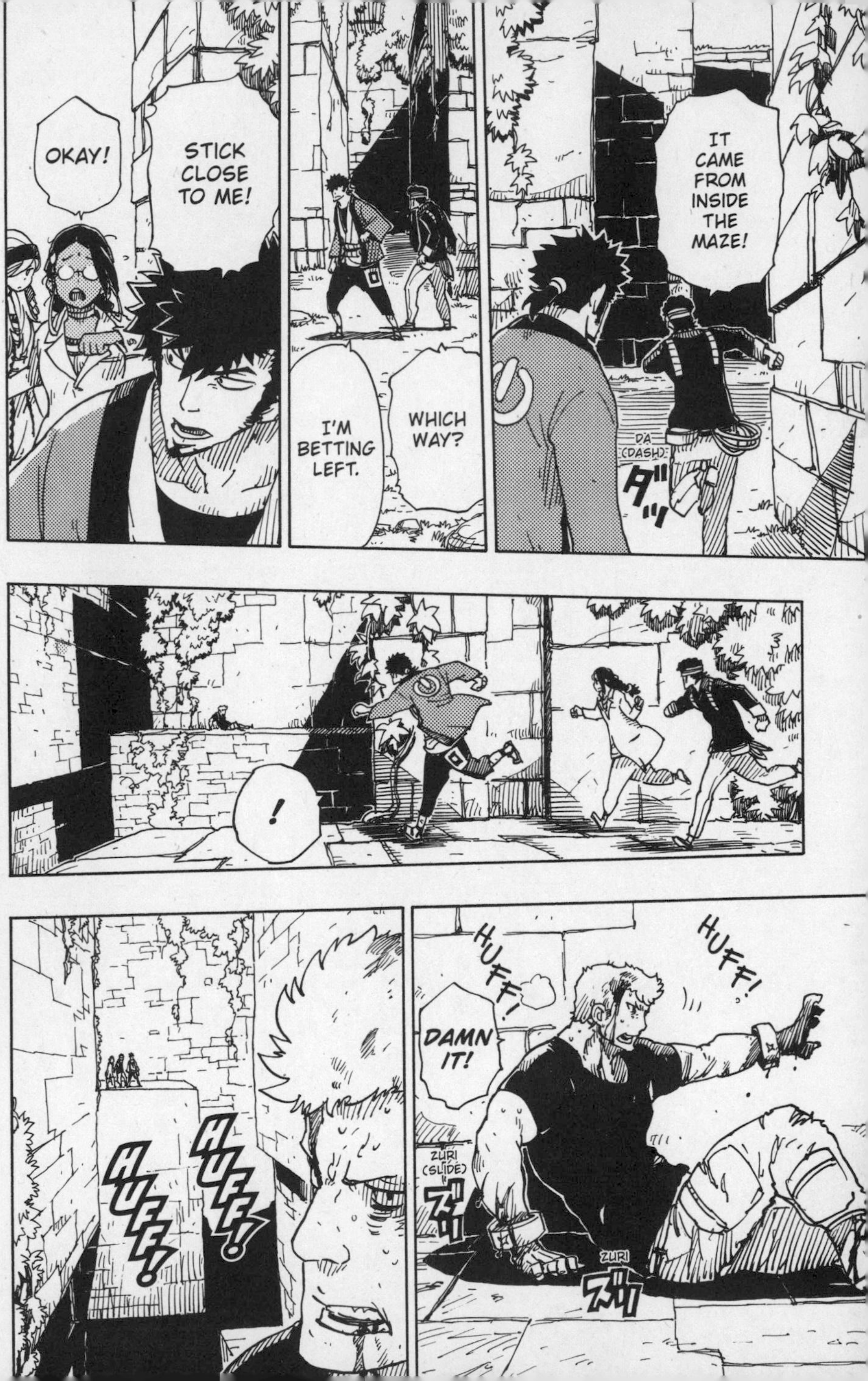
IT CAME FROM INSIDE THE MAZE!
DA (DASH)
ダッ
WHICH WAY?
I'M BETTING LEFT.
STICK CLOSE TO ME!
OKAY!
!
HUFF!
HUFF!
DAMN IT!
ZURI (SLIDE)
ズリ
ZURI
ズリ
HUFF!
HUFF!

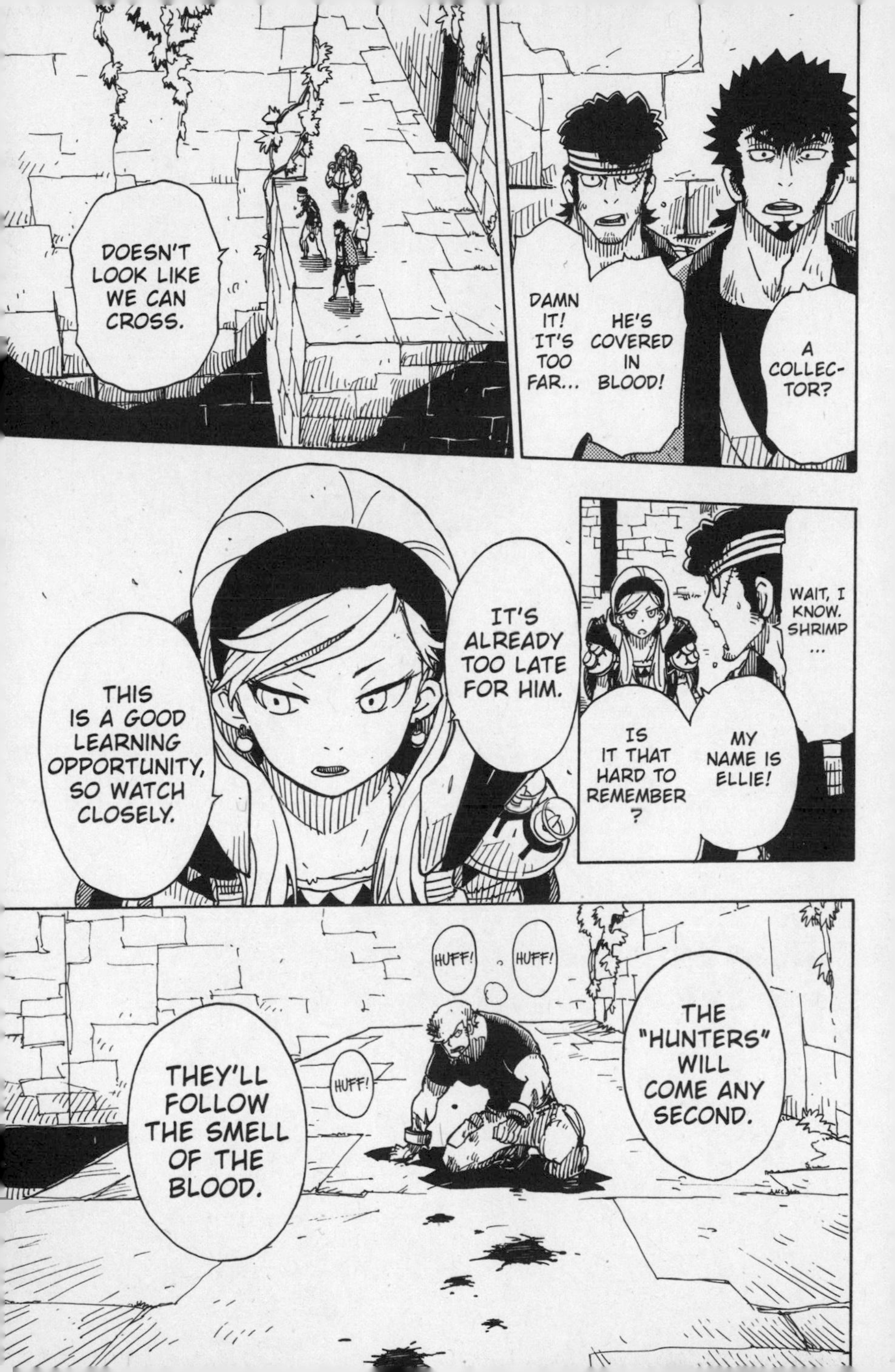
A COLLECTOR?
HE'S COVERED IN BLOOD!
DAMN IT! IT'S TOO FAR...
DOESN'T LOOK LIKE WE CAN CROSS.
WAIT, I KNOW. SHRIMP ...
MY NAME IS ELLIE!
IS IT THAT HARD TO REMEMBER?
IT'S ALREADY TOO LATE FOR HIM.
THIS IS A GOOD LEARNING OPPORTUNITY, SO WATCH CLOSELY.
HUFF!
HUFF!
HUFF!
THE "HUNTERS" WILL COME ANY SECOND.
THEY'LL FOLLOW THE SMELL OF THE BLOOD.

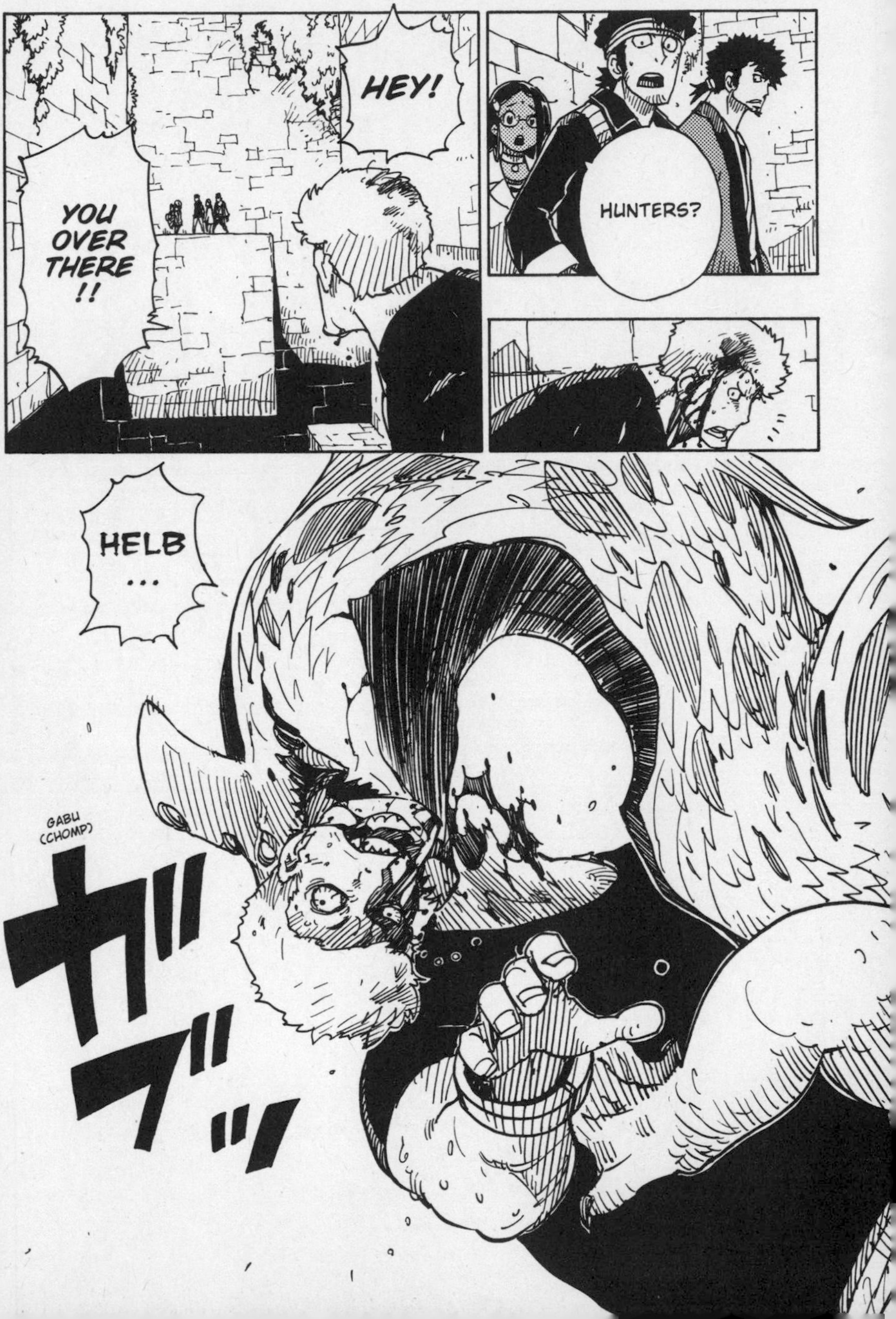
HUNTERS?
HEY!
YOU OVER THERE!!
HELB...
GABU (CHOMP)
ガブッ

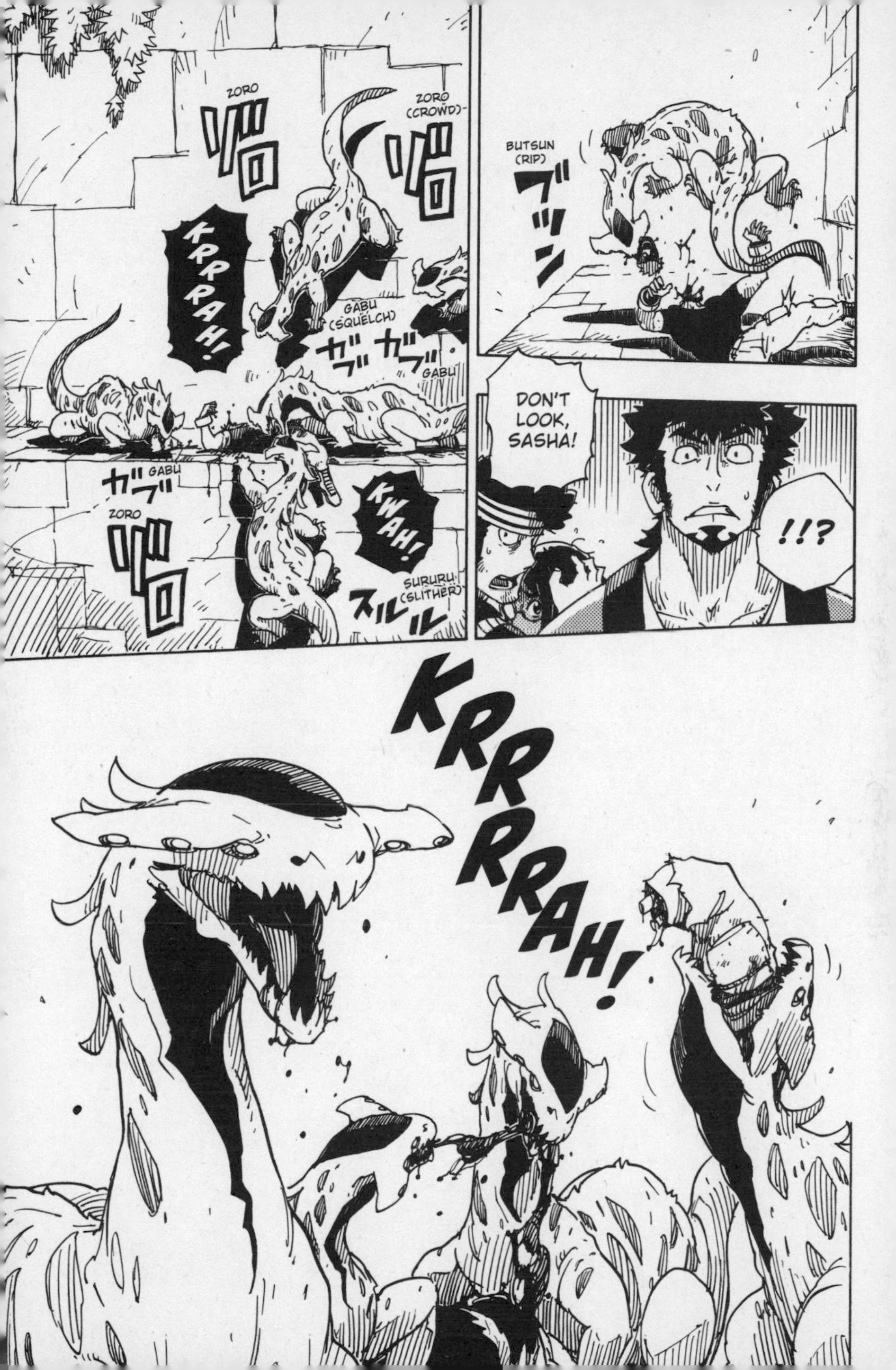
BUTSUN (RIP)
ブツン
DON'T LOOK, SASHA!
!!?
ZORO (CROWD)
ゾロ
ZORO
ゾロ
KRRRAH!
GABU (SQUELCH)
ガブ
ガブ
GABU
KWAH!
GABU
ガブ
ZORO
ゾロ
SURURU (SLITHER)
スルル
KRRRRAH!

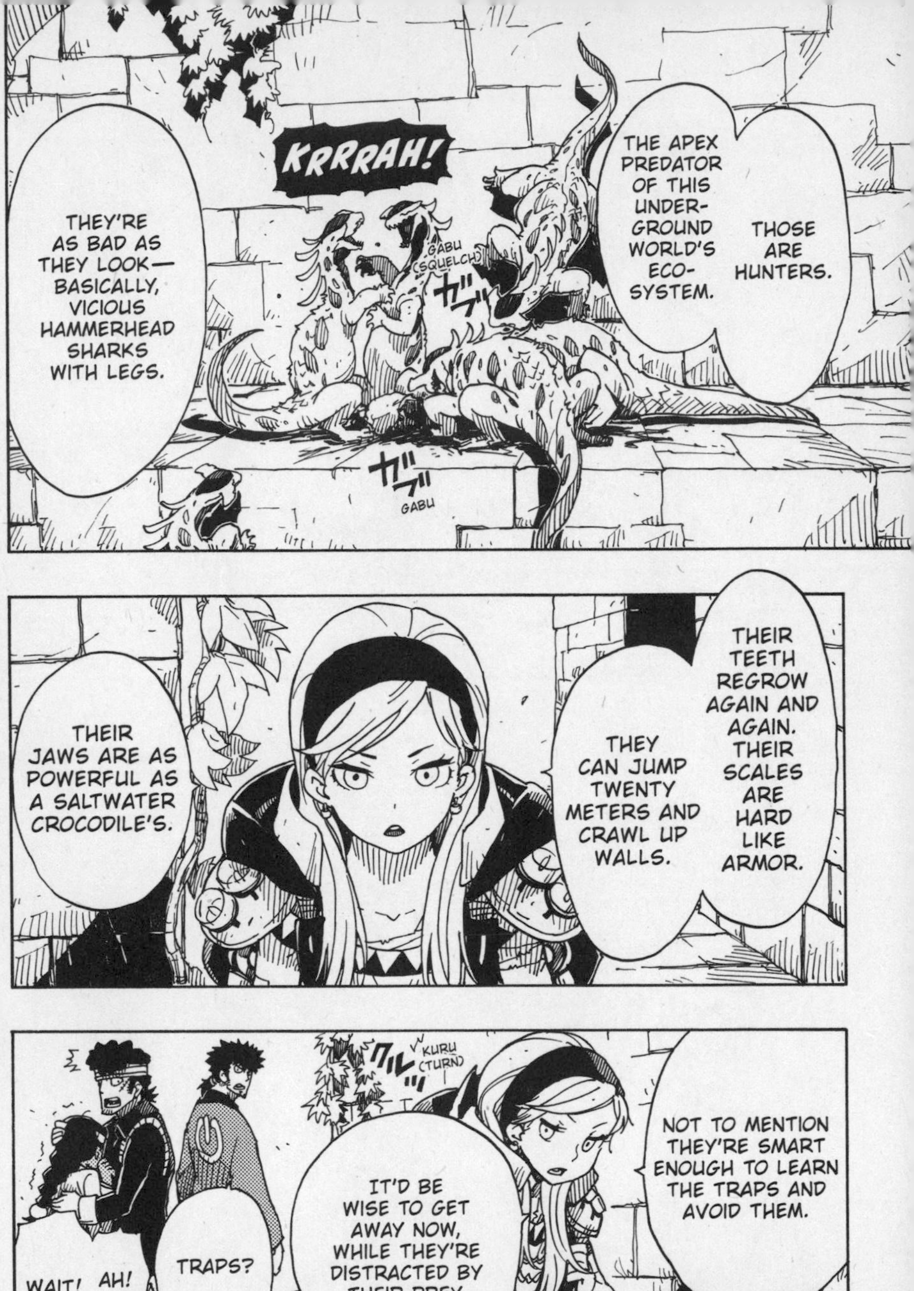
THOSE ARE HUNTERS.
THE APEX PREDATOR OF THIS UNDER-GROUND WORLD'S ECO-SYSTEM.
KRRRAH!
GABU (SQUELCH)
THEY'RE AS BAD AS THEY LOOK—BASICALLY, VICIOUS HAMMERHEAD SHARKS WITH LEGS.
GABU
THEIR TEETH REGROW AGAIN AND AGAIN. THEIR SCALES ARE HARD LIKE ARMOR.
THEY CAN JUMP TWENTY METERS AND CRAWL UP WALLS.
THEIR JAWS ARE AS POWERFUL AS A SALTWATER CROCODILE'S.
NOT TO MENTION THEY'RE SMART ENOUGH TO LEARN THE TRAPS AND AVOID THEM.
KURU (TURN)
IT'D BE WISE TO GET AWAY NOW, WHILE THEY'RE DISTRACTED BY THEIR PREY.
TRAPS?
AH!
WAIT!

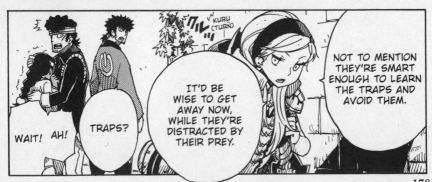

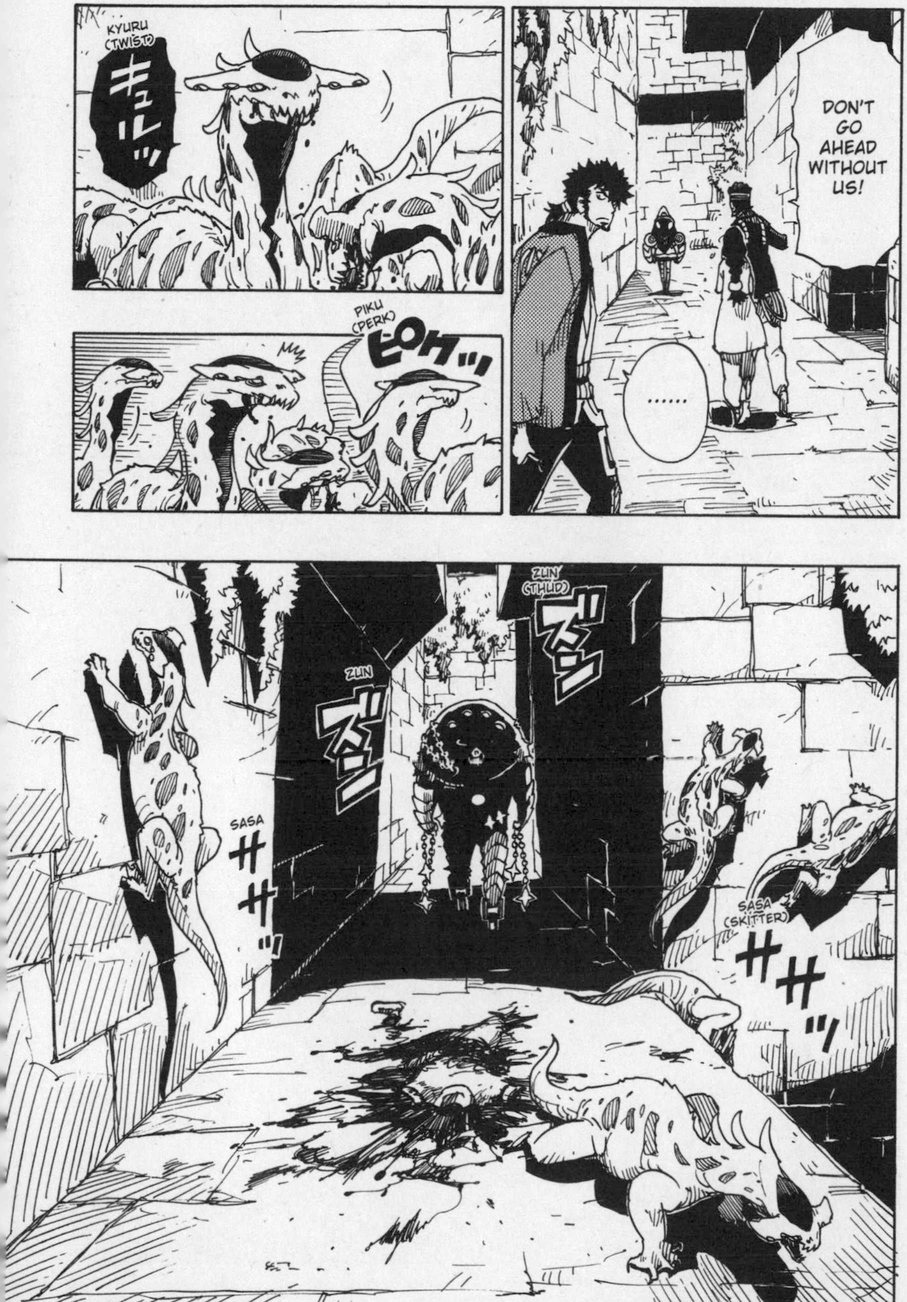
DON'T GO AHEAD WITHOUT US!
......
KYURU (TWIST)
キュルッ
PIKU (PERK)
ピクッ
ZUN (THUD)
ズシン
ZUN
ズシン
SASA (SKITTER)
ササッ
SASA
ササッ

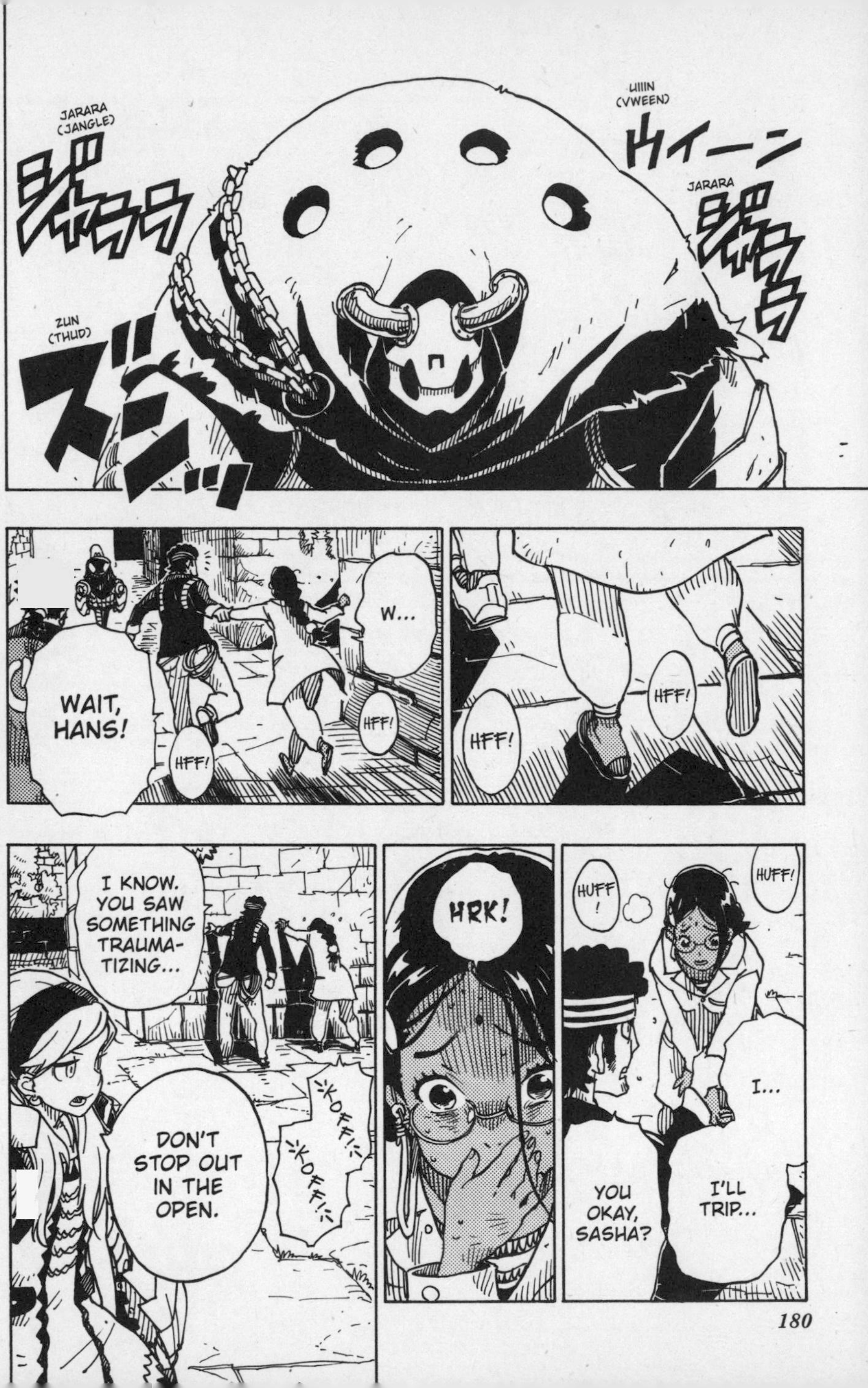
UIIIN (VWEEN)
ウイーン
JARARA
ジャララ
JARARA (JANGLE)
ジャララ
ZUN (THUD)
ズン
HFF!
HFF!
W...
HFF!
WAIT, HANS!
HFF!
HUFF!
HUFF!
I...
I'LL TRIP...
YOU OKAY, SASHA?
HRK!
I KNOW. YOU SAW SOMETHING TRAUMATIZING...
KOFF! KOFF!
DON'T STOP OUT IN THE OPEN.

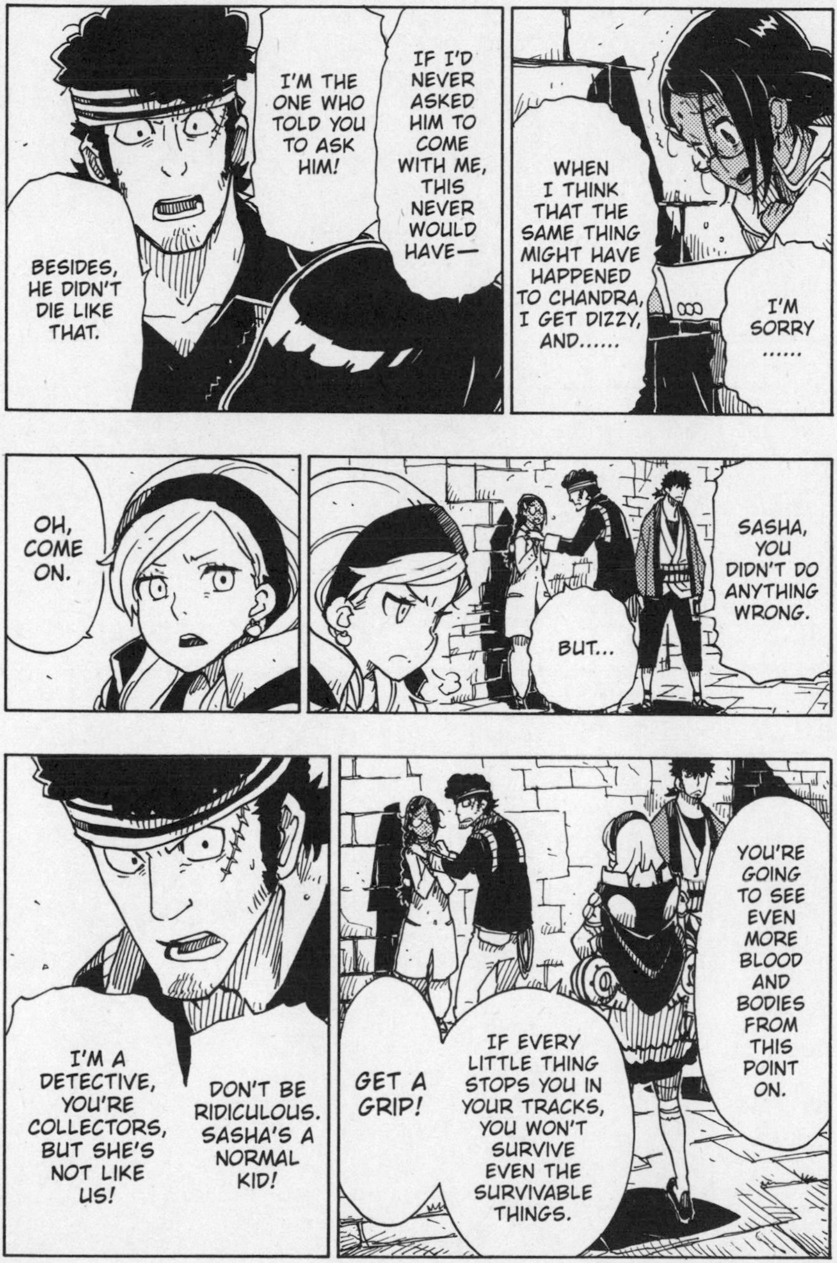
WHEN I THINK THAT THE SAME THING MIGHT HAVE HAPPENED TO CHANDRA, I GET DIZZY, AND......
I'M SORRY ......
IF I'D NEVER ASKED HIM TO COME WITH ME, THIS NEVER WOULD HAVE—
I'M THE ONE WHO TOLD YOU TO ASK HIM!
BESIDES, HE DIDN'T DIE LIKE THAT.
SASHA, YOU DIDN'T DO ANYTHING WRONG.
BUT...
OH, COME ON.
YOU'RE GOING TO SEE EVEN MORE BLOOD AND BODIES FROM THIS POINT ON.
IF EVERY LITTLE THING STOPS YOU IN YOUR TRACKS, YOU WON'T SURVIVE EVEN THE SURVIVABLE THINGS.
GET A GRIP!
DON'T BE RIDICULOUS. SASHA'S A NORMAL KID!
I'M A DETECTIVE, YOU'RE COLLECTORS, BUT SHE'S NOT LIKE US!

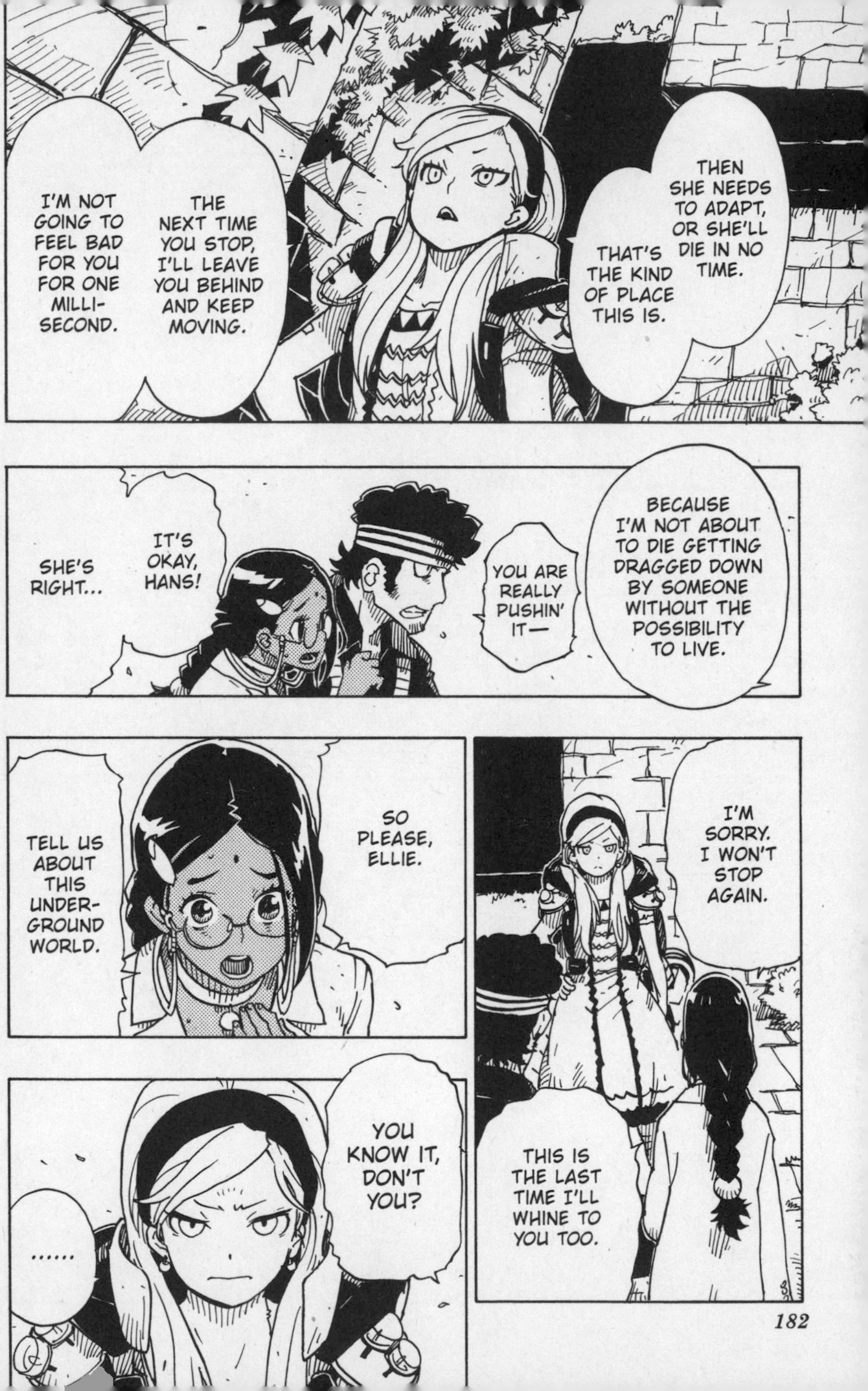
THEN SHE NEEDS TO ADAPT, OR SHE'LL DIE IN NO TIME.
THAT'S THE KIND OF PLACE THIS IS.
THE NEXT TIME YOU STOP, I'LL LEAVE YOU BEHIND AND KEEP MOVING.
I'M NOT GOING TO FEEL BAD FOR YOU FOR ONE MILLI-SECOND.
BECAUSE I'M NOT ABOUT TO DIE GETTING DRAGGED DOWN BY SOMEONE WITHOUT THE POSSIBILITY TO LIVE.
YOU ARE REALLY PUSHIN' IT—
IT'S OKAY, HANS!
SHE'S RIGHT...
I'M SORRY. I WON'T STOP AGAIN.
THIS IS THE LAST TIME I'LL WHINE TO YOU TOO.
SO PLEASE, ELLIE.
TELL US ABOUT THIS UNDER-GROUND WORLD.
YOU KNOW IT, DON'T YOU?
......

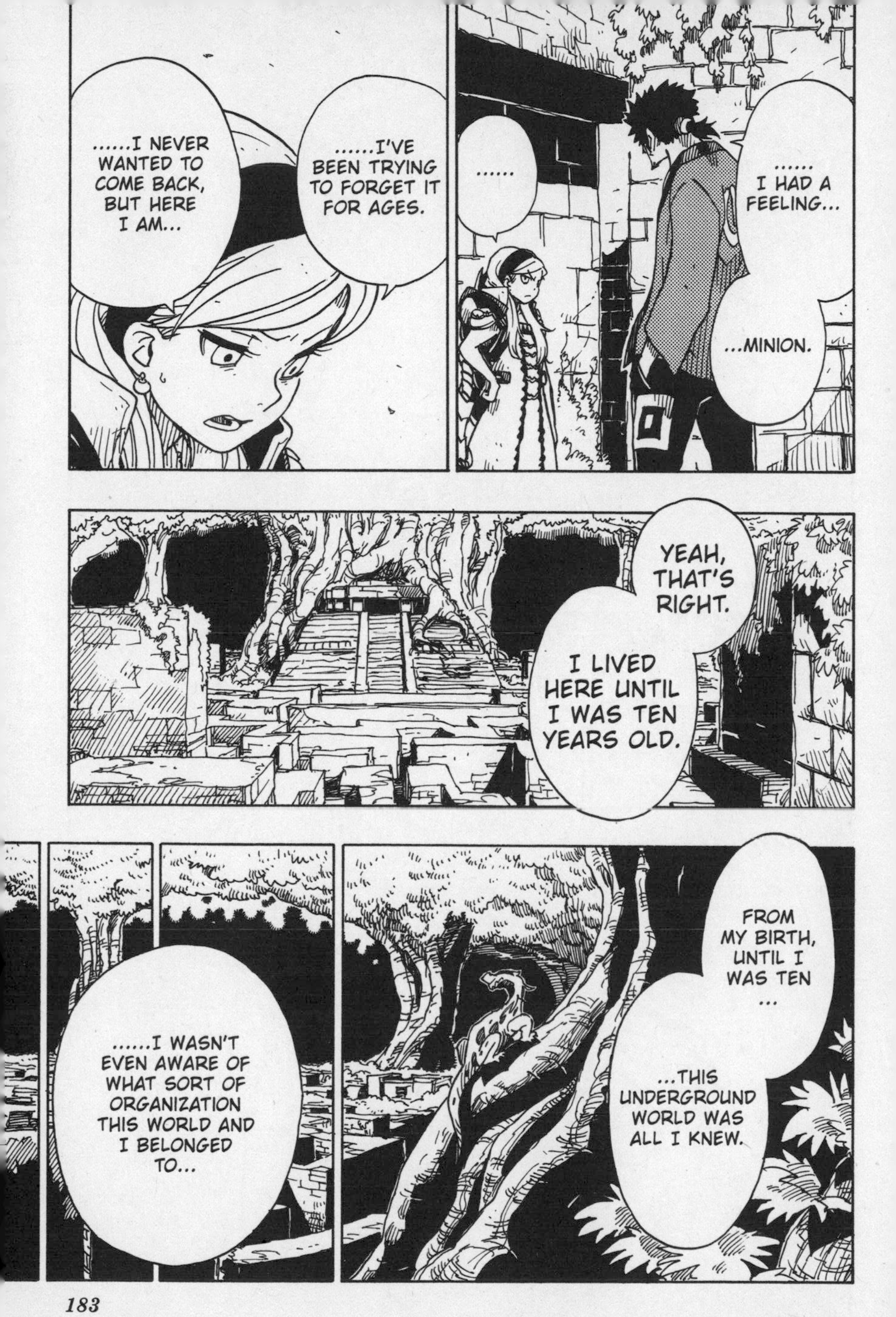
......I HAD A FEELING...
...MINION.
......
......I'VE BEEN TRYING TO FORGET IT FOR AGES.
......I NEVER WANTED TO COME BACK, BUT HERE I AM...
YEAH, THAT'S RIGHT.
I LIVED HERE UNTIL I WAS TEN YEARS OLD.
FROM MY BIRTH, UNTIL I WAS TEN ...
...THIS UNDERGROUND WORLD WAS ALL I KNEW.
......I WASN'T EVEN AWARE OF WHAT SORT OF ORGANIZATION THIS WORLD AND I BELONGED TO...

......

FUWA
(DRIFT)

PARA
(CRINKLE)

JIWAAAA
(SPREAD)

KURU
(TWIST)

A
LEAF.

WHATCHA
LOOKIN'
AT?

UNO.

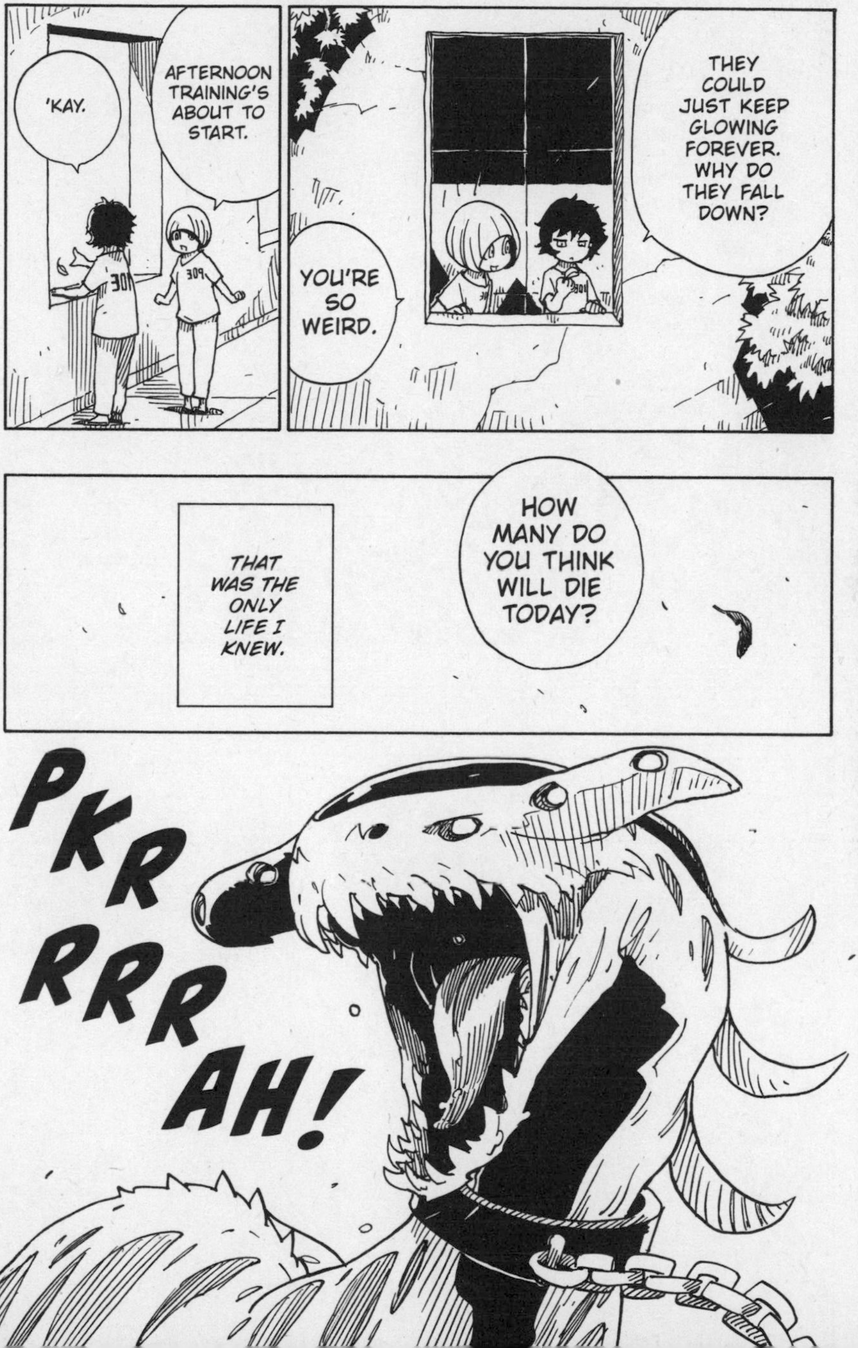
AFTERNOON TRAINING'S ABOUT TO START.
'KAY.
THEY COULD JUST KEEP GLOWING FOREVER. WHY DO THEY FALL DOWN?
YOU'RE SO WEIRD.
HOW MANY DO YOU THINK WILL DIE TODAY?
THAT WAS THE ONLY LIFE I KNEW.
PKRRRRRAH!

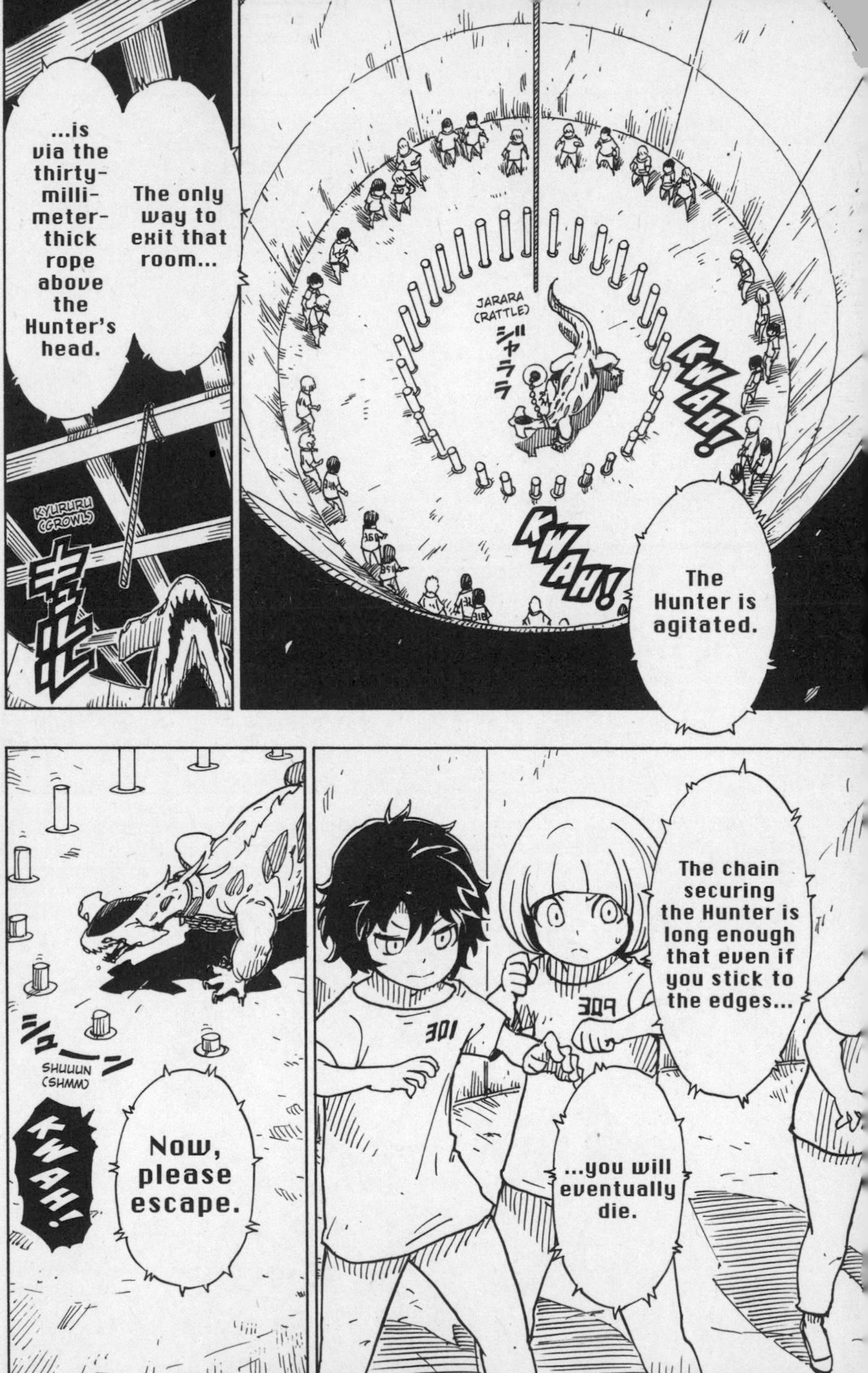
The Hunter is agitated.
KWAH!
KWAH!
ジャララ
JARARA (RATTLE)
The only way to exit that room...
...is via the thirty-millimeter-thick rope above the Hunter's head.
KYURURU (GROWL)
The chain securing the Hunter is long enough that even if you stick to the edges...
...you will eventually die.
301
309
Now, please escape.
シューン
SHUUUN (SHMM)
KWAH!

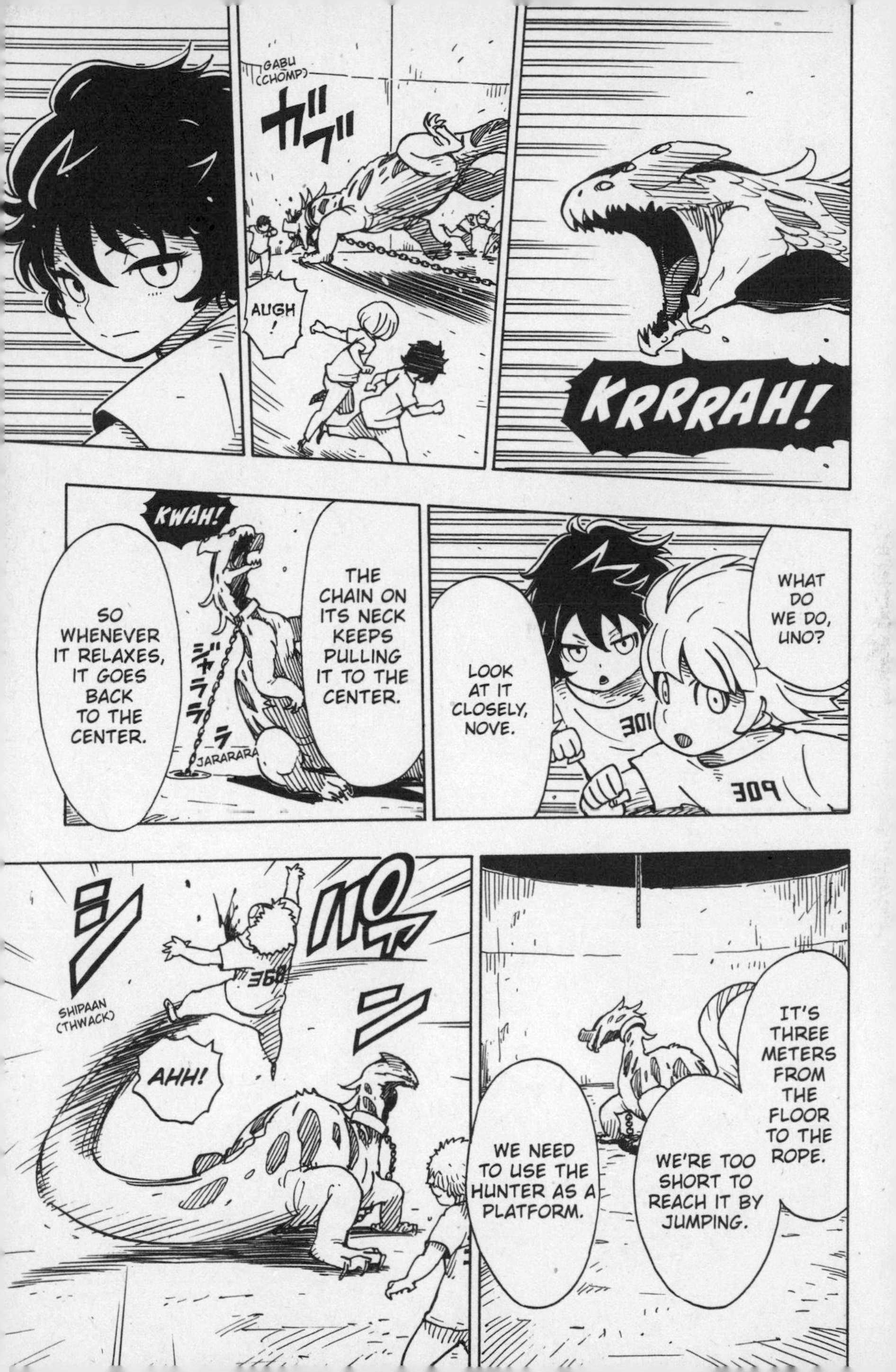
KRRRAH!
GABU (CHOMP)
ガブ
AUGH!
WHAT DO WE DO, UNO?
LOOK AT IT CLOSELY, NOVE.
KWAH!
THE CHAIN ON ITS NECK KEEPS PULLING IT TO THE CENTER.
SO WHENEVER IT RELAXES, IT GOES BACK TO THE CENTER.
JARARARA
IT'S THREE METERS FROM THE FLOOR TO THE ROPE.
WE'RE TOO SHORT TO REACH IT BY JUMPING.
WE NEED TO USE THE HUNTER AS A PLATFORM.
SHIPAAN (THWACK)
AHH!

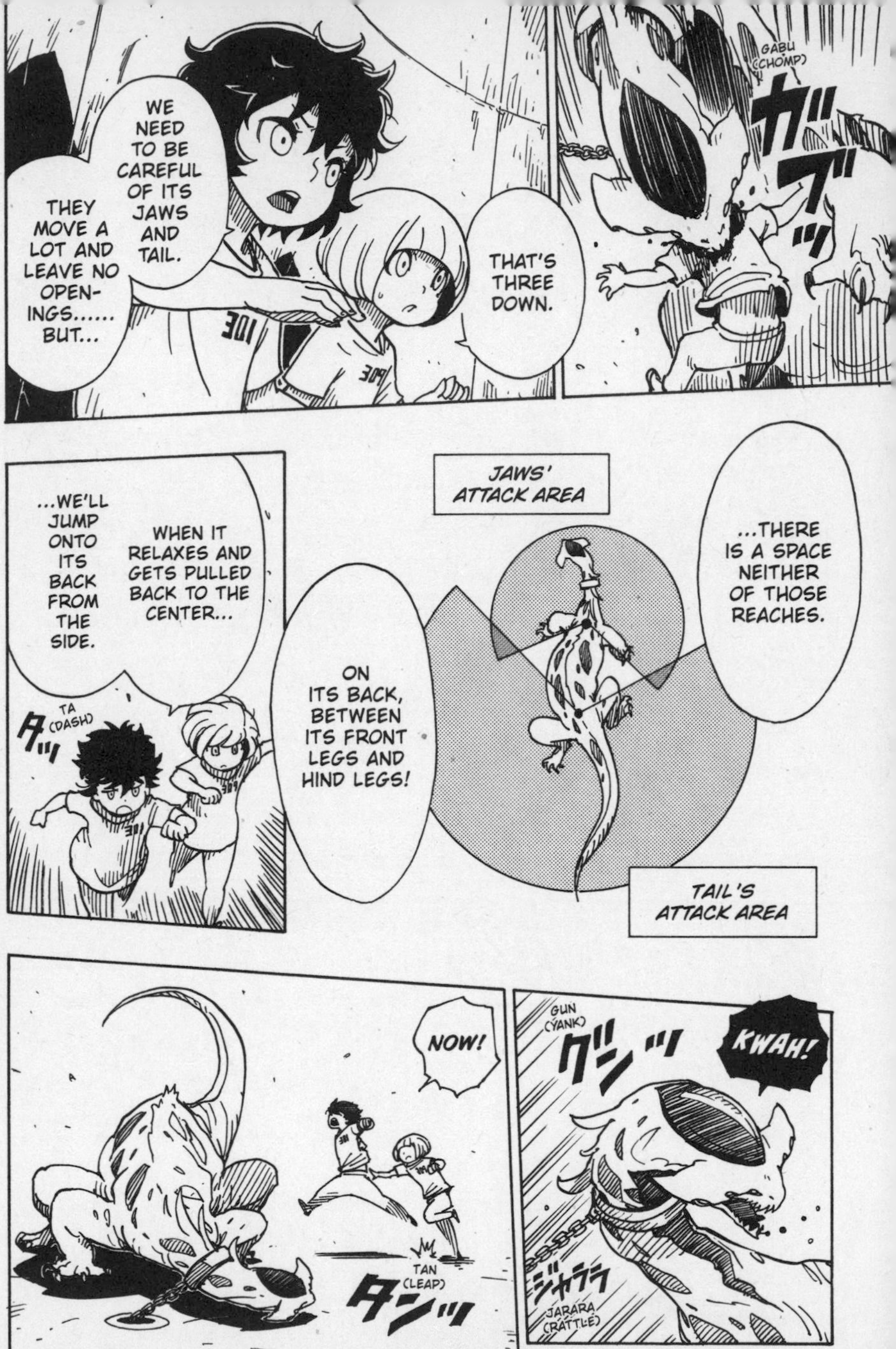
GABU (CHOMP)
THAT'S THREE DOWN.
WE NEED TO BE CAREFUL OF ITS JAWS AND TAIL.
THEY MOVE A LOT AND LEAVE NO OPENINGS...... BUT...
...THERE IS A SPACE NEITHER OF THOSE REACHES.
JAWS' ATTACK AREA
TAIL'S ATTACK AREA
ON ITS BACK, BETWEEN ITS FRONT LEGS AND HIND LEGS!
WHEN IT RELAXES AND GETS PULLED BACK TO THE CENTER...
...WE'LL JUMP ONTO ITS BACK FROM THE SIDE.
TA (DASH)
GUN (YANK)
KWAH!
JARARA (RATTLE)
NOW!
TAN (LEAP)

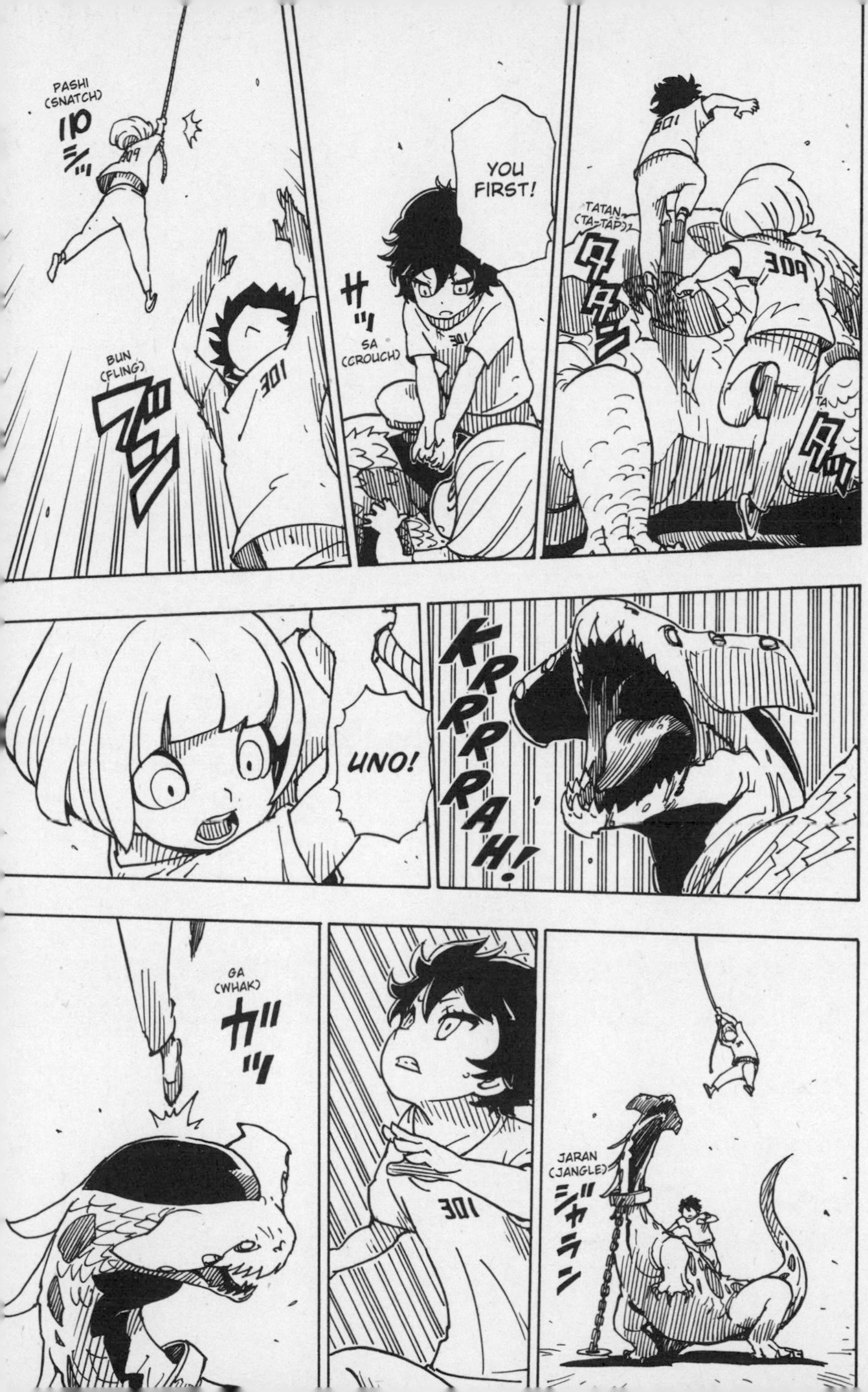
TATAN (TA-TAP)
TA
YOU FIRST!
SA (CROUCH)
PASHI (SNATCH)
BUN (FLING)
KRRRRAH!
UNO!
JARAN (JANGLE)
GA (WHAK)

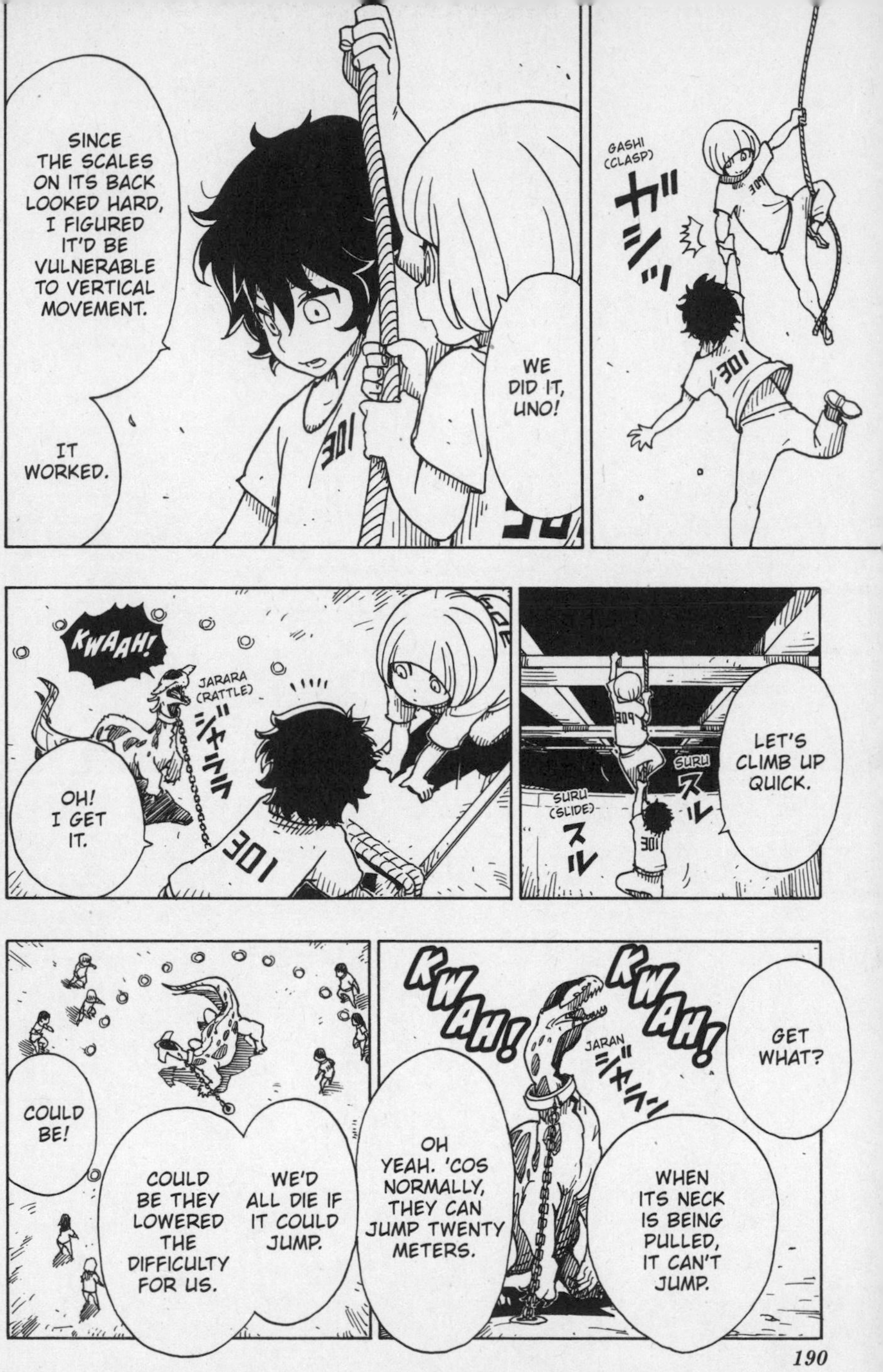
GASHI (CLASP)
WE DID IT, UNO!
SINCE THE SCALES ON ITS BACK LOOKED HARD, I FIGURED IT'D BE VULNERABLE TO VERTICAL MOVEMENT.
IT WORKED.
LET'S CLIMB UP QUICK.
SURU
SURU (SLIDE)
KWAAH!
JARARA (RATTLE)
OH! I GET IT.
GET WHAT?
KWAH! KWAH!
JARAN
WHEN ITS NECK IS BEING PULLED, IT CAN'T JUMP.
OH YEAH. 'COS NORMALLY, THEY CAN JUMP TWENTY METERS.
WE'D ALL DIE IF IT COULD JUMP.
COULD BE THEY LOWERED THE DIFFICULTY FOR US.
COULD BE!

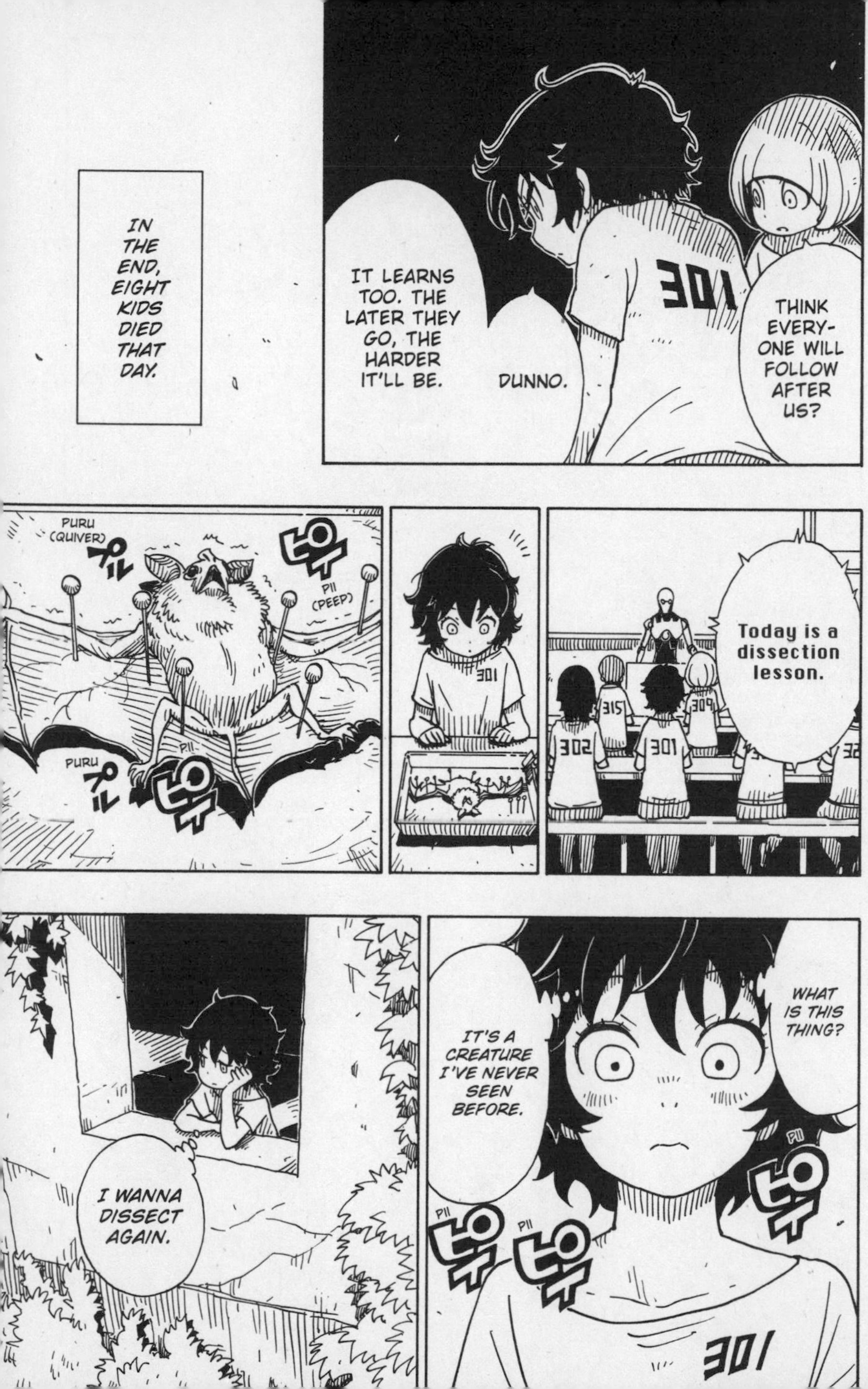
THINK EVERYONE WILL FOLLOW AFTER US?
DUNNO.
IT LEARNS TOO. THE LATER THEY GO, THE HARDER IT'LL BE.
IN THE END, EIGHT KIDS DIED THAT DAY.
Today is a dissection lesson.
ピィ
PII (PEEP)
プル
PURU (QUIVER)
ピィ
PII
プル
PURU
WHAT IS THIS THING?
IT'S A CREATURE I'VE NEVER SEEN BEFORE.
ピィ
PII
ピィ
PII
ピィ
PII
I WANNA DISSECT AGAIN.

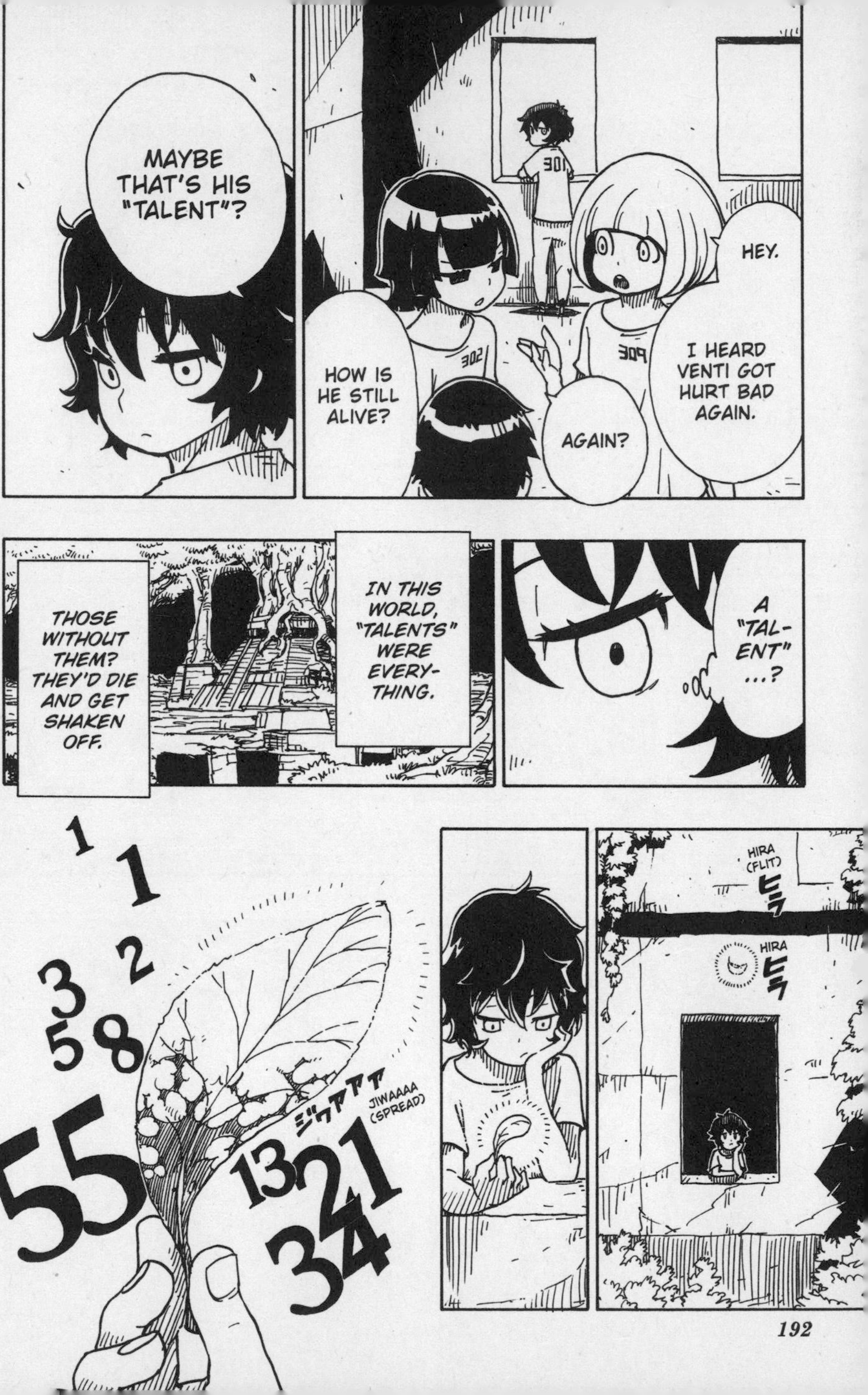
HEY.
I HEARD VENTI GOT HURT BAD AGAIN.
AGAIN?
HOW IS HE STILL ALIVE?
MAYBE THAT'S HIS "TALENT"?
A "TAL-ENT"...?
IN THIS WORLD, "TALENTS" WERE EVERY-THING.
THOSE WITHOUT THEM? THEY'D DIE AND GET SHAKEN OFF.
HIRA (FLIT)
HIRA
JIWAAAA (SPREAD)
1 1 2 3 5 8 13 21 34 55

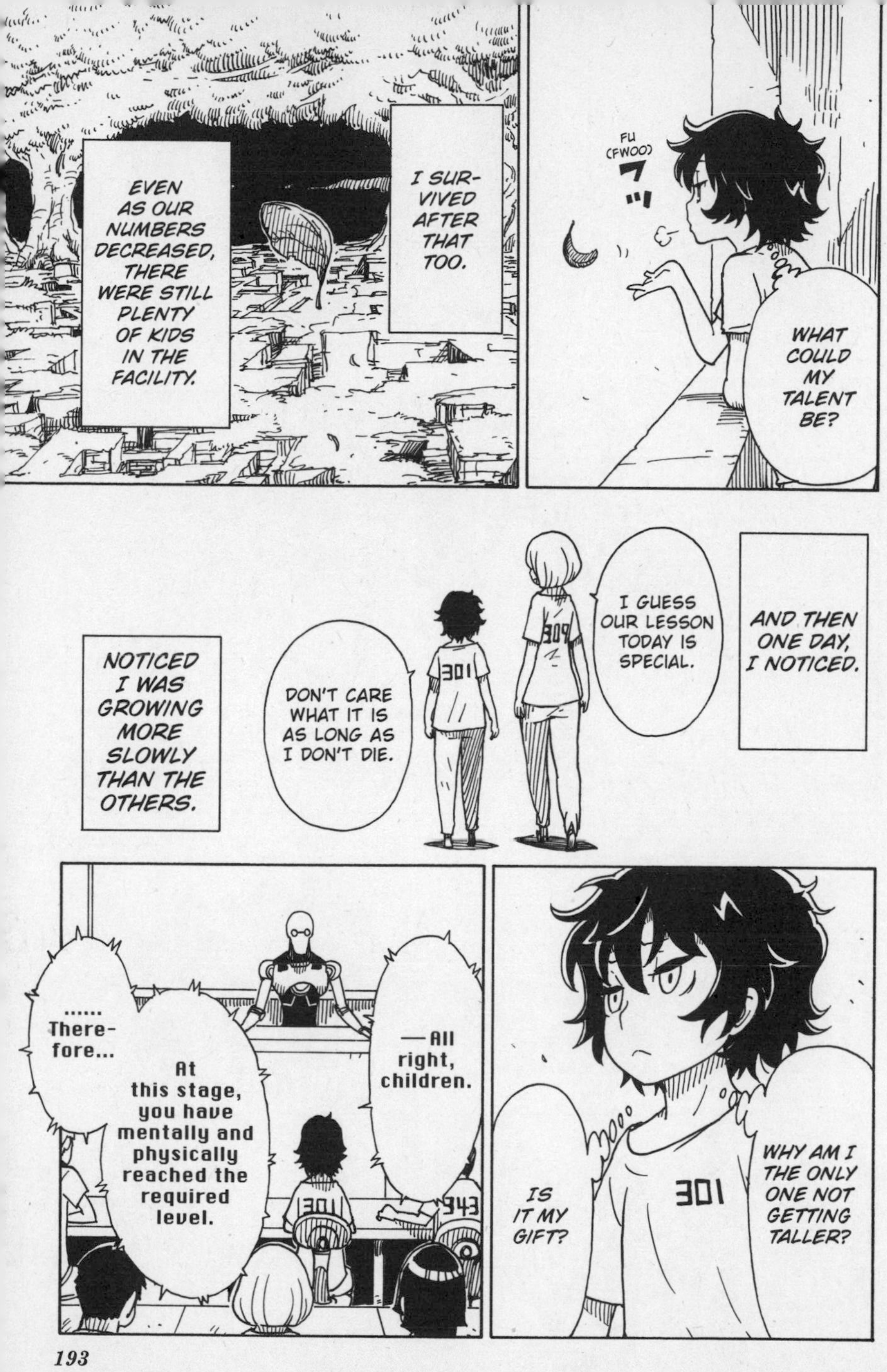
FU (FWOO)
WHAT COULD MY TALENT BE?
I SURVIVED AFTER THAT TOO.
EVEN AS OUR NUMBERS DECREASED, THERE WERE STILL PLENTY OF KIDS IN THE FACILITY.
AND THEN ONE DAY, I NOTICED.
I GUESS OUR LESSON TODAY IS SPECIAL.
DON'T CARE WHAT IT IS AS LONG AS I DON'T DIE.
NOTICED I WAS GROWING MORE SLOWLY THAN THE OTHERS.
WHY AM I THE ONLY ONE NOT GETTING TALLER?
IS IT MY GIFT?
—All right, children.
At this stage, you have mentally and physically reached the required level.
...... Therefore...

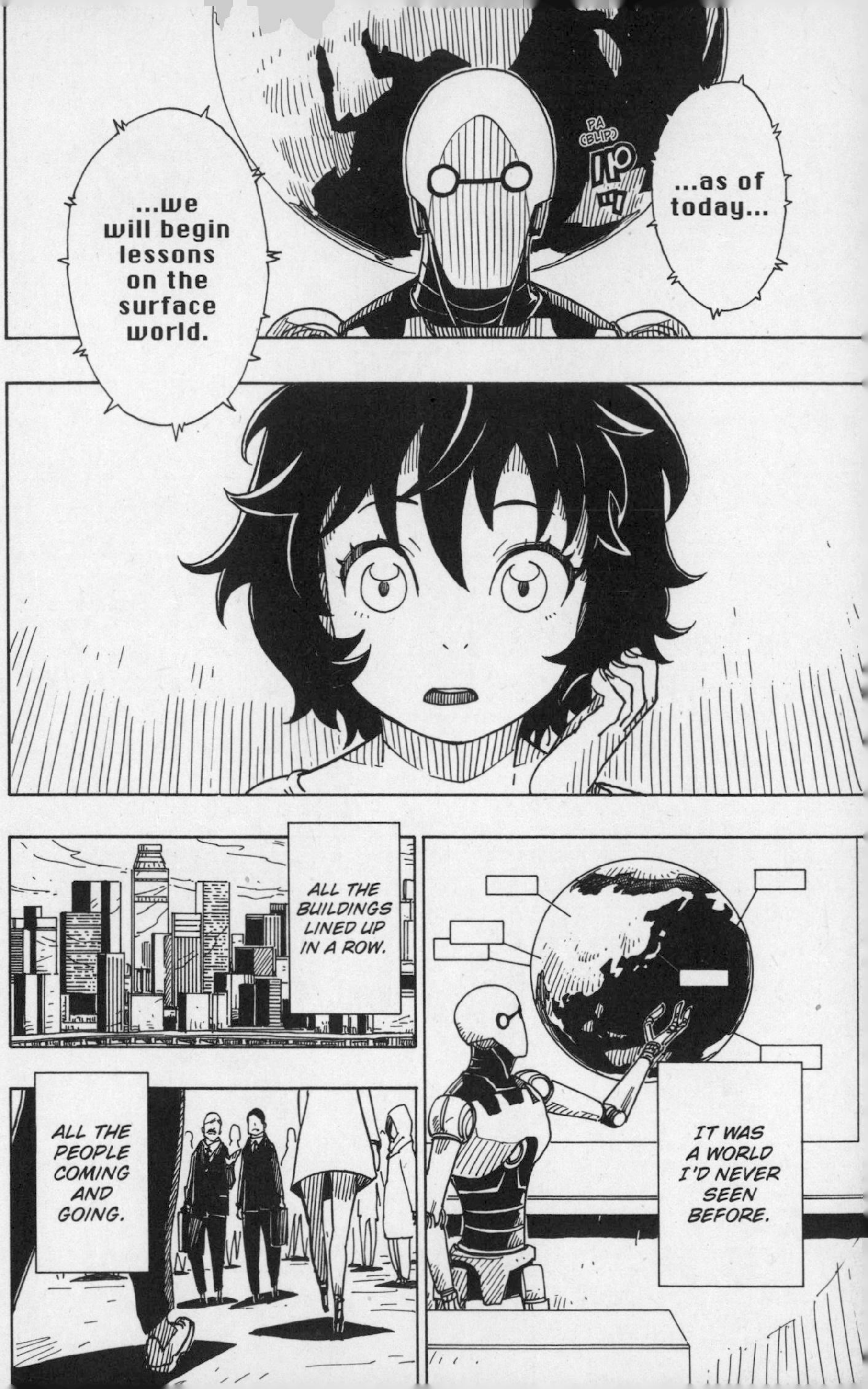
...as of today...
PA (BLIP)
...we will begin lessons on the surface world.
ALL THE BUILDINGS LINED UP IN A ROW.
ALL THE PEOPLE COMING AND GOING.
IT WAS A WORLD I'D NEVER SEEN BEFORE.

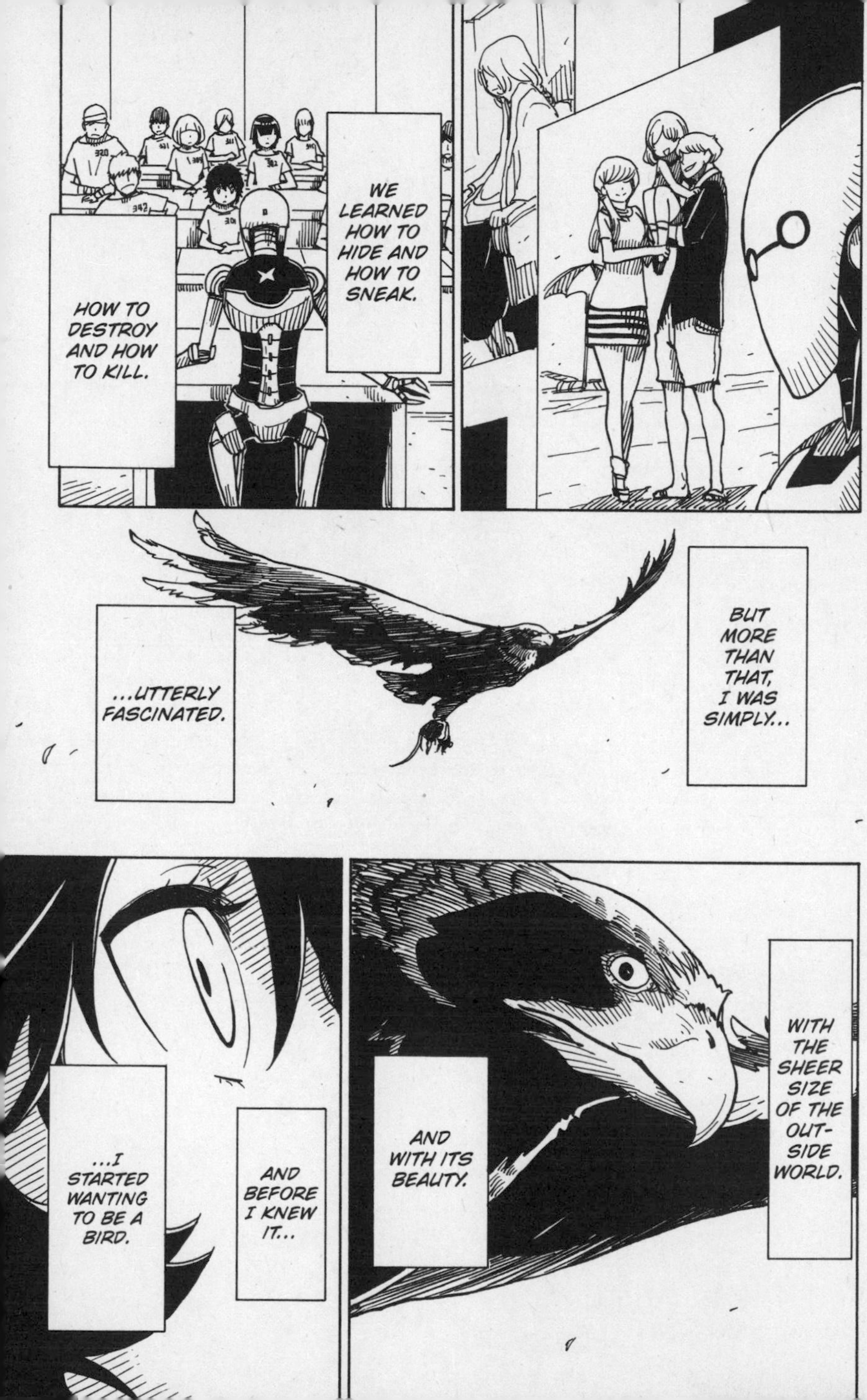
WE LEARNED HOW TO HIDE AND HOW TO SNEAK.
HOW TO DESTROY AND HOW TO KILL.
BUT MORE THAN THAT, I WAS SIMPLY...
...UTTERLY FASCINATED.
WITH THE SHEER SIZE OF THE OUT-SIDE WORLD.
AND WITH ITS BEAUTY.
AND BEFORE I KNEW IT...
...I STARTED WANTING TO BE A BIRD.

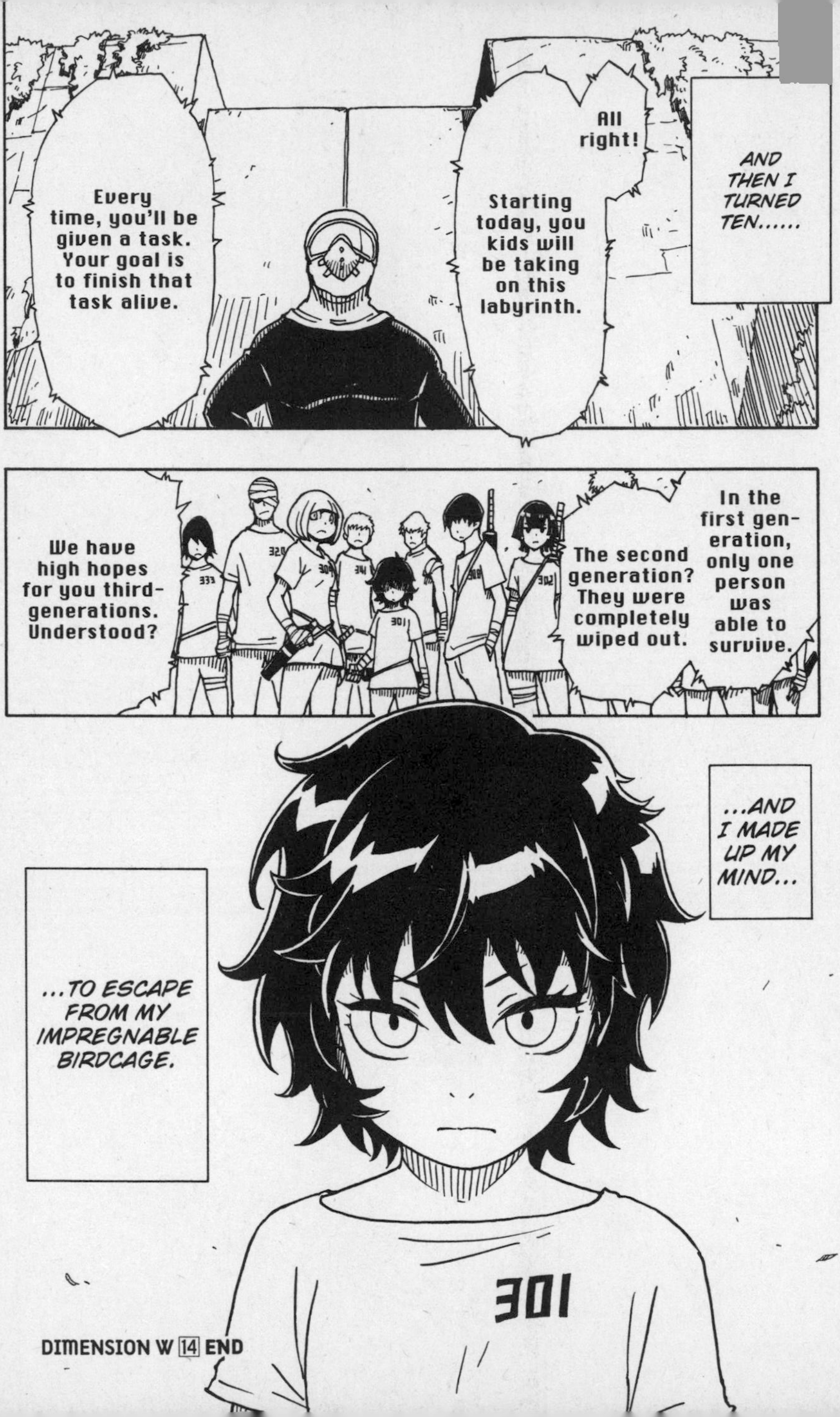
AND THEN I TURNED TEN......
All right!
Starting today, you kids will be taking on this labyrinth.
Every time, you'll be given a task. Your goal is to finish that task alive.
In the first generation, only one person was able to survive.
The second generation? They were completely wiped out.
We have high hopes for you third-generations. Understood?
...AND I MADE UP MY MIND...
...TO ESCAPE FROM MY IMPREGNABLE BIRDCAGE.
301
DIMENSION W 14 END

Dimension W

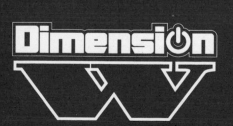

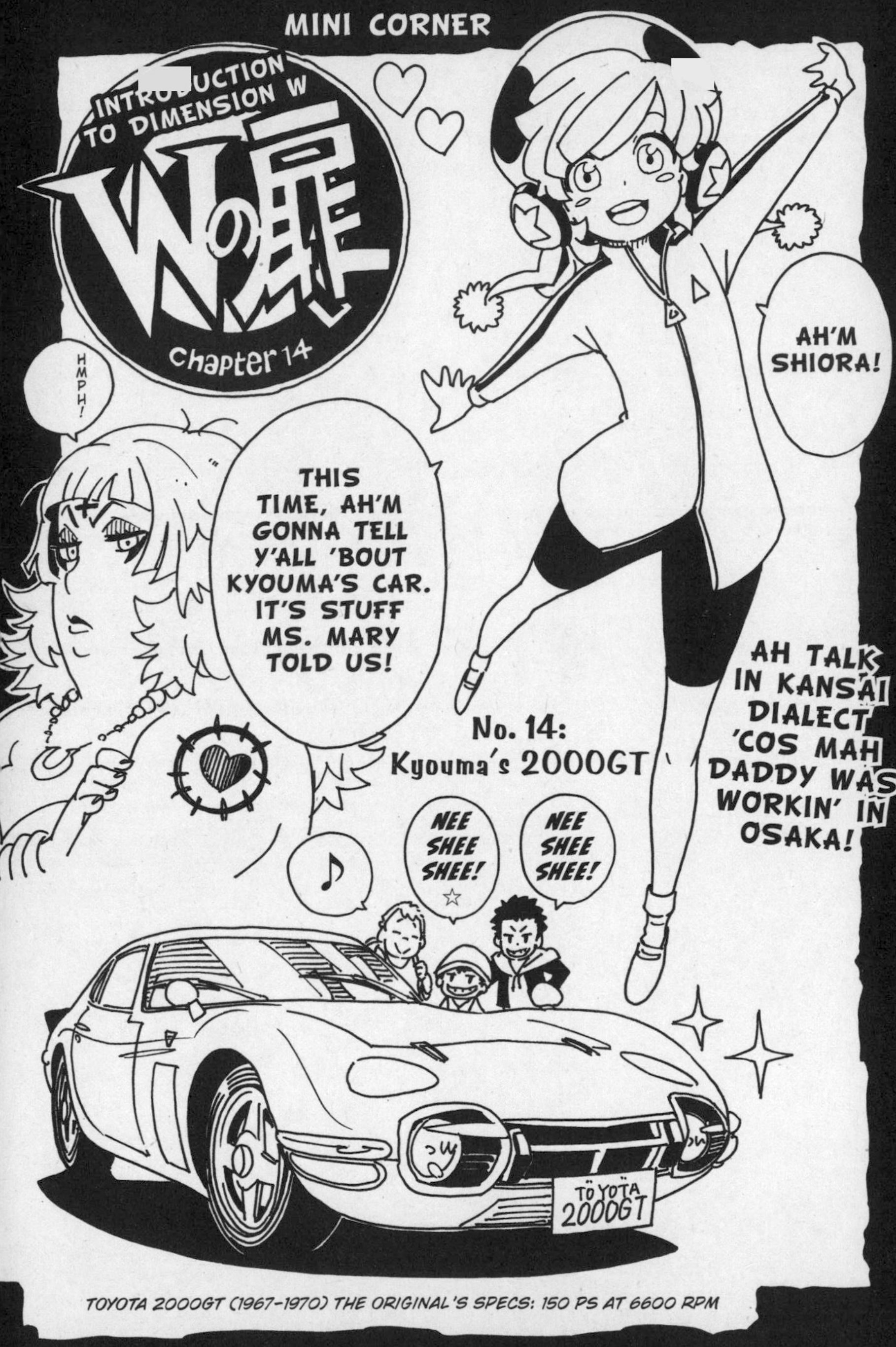
MINI CORNER
INTRODUCTION TO DIMENSION W
Chapter 14
AH'M SHIORA!
HMPH!
THIS TIME, AH'M GONNA TELL Y'ALL 'BOUT KYOUMA'S CAR. IT'S STUFF MS. MARY TOLD US!
AH TALK IN KANSAI DIALECT 'COS MAH DADDY WAS WORKIN' IN OSAKA!
No. 14: Kyouma's 2000GT
NEE SHEE SHEE! ☆
NEE SHEE SHEE!
♪
TOYOTA 2000GT
TOYOTA 2000GT (1967-1970) THE ORIGINAL'S SPECS: 150 PS AT 6600 RPM

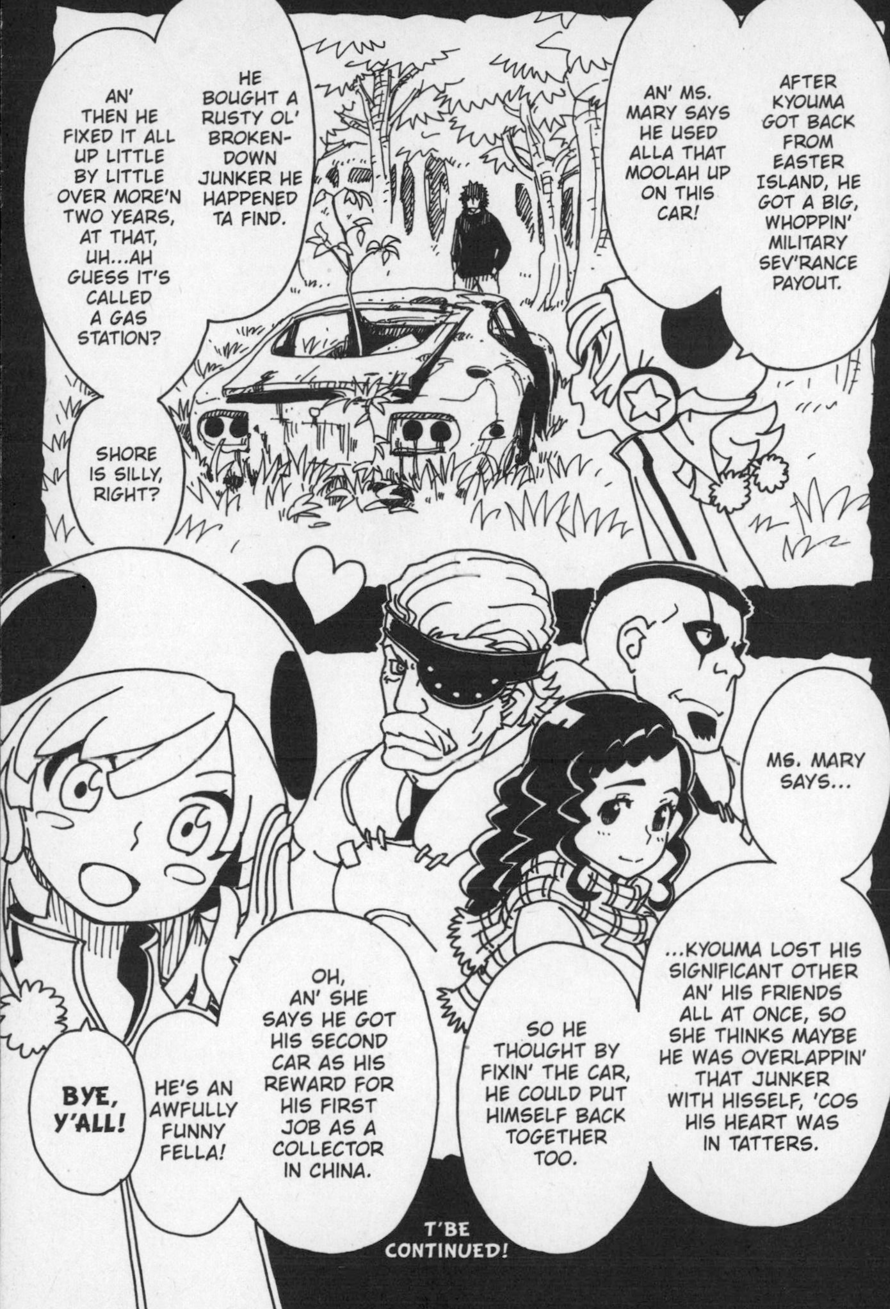

AFTER KYOUMA GOT BACK FROM EASTER ISLAND, HE GOT A BIG, WHOPPIN' MILITARY SEV'RANCE PAYOUT.
AN' MS. MARY SAYS HE USED ALLA THAT MOOLAH UP ON THIS CAR!
HE BOUGHT A RUSTY OL' BROKEN-DOWN JUNKER HE HAPPENED TA FIND.
AN' THEN HE FIXED IT ALL UP LITTLE BY LITTLE OVER MORE'N TWO YEARS, AT THAT, UH...AH GUESS IT'S CALLED A GAS STATION?
SHORE IS SILLY, RIGHT?
MS. MARY SAYS...
...KYOUMA LOST HIS SIGNIFICANT OTHER AN' HIS FRIENDS ALL AT ONCE, SO SHE THINKS MAYBE HE WAS OVERLAPPIN' THAT JUNKER WITH HISSELF, 'COS HIS HEART WAS IN TATTERS.
SO HE THOUGHT BY FIXIN' THE CAR, HE COULD PUT HIMSELF BACK TOGETHER TOO.
OH, AN' SHE SAYS HE GOT HIS SECOND CAR AS HIS REWARD FOR HIS FIRST JOB AS A COLLECTOR IN CHINA.
HE'S AN AWFULLY FUNNY FELLA!
BYE, Y'ALL!
T'BE CONTINUED!

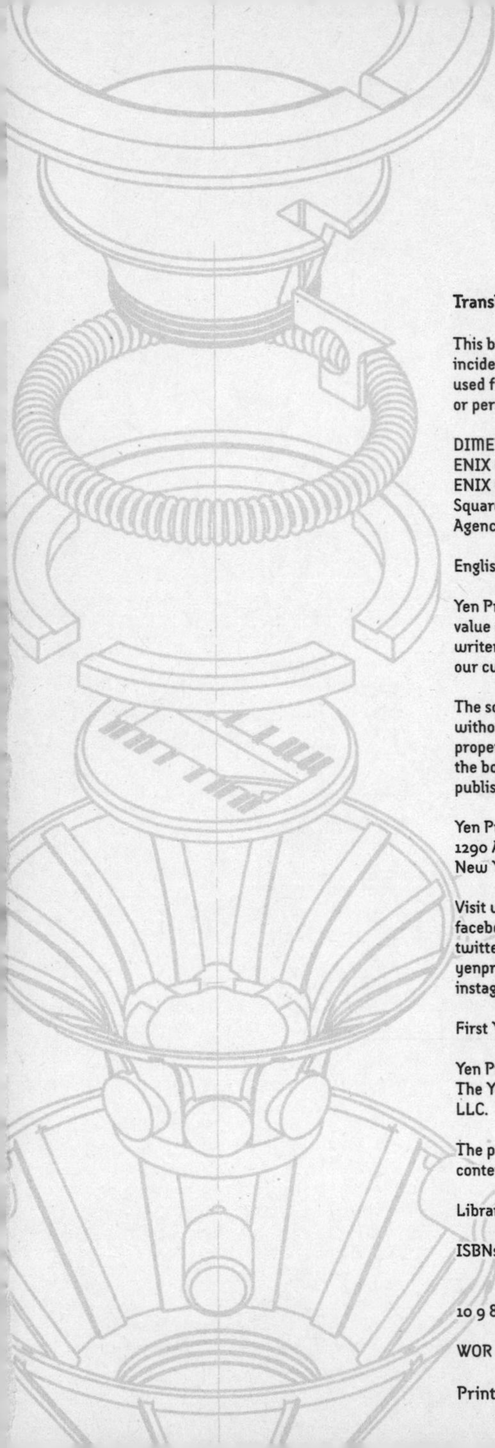

Dimension W

by YUJI IWAHARA

Translation: Amanda Haley • Lettering: Phil Christie

This book is a work of fiction. Names, characters, places, and incidents are the product of the author's imagination or are used fictitiously. Any resemblance to actual events, locales, or persons, living or dead, is coincidental.

DIMENSION W Volume 14 ©2018 YUJI IWAHARA/SQUARE ENIX CO., LTD. First published in Japan in 2018 by SQUARE ENIX CO., LTD. English translation rights arranged with Square Enix Co., Ltd. and Yen Press, LLC through Tuttle-Mori Agency, Inc.

English translation © 2019 by SQUARE ENIX CO., LTD.

Yen Press
1290 Avenue of the Americas
New York, NY 10104

Visit us at yenpress.com
facebook.com/yenpress
twitter.com/yenpress
yenpress.tumblr.com
instagram.com/yenpress

First Yen Press Edition: May 2019

Yen Press is an imprint of Yen Press, LLC.
The Yen Press name and logo are trademarks of Yen Press, LLC.

The publisher is not responsible for websites (or their content) that are not owned by the publisher.

Library of Congress Control Number: 2015956889

ISBNs: 978-1-9753-8274-2 (paperback)
       978-1-9753-8275-9 (ebook)

10 9 8 7 6 5 4 3 2 1

WOR

Printed in the United States of America

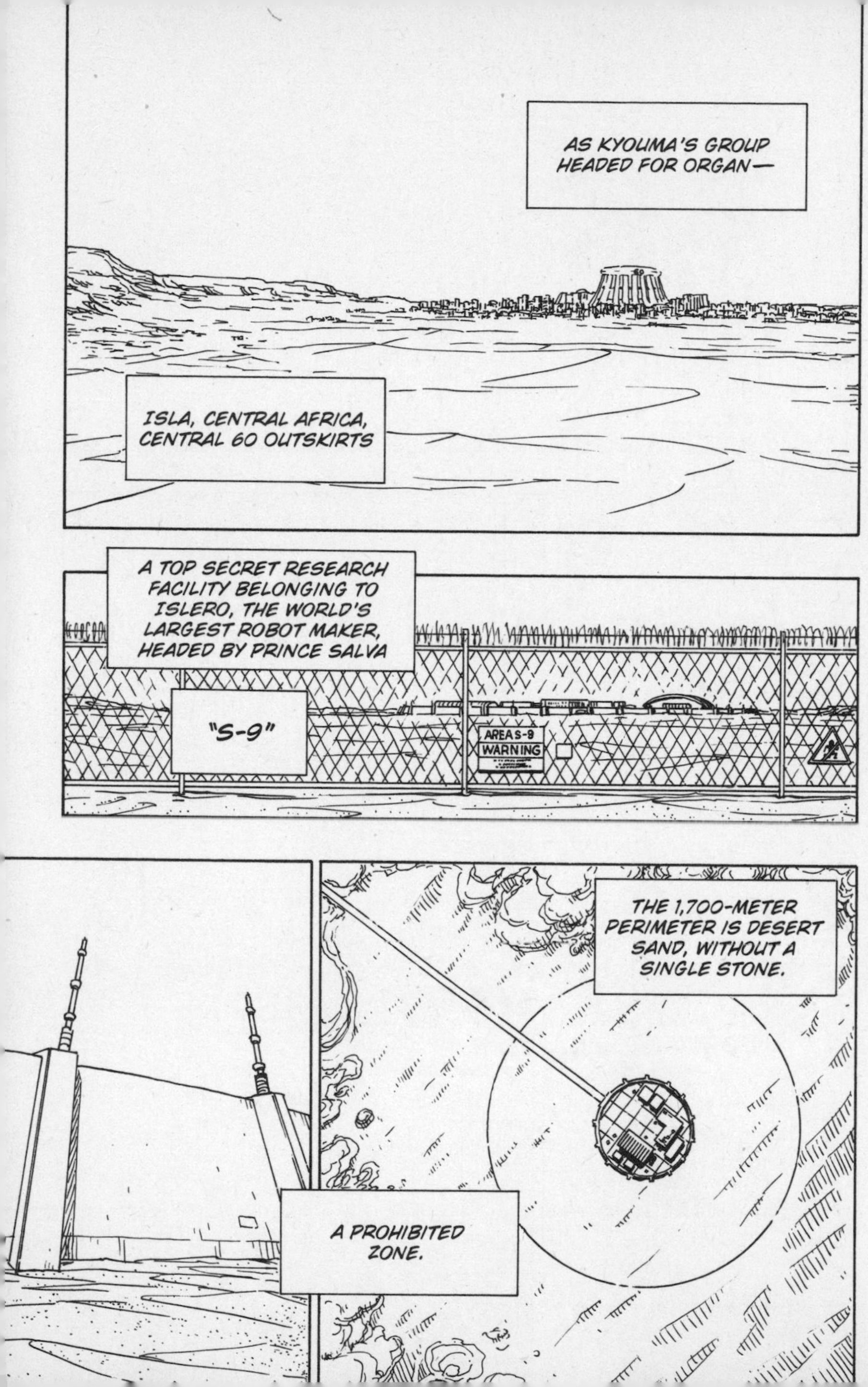
AS KYOUMA'S GROUP HEADED FOR ORGAN—
ISLA, CENTRAL AFRICA, CENTRAL 60 OUTSKIRTS
A TOP SECRET RESEARCH FACILITY BELONGING TO ISLERO, THE WORLD'S LARGEST ROBOT MAKER, HEADED BY PRINCE SALVA
"S-9"
AREA S-9
WARNING
THE 1,700-METER PERIMETER IS DESERT SAND, WITHOUT A SINGLE STONE.
A PROHIBITED ZONE.

SARA
(RUSTLE)

SARA

SARA

サラ サラ サラ

MOKO
(BULGE)
モワッ

HYU
(FLING)

ANOTHER
BIRD?

SOME-
THING
HIT THE
SHIELD.

BACHII
(BZZZT)

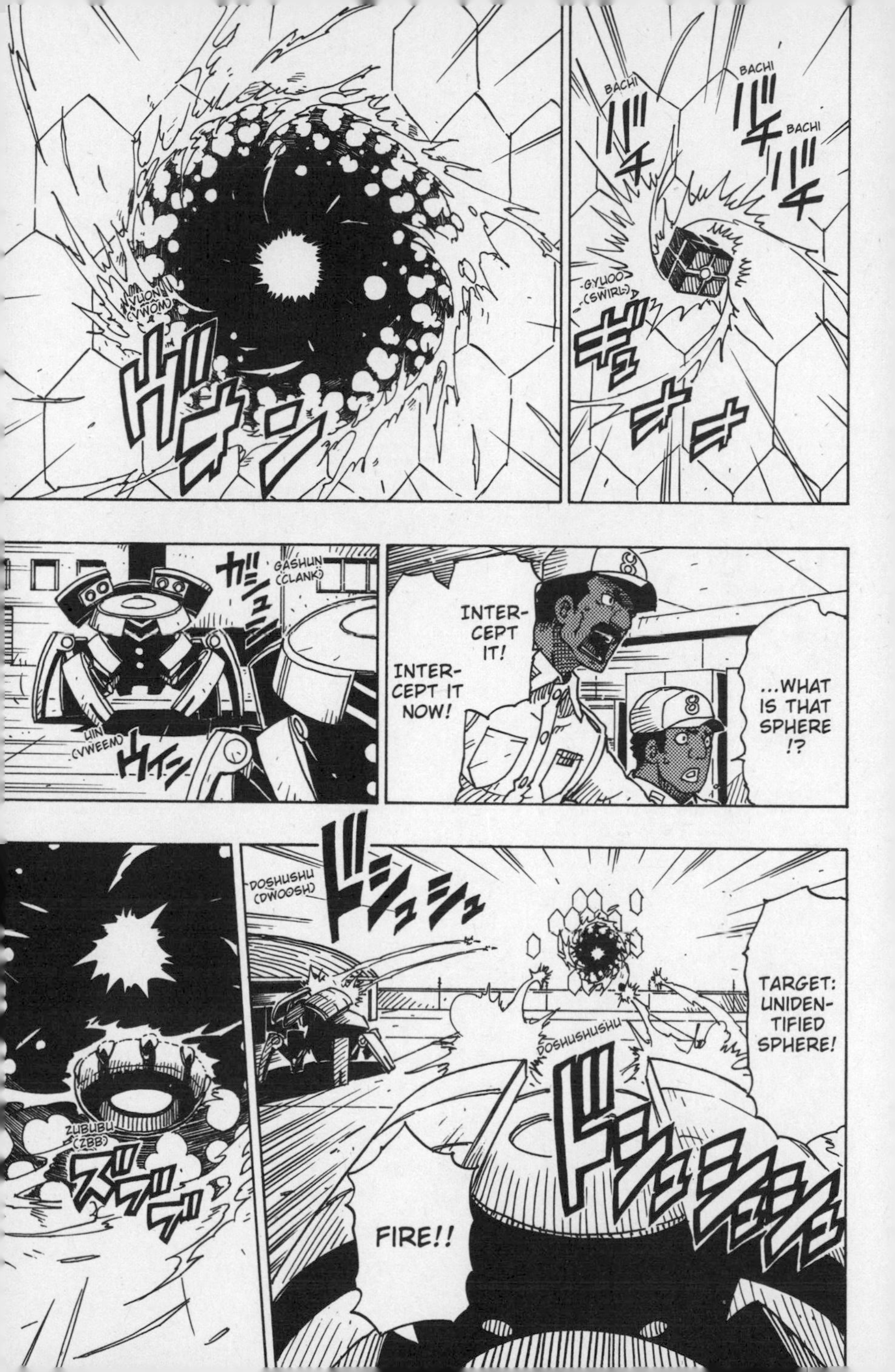
BACHI
BACHI
BACHI
GYUOO (SWIRL)
VUON (VWOM)
...WHAT IS THAT SPHERE !?
INTER-CEPT IT!
INTER-CEPT IT NOW!
GASHUN (CLANK)
UIN (VWEEM)
DOSHUSHU (DWOOSH)
TARGET: UNIDEN-TIFIED SPHERE!
DOSHUSHUSHU
FIRE!!
ZUBUBU (ZBB)

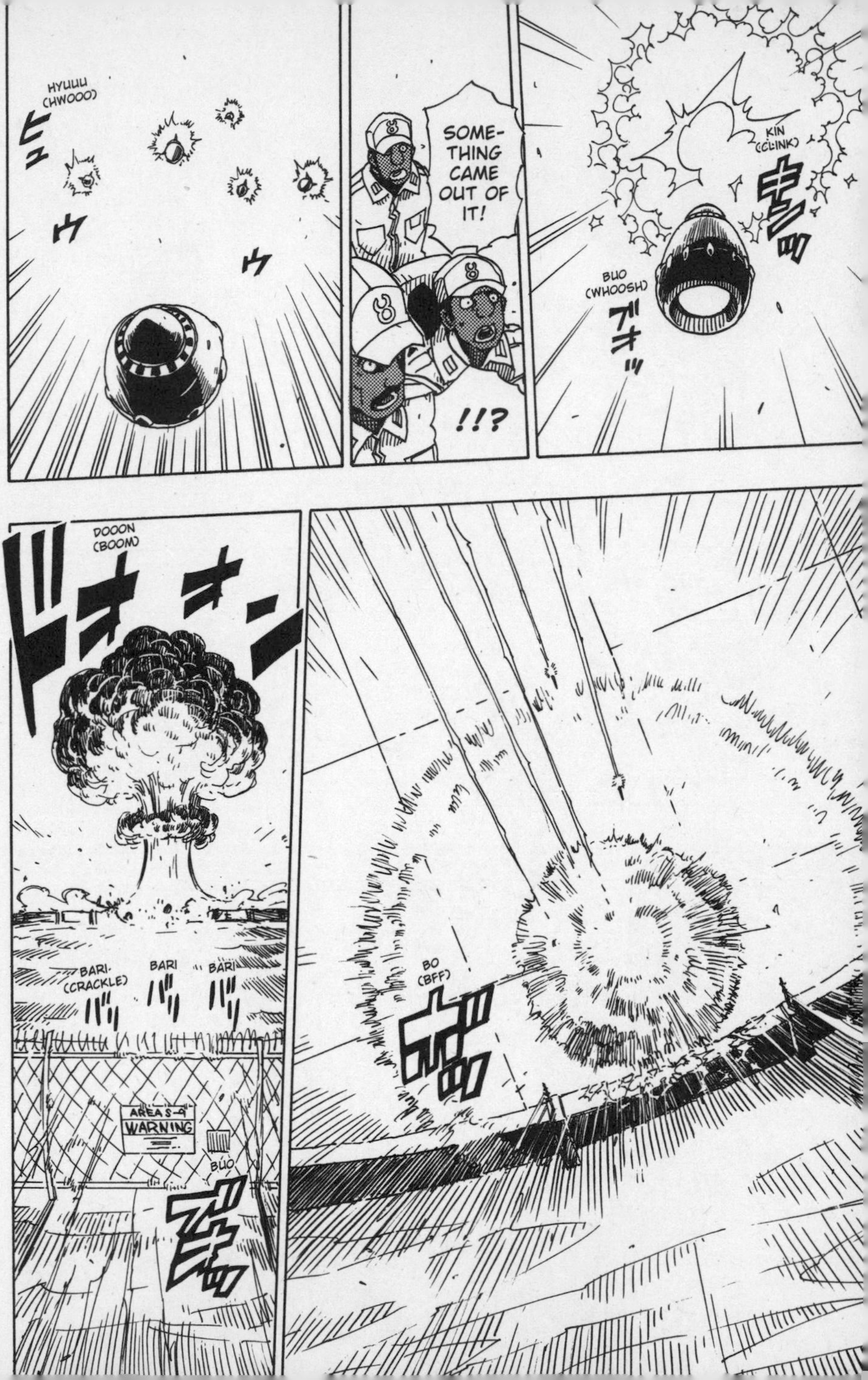
KIN (CLINK)
BUO (WHOOSH)
SOMETHING CAME OUT OF IT!
!!?
HYUUU (HWOOO)
BO (BFF)
DOOON (BOOM)
BARI (CRACKLE) BARI BARI
AREA S-4
WARNING
BUO

GOGOGOGOGOGO
(RUMBLE)

ゴ゛ ゴ゛ ゴ゛ ゴ゛ ゴ゛

ZAPA
(BURST)

ザバ
ッ

KASHA
(CLICK)

カシャ

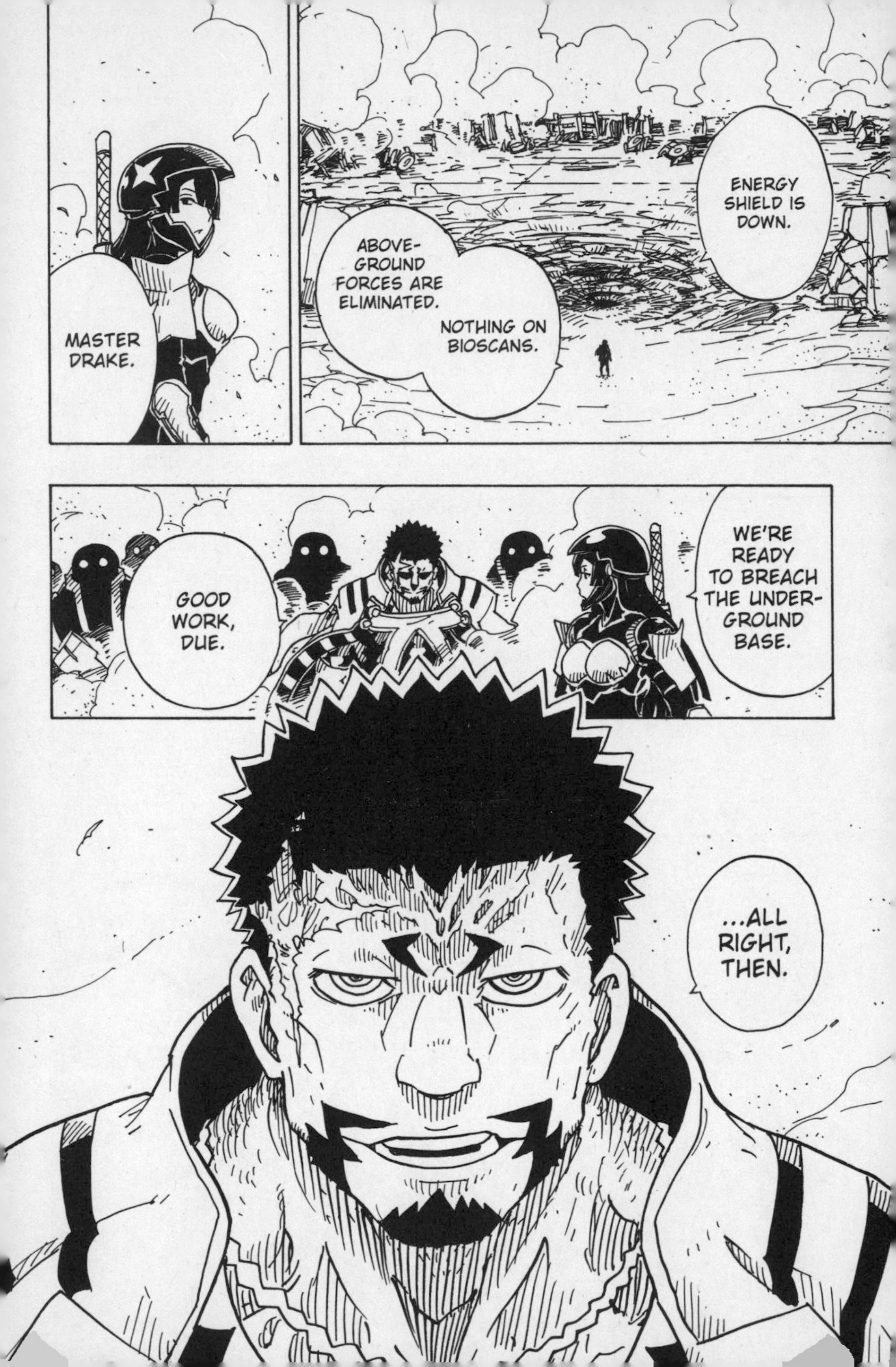
ENERGY SHIELD IS DOWN.
ABOVE-GROUND FORCES ARE ELIMINATED.
NOTHING ON BIOSCANS.
MASTER DRAKE.
WE'RE READY TO BREACH THE UNDERGROUND BASE.
GOOD WORK, DUE.
...ALL RIGHT, THEN.

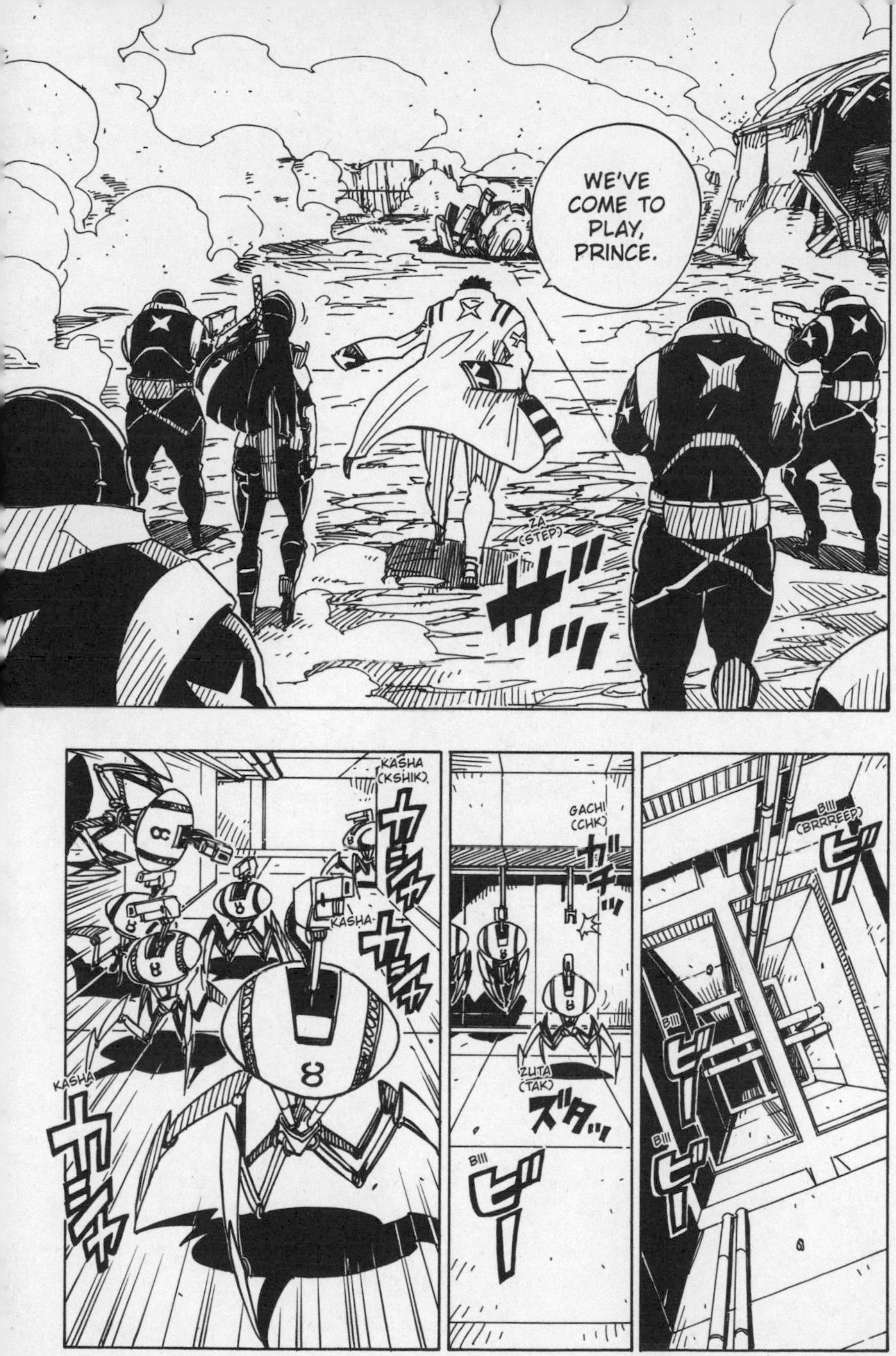
WE'VE COME TO PLAY, PRINCE.
ZA (STEP)
ザッ
BIII (BRRREEP)
ビー
BIII
ビー
BIII
ビー
GACHI (CHK)
ガチッ
ZUTA (TAK)
ズタッ
BIII
ビー
KASHA (KSHIK)
カシャ
KASHA
カシャ
KASHA
カシャ

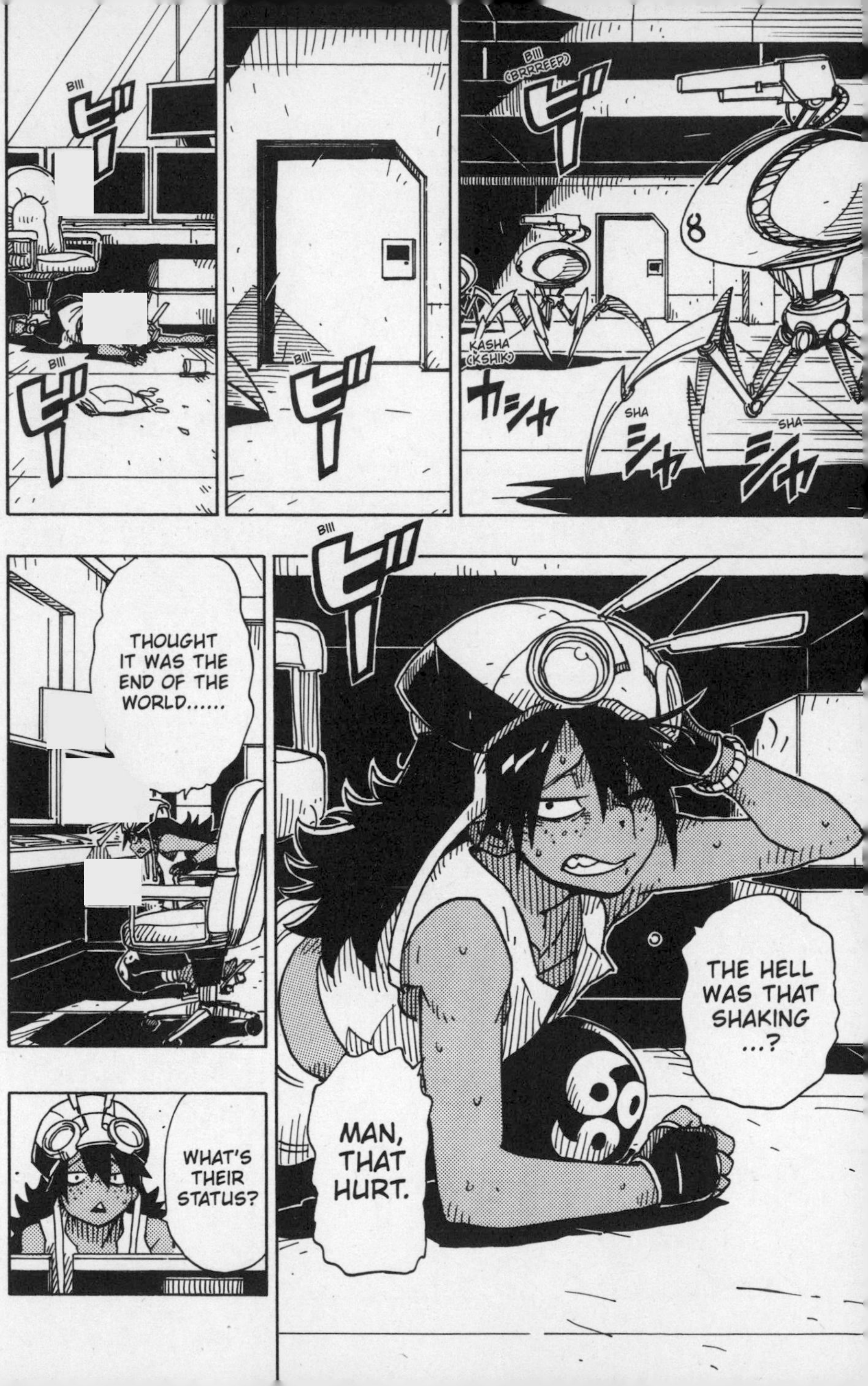
BIII (BRRREEP)
ビ
KASHA (KSHIK)
カシャ
SHA
シャ
SHA
シャ
BIII
ビ
BIII
ビ
BIII
ビ
BIII
ビ
THE HELL WAS THAT SHAKING ...?
MAN, THAT HURT.
THOUGHT IT WAS THE END OF THE WORLD......
WHAT'S THEIR STATUS?

GODOPÓ
(BLUB)

UIM
(VWEEM)

PRINCE
SALVA!

KOOROGI.

LOOKS
LIKE
THEY'RE
IN ONE
PIECE.

...
WHEW.

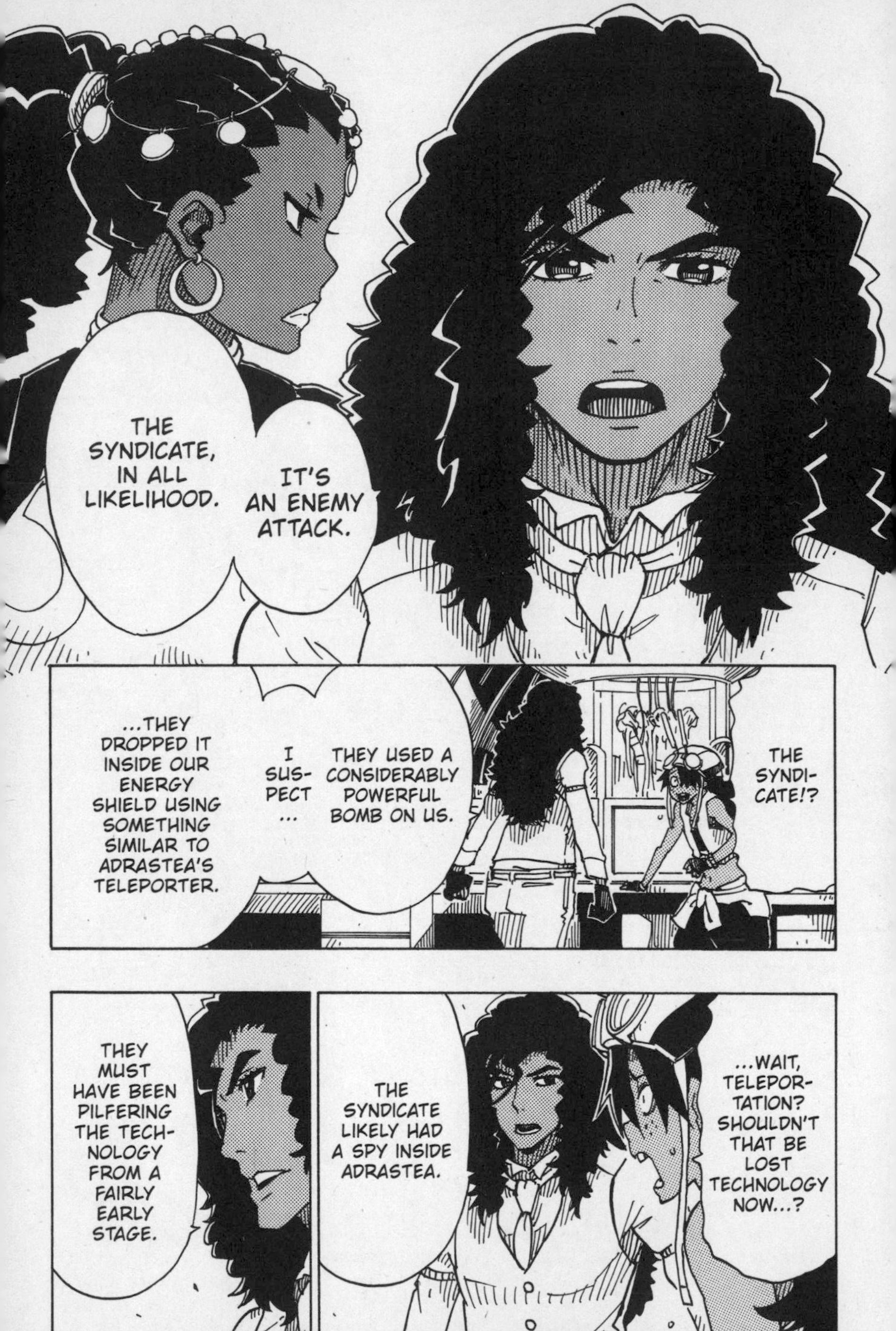
IT'S AN ENEMY ATTACK.
THE SYNDICATE, IN ALL LIKELIHOOD.
THE SYNDICATE!?
THEY USED A CONSIDERABLY POWERFUL BOMB ON US.
I SUSPECT...
...THEY DROPPED IT INSIDE OUR ENERGY SHIELD USING SOMETHING SIMILAR TO ADRASTEA'S TELEPORTER.
...WAIT, TELEPORTATION? SHOULDN'T THAT BE LOST TECHNOLOGY NOW...?
THE SYNDICATE LIKELY HAD A SPY INSIDE ADRASTEA.
THEY MUST HAVE BEEN PILFERING THE TECHNOLOGY FROM A FAIRLY EARLY STAGE.

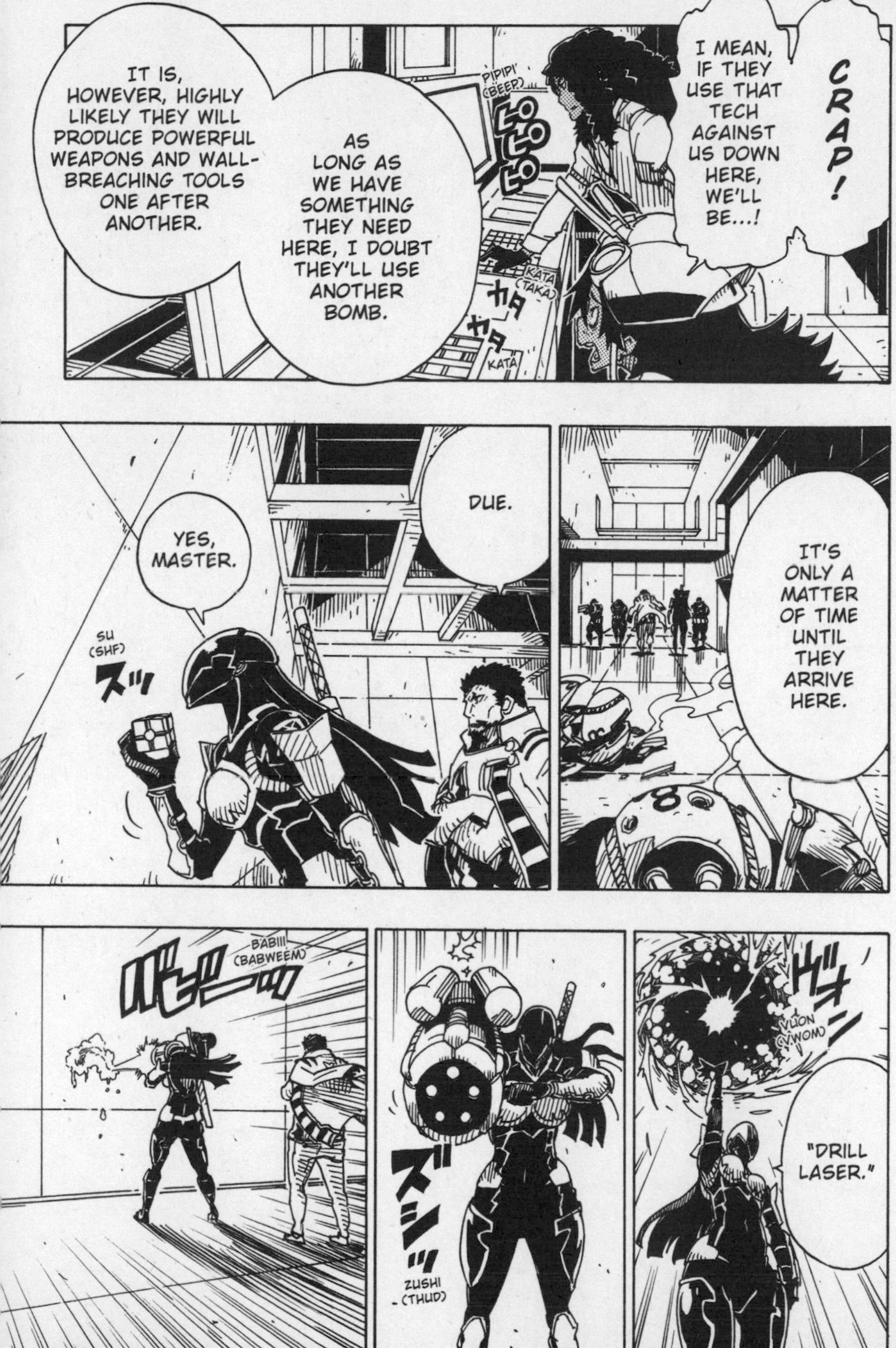
CRAP!
I MEAN, IF THEY USE THAT TECH AGAINST US DOWN HERE, WE'LL BE...!
PIPIPI (BEEP)
KATA (TAKA)
KATA
AS LONG AS WE HAVE SOMETHING THEY NEED HERE, I DOUBT THEY'LL USE ANOTHER BOMB.
IT IS, HOWEVER, HIGHLY LIKELY THEY WILL PRODUCE POWERFUL WEAPONS AND WALL-BREACHING TOOLS ONE AFTER ANOTHER.
IT'S ONLY A MATTER OF TIME UNTIL THEY ARRIVE HERE.
DUE.
YES, MASTER.
SU (SHF)
VUON (VWOM)
"DRILL LASER."
ZUSHI (THUD)
BABIII (BABWEEM)

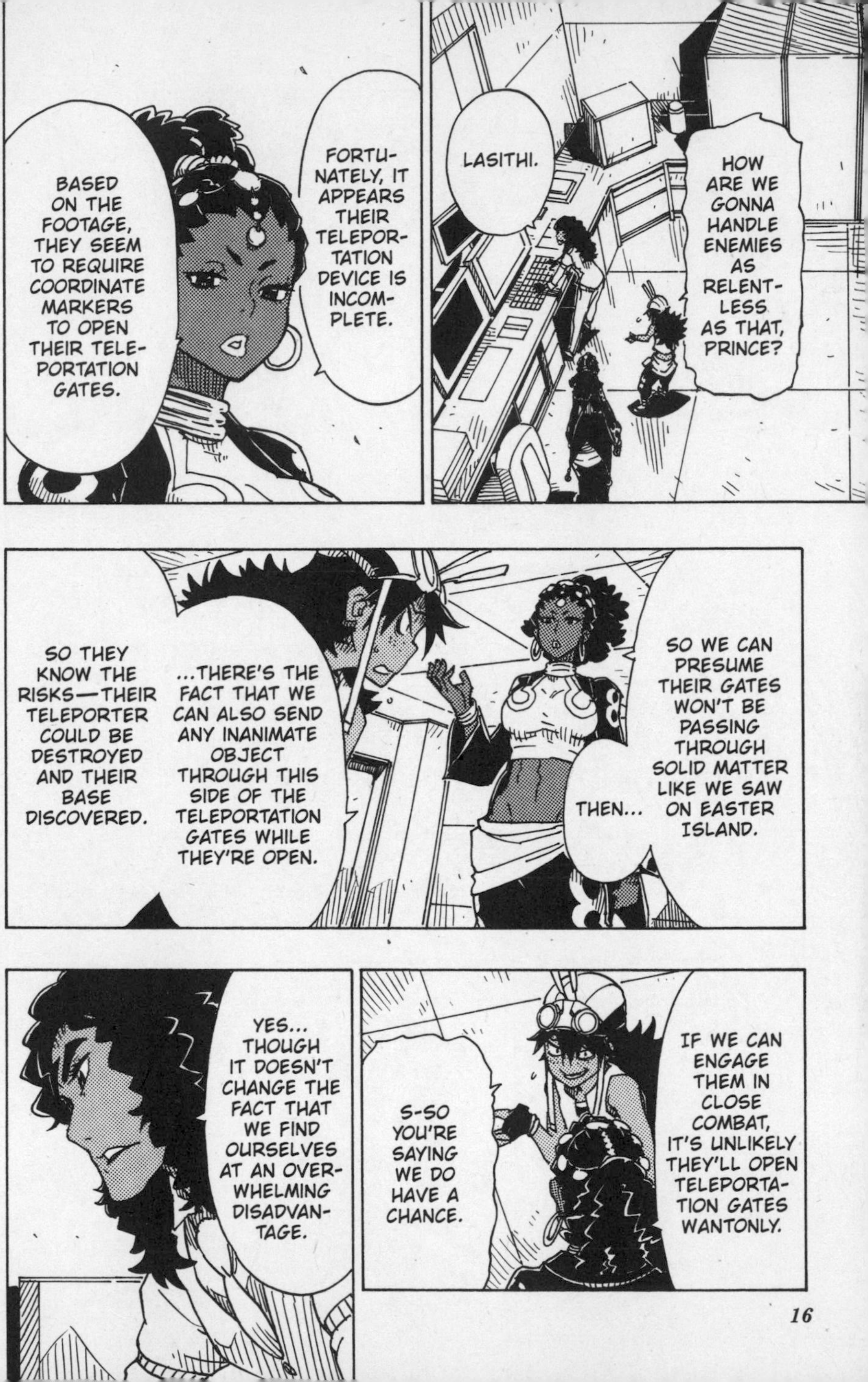

HOW ARE WE GONNA HANDLE ENEMIES AS RELENTLESS AS THAT, PRINCE?
LASITHI.
FORTUNATELY, IT APPEARS THEIR TELEPORTATION DEVICE IS INCOMPLETE.
BASED ON THE FOOTAGE, THEY SEEM TO REQUIRE COORDINATE MARKERS TO OPEN THEIR TELEPORTATION GATES.
SO WE CAN PRESUME THEIR GATES WON'T BE PASSING THROUGH SOLID MATTER LIKE WE SAW ON EASTER ISLAND.
THEN...
...THERE'S THE FACT THAT WE CAN ALSO SEND ANY INANIMATE OBJECT THROUGH THIS SIDE OF THE TELEPORTATION GATES WHILE THEY'RE OPEN.
SO THEY KNOW THE RISKS—THEIR TELEPORTER COULD BE DESTROYED AND THEIR BASE DISCOVERED.
IF WE CAN ENGAGE THEM IN CLOSE COMBAT, IT'S UNLIKELY THEY'LL OPEN TELEPORTATION GATES WANTONLY.
S-SO YOU'RE SAYING WE DO HAVE A CHANCE.
YES... THOUGH IT DOESN'T CHANGE THE FACT THAT WE FIND OURSELVES AT AN OVERWHELMING DISADVANTAGE.

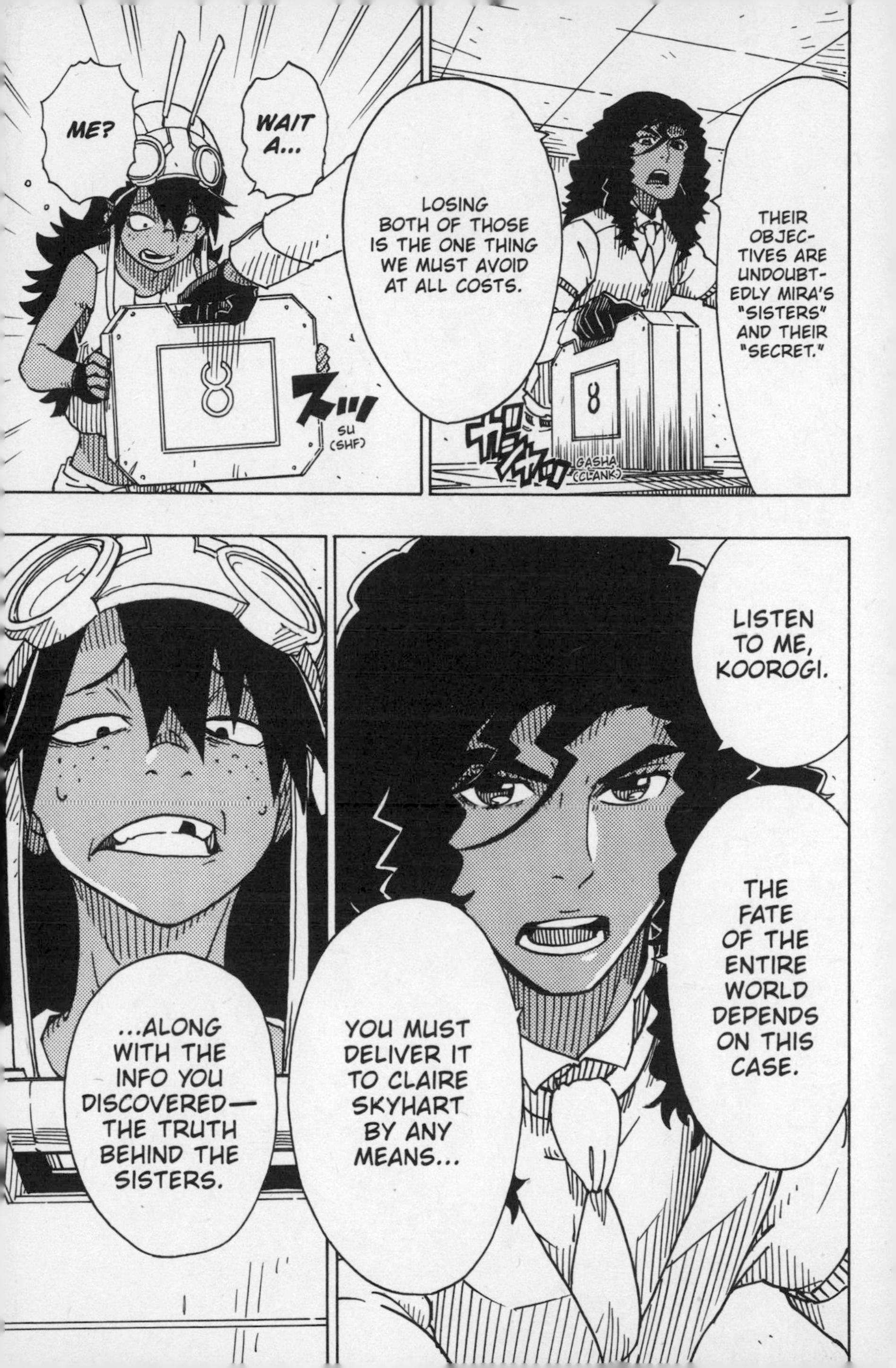
THEIR OBJECTIVES ARE UNDOUBTEDLY MIRA'S "SISTERS" AND THEIR "SECRET."
LOSING BOTH OF THOSE IS THE ONE THING WE MUST AVOID AT ALL COSTS.
GASHA (CLANK)
WAIT A...
ME?
SU (SHF)
LISTEN TO ME, KOOROGI.
THE FATE OF THE ENTIRE WORLD DEPENDS ON THIS CASE.
YOU MUST DELIVER IT TO CLAIRE SKYHART BY ANY MEANS...
...ALONG WITH THE INFO YOU DISCOVERED—THE TRUTH BEHIND THE SISTERS.

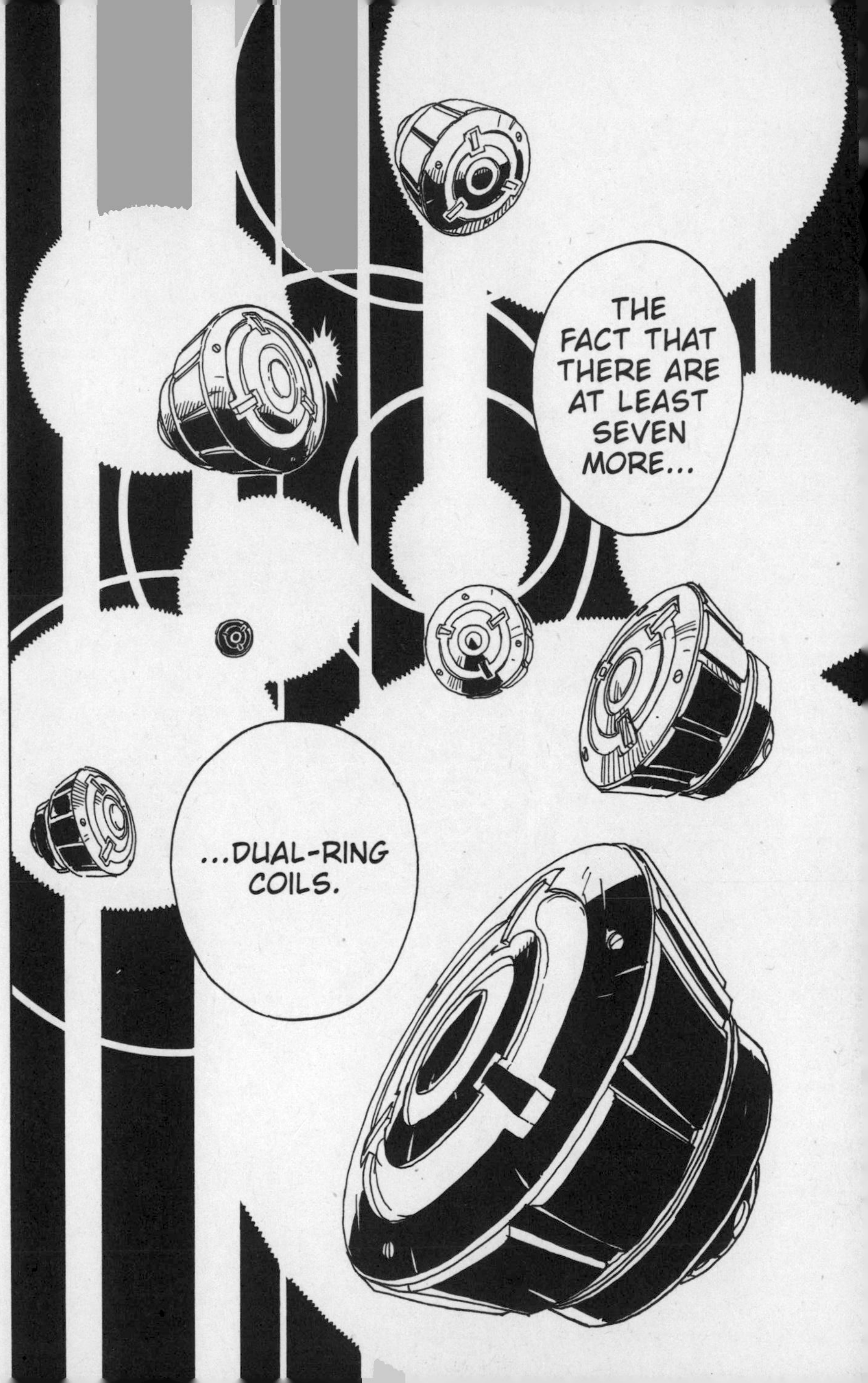
THE FACT THAT THERE ARE AT LEAST SEVEN MORE...
...DUAL-RING COILS.

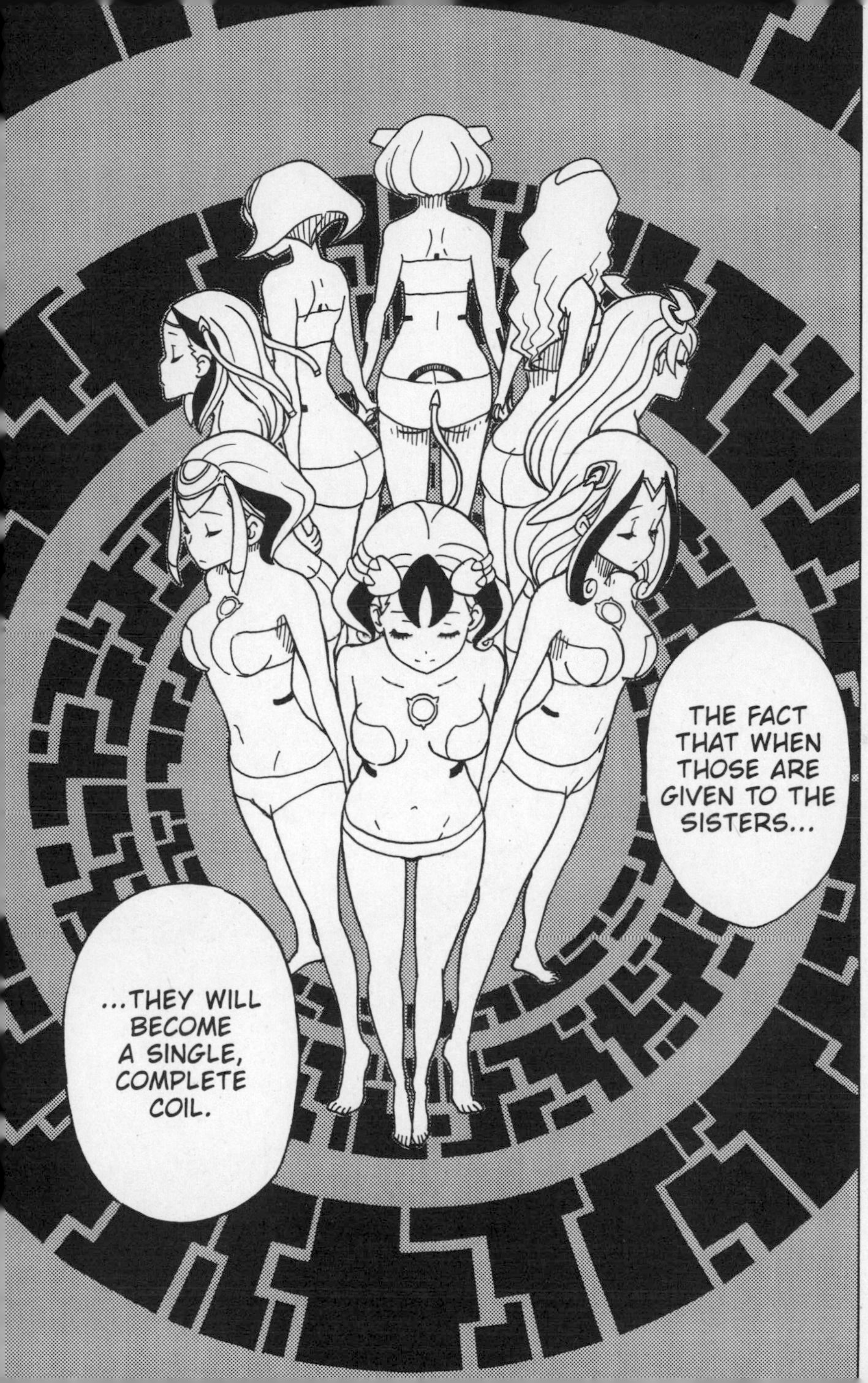
THE FACT THAT WHEN THOSE ARE GIVEN TO THE SISTERS...
...THEY WILL BECOME A SINGLE, COMPLETE COIL.

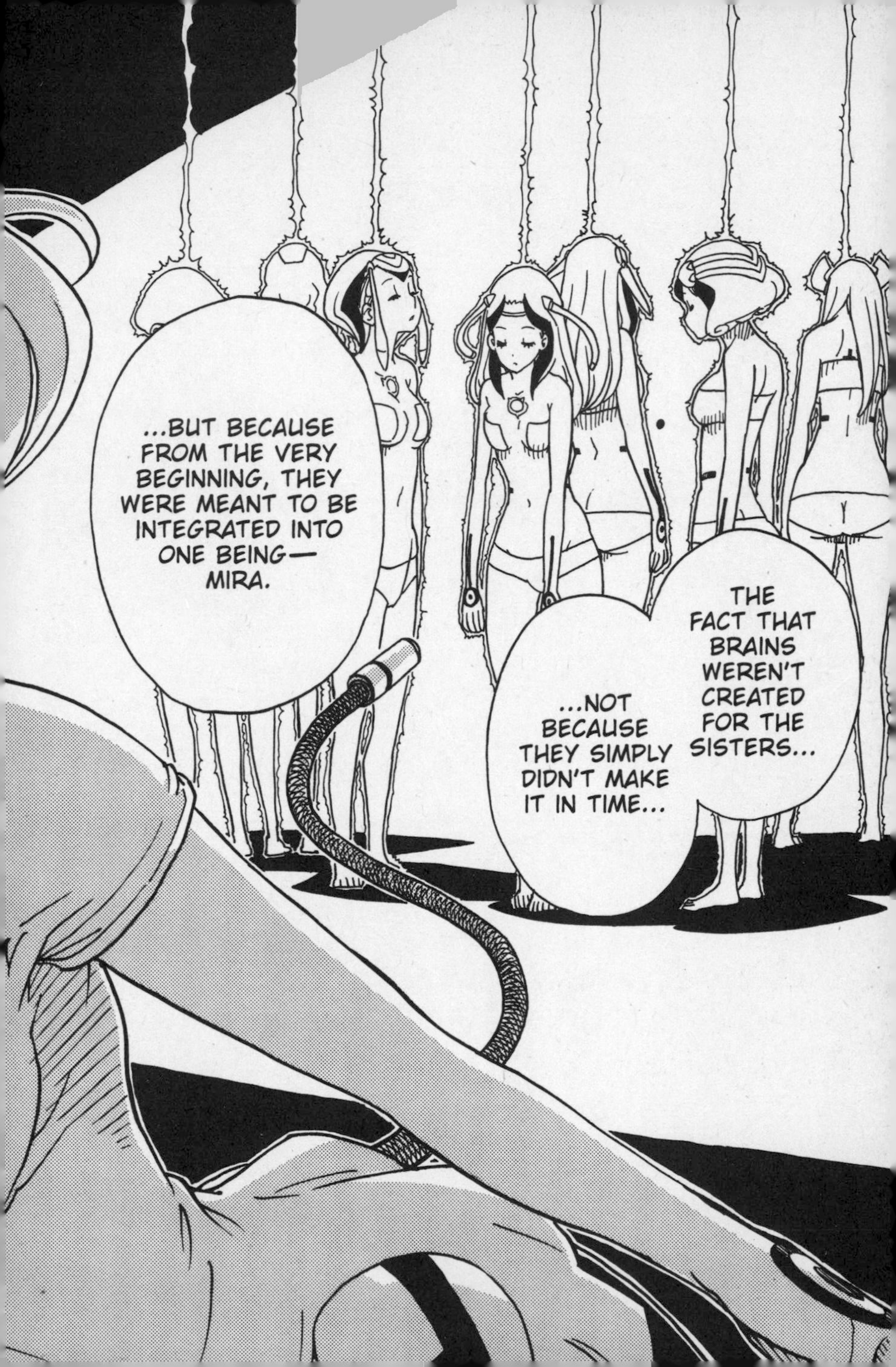
THE FACT THAT BRAINS WEREN'T CREATED FOR THE SISTERS...
...NOT BECAUSE THEY SIMPLY DIDN'T MAKE IT IN TIME...
...BUT BECAUSE FROM THE VERY BEGINNING, THEY WERE MEANT TO BE INTEGRATED INTO ONE BEING—MIRA.

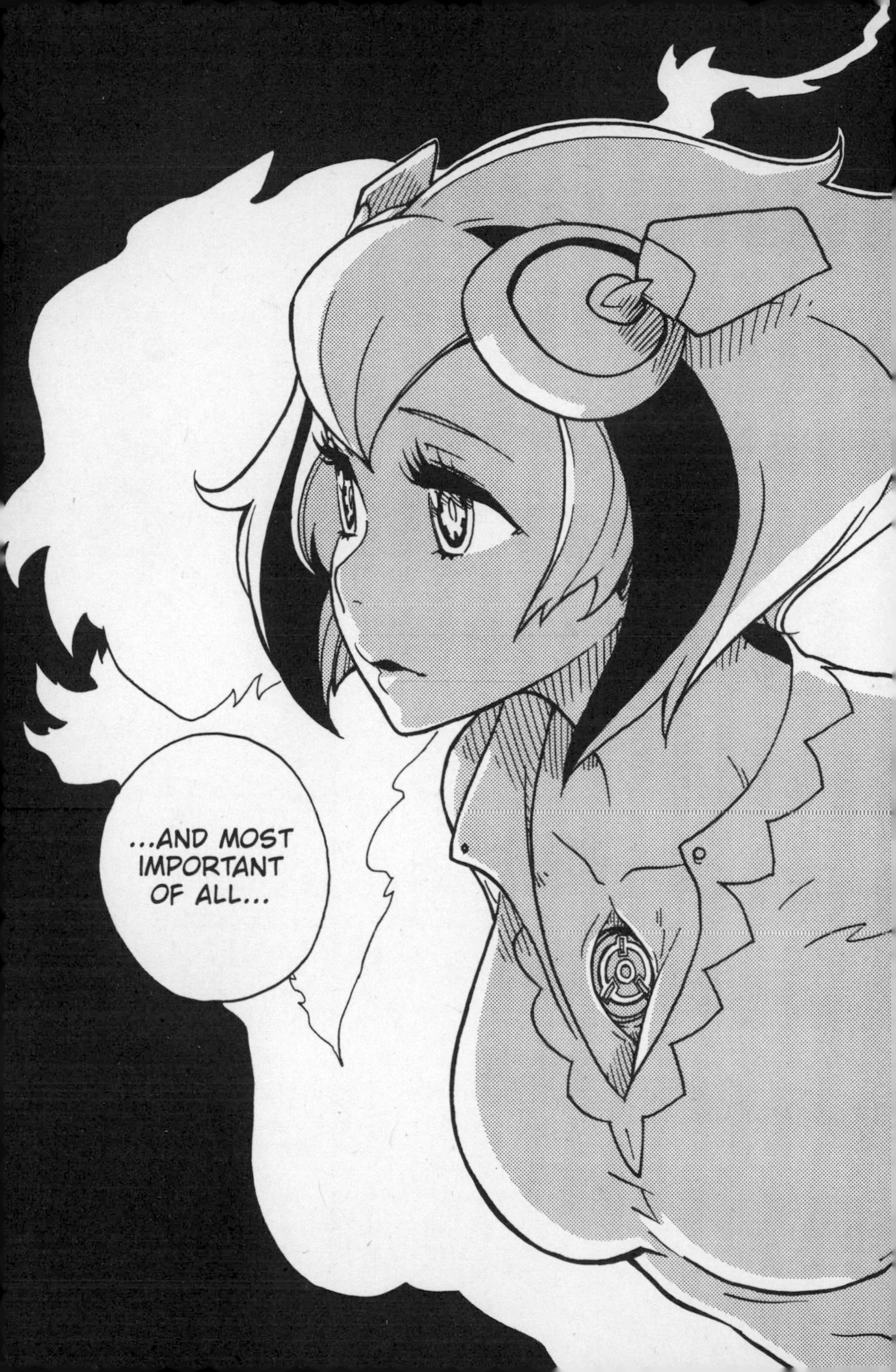
...AND MOST IMPORTANT OF ALL...

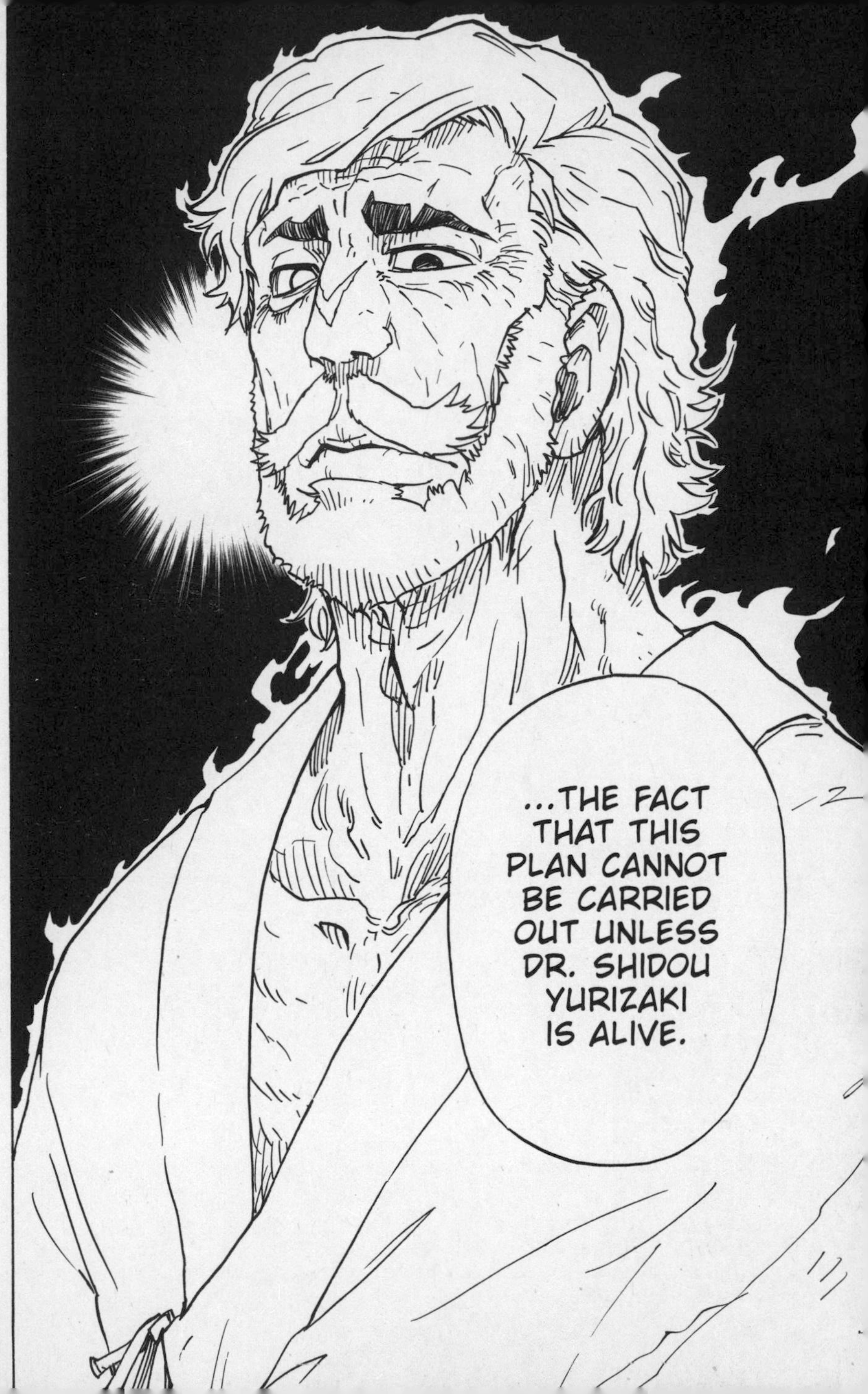
...THE FACT THAT THIS PLAN CANNOT BE CARRIED OUT UNLESS DR. SHIDOU YURIZAKI IS ALIVE.

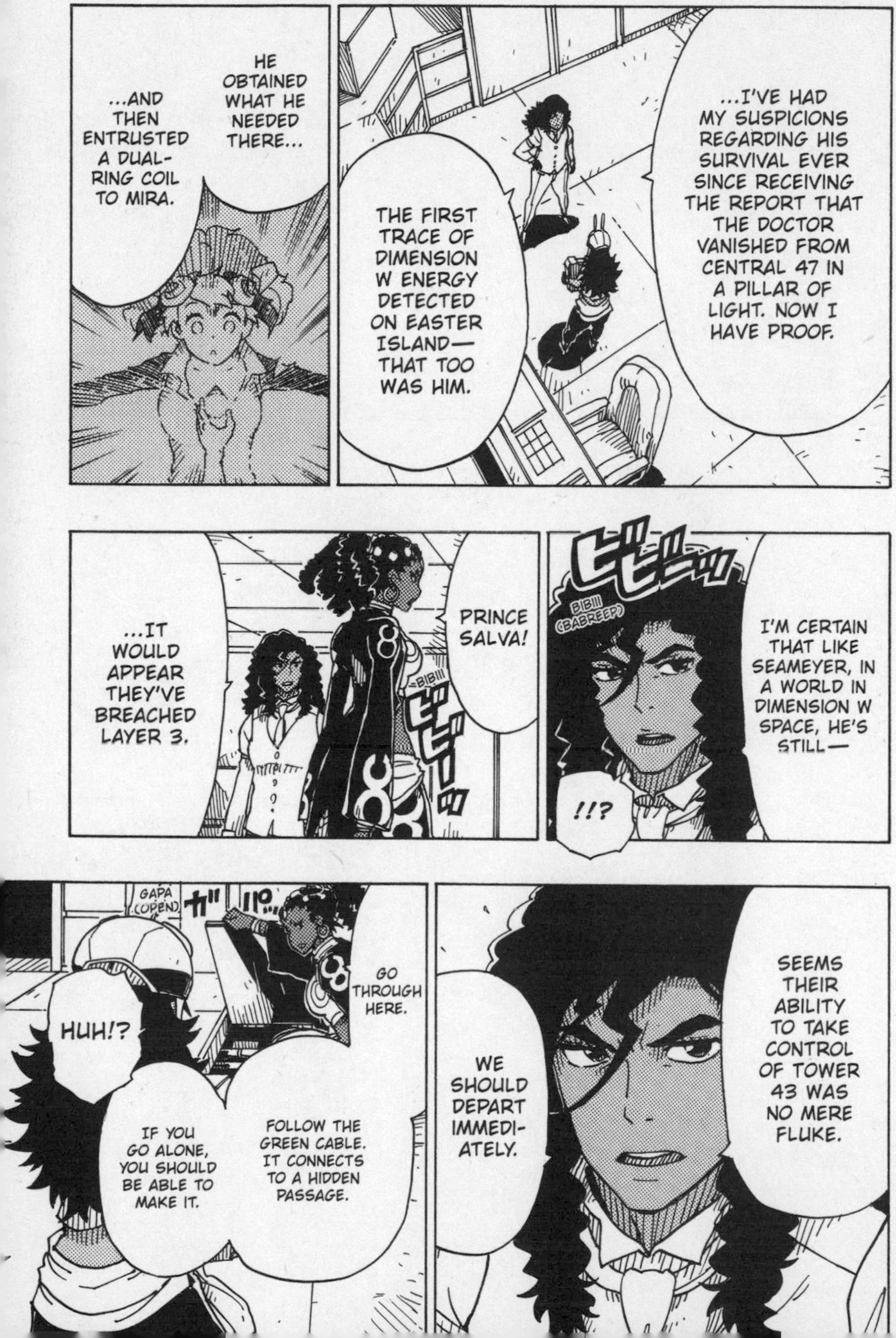
...I'VE HAD MY SUSPICIONS REGARDING HIS SURVIVAL EVER SINCE RECEIVING THE REPORT THAT THE DOCTOR VANISHED FROM CENTRAL 47 IN A PILLAR OF LIGHT. NOW I HAVE PROOF.
THE FIRST TRACE OF DIMENSION W ENERGY DETECTED ON EASTER ISLAND— THAT TOO WAS HIM.
HE OBTAINED WHAT HE NEEDED THERE...
...AND THEN ENTRUSTED A DUAL-RING COIL TO MIRA.
BIBIII (BABREEP)
I'M CERTAIN THAT LIKE SEAMEYER, IN A WORLD IN DIMENSION W SPACE, HE'S STILL—
!!?
PRINCE SALVA!
BIBIII
...IT WOULD APPEAR THEY'VE BREACHED LAYER 3.
SEEMS THEIR ABILITY TO TAKE CONTROL OF TOWER 43 WAS NO MERE FLUKE.
WE SHOULD DEPART IMMEDIATELY.
GO THROUGH HERE.
GAPA (OPEN)
HUH!?
FOLLOW THE GREEN CABLE. IT CONNECTS TO A HIDDEN PASSAGE.
IF YOU GO ALONE, YOU SHOULD BE ABLE TO MAKE IT.

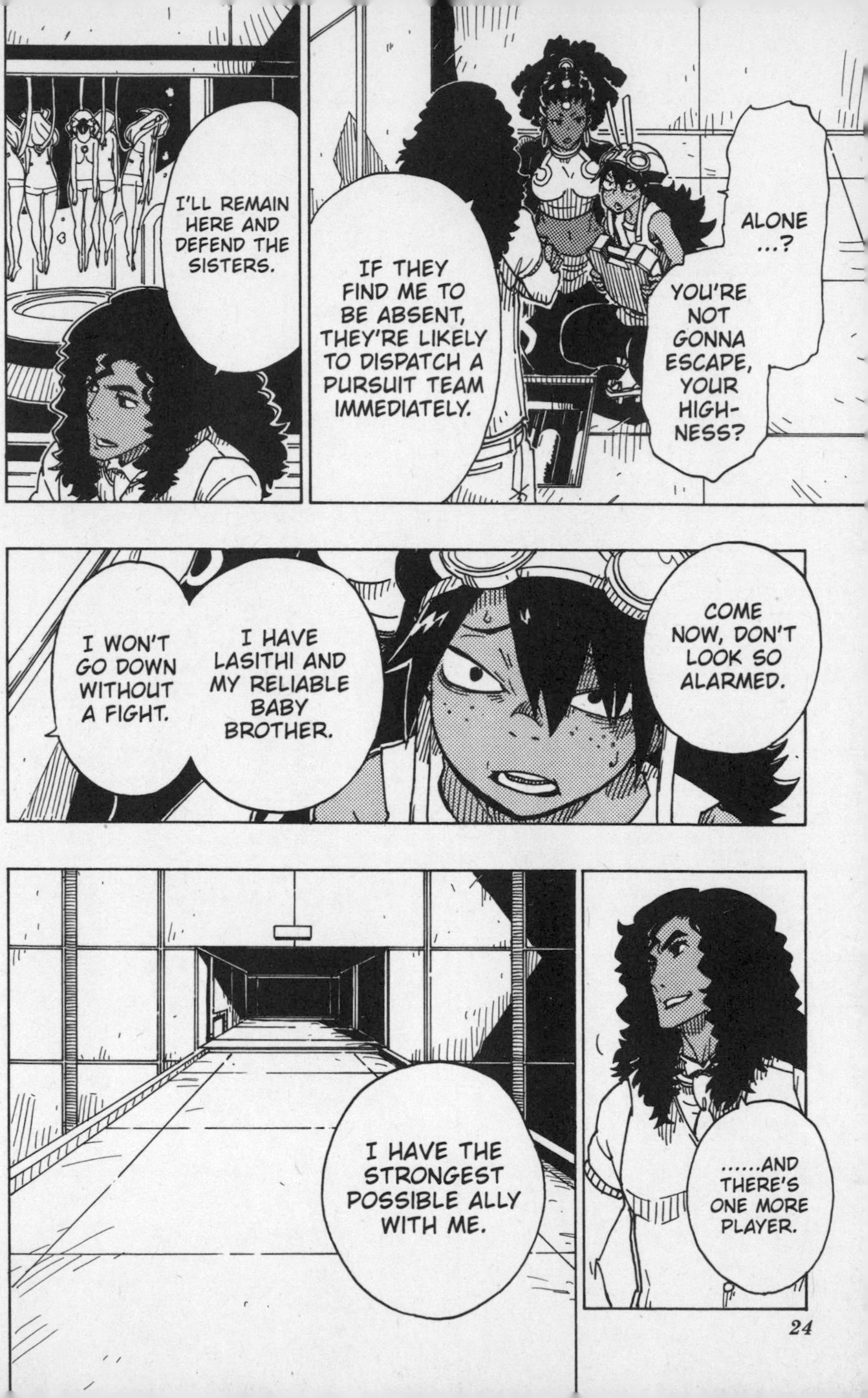
ALONE ...?
YOU'RE NOT GONNA ESCAPE, YOUR HIGH-NESS?
IF THEY FIND ME TO BE ABSENT, THEY'RE LIKELY TO DISPATCH A PURSUIT TEAM IMMEDIATELY.
I'LL REMAIN HERE AND DEFEND THE SISTERS.
COME NOW, DON'T LOOK SO ALARMED.
I HAVE LASITHI AND MY RELIABLE BABY BROTHER.
I WON'T GO DOWN WITHOUT A FIGHT.
......AND THERE'S ONE MORE PLAYER.
I HAVE THE STRONGEST POSSIBLE ALLY WITH ME.

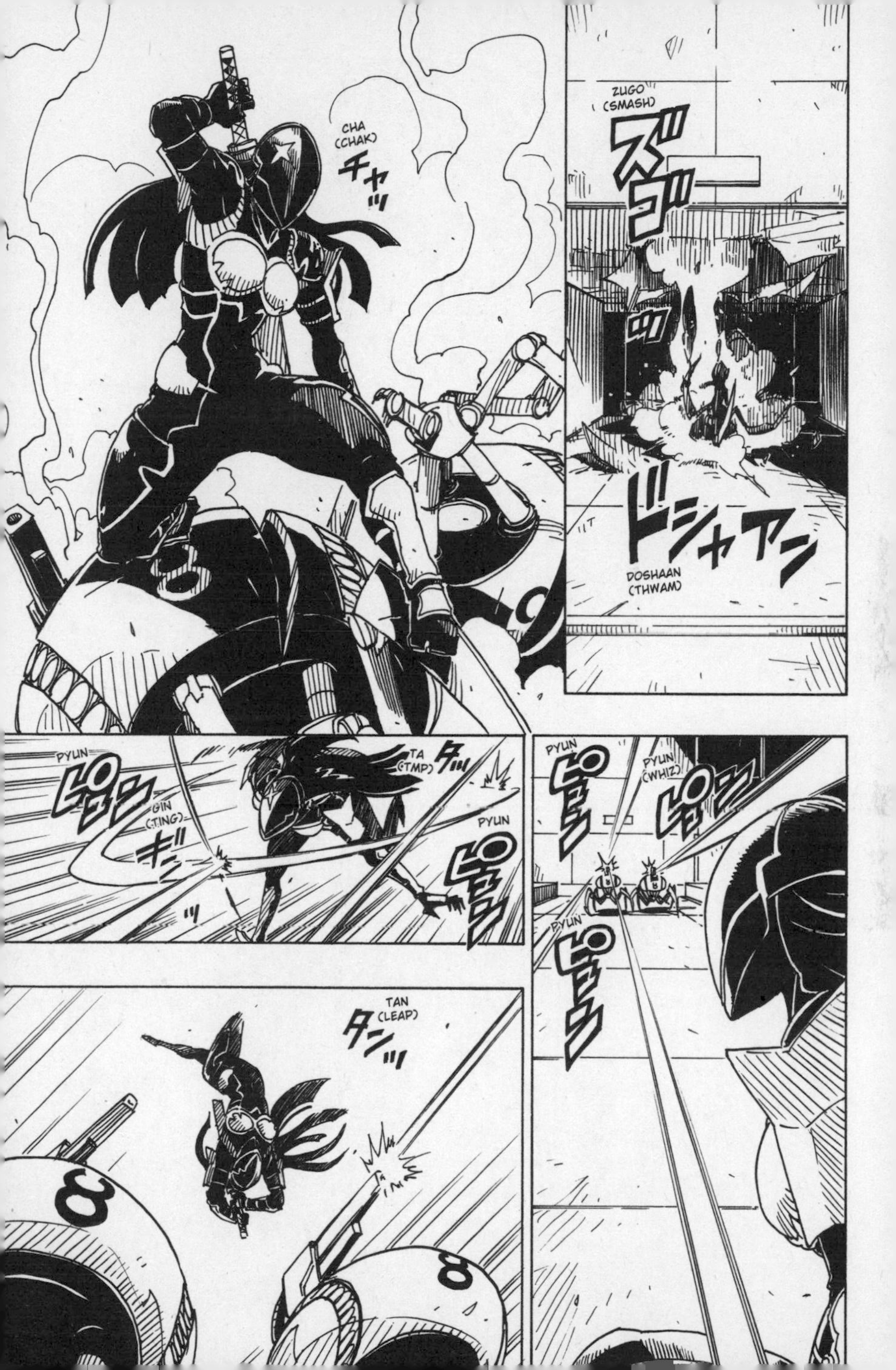
ZUGO (SMASH)
ズゴ
ドシャアン
DOSHAAN (THWAM)
CHA (CHAK)
チャッ
PYUN
PYUN (WHIZ)
PYUN
PYUN
TA (TMP)
PYUN
GIN (TING)
PYUN
TAN (LEAP)
タンッ

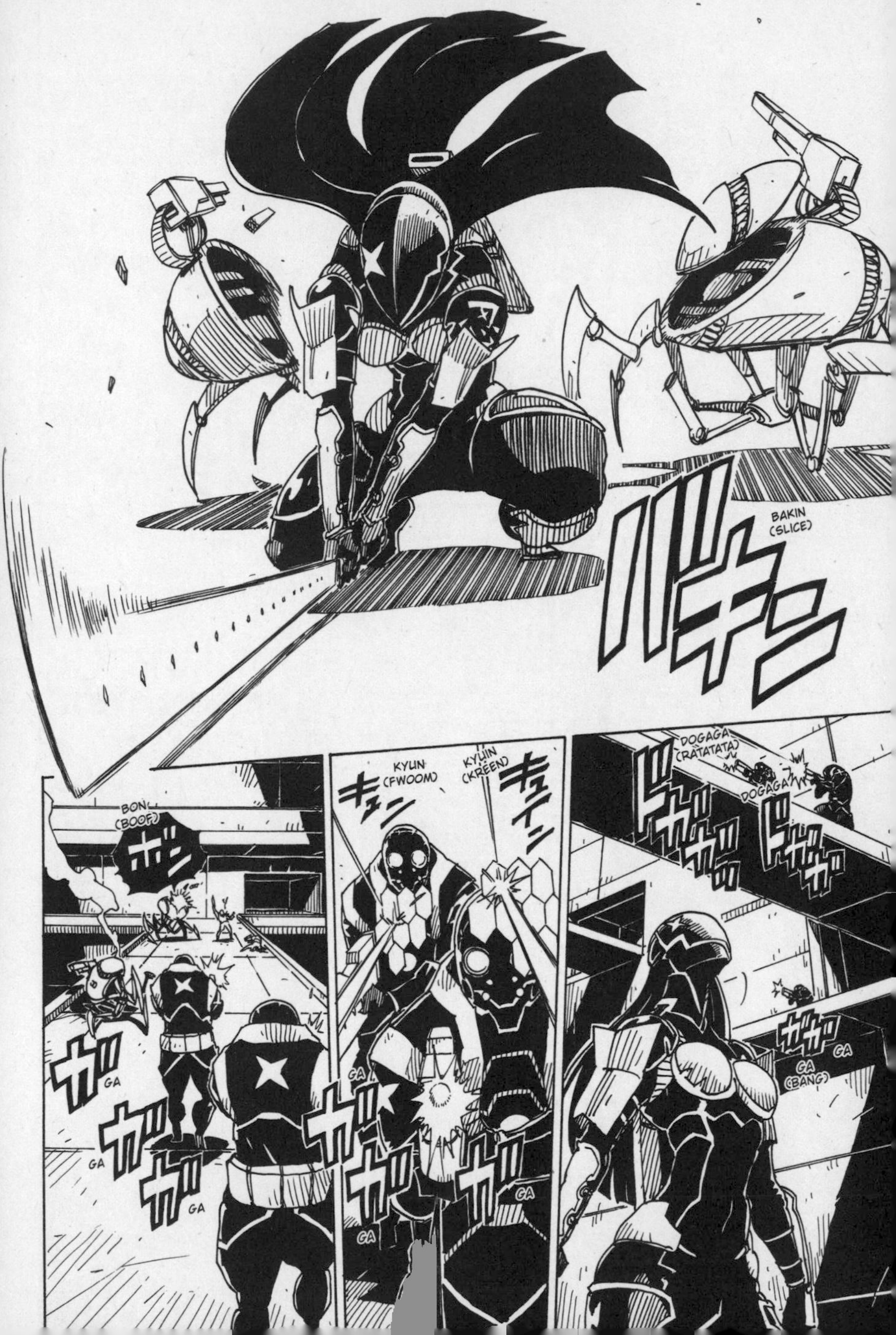

BAKIN
(SLICE)
DOGAGA
(RATATATA)
DOGAGA
GA
GA
(BANG)
KYUN
(FWOOM)
KYUIN
(KREEN)
GA
GA
GA
BON
(BOOF)
GA
GA
GA

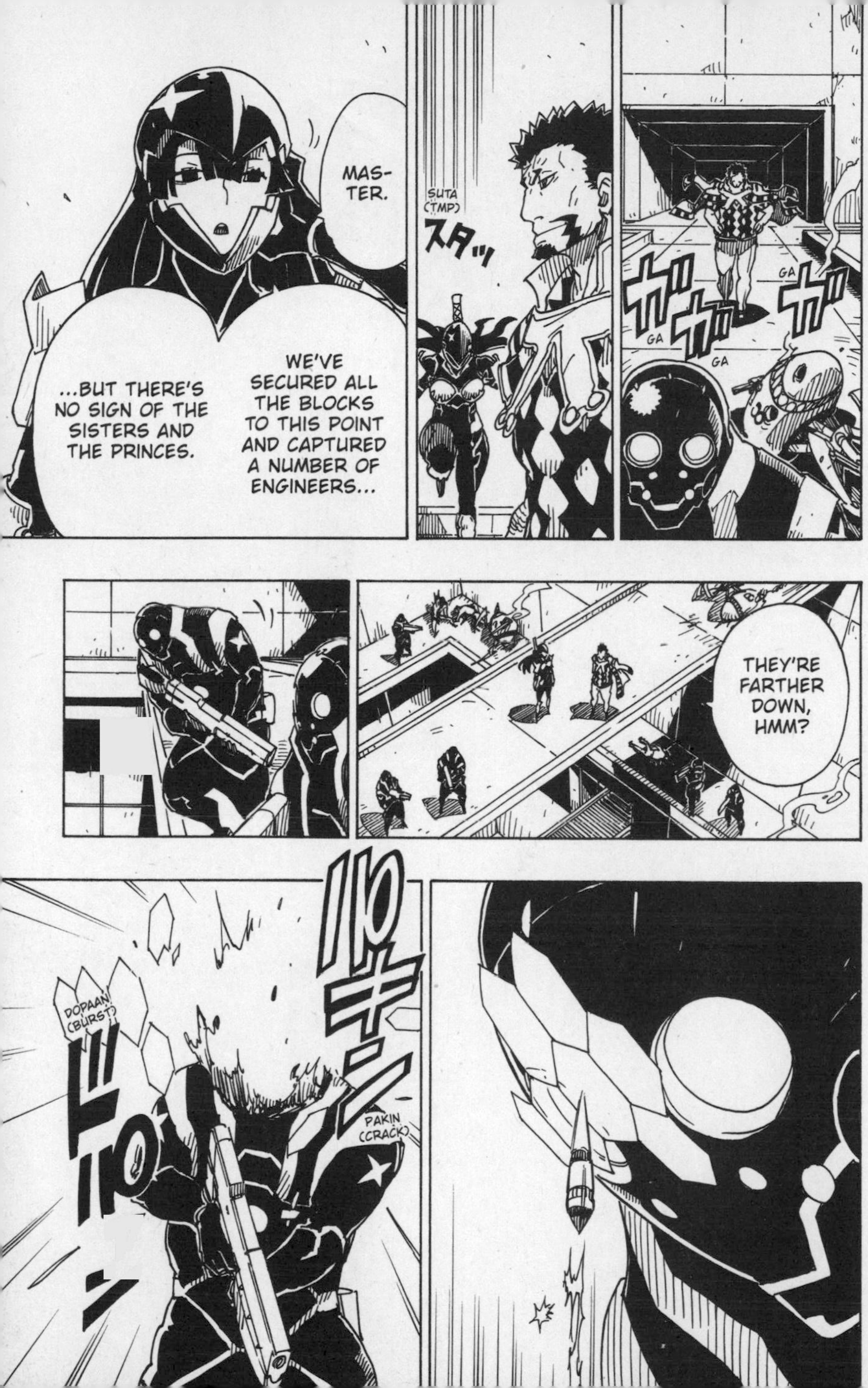

GA
GA
GA
SUTA (TMP)
スタッ
MAS-TER.
WE'VE SECURED ALL THE BLOCKS TO THIS POINT AND CAPTURED A NUMBER OF ENGINEERS...
...BUT THERE'S NO SIGN OF THE SISTERS AND THE PRINCES.
THEY'RE FARTHER DOWN, HMM?
PAKIN (CRACK)
DOPAAN (BURST)

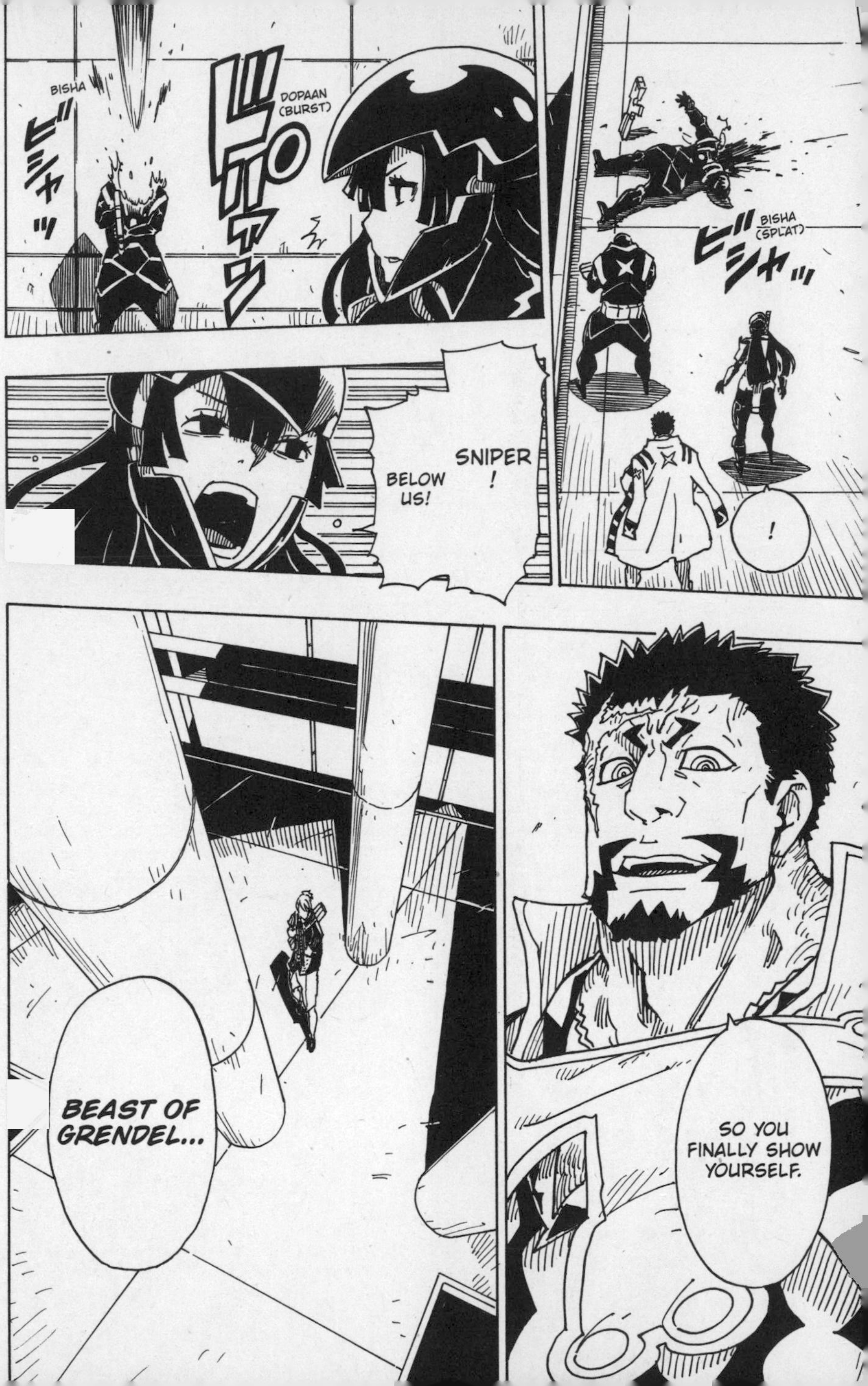
BISHA (SPLAT)
ビシャッ
!
DOPAAN (BURST)
ドパァン
BISHA
ビシャッ
SNIPER!
BELOW US!
SO YOU FINALLY SHOW YOURSELF.
BEAST OF GRENDEL...

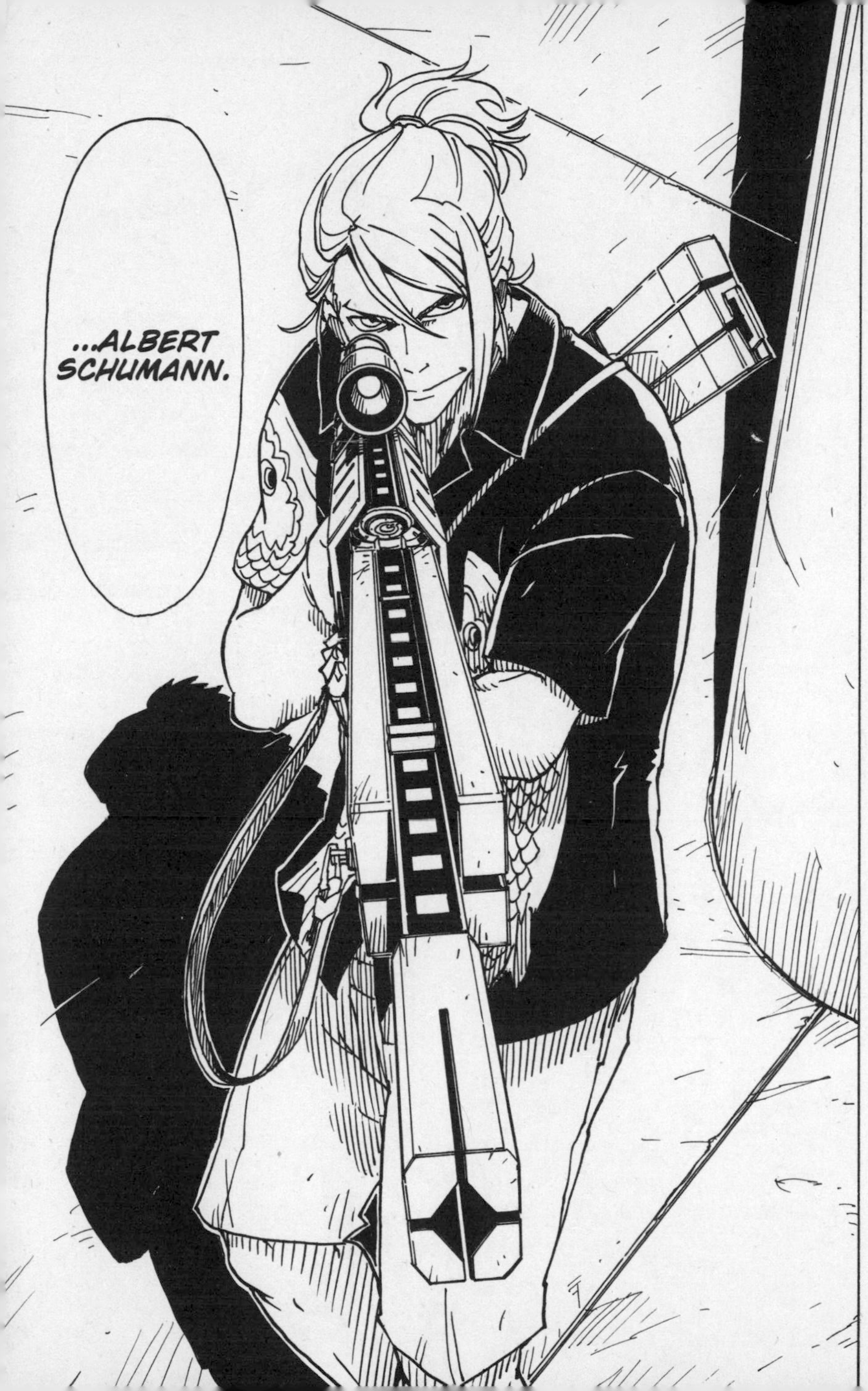
...ALBERT SCHUMANN.

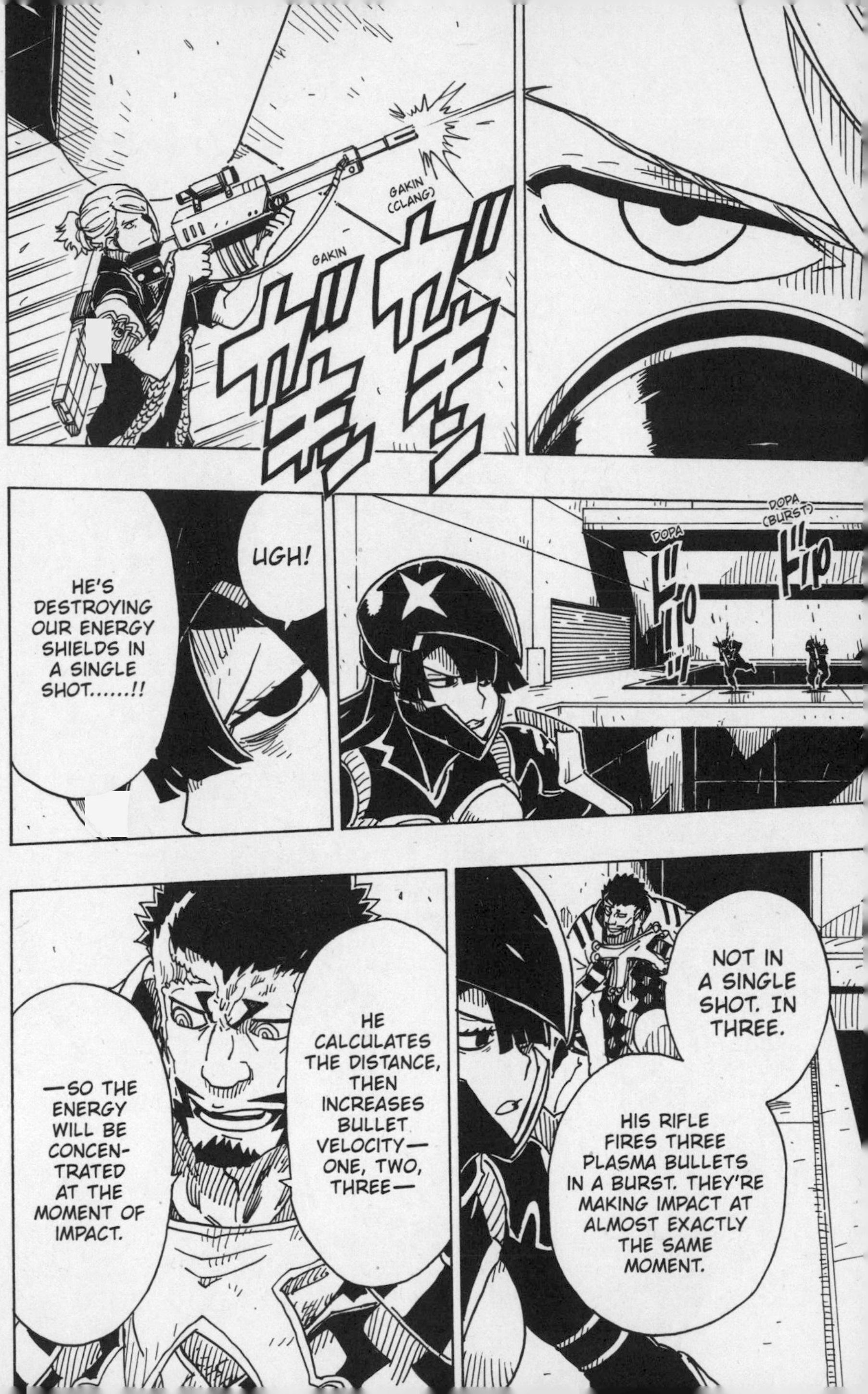
GAKIN (CLANG)
GAKIN
DOPA (BURST)
DOPA
UGH!
HE'S DESTROYING OUR ENERGY SHIELDS IN A SINGLE SHOT......!!
NOT IN A SINGLE SHOT. IN THREE.
HIS RIFLE FIRES THREE PLASMA BULLETS IN A BURST. THEY'RE MAKING IMPACT AT ALMOST EXACTLY THE SAME MOMENT.
HE CALCULATES THE DISTANCE, THEN INCREASES BULLET VELOCITY—ONE, TWO, THREE—
—SO THE ENERGY WILL BE CONCEN-TRATED AT THE MOMENT OF IMPACT.

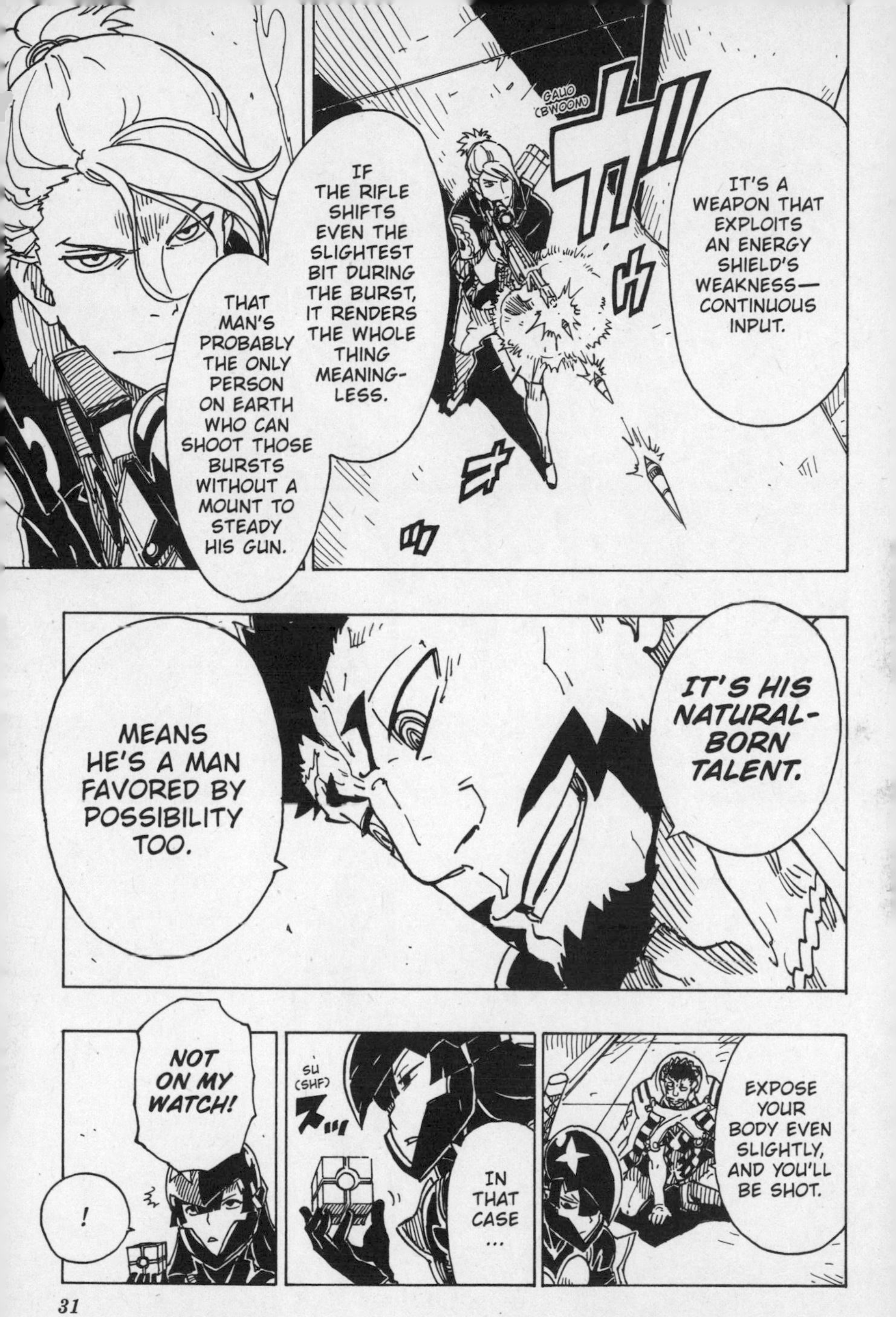
GALIO (BWOOM)
IT'S A WEAPON THAT EXPLOITS AN ENERGY SHIELD'S WEAKNESS—CONTINUOUS INPUT.
IF THE RIFLE SHIFTS EVEN THE SLIGHTEST BIT DURING THE BURST, IT RENDERS THE WHOLE THING MEANING-LESS.
THAT MAN'S PROBABLY THE ONLY PERSON ON EARTH WHO CAN SHOOT THOSE BURSTS WITHOUT A MOUNT TO STEADY HIS GUN.
IT'S HIS NATURAL-BORN TALENT.
MEANS HE'S A MAN FAVORED BY POSSIBILITY TOO.
EXPOSE YOUR BODY EVEN SLIGHTLY, AND YOU'LL BE SHOT.
IN THAT CASE ...
SU (SHF)
NOT ON MY WATCH!
!

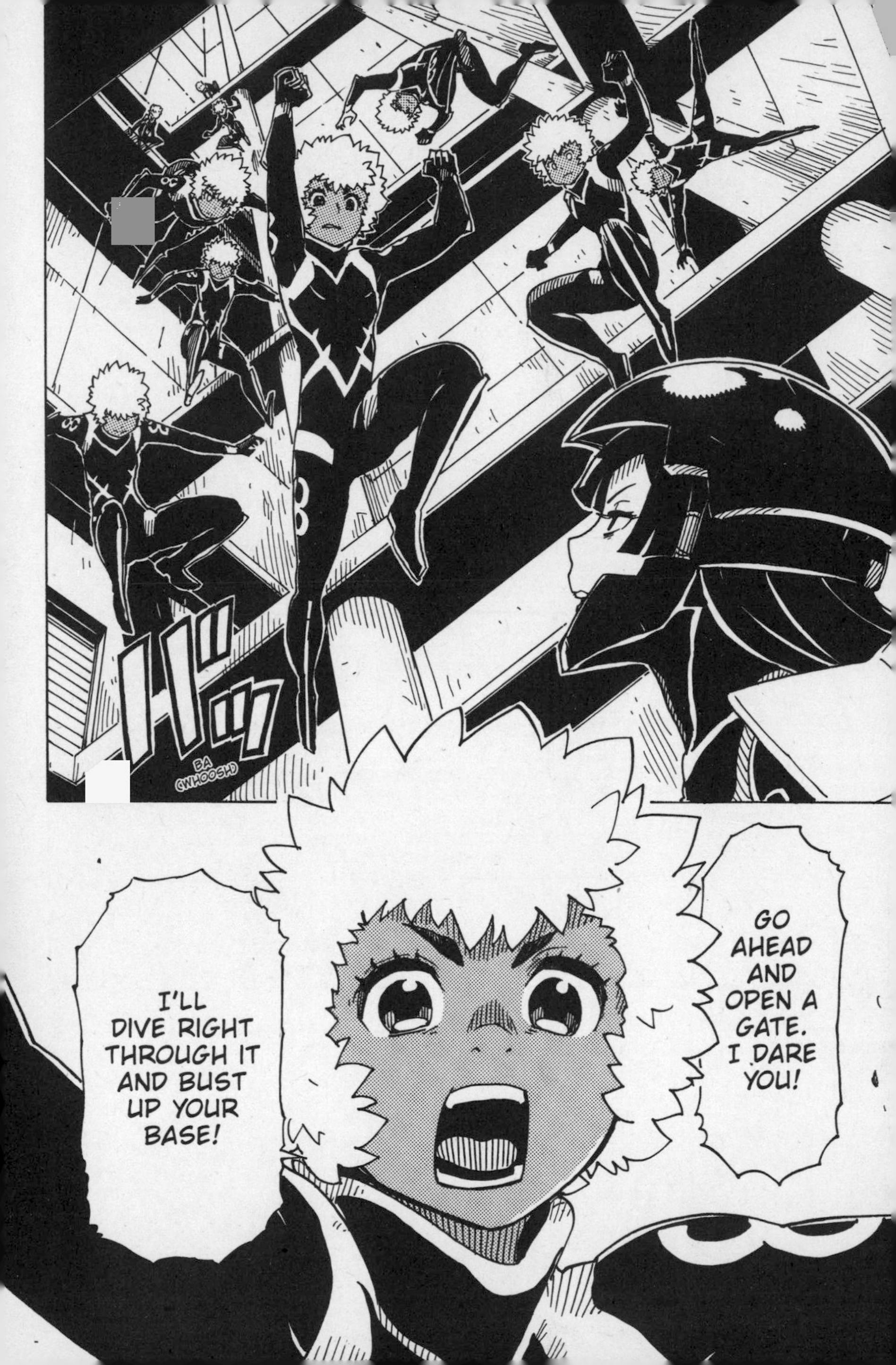
BA (WHOOSH)
GO AHEAD AND OPEN A GATE. I DARE YOU!
I'LL DIVE RIGHT THROUGH IT AND BUST UP YOUR BASE!

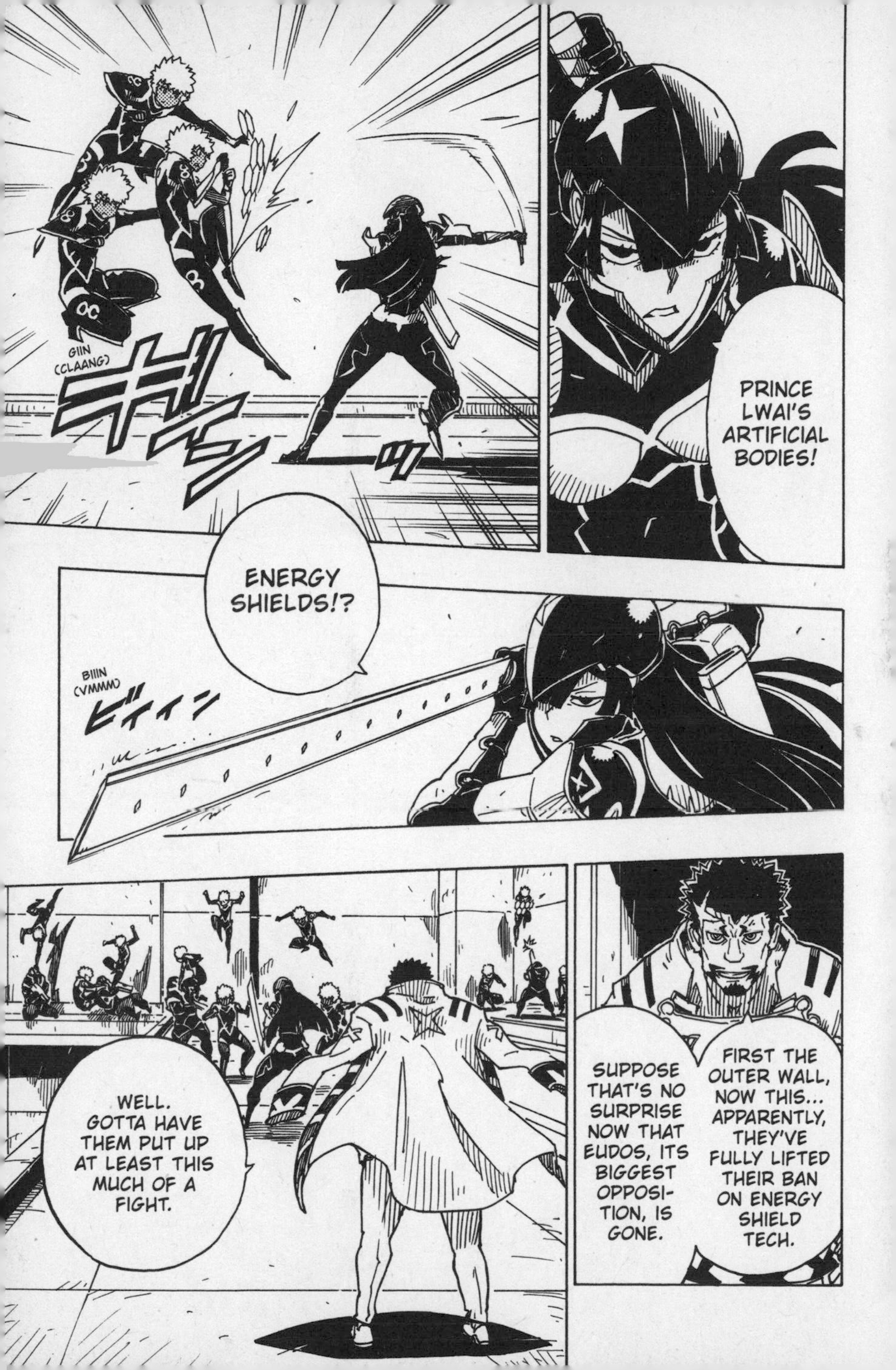
PRINCE LWAI'S ARTIFICIAL BODIES!
GIIN (CLAANG)
ENERGY SHIELDS!?
BIIN (VMMM)
FIRST THE OUTER WALL, NOW THIS... APPARENTLY, THEY'VE FULLY LIFTED THEIR BAN ON ENERGY SHIELD TECH.
SUPPOSE THAT'S NO SURPRISE NOW THAT EUDOS, ITS BIGGEST OPPOSITION, IS GONE.
WELL. GOTTA HAVE THEM PUT UP AT LEAST THIS MUCH OF A FIGHT.

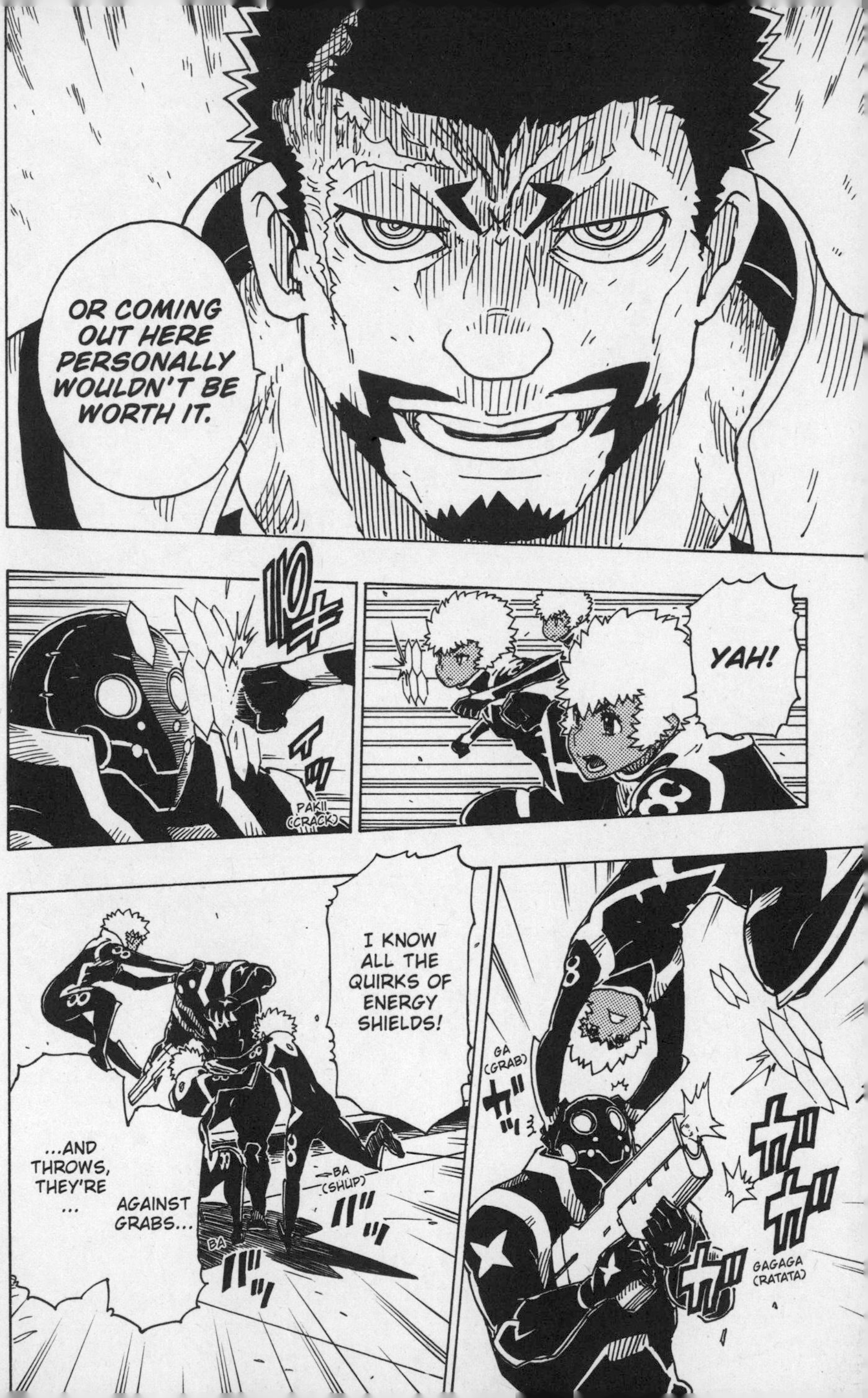
OR COMING OUT HERE PERSONALLY WOULDN'T BE WORTH IT.
YAH!
PAKI! (CRACK)
GAGAGA (RATATA)
GA (GRAB)
I KNOW ALL THE QUIRKS OF ENERGY SHIELDS!
BA (SHUP)
AGAINST GRABS...
...AND THROWS, THEY'RE ...
BA

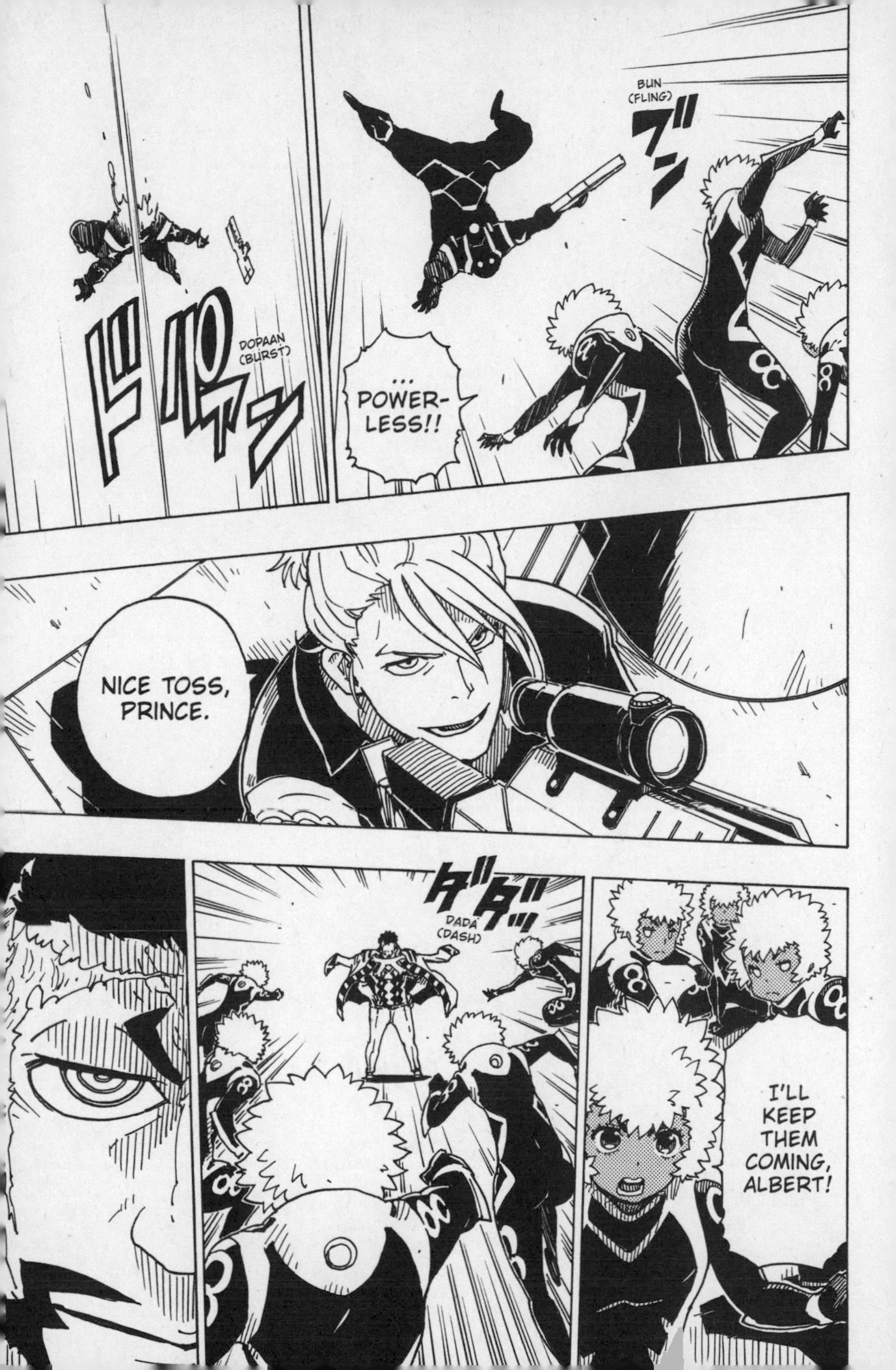
BUN (FLING)
ブン
... POWER-LESS!!
ドパァン
DOPAAN (BURST)
NICE TOSS, PRINCE.
I'LL KEEP THEM COMING, ALBERT!
ダダッ
DADA (DASH)

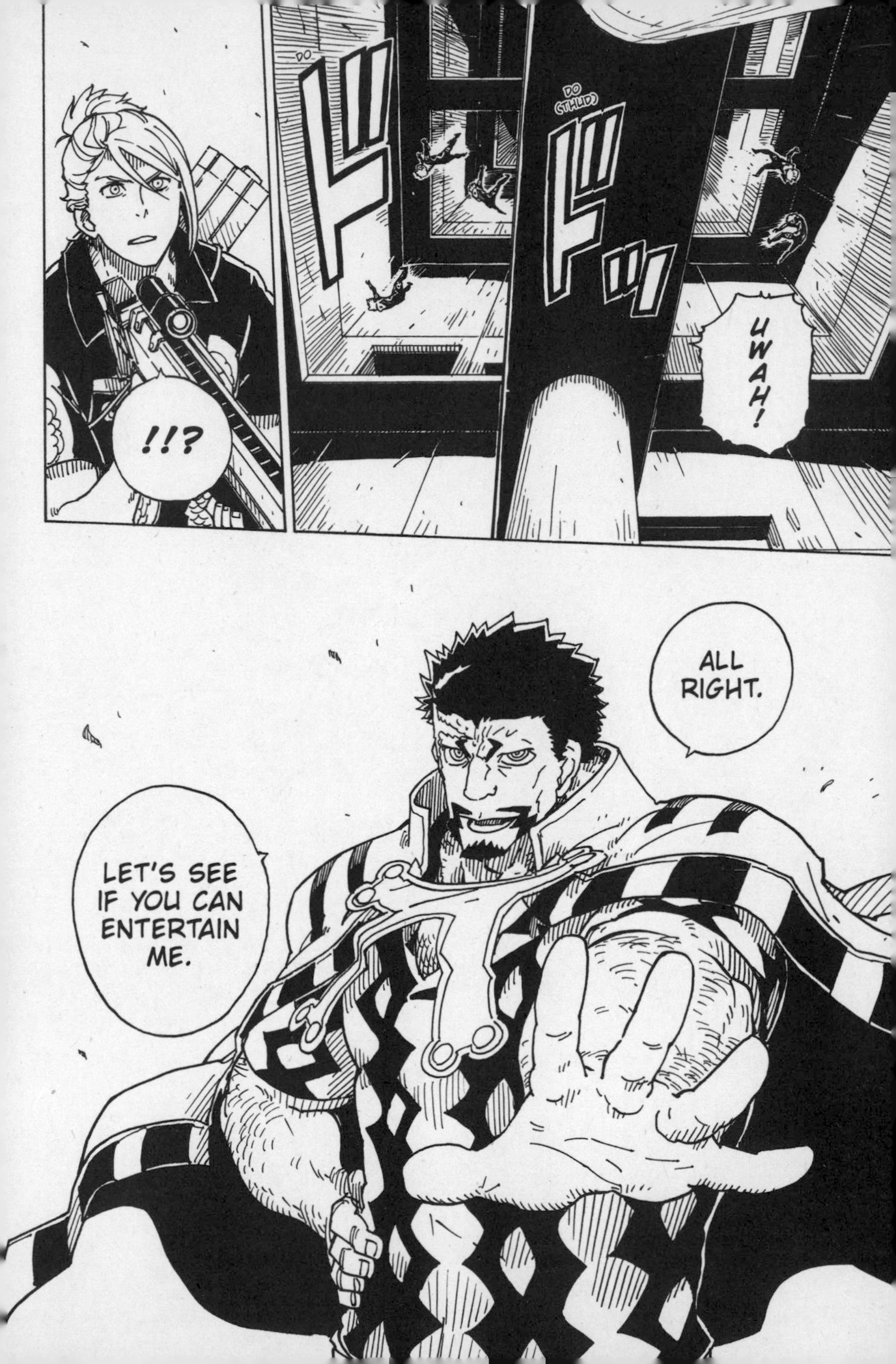
UWAH!
DO (THUD)
DO
!!?
ALL RIGHT.
LET'S SEE IF YOU CAN ENTERTAIN ME.

FILE.98
BEAST HUNT

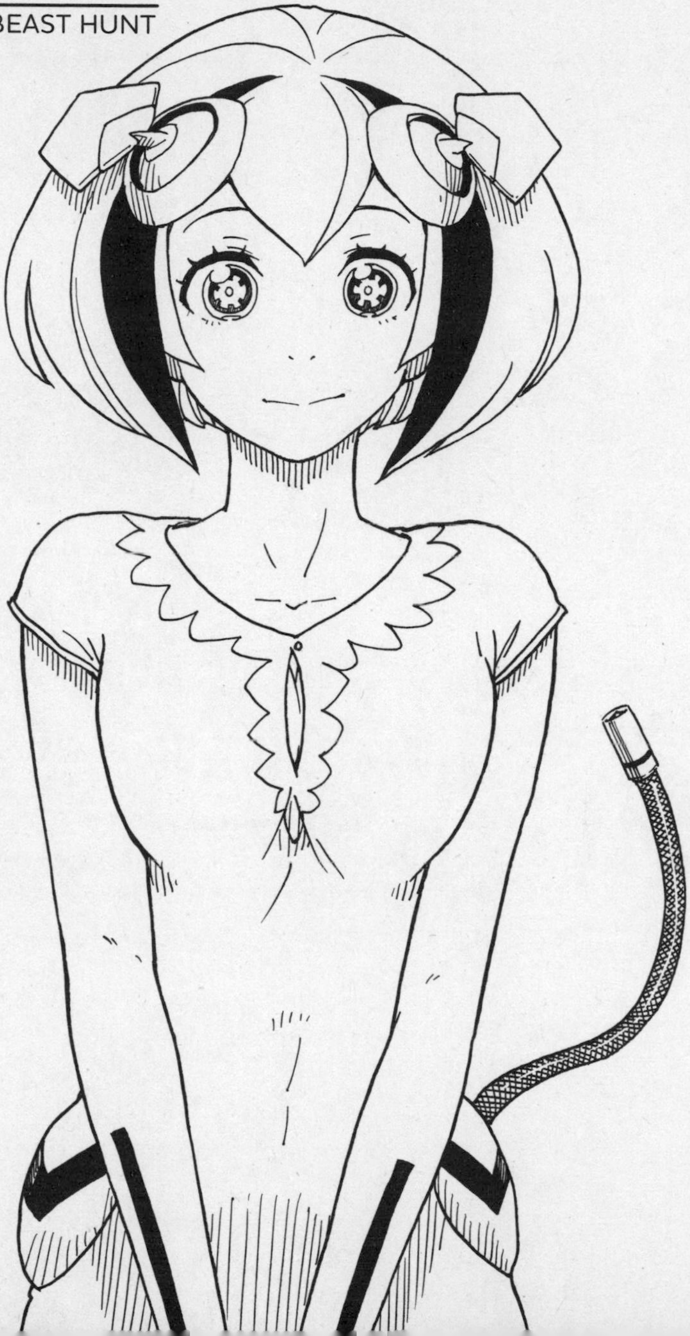

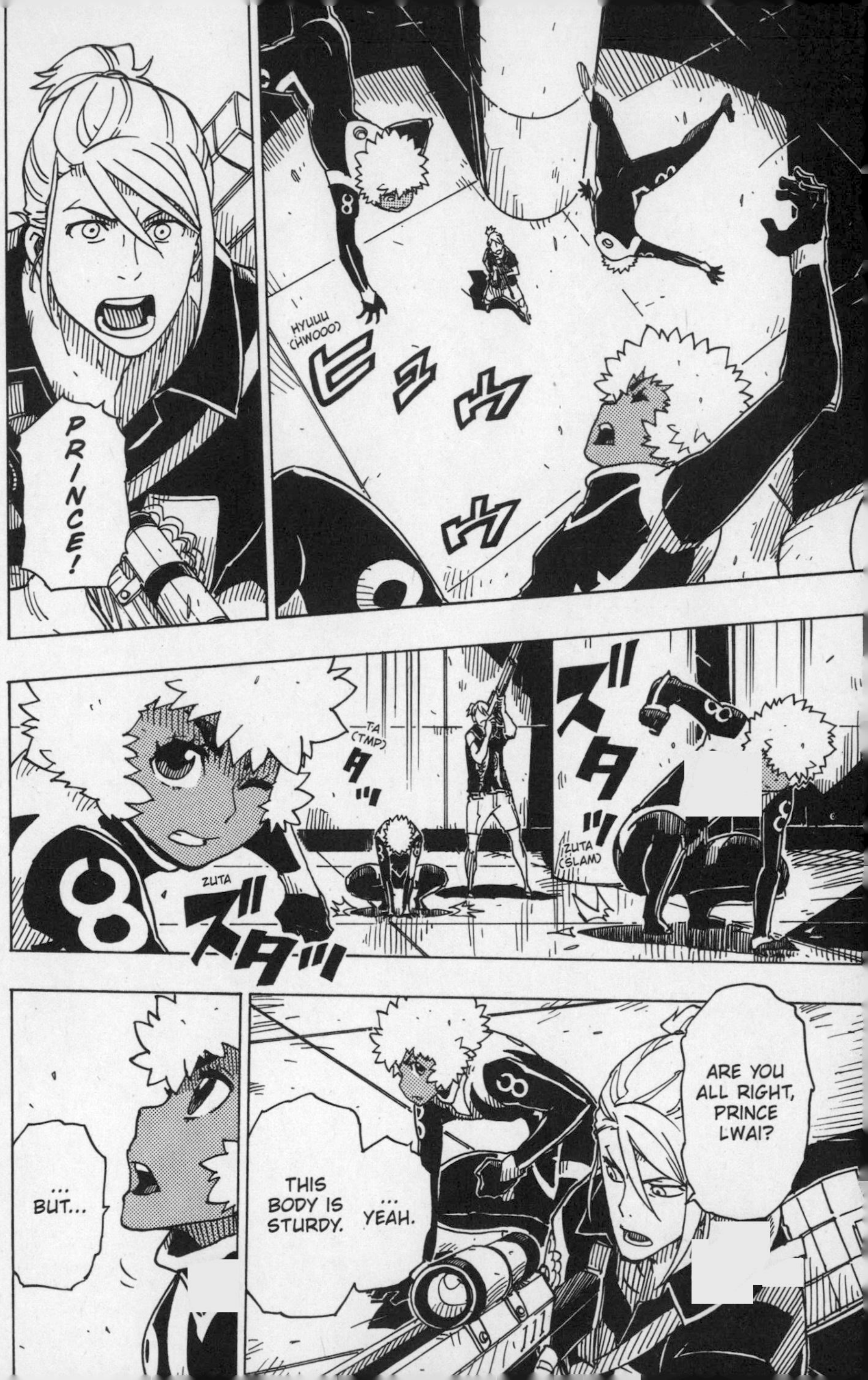
HYUUU (HWOOO)
PRINCE!
ZUTA (SLAM)
TA (TMP)
ZUTA
ARE YOU ALL RIGHT, PRINCE LWAI?
... YEAH.
THIS BODY IS STURDY.
... BUT...

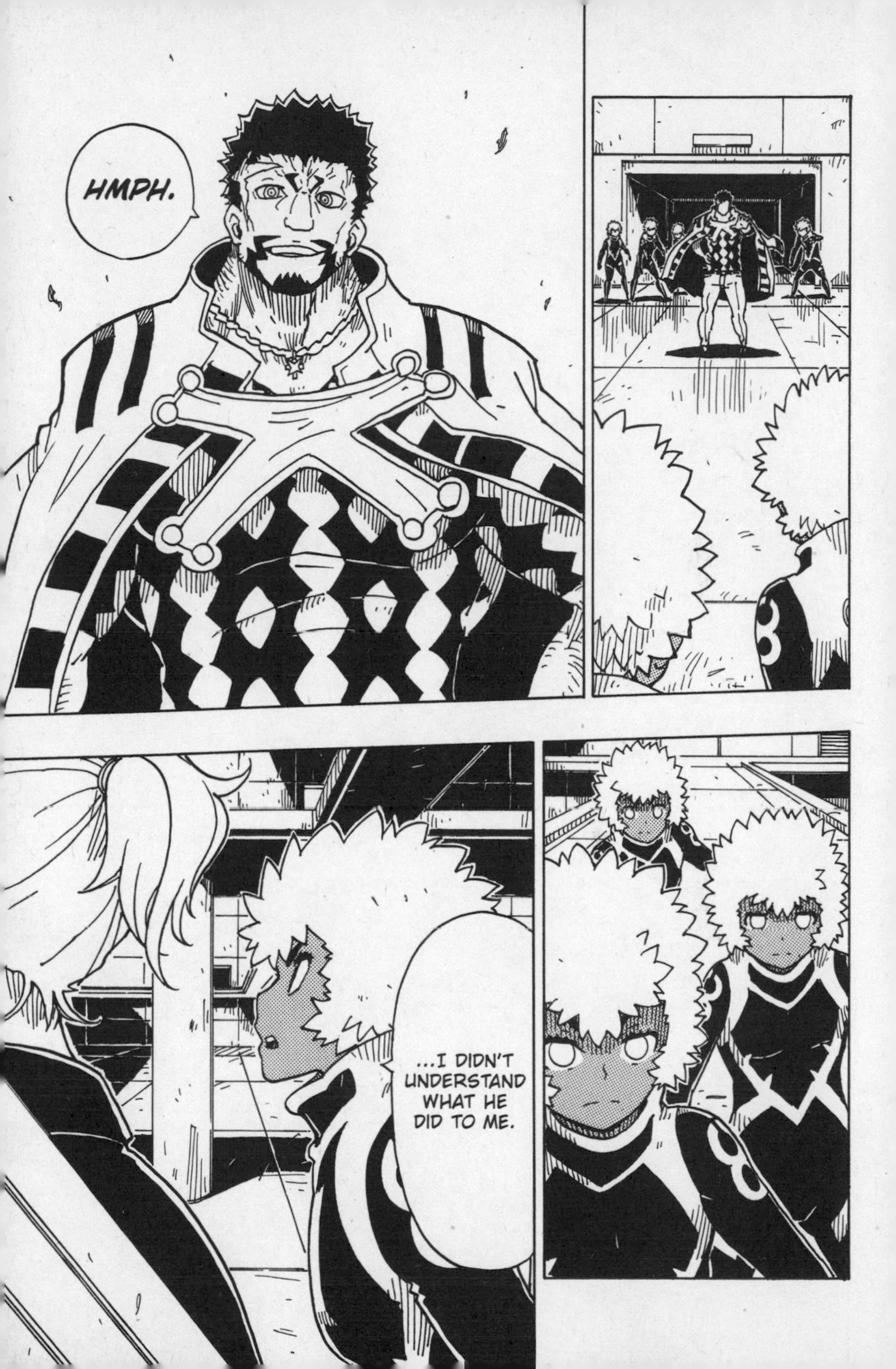
HMPH.
...I DIDN'T UNDERSTAND WHAT HE DID TO ME.

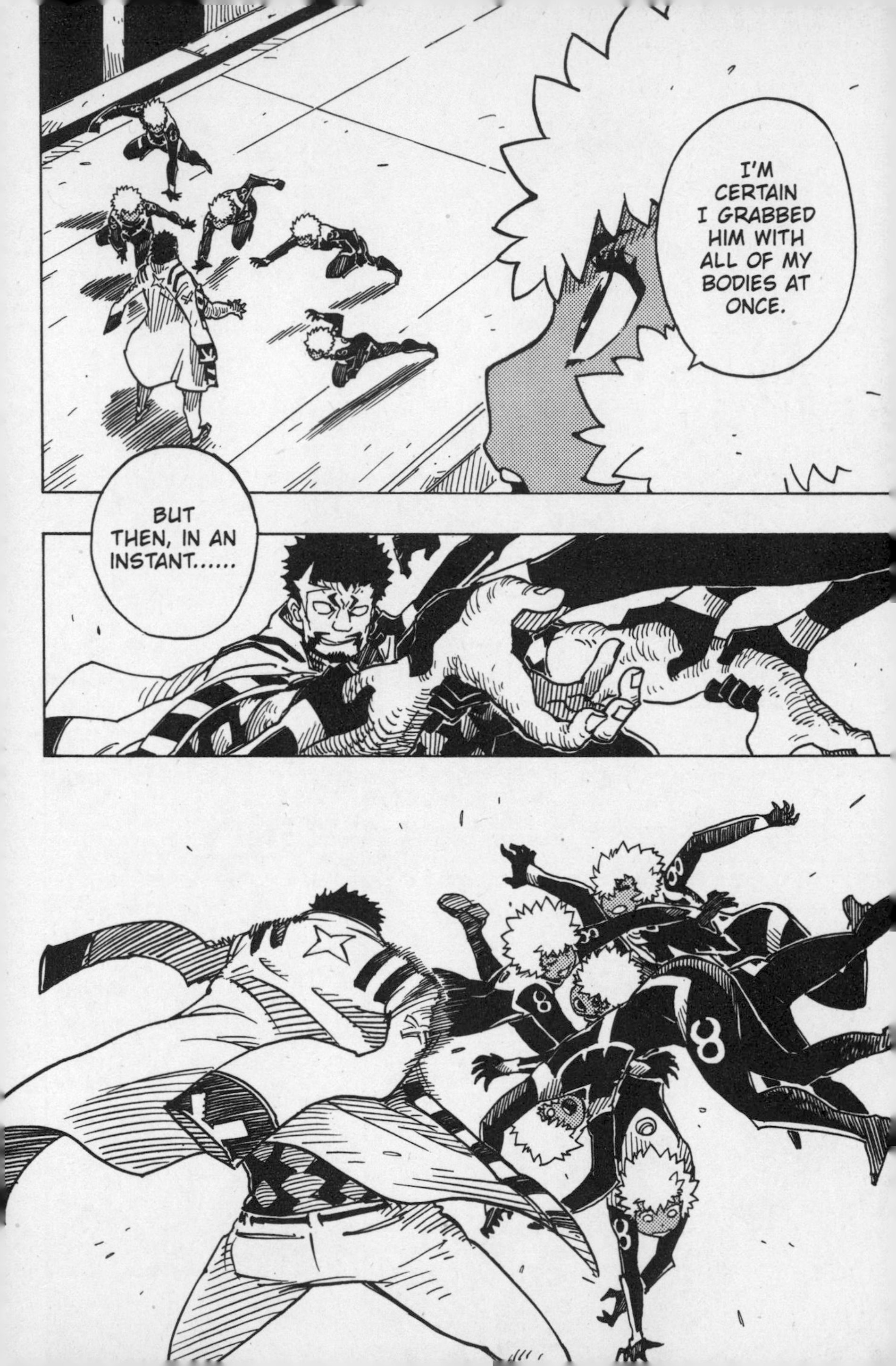
I'M CERTAIN I GRABBED HIM WITH ALL OF MY BODIES AT ONCE.
BUT THEN, IN AN INSTANT......

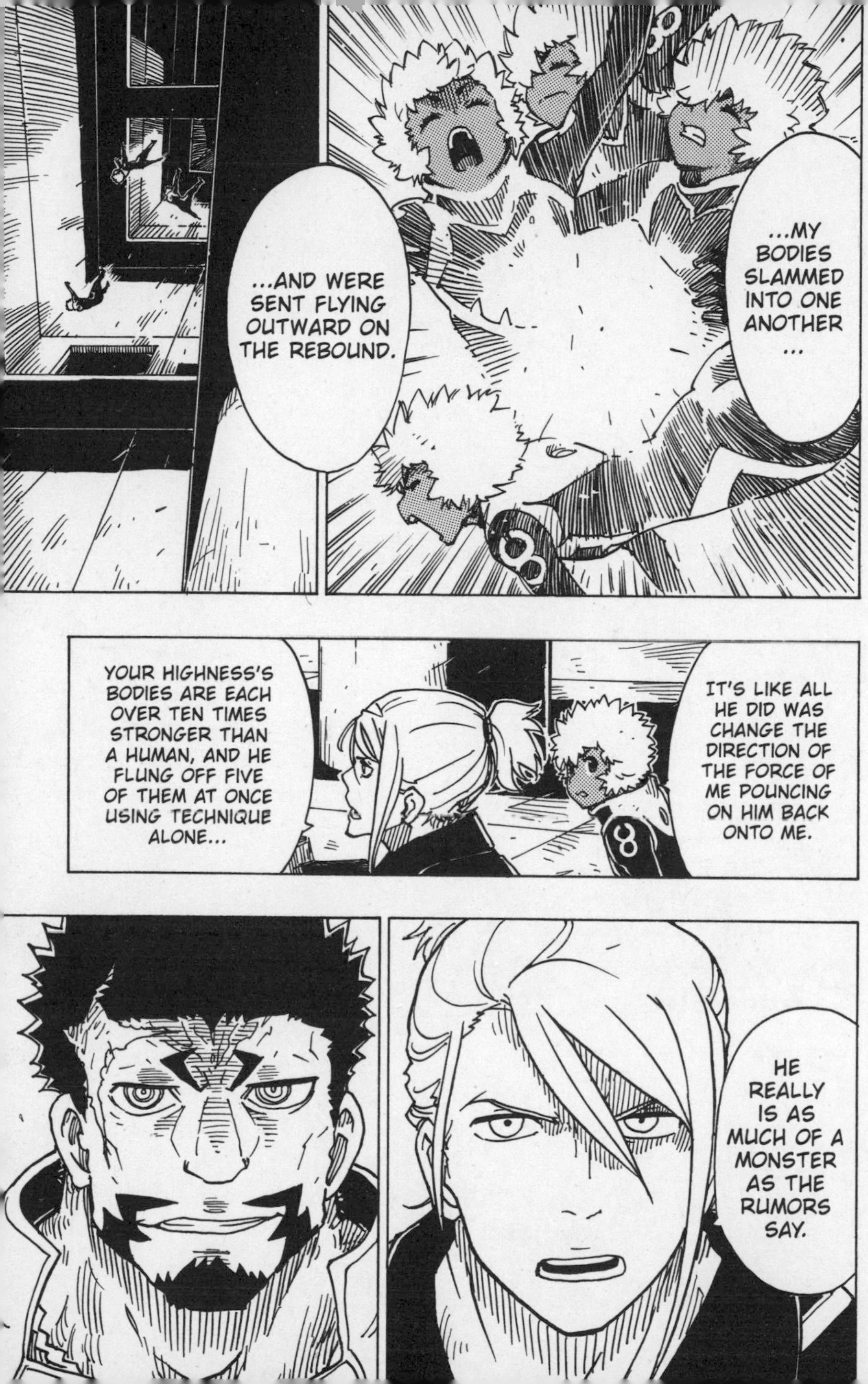
...MY BODIES SLAMMED INTO ONE ANOTHER...
...AND WERE SENT FLYING OUTWARD ON THE REBOUND.
IT'S LIKE ALL HE DID WAS CHANGE THE DIRECTION OF THE FORCE OF ME POUNCING ON HIM BACK ONTO ME.
YOUR HIGHNESS'S BODIES ARE EACH OVER TEN TIMES STRONGER THAN A HUMAN, AND HE FLUNG OFF FIVE OF THEM AT ONCE USING TECHNIQUE ALONE...
HE REALLY IS AS MUCH OF A MONSTER AS THE RUMORS SAY.

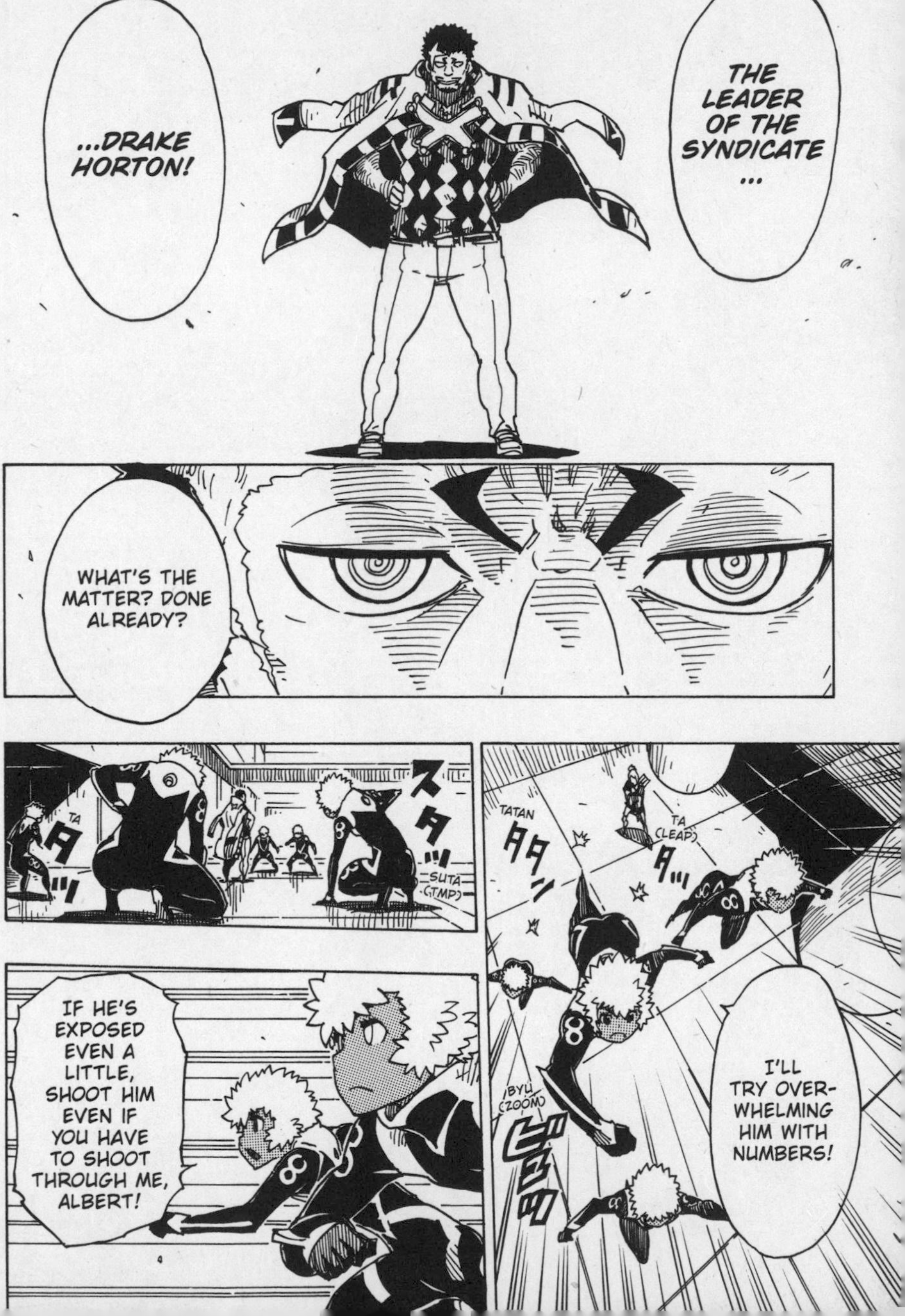
THE LEADER OF THE SYNDICATE ...
...DRAKE HORTON!
WHAT'S THE MATTER? DONE ALREADY?
TA (LEAP)
TATAN
I'LL TRY OVER-WHELMING HIM WITH NUMBERS!
BYU (ZOOM)
SUTA (TMP)
TA
IF HE'S EXPOSED EVEN A LITTLE, SHOOT HIM EVEN IF YOU HAVE TO SHOOT THROUGH ME, ALBERT!

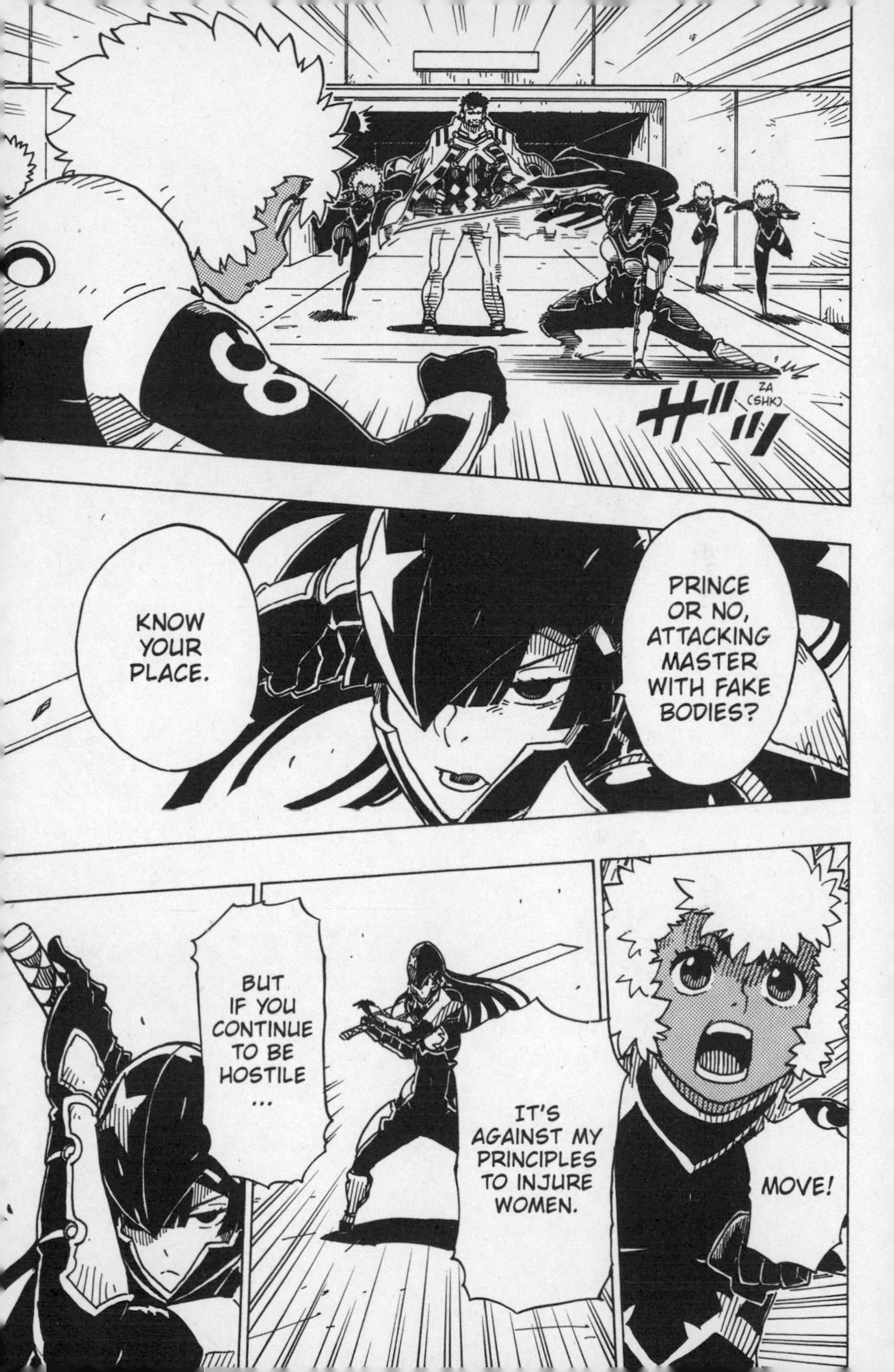
ザッ
ZA
(SHK)
PRINCE OR NO, ATTACKING MASTER WITH FAKE BODIES?
KNOW YOUR PLACE.
MOVE!
BUT IF YOU CONTINUE TO BE HOSTILE ...
IT'S AGAINST MY PRINCIPLES TO INJURE WOMEN.

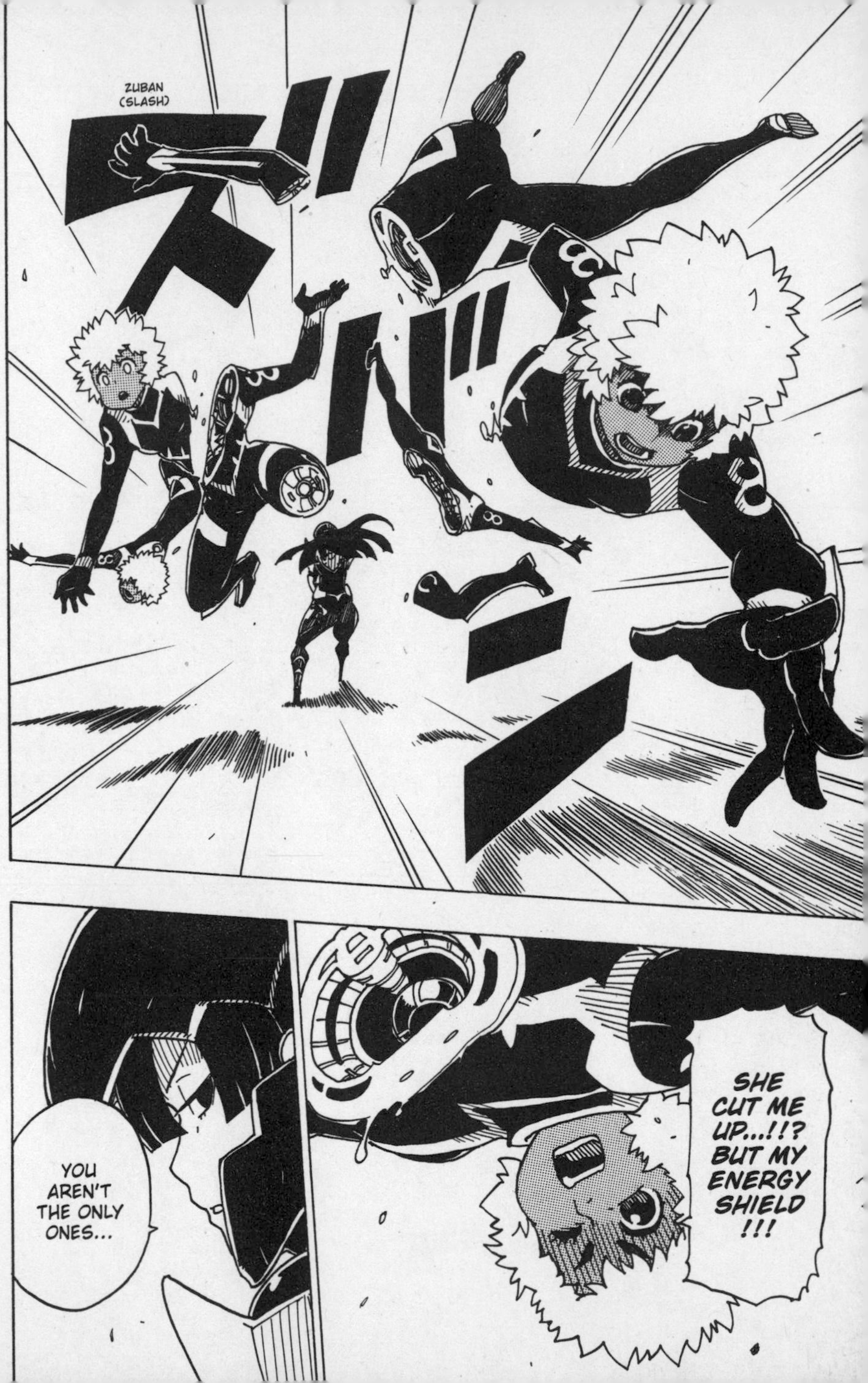
ZUBAN
(SLASH)
SHE CUT ME UP...!!? BUT MY ENERGY SHIELD !!!
YOU AREN'T THE ONLY ONES...

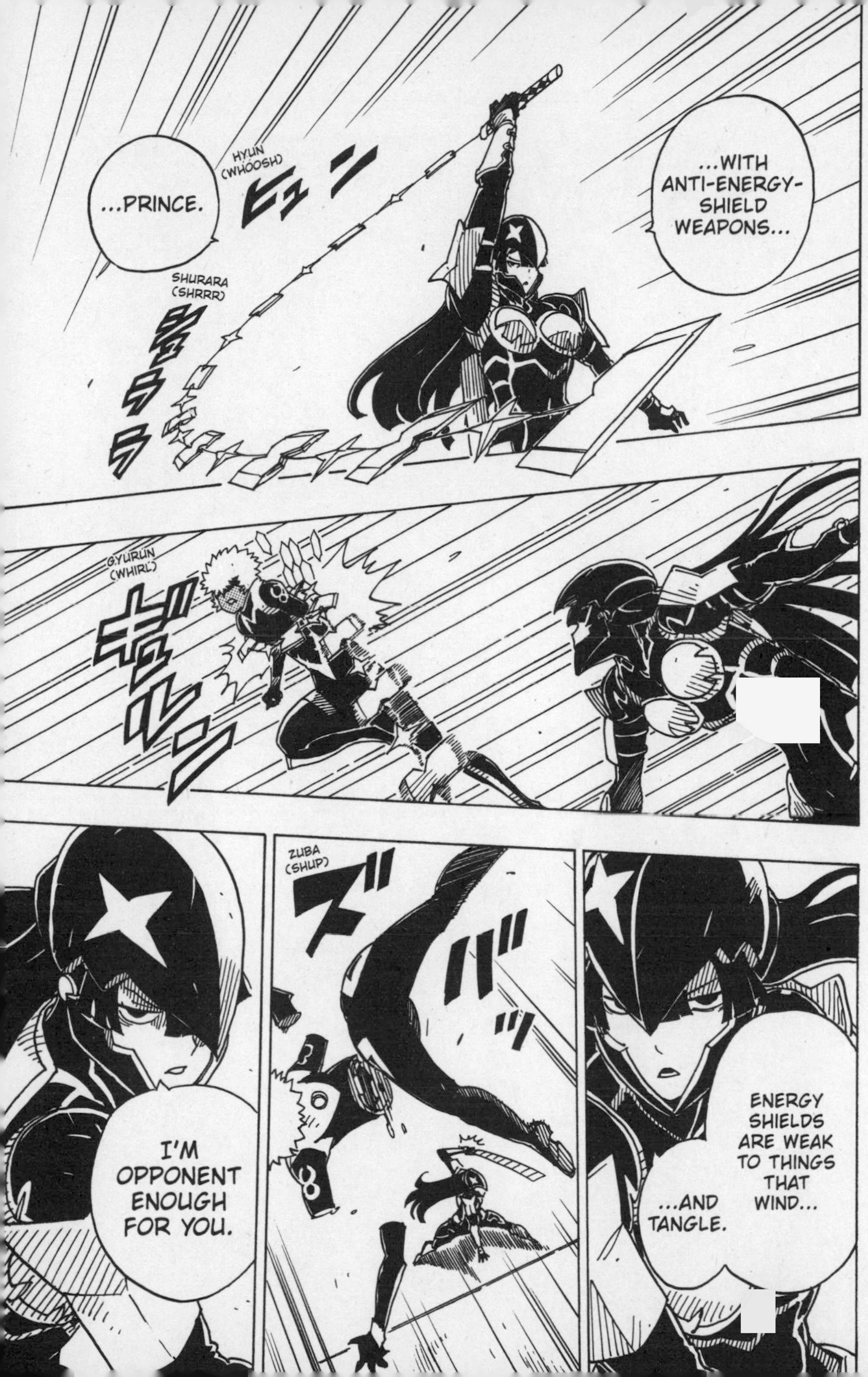
...WITH ANTI-ENERGY-SHIELD WEAPONS...
HYUN (WHOOSH)
...PRINCE.
SHURARA (SHRRR)
GYURUN (WHIRL)
ENERGY SHIELDS ARE WEAK TO THINGS THAT WIND...
...AND TANGLE.
ZUBA (SHUP)
I'M OPPONENT ENOUGH FOR YOU.

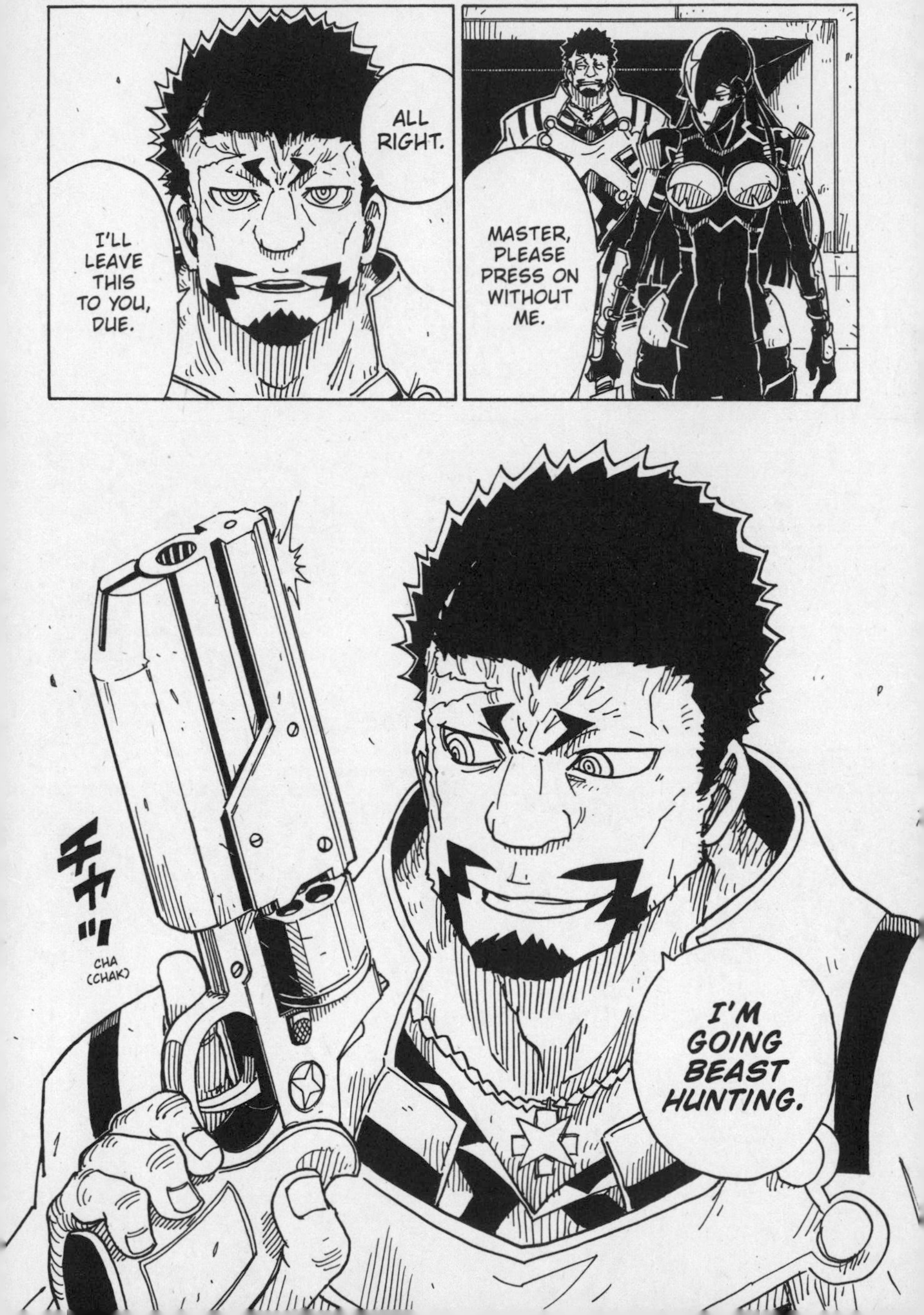
MASTER, PLEASE PRESS ON WITHOUT ME.
ALL RIGHT.
I'LL LEAVE THIS TO YOU, DUE.
チャッ
CHA (CHAK)
I'M GOING BEAST HUNTING.

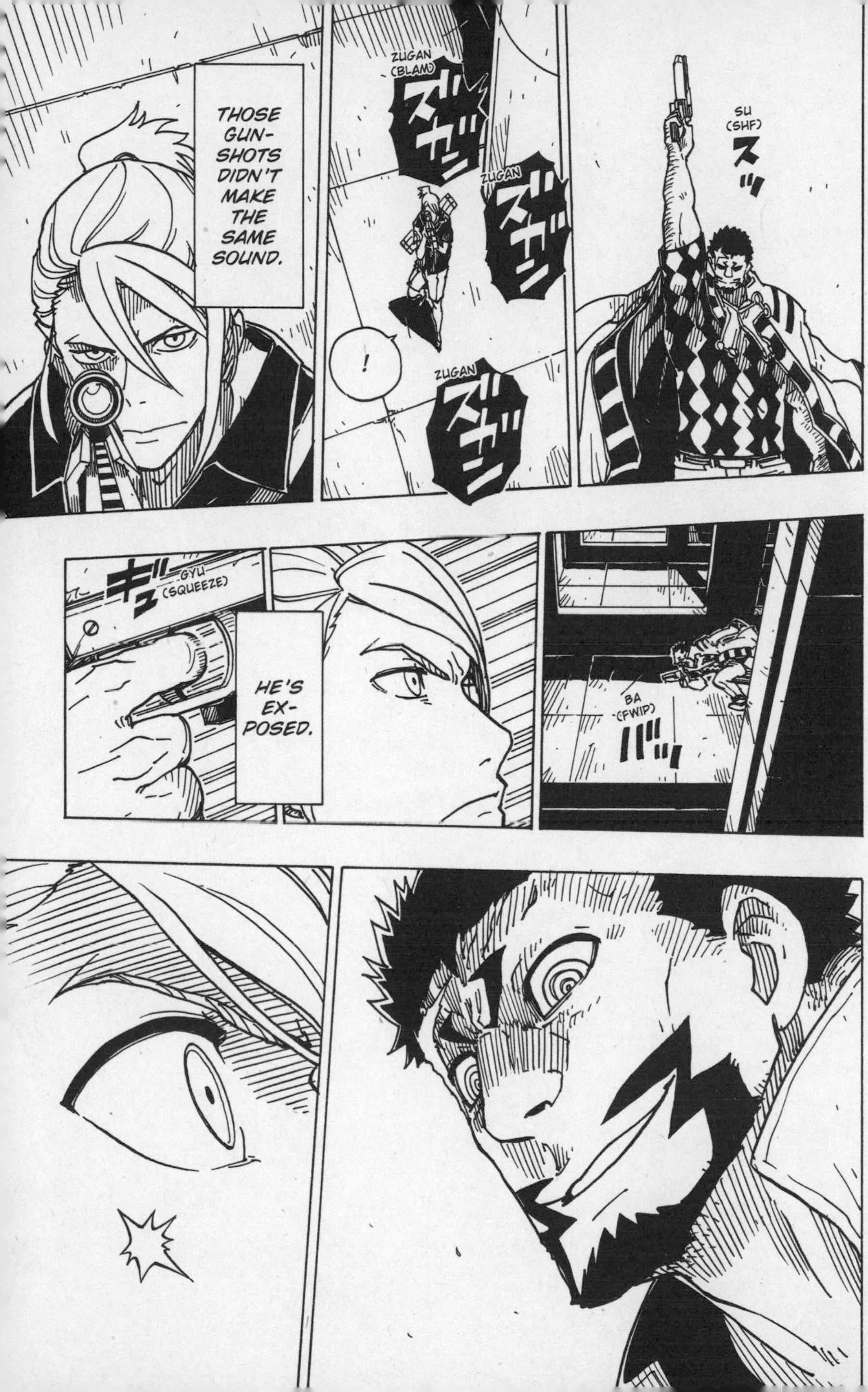
SU (SHF)
スッ
ZUGAN (BLAM)
ズガン
ZUGAN
ズガン
!
ZUGAN
ズガン
THOSE GUN-SHOTS DIDN'T MAKE THE SAME SOUND.
BA (FWIP)
バッ
HE'S EX-POSED.
GYU (SQUEEZE)
ギュ

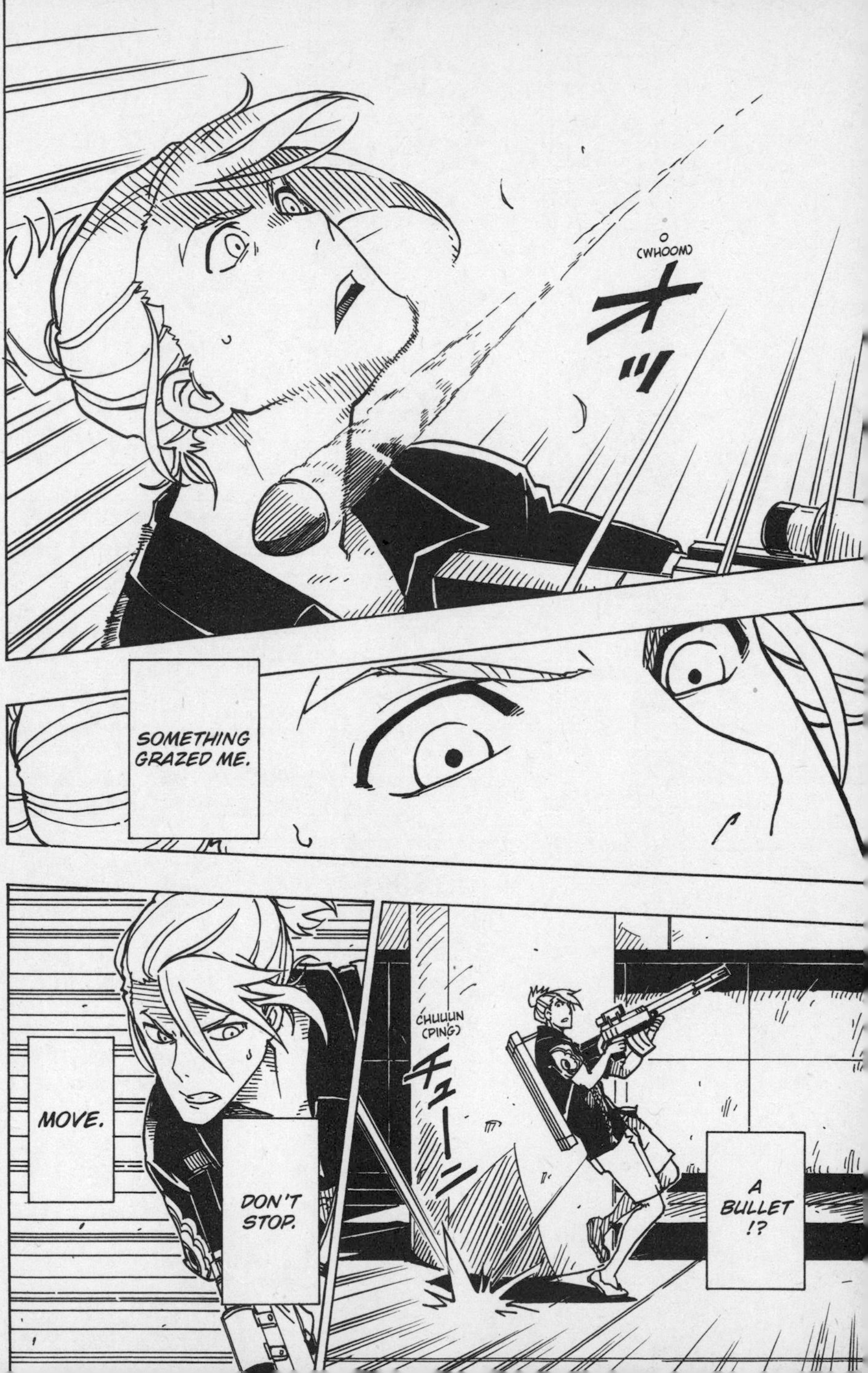
(WHOOM)
オッ
SOMETHING GRAZED ME.
A BULLET !?
CHUUUN (PING)
チュー
MOVE.
DON'T STOP.

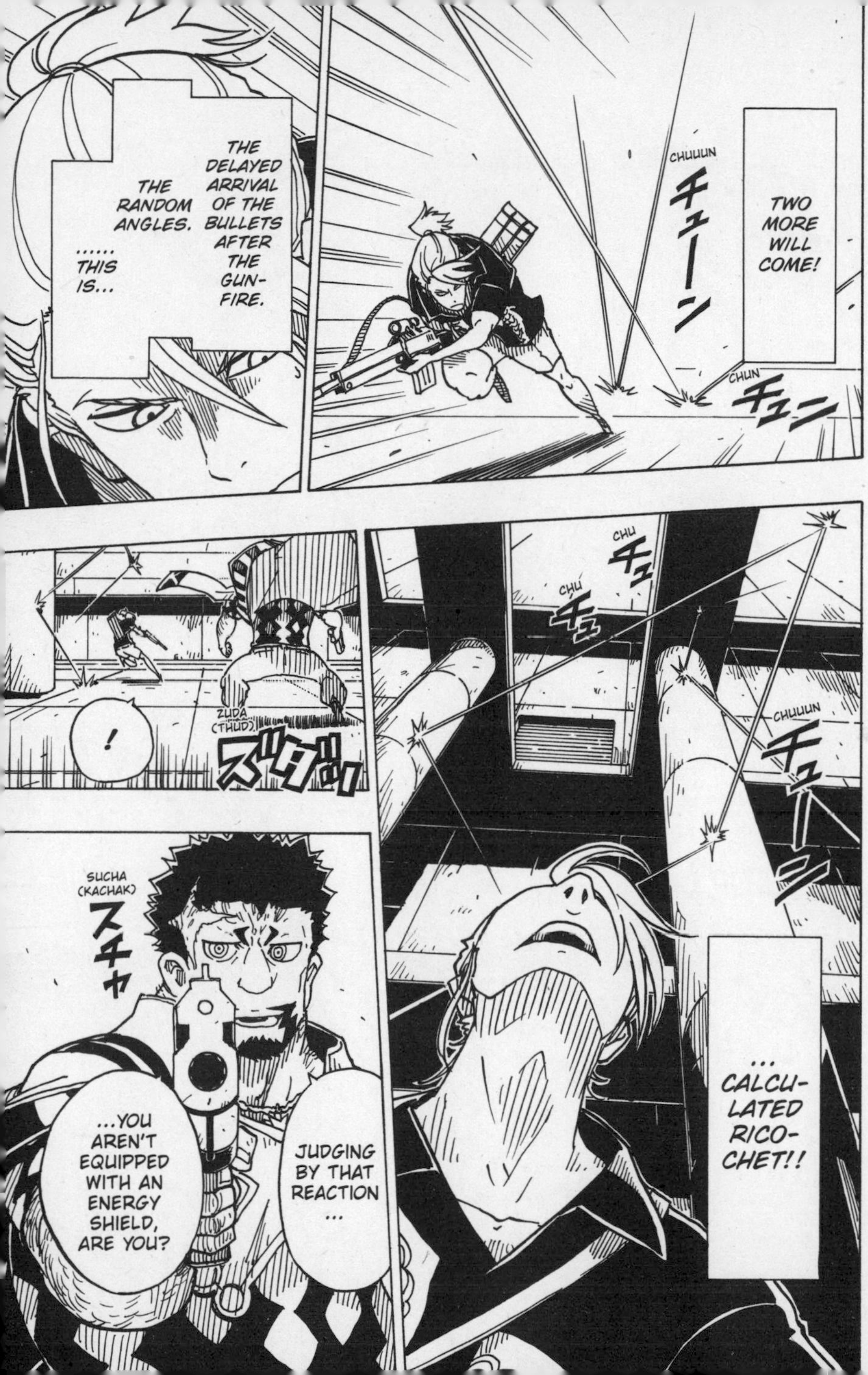
TWO MORE WILL COME!
CHUUUN
チューン
CHUN
チュン
THE DELAYED ARRIVAL OF THE BULLETS AFTER THE GUNFIRE.
THE RANDOM ANGLES.
...... THIS IS...
CHU
チュ
CHU
チュ
CHUUUN
チューン
... CALCULATED RICOCHET!!
!
ZUDA (THUD)
ズダッ
SUCHA (KACHAK)
スチャ
JUDGING BY THAT REACTION ...
...YOU AREN'T EQUIPPED WITH AN ENERGY SHIELD, ARE YOU?

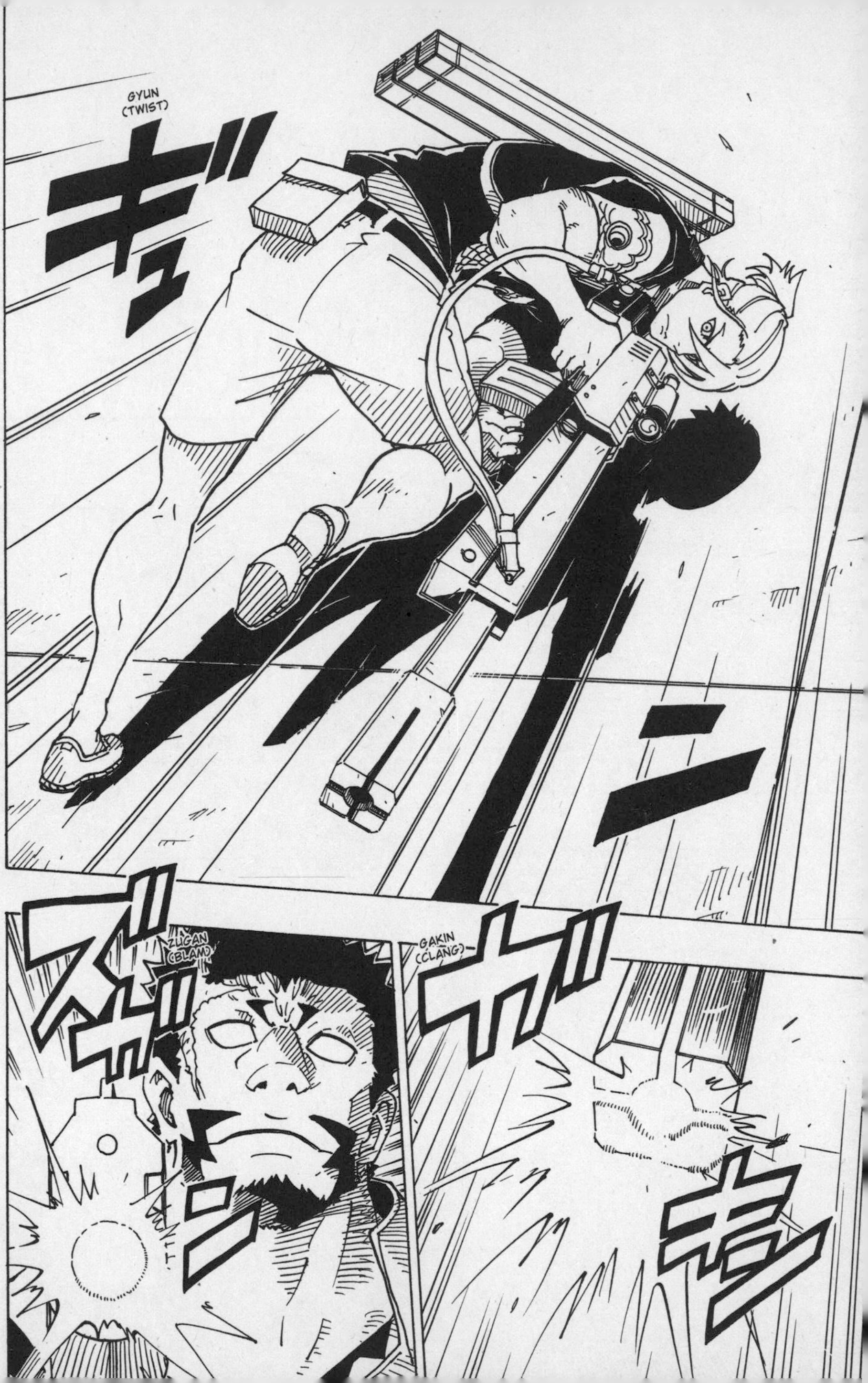
GYUN (TWIST)
GAKIN (CLANG)
ZUGAN (BLAM)

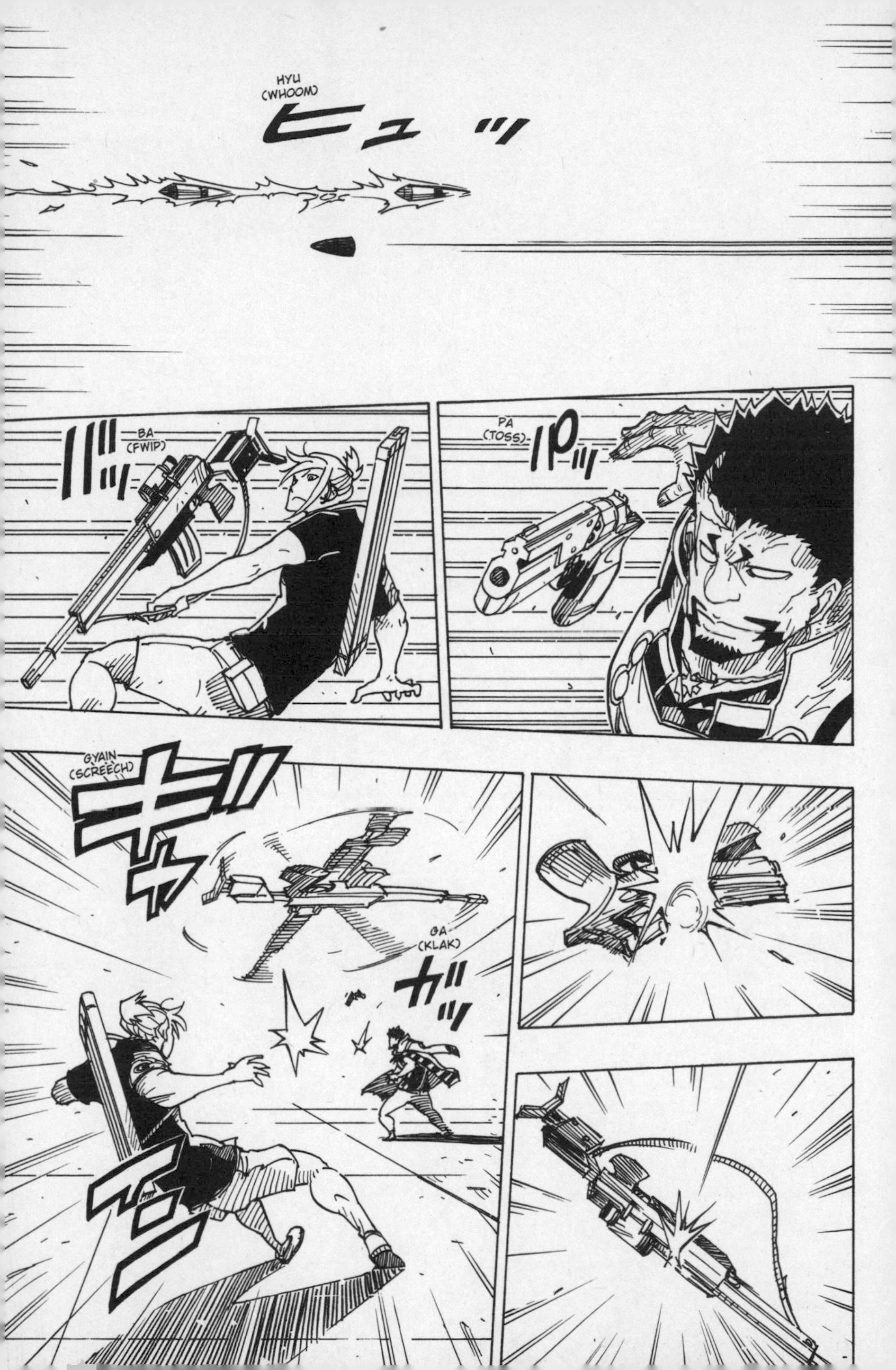
HYU
(WHOOM)
PA
(TOSS)
BA
(FWIP)
GYAIN
(SCREECH)
GA
(KLAK)

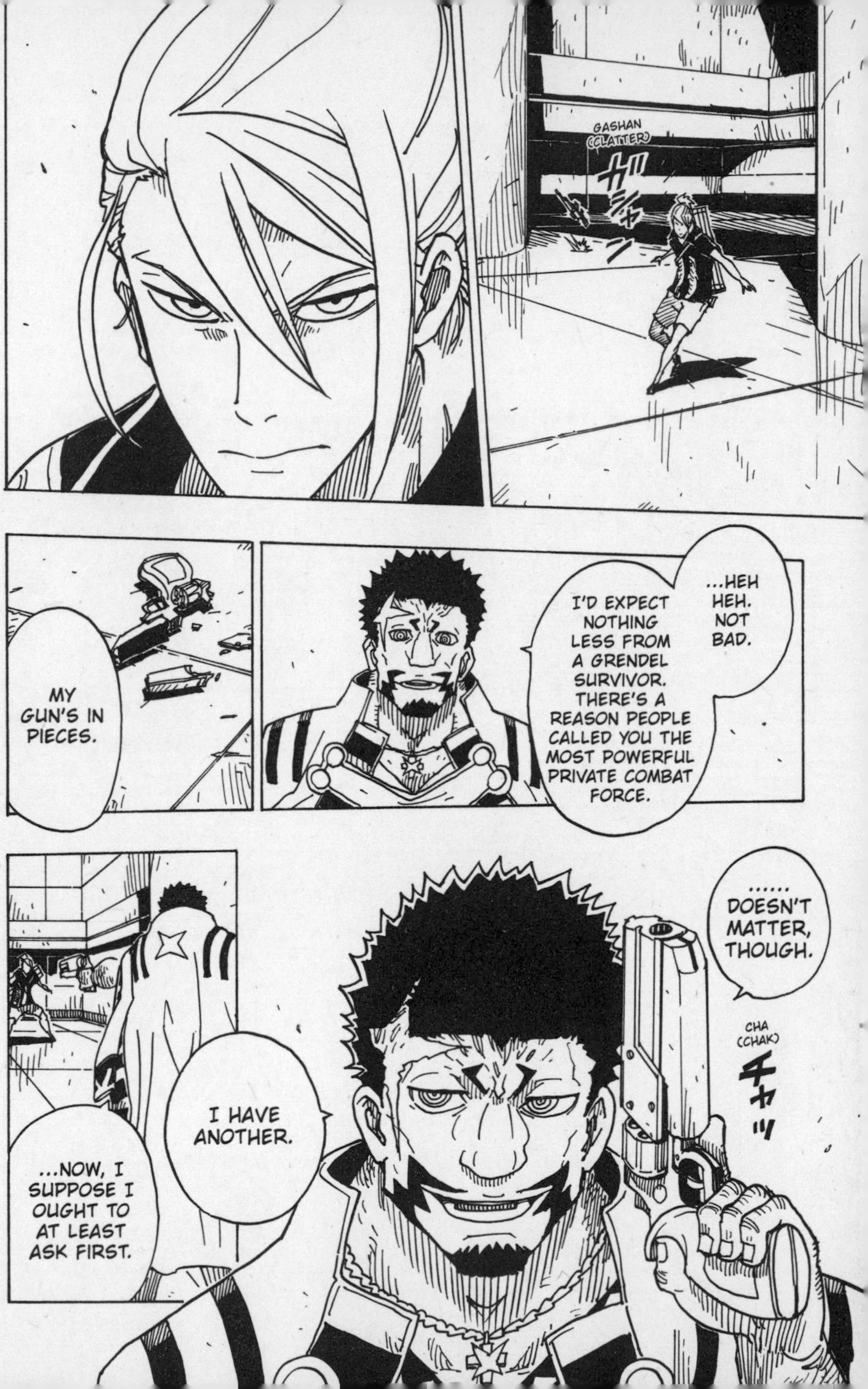

GASHAN (CLATTER)
...HEH HEH. NOT BAD.
I'D EXPECT NOTHING LESS FROM A GRENDEL SURVIVOR. THERE'S A REASON PEOPLE CALLED YOU THE MOST POWERFUL PRIVATE COMBAT FORCE.
MY GUN'S IN PIECES.
...... DOESN'T MATTER, THOUGH.
CHA (CHAK)
I HAVE ANOTHER.
...NOW, I SUPPOSE I OUGHT TO AT LEAST ASK FIRST.

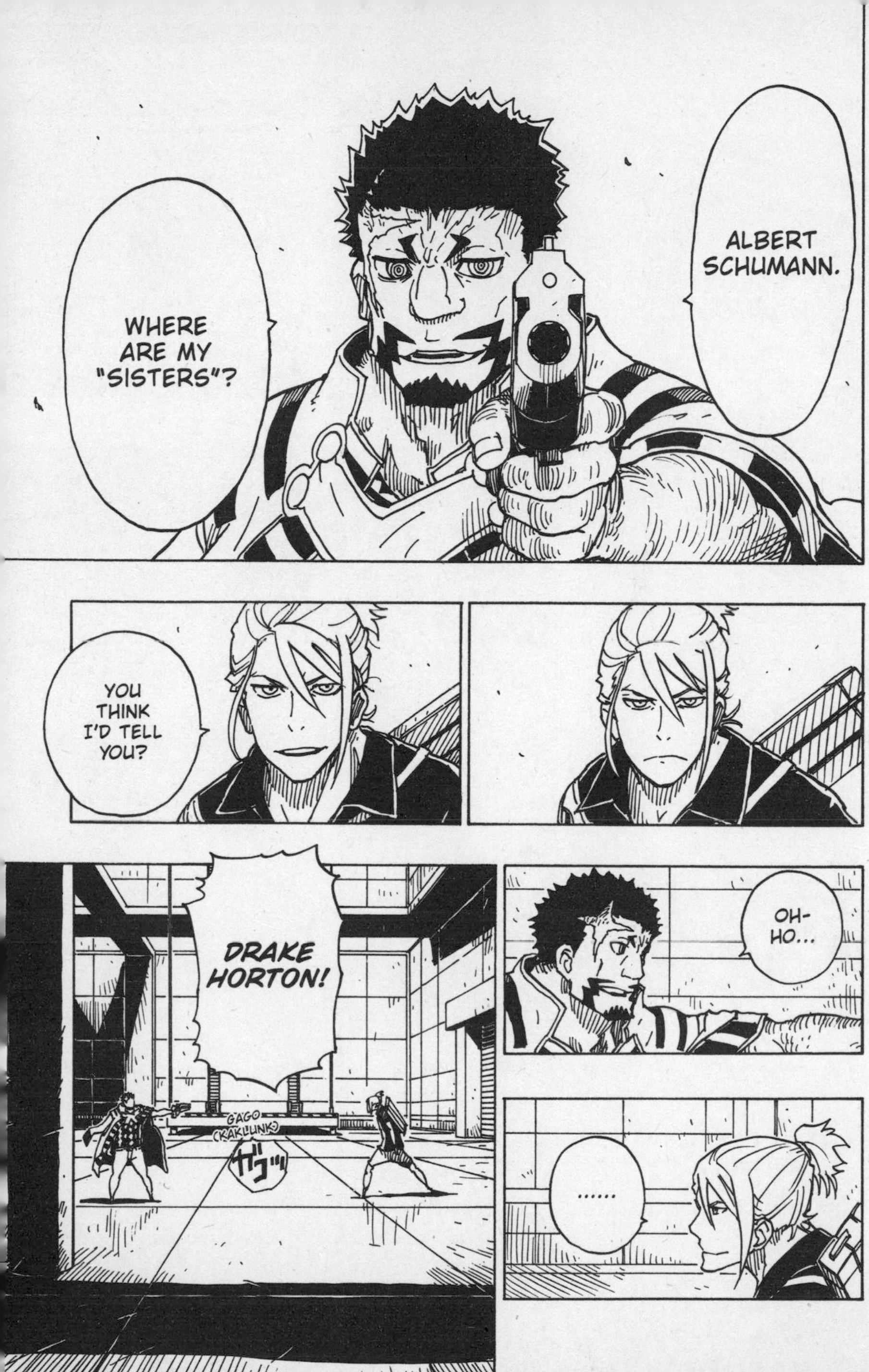
ALBERT SCHUMANN.
WHERE ARE MY "SISTERS"?
YOU THINK I'D TELL YOU?
OH-HO...
......
DRAKE HORTON!
GAGO (KAKLUNK)
ガゴッ

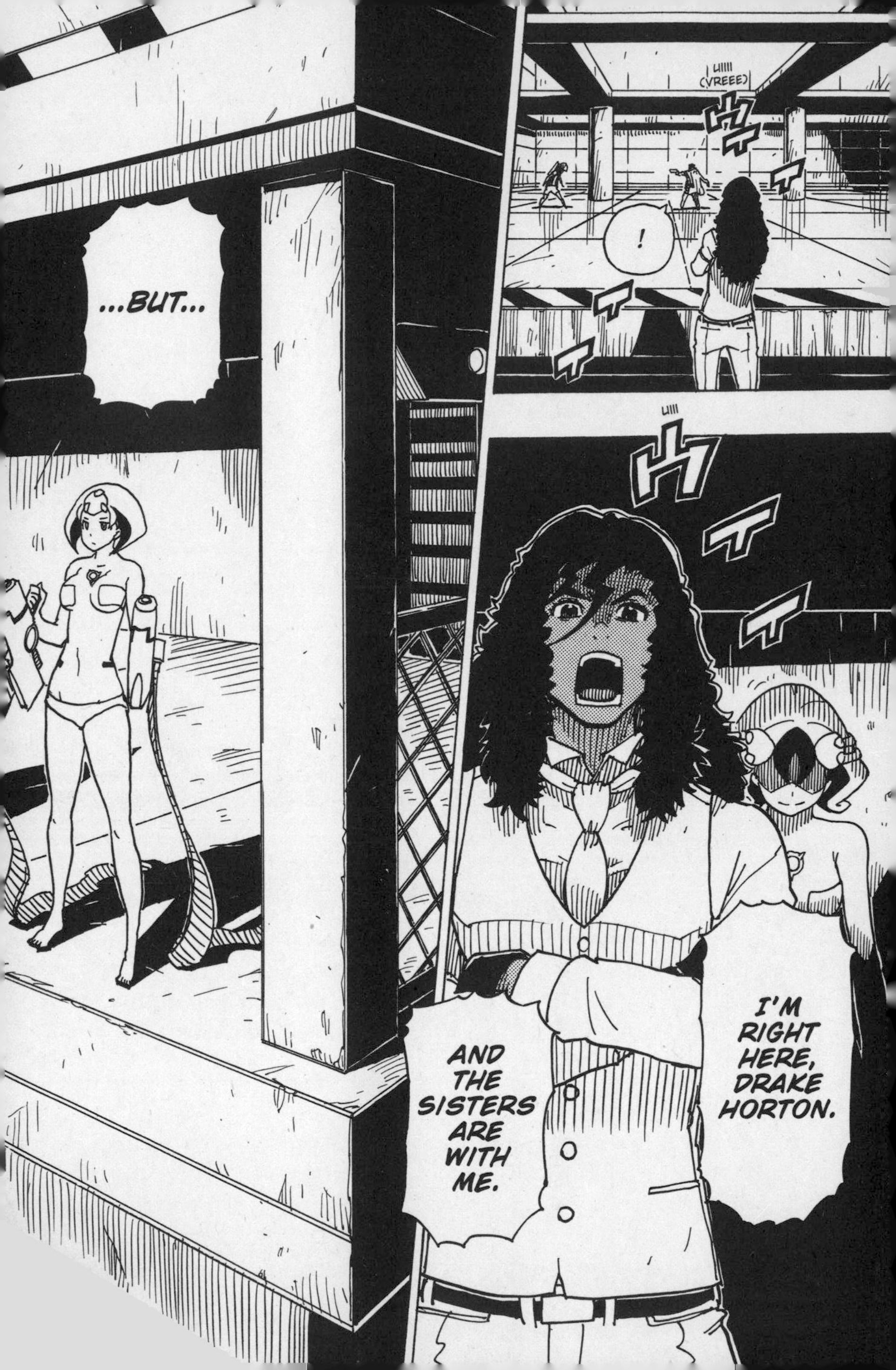
UIIII
(VREEE)
!
UIIII
I'M RIGHT HERE, DRAKE HORTON.
AND THE SISTERS ARE WITH ME.
...BUT...

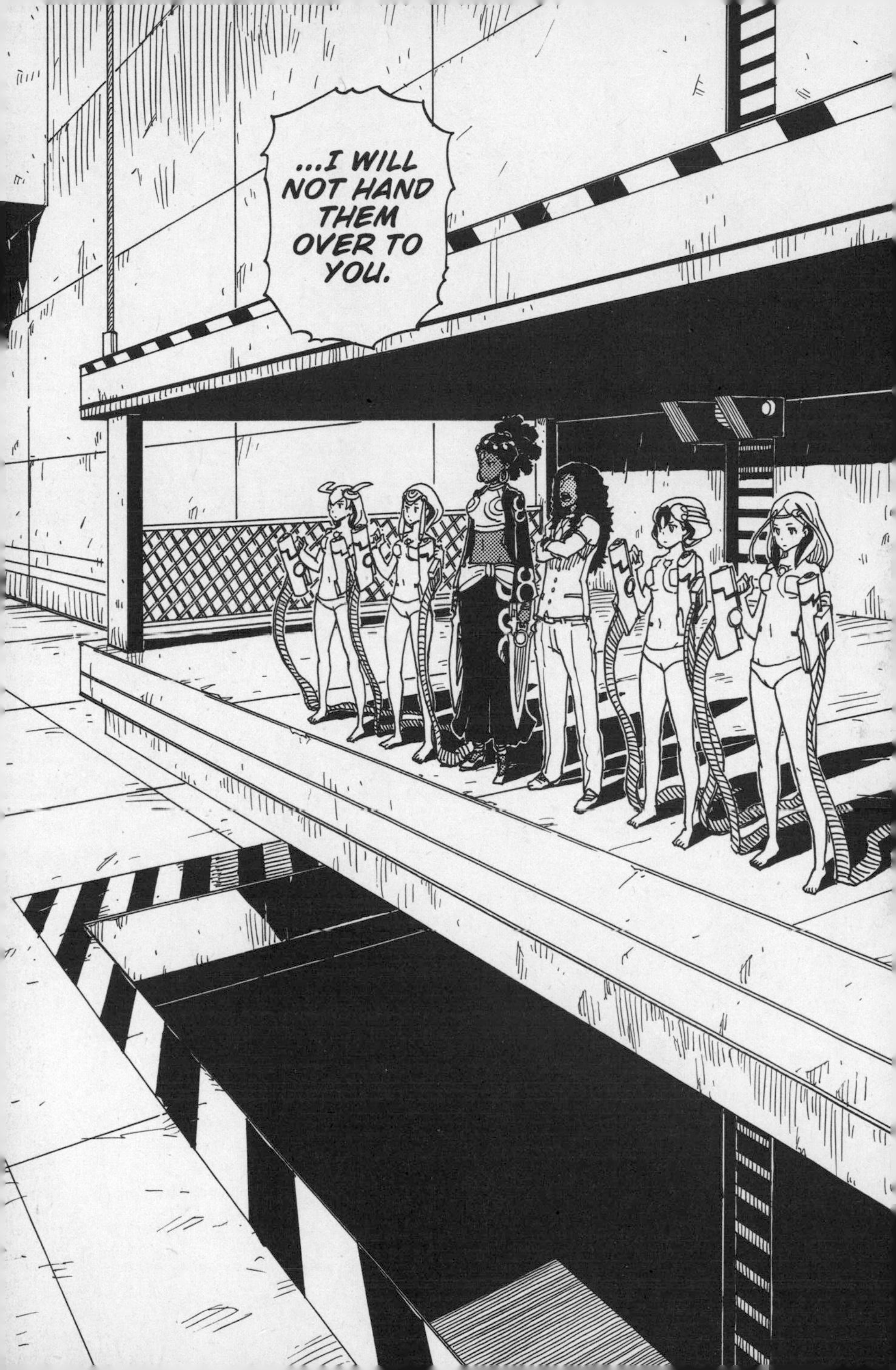
...I WILL NOT HAND THEM OVER TO YOU.

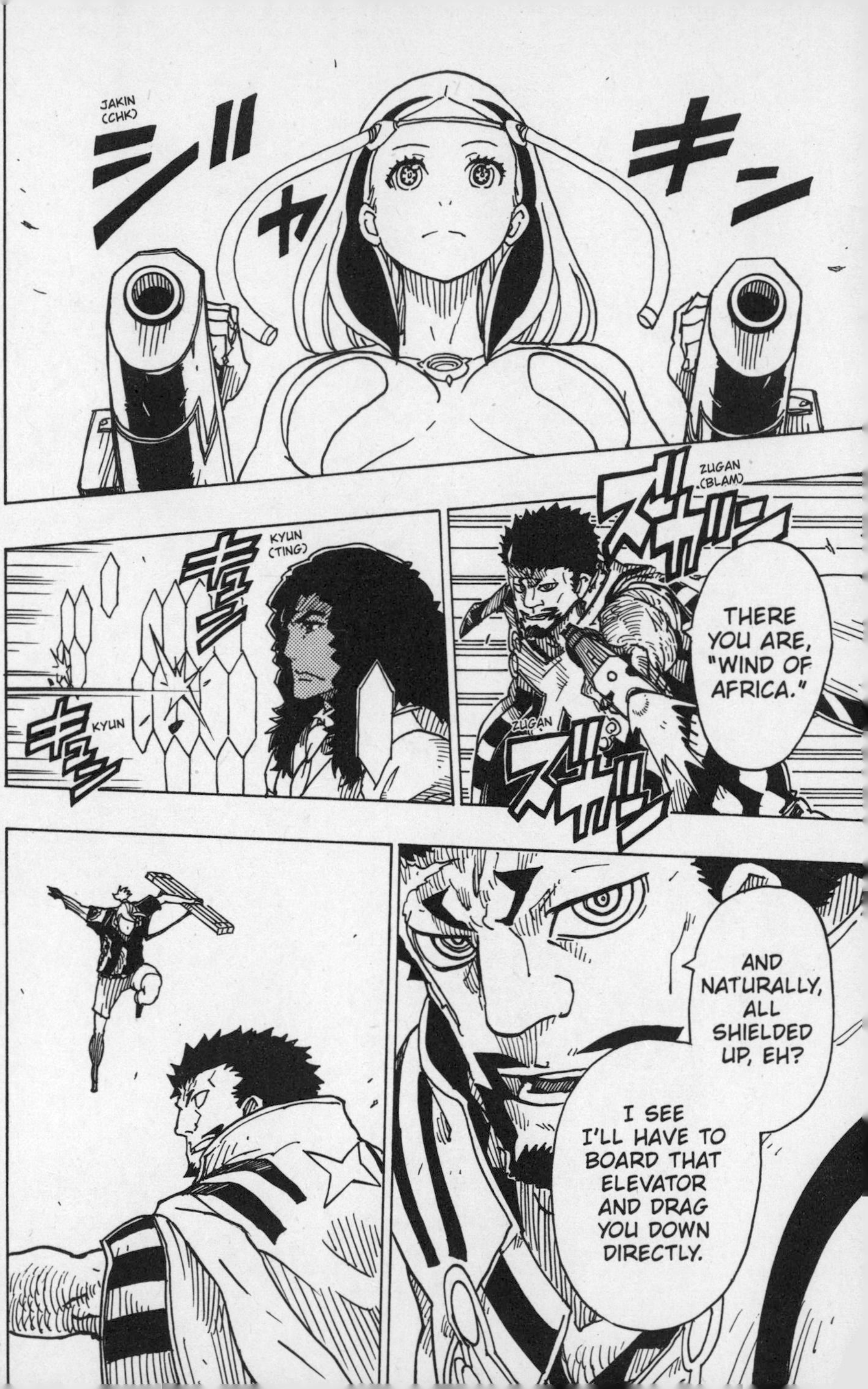

JAKIN (CHK)
ZUGAN (BLAM)
THERE YOU ARE, "WIND OF AFRICA."
ZUGAN
KYUN (TING)
KYUN
AND NATURALLY, ALL SHIELDED UP, EH?
I SEE I'LL HAVE TO BOARD THAT ELEVATOR AND DRAG YOU DOWN DIRECTLY.

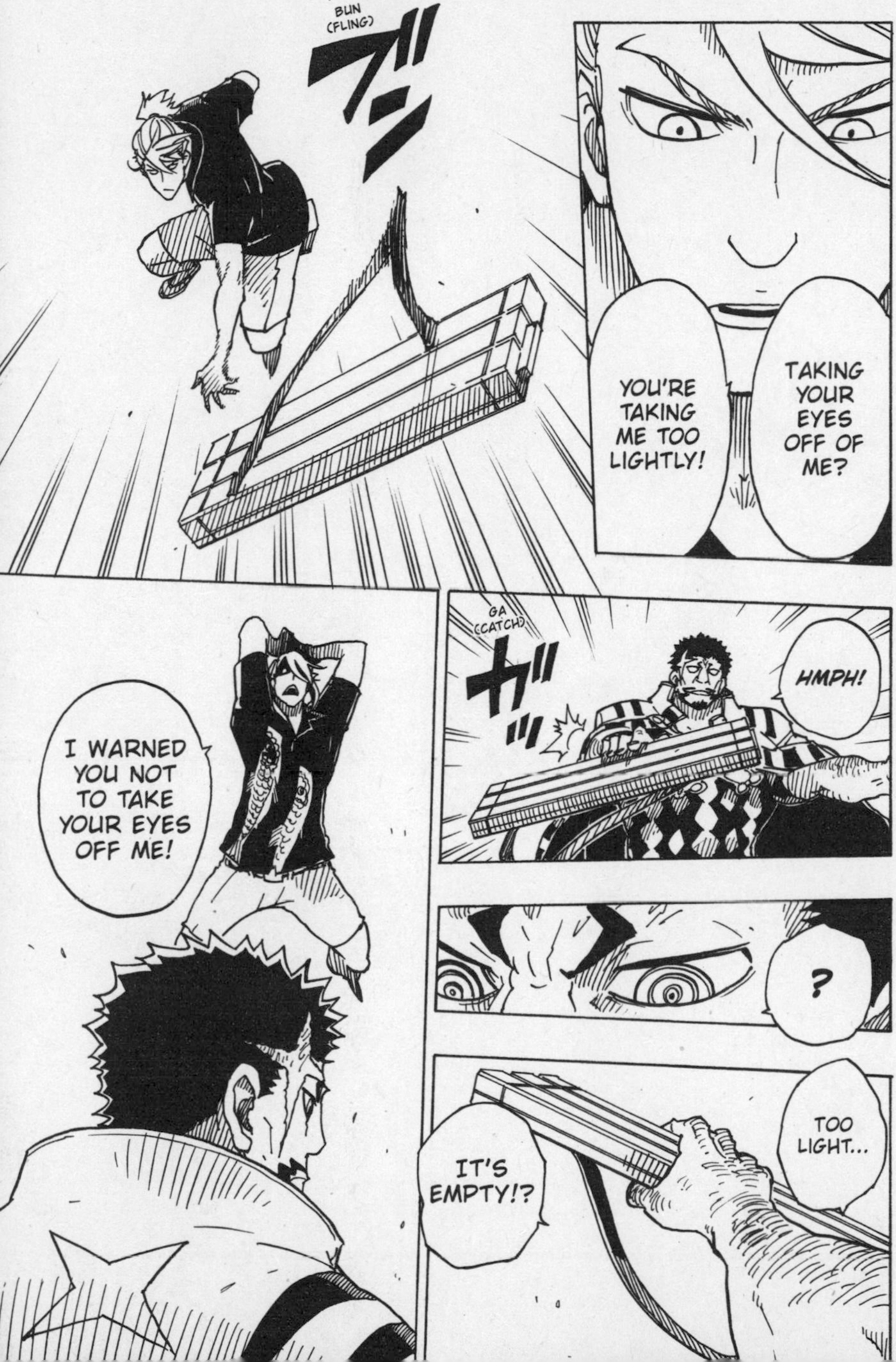
TAKING YOUR EYES OFF OF ME?
YOU'RE TAKING ME TOO LIGHTLY!
BUN (FLING)
GA (CATCH)
HMPH!
?
TOO LIGHT...
IT'S EMPTY!?
I WARNED YOU NOT TO TAKE YOUR EYES OFF ME!

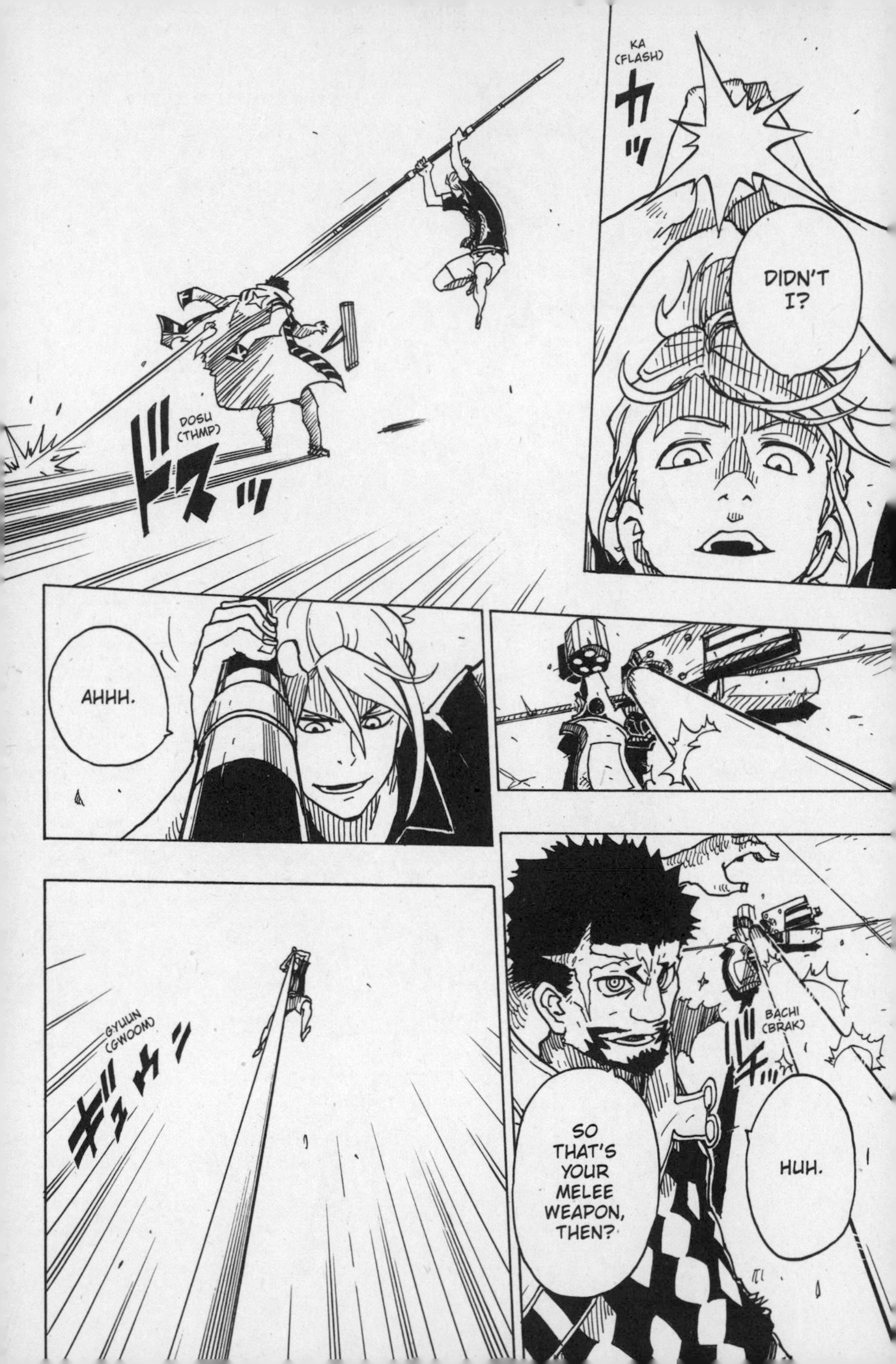
KA (FLASH)
カッ
DIDN'T I?
DOSU (THMP)
ドスッ
AHHH.
BACHI (BRAK)
HUH.
SO THAT'S YOUR MELEE WEAPON, THEN?
GYUUN (GWOOM)

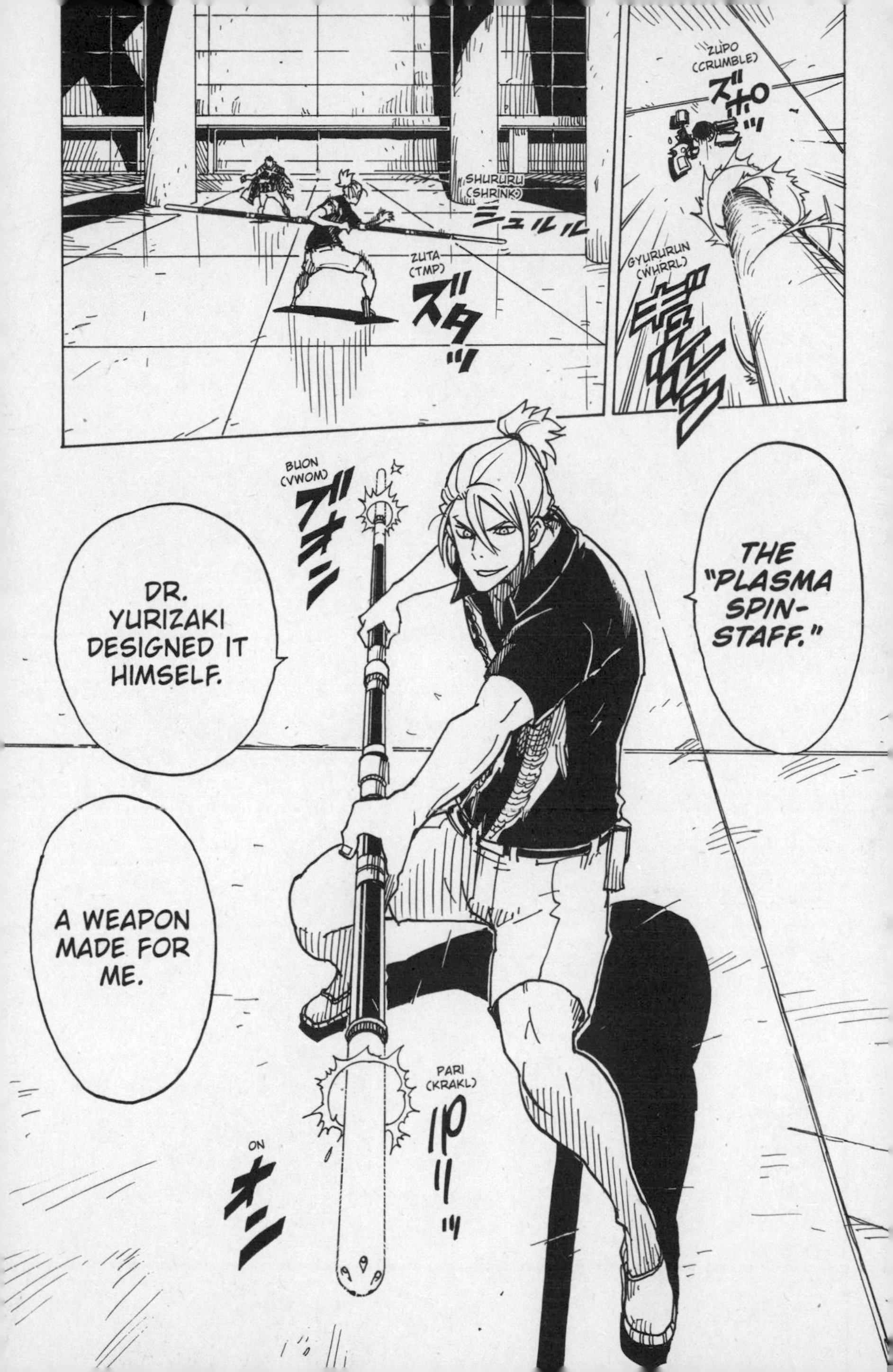
ZUPO (CRUMBLE)
GYURURUN (WHRRL)
SHURURU (SHRINK)
ZUTA (TMP)
THE "PLASMA SPIN-STAFF."
BUON (VWOM)
DR. YURIZAKI DESIGNED IT HIMSELF.
A WEAPON MADE FOR ME.
PARI (KRAKL)
ON

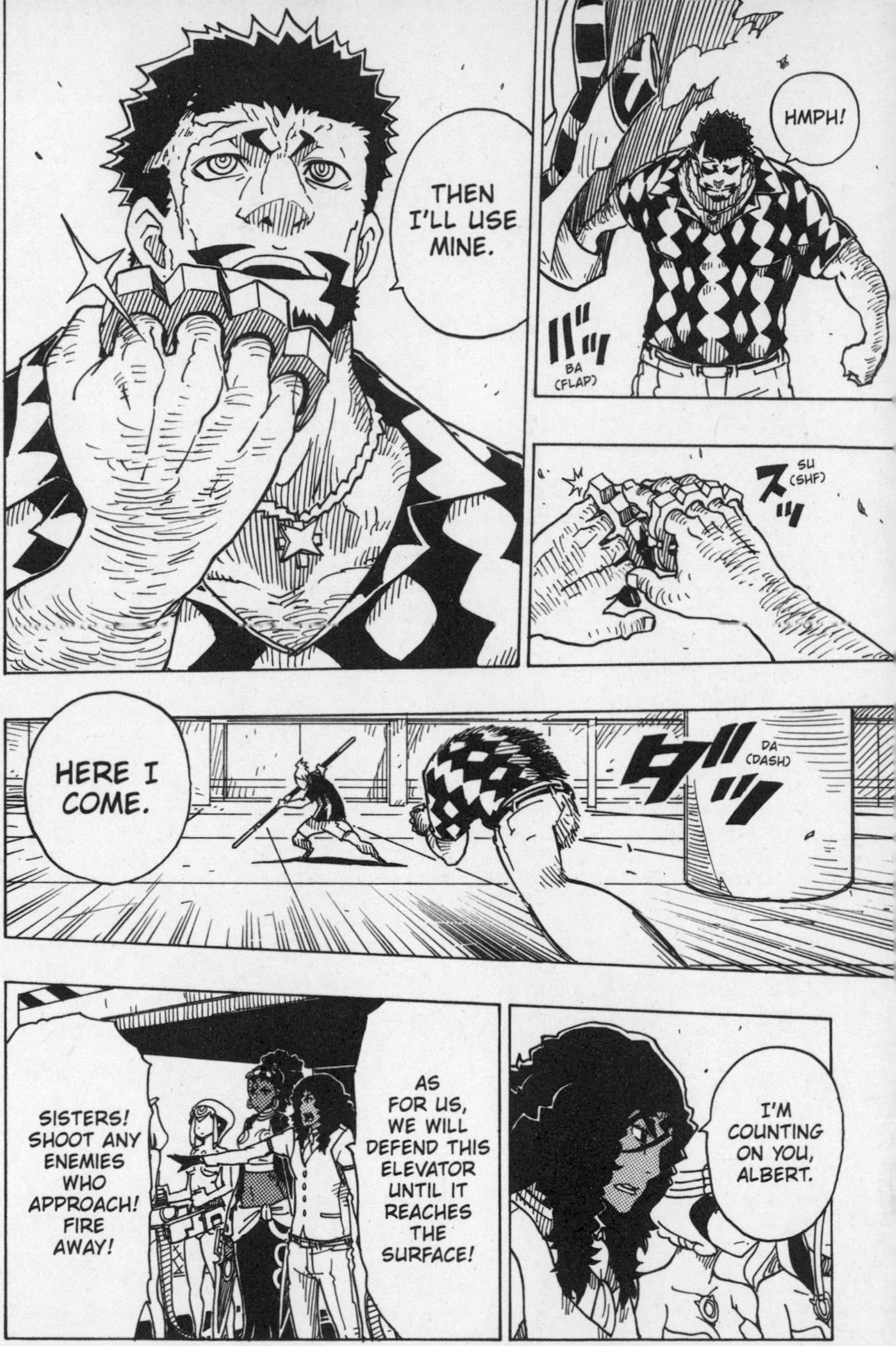
HMPH!
BA (FLAP)
SU (SHF)
THEN I'LL USE MINE.
DA (DASH)
HERE I COME.
I'M COUNTING ON YOU, ALBERT.
AS FOR US, WE WILL DEFEND THIS ELEVATOR UNTIL IT REACHES THE SURFACE!
SISTERS! SHOOT ANY ENEMIES WHO APPROACH! FIRE AWAY!

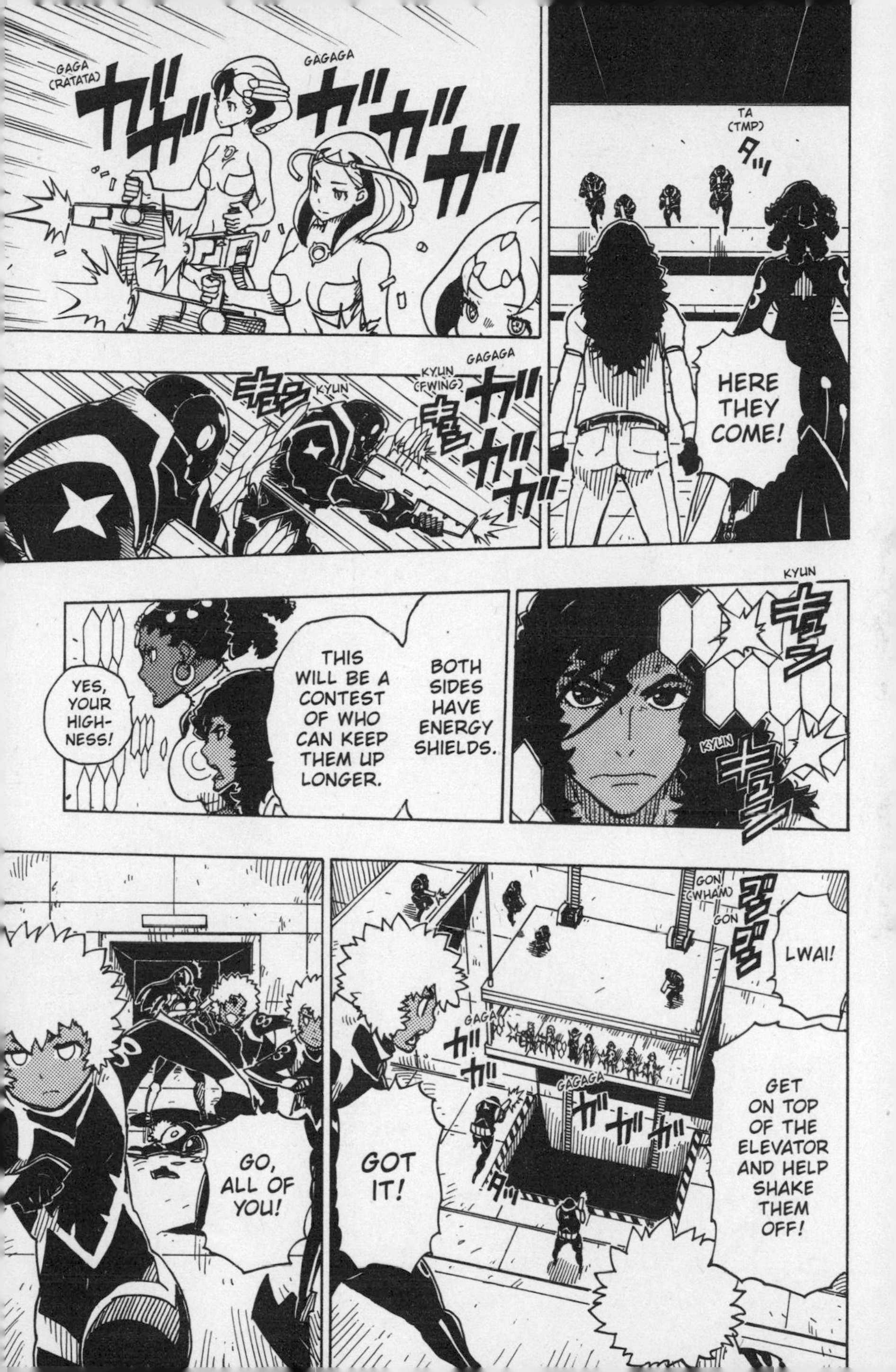
TA
(TMP)
HERE THEY COME!
GAGA
(RATATA)
GAGAGA
GAGAGA
KYUN
(FWING)
KYUN
KYUN
KYUN
BOTH SIDES HAVE ENERGY SHIELDS.
THIS WILL BE A CONTEST OF WHO CAN KEEP THEM UP LONGER.
YES, YOUR HIGH-NESS!
GON
(WHAM)
GON
LWAI!
GET ON TOP OF THE ELEVATOR AND HELP SHAKE THEM OFF!
GAGA
GAGAGA
GOT IT!
GO, ALL OF YOU!

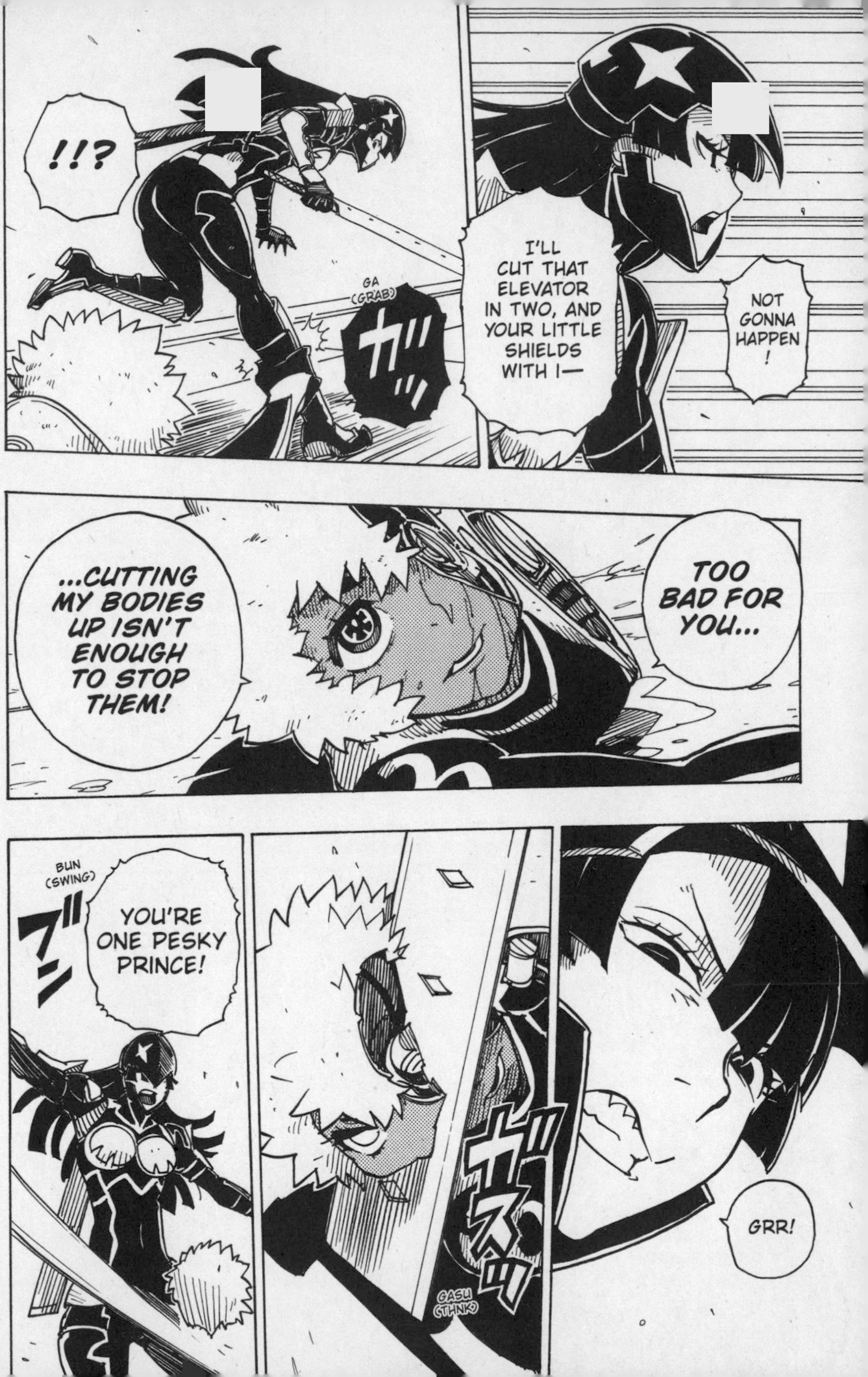
I'LL CUT THAT ELEVATOR IN TWO, AND YOUR LITTLE SHIELDS WITH I—
NOT GONNA HAPPEN!
GA (GRAB)
!!?
TOO BAD FOR YOU...
...CUTTING MY BODIES UP ISN'T ENOUGH TO STOP THEM!
GRR!
GASU (THNK)
BUN (SWING)
YOU'RE ONE PESKY PRINCE!

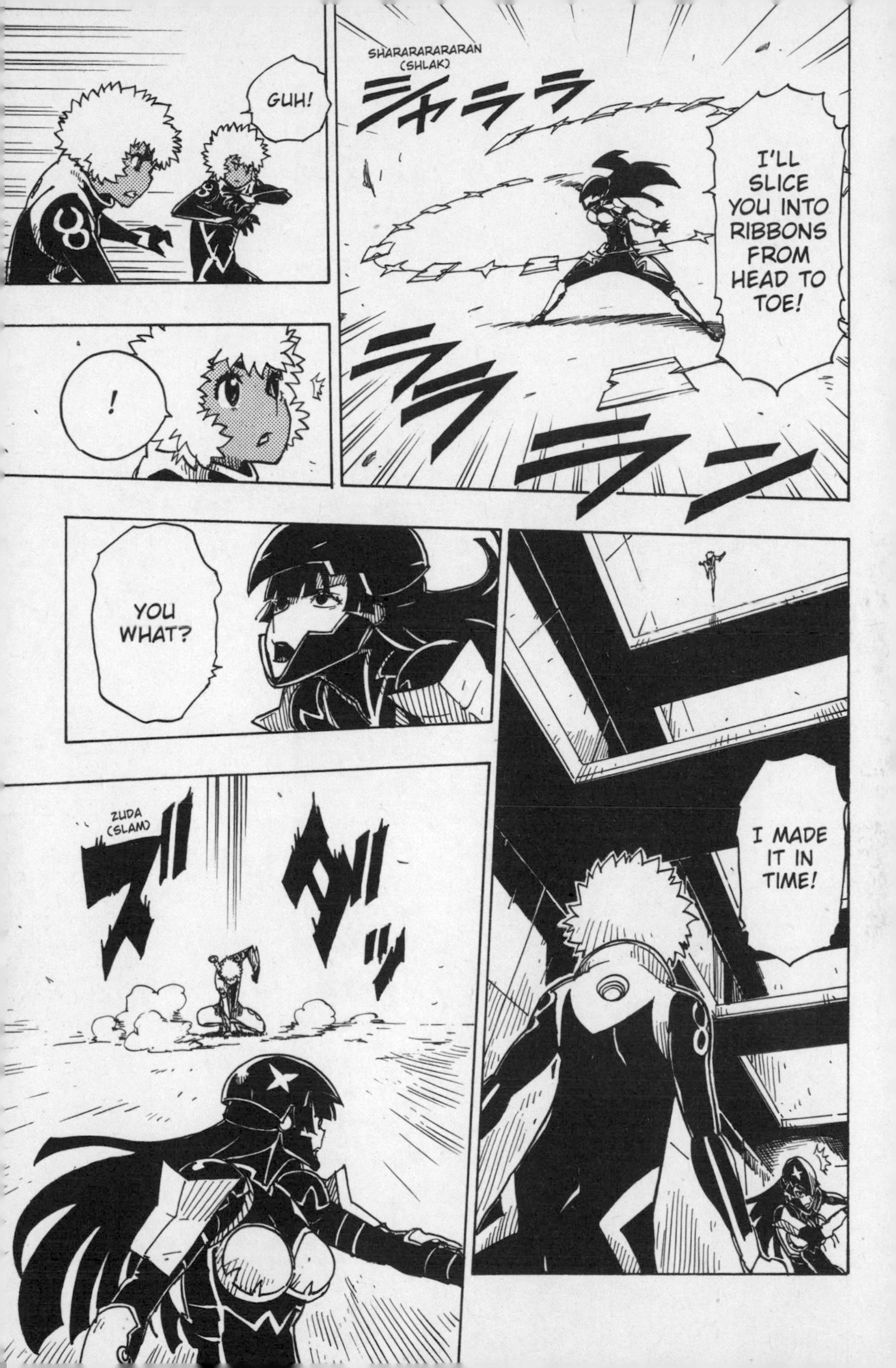
SHARARARARARAN (SHLAK)
シャラララララン
I'LL SLICE YOU INTO RIBBONS FROM HEAD TO TOE!
GUH!
!
I MADE IT IN TIME!
YOU WHAT?
ZUDA (SLAM)
ズダッ

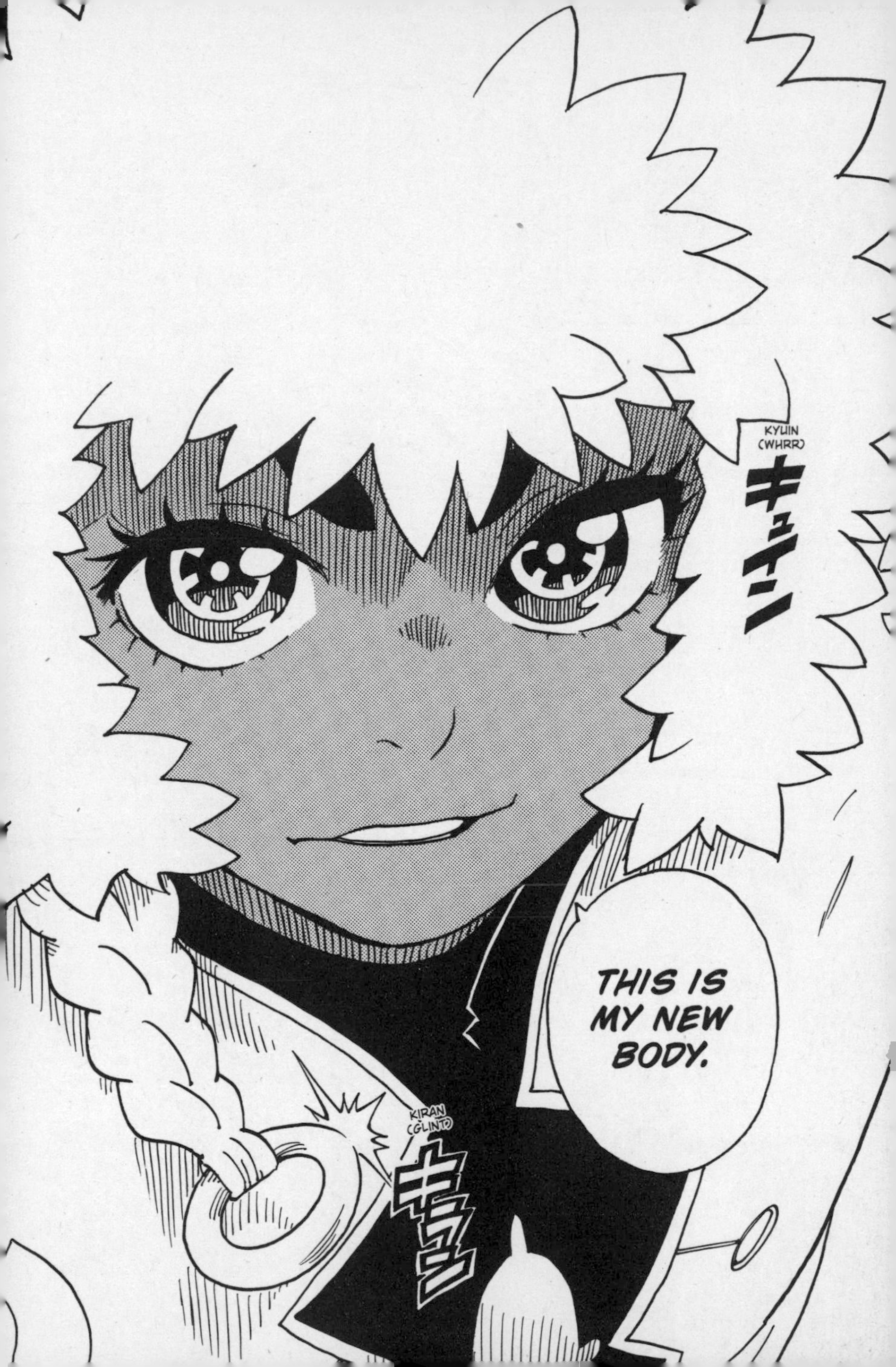
KYUIN (WHRR)
キュイン
THIS IS MY NEW BODY.
KIRAN (GLINT)
キラン

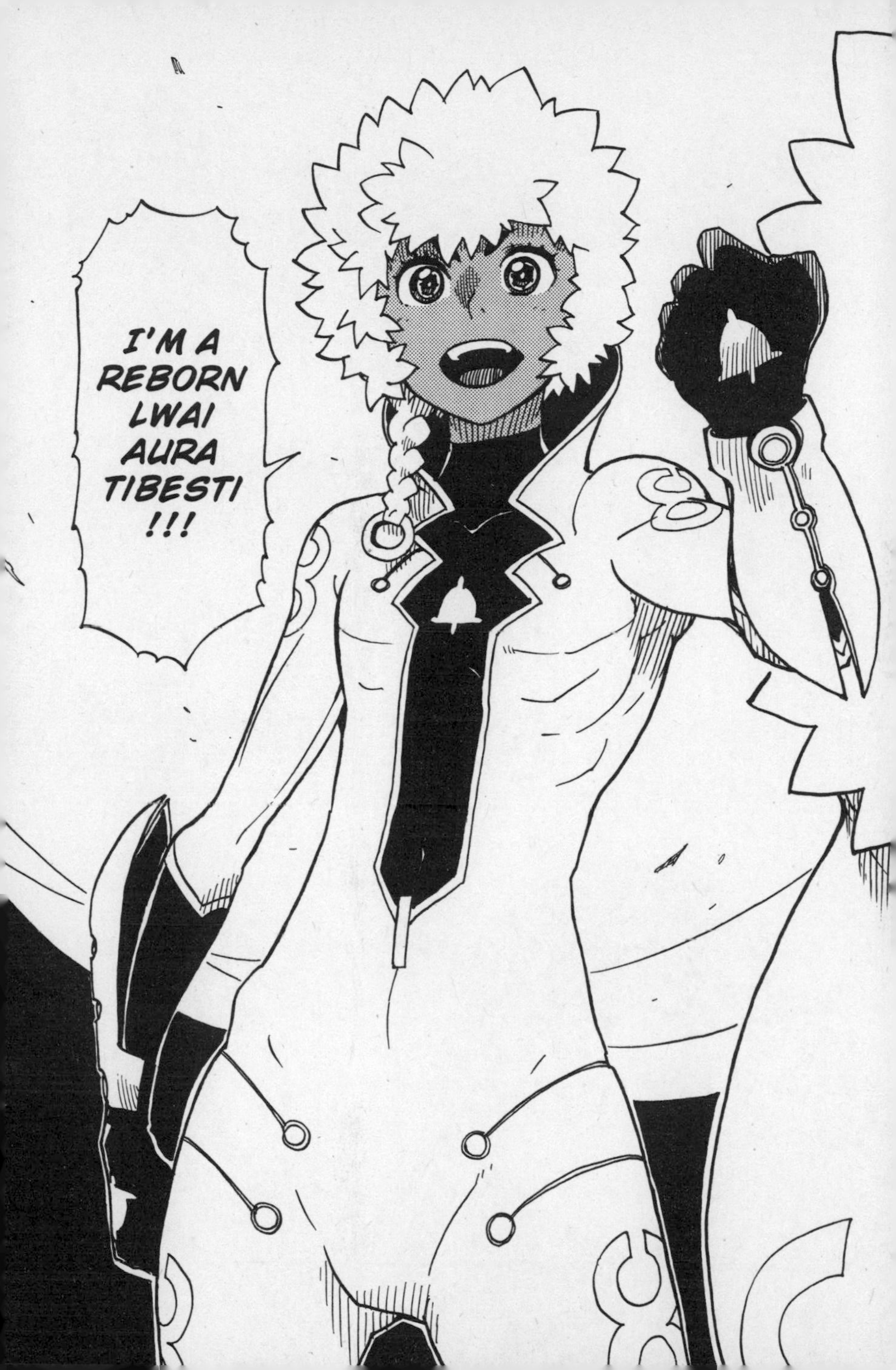
I'M A REBORN LWAI AURA TIBESTI !!!

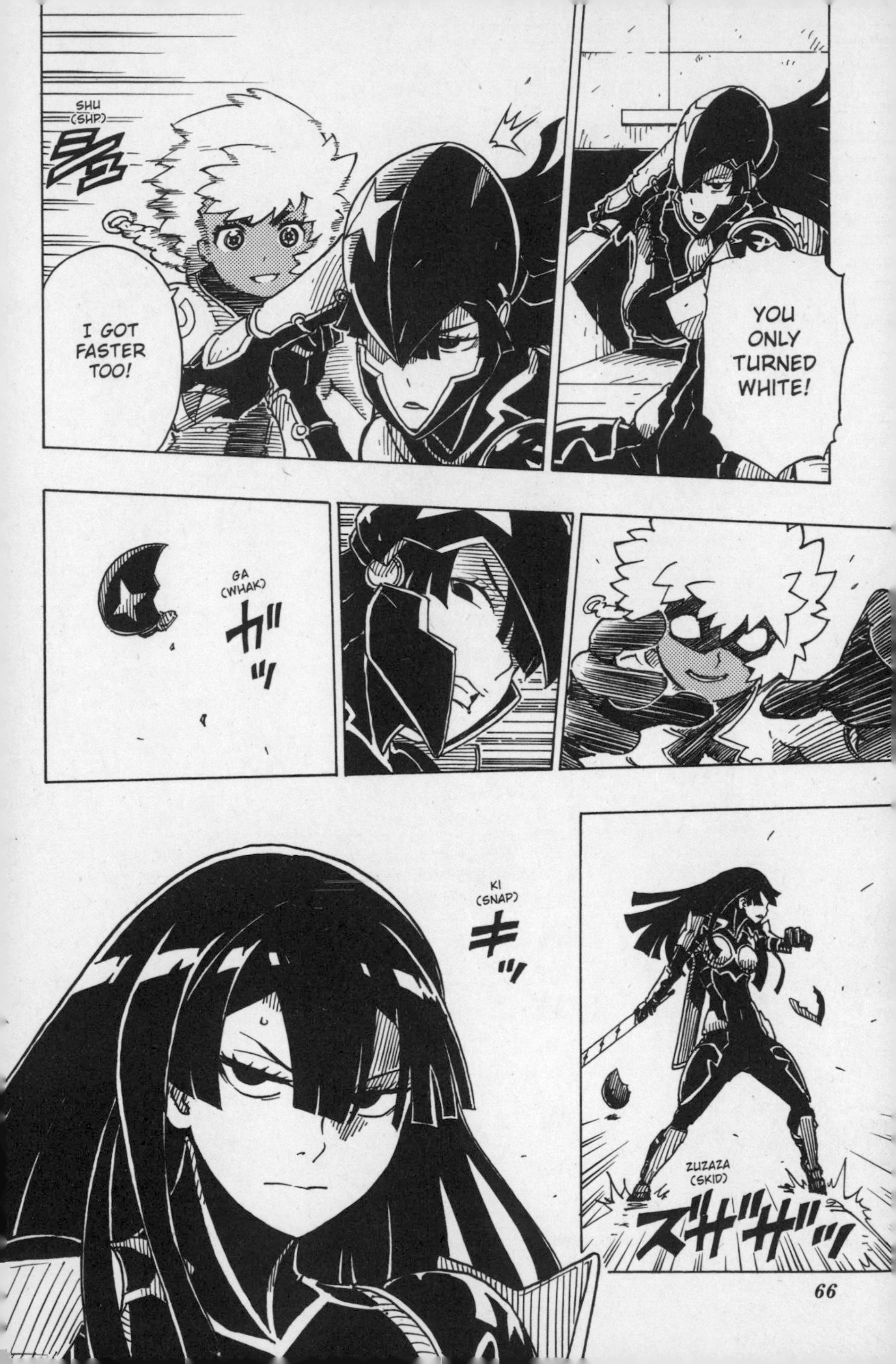
YOU ONLY TURNED WHITE!
SHU (SHP)
I GOT FASTER TOO!
GA (WHAK)
ZUZAZA (SKID)
KI (SNAP)

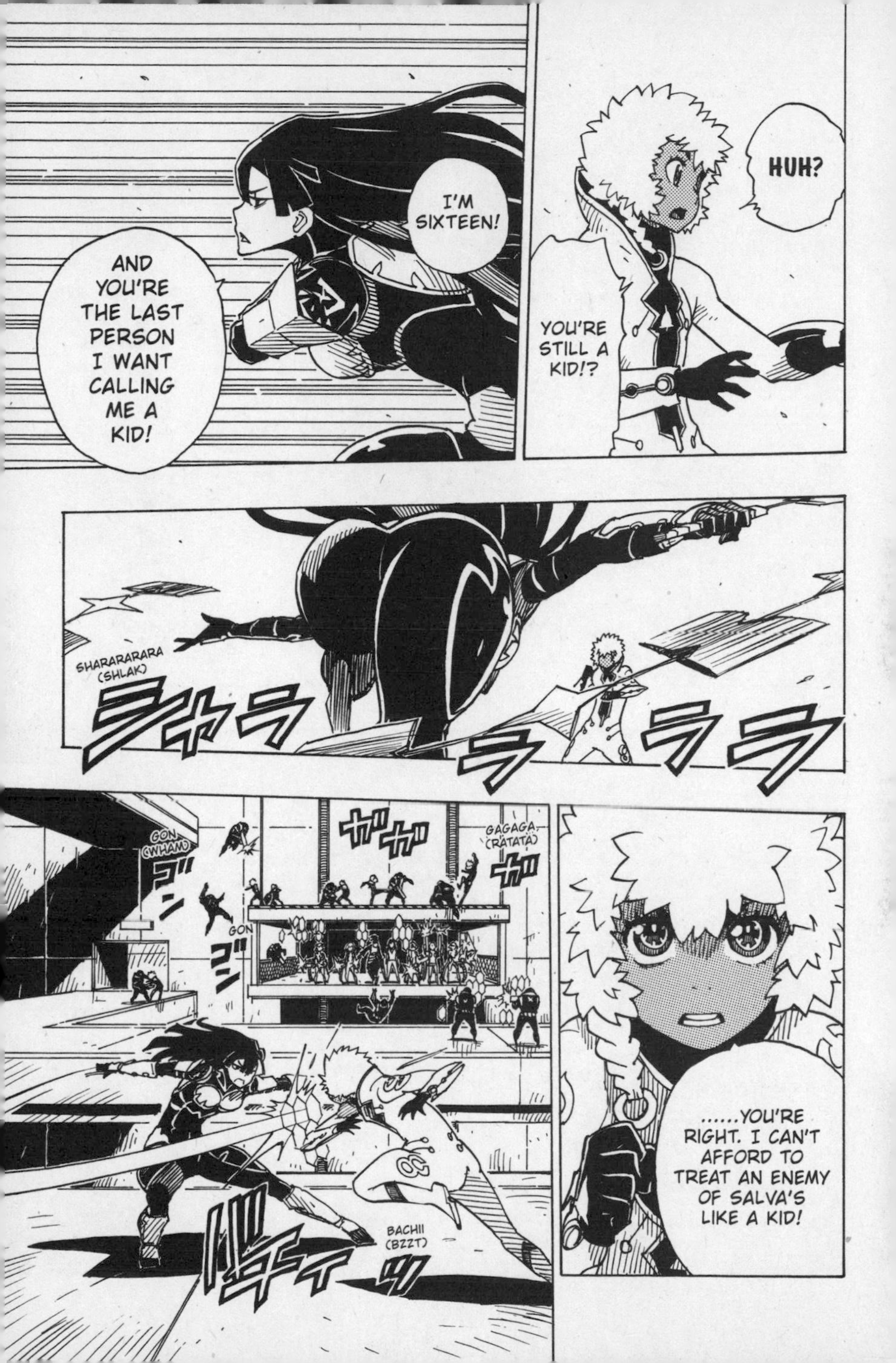
HUH?
YOU'RE STILL A KID!?
I'M SIXTEEN!
AND YOU'RE THE LAST PERSON I WANT CALLING ME A KID!
SHARARARARA (SHLAK)
......YOU'RE RIGHT. I CAN'T AFFORD TO TREAT AN ENEMY OF SALVA'S LIKE A KID!
GAGAGA (RATATA)
GON (WHAM)
GON
BACHII (BZZT)

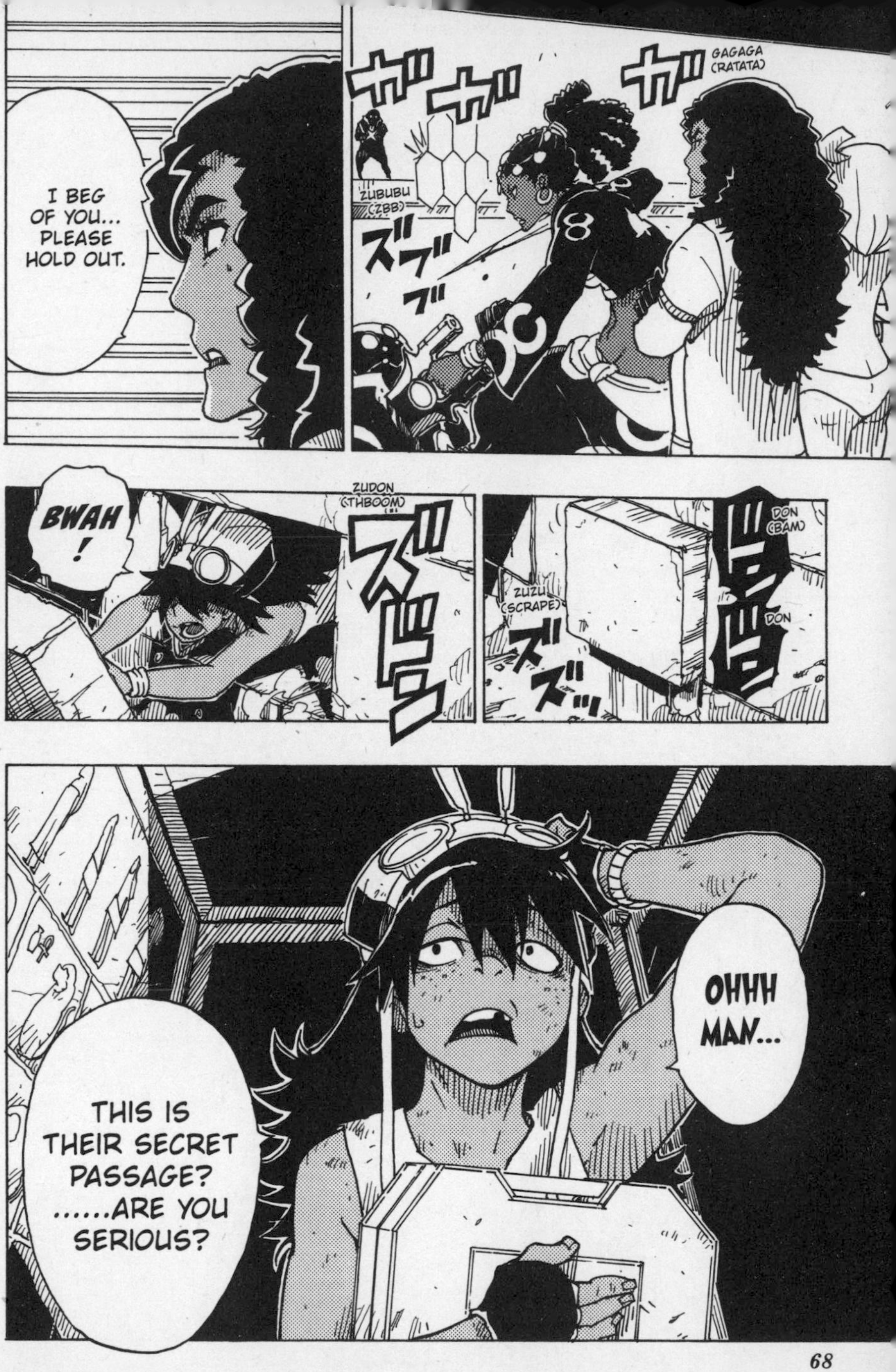
GAGAGA (RATATA)
ZUBUBU (ZBB)
I BEG OF YOU... PLEASE HOLD OUT.
DON (BAM)
DON
ZUZU (SCRAPE)
ZUDON (THBOOM)
BWAH!
OHHH MAN...
THIS IS THEIR SECRET PASSAGE? ......ARE YOU SERIOUS?

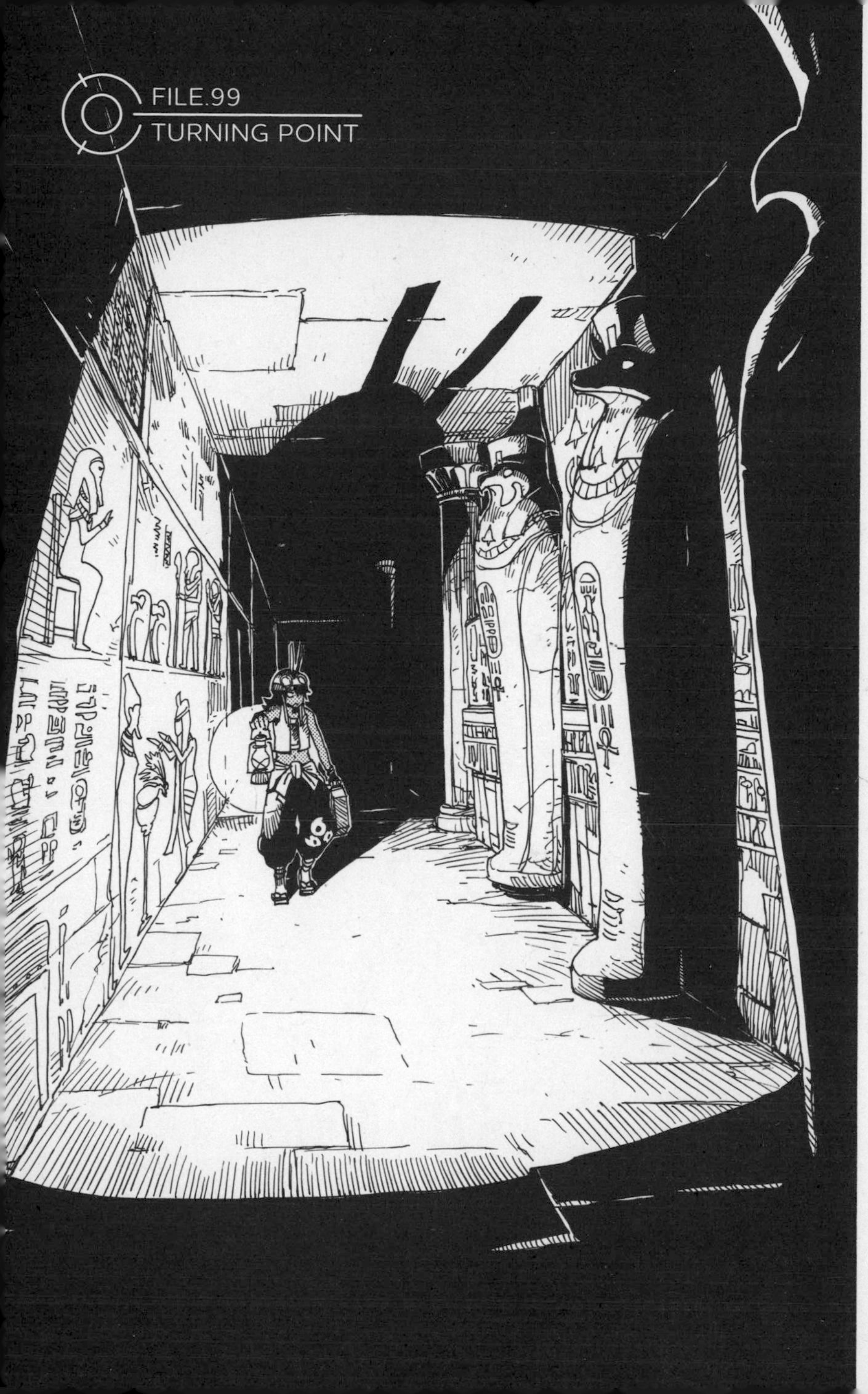
FILE.99
TURNING POINT

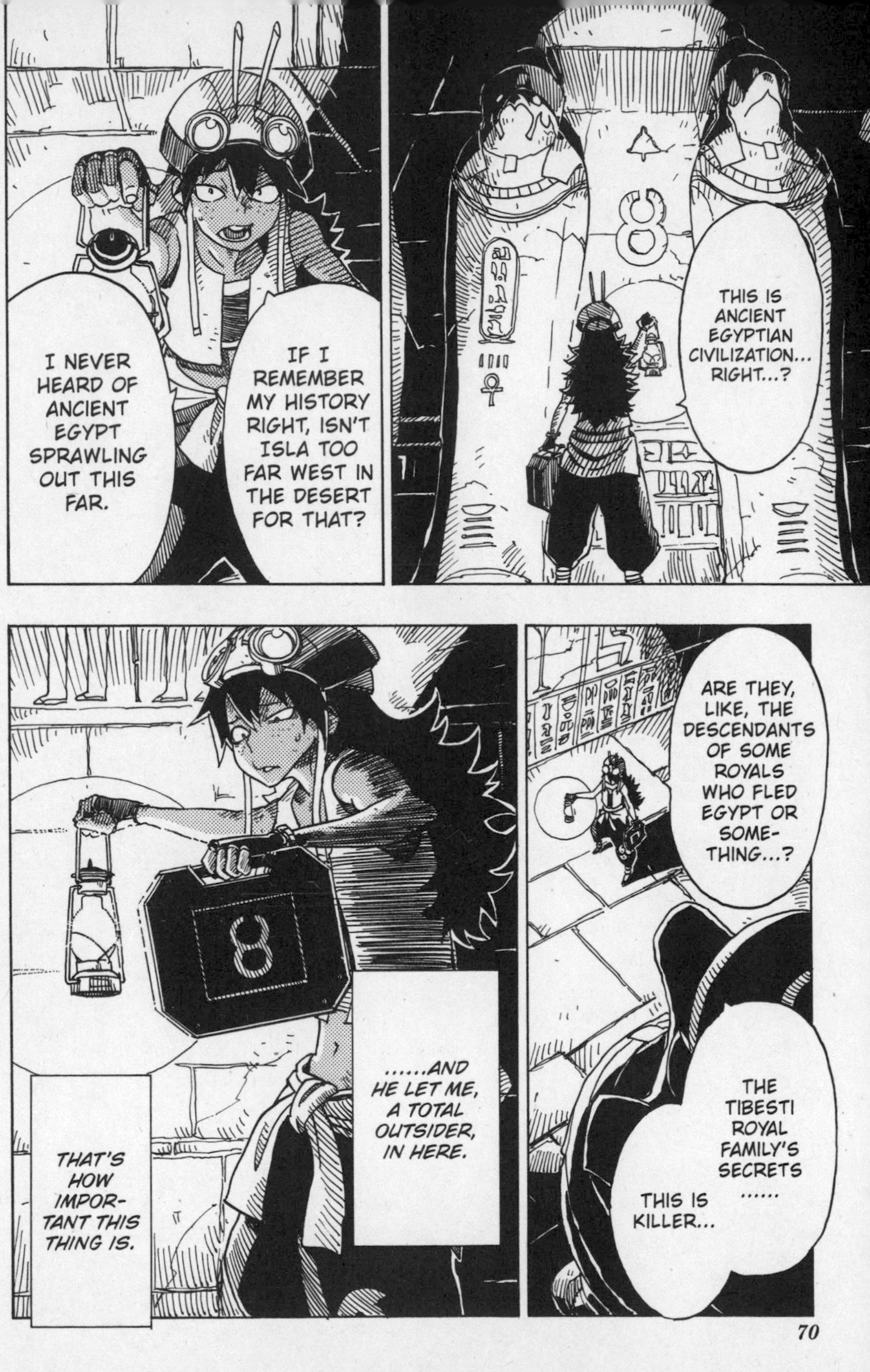
THIS IS ANCIENT EGYPTIAN CIVILIZATION... RIGHT...?
IF I REMEMBER MY HISTORY RIGHT, ISN'T ISLA TOO FAR WEST IN THE DESERT FOR THAT?
I NEVER HEARD OF ANCIENT EGYPT SPRAWLING OUT THIS FAR.
ARE THEY, LIKE, THE DESCENDANTS OF SOME ROYALS WHO FLED EGYPT OR SOME-THING...?
THE TIBESTI ROYAL FAMILY'S SECRETS ......
THIS IS KILLER...
......AND HE LET ME, A TOTAL OUTSIDER, IN HERE.
THAT'S HOW IMPOR-TANT THIS THING IS.

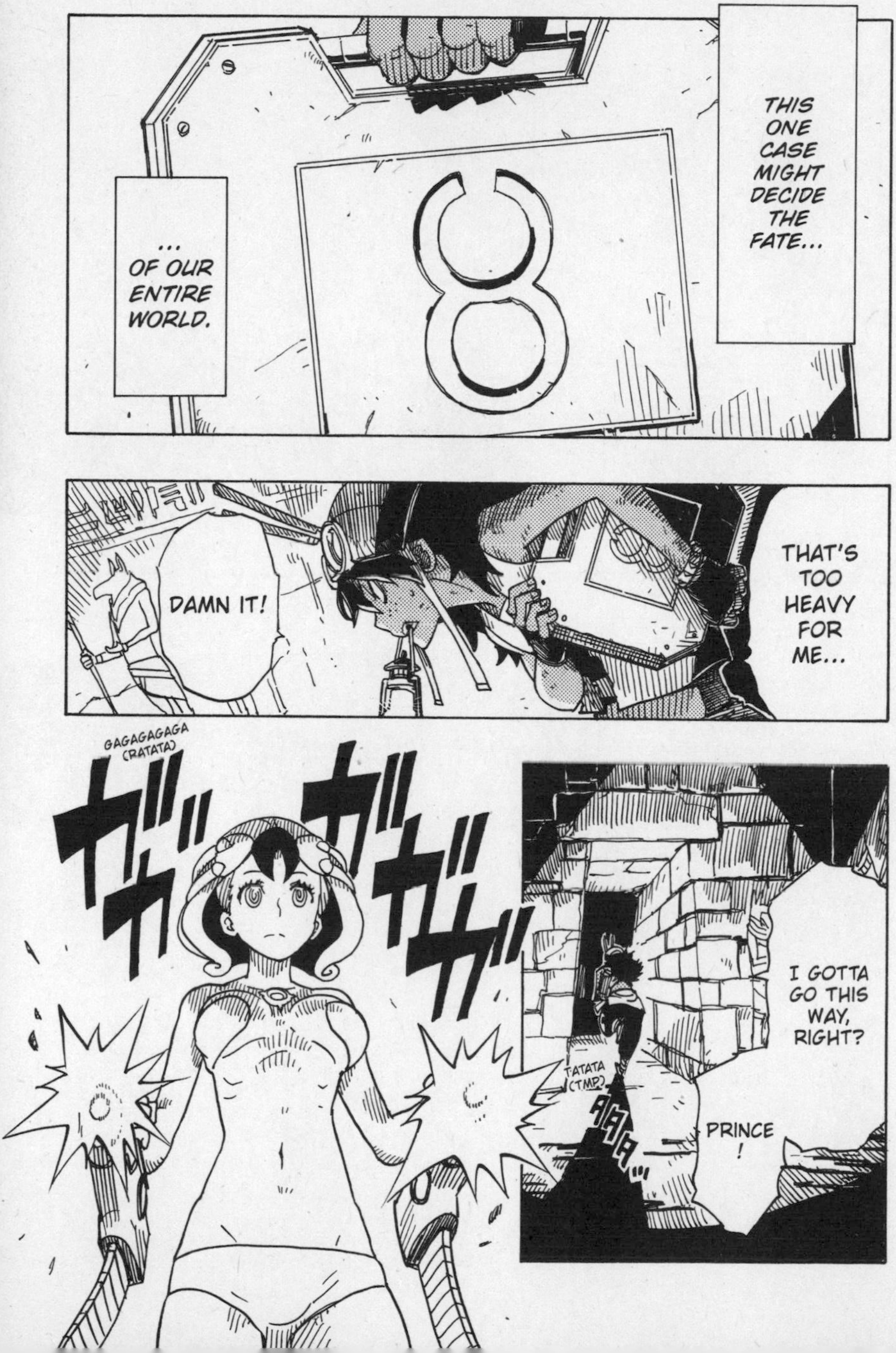
THIS ONE CASE MIGHT DECIDE THE FATE...
... OF OUR ENTIRE WORLD.
THAT'S TOO HEAVY FOR ME...
DAMN IT!
I GOTTA GO THIS WAY, RIGHT?
TATATA (TMP)
PRINCE!
GAGAGAGAGA (RATATA)

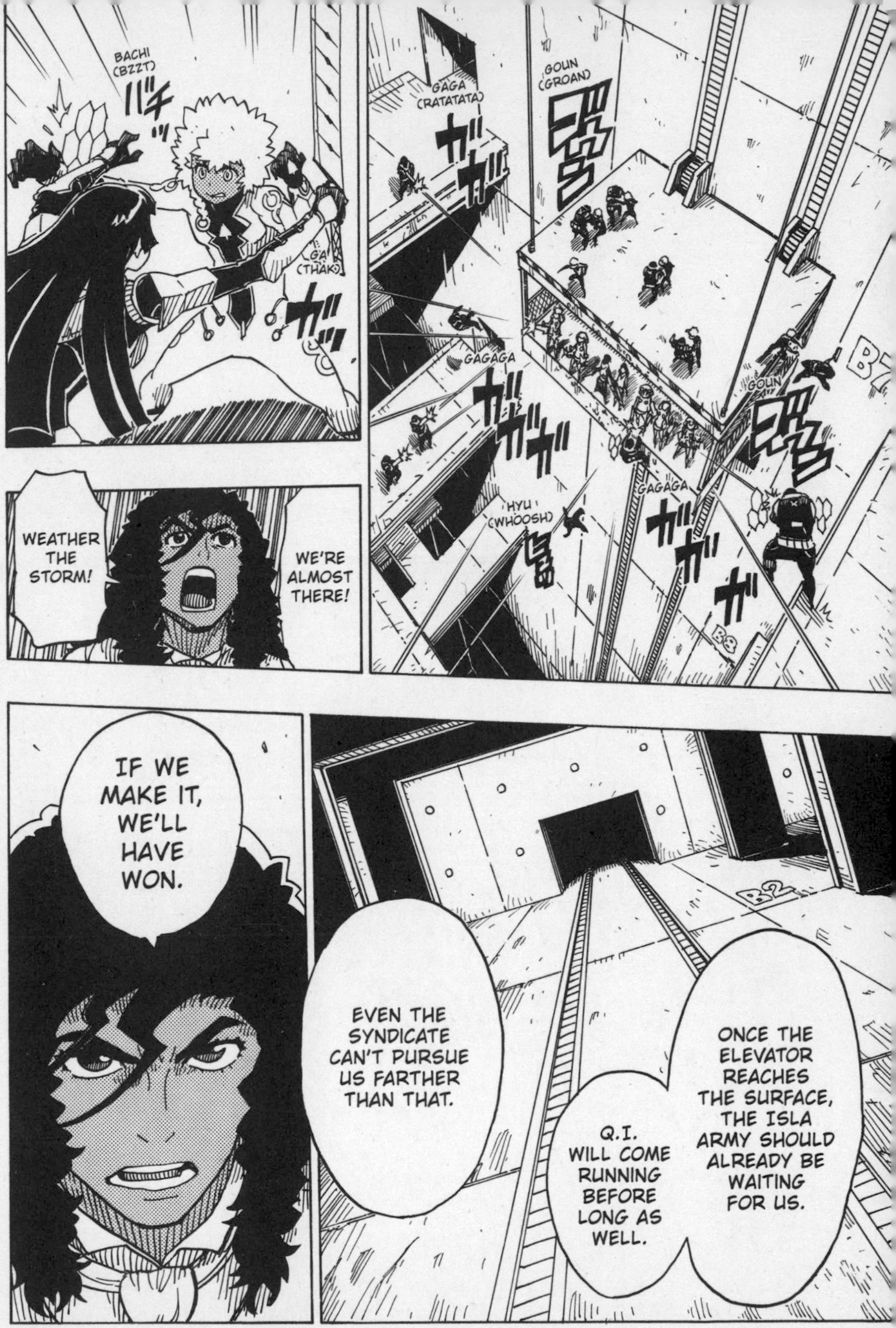
GOUN (GROAN)
GAGA (RATATATA)
B7
GOUN
GAGAGA
GAGAGA
HYU (WHOOSH)
B8
BACHI (BZZT)
GA (THAK)
WE'RE ALMOST THERE!
WEATHER THE STORM!
ONCE THE ELEVATOR REACHES THE SURFACE, THE ISLA ARMY SHOULD ALREADY BE WAITING FOR US.
Q.I. WILL COME RUNNING BEFORE LONG AS WELL.
EVEN THE SYNDICATE CAN'T PURSUE US FARTHER THAN THAT.
B2
IF WE MAKE IT, WE'LL HAVE WON.

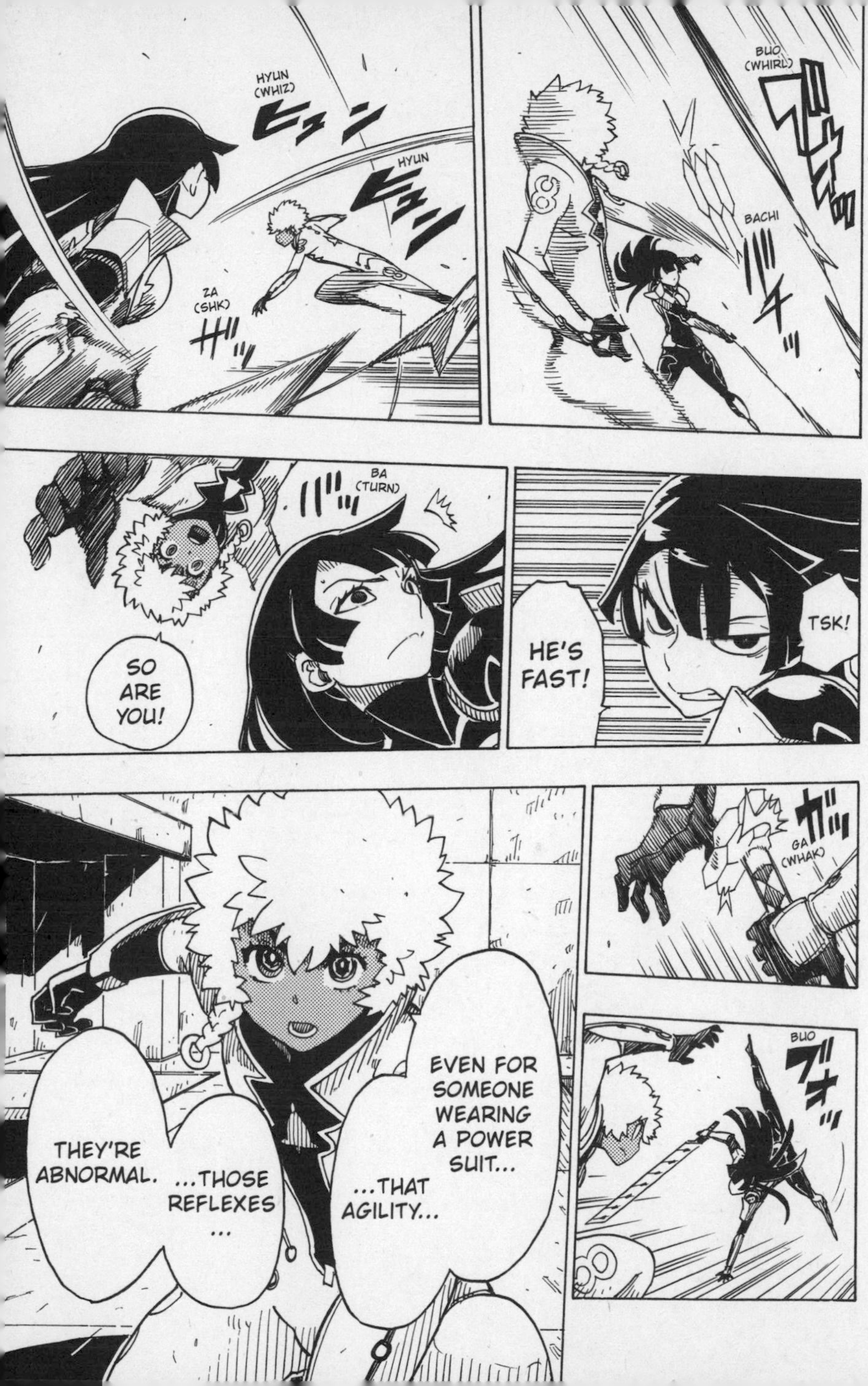
BUO (WHIRL)
BACHI
HYUN (WHIZ)
HYUN
ZA (SHK)
TSK!
HE'S FAST!
BA (TURN)
SO ARE YOU!
GA (WHAK)
BUO
EVEN FOR SOMEONE WEARING A POWER SUIT...
...THAT AGILITY...
...THOSE REFLEXES ...
THEY'RE ABNORMAL.

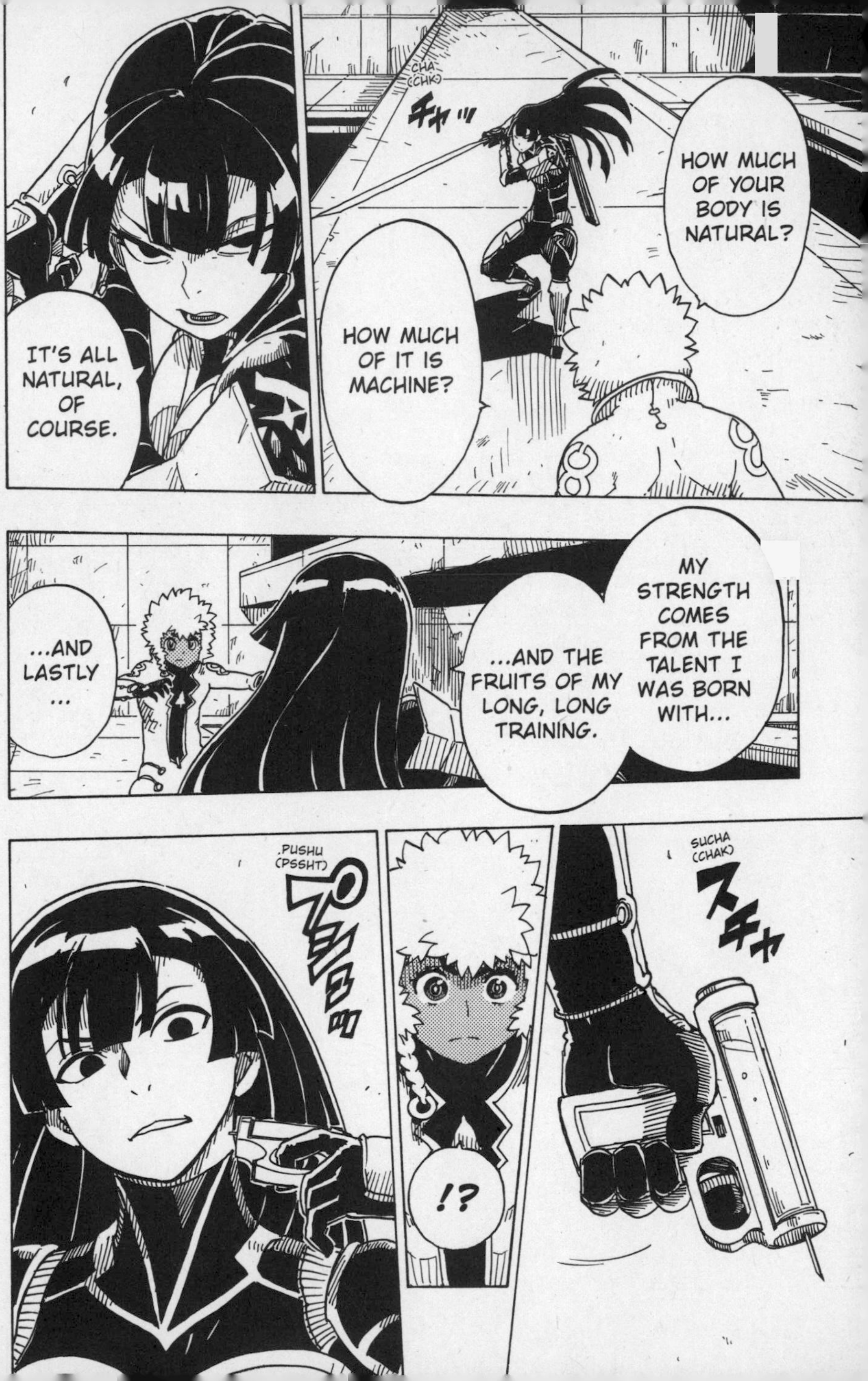
CHA (CHK)
チャッ
HOW MUCH OF YOUR BODY IS NATURAL?
HOW MUCH OF IT IS MACHINE?
IT'S ALL NATURAL, OF COURSE.
MY STRENGTH COMES FROM THE TALENT I WAS BORN WITH...
...AND THE FRUITS OF MY LONG, LONG TRAINING.
...AND LASTLY ...
SUCHA (CHAK)
スチャ
!?
PUSHU (PSSHT)

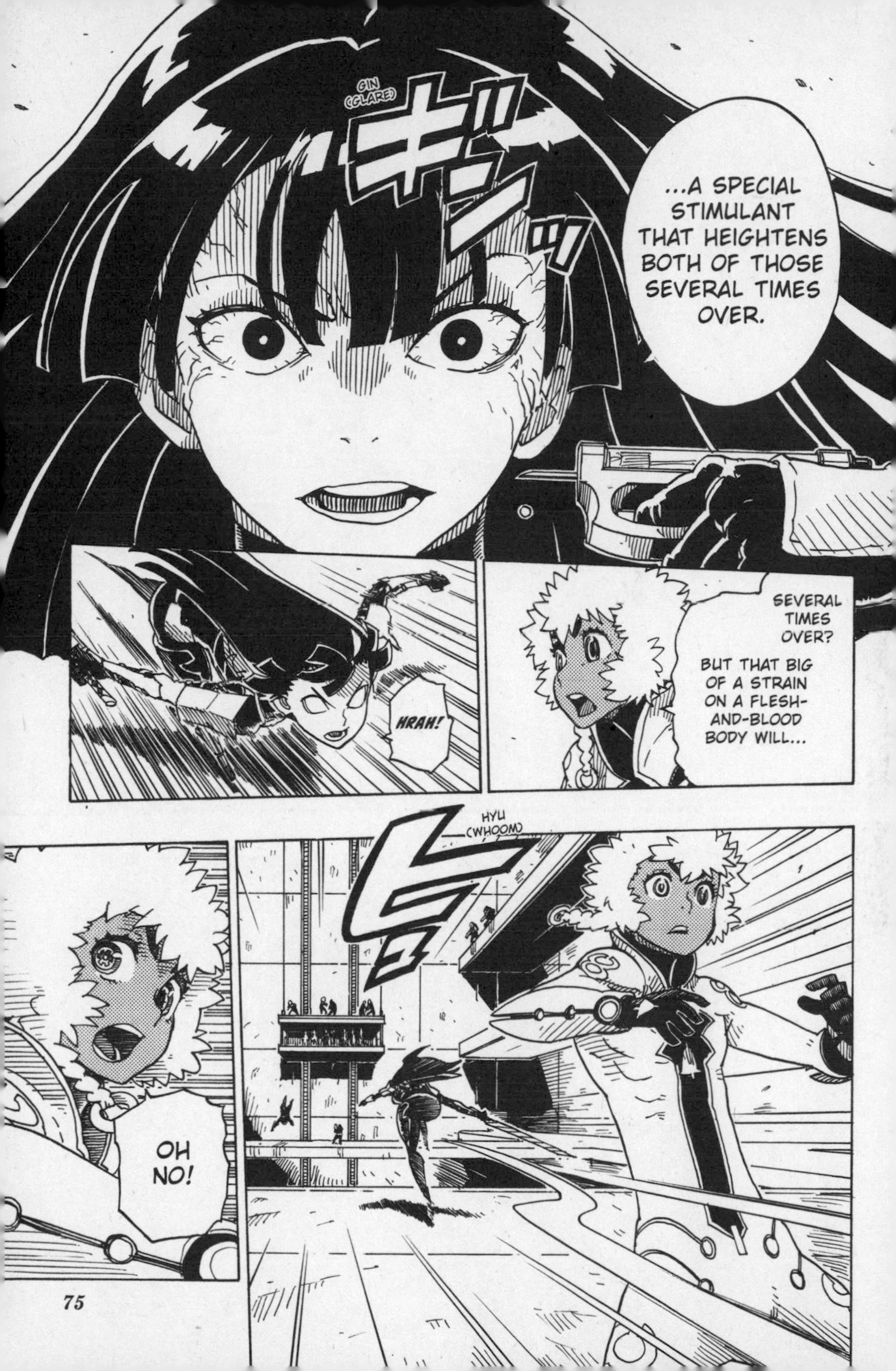
...A SPECIAL STIMULANT THAT HEIGHTENS BOTH OF THOSE SEVERAL TIMES OVER.
GIN (GLARE)
SEVERAL TIMES OVER?
BUT THAT BIG OF A STRAIN ON A FLESH-AND-BLOOD BODY WILL...
HRAH!
HYU (WHOOM)
OH NO!

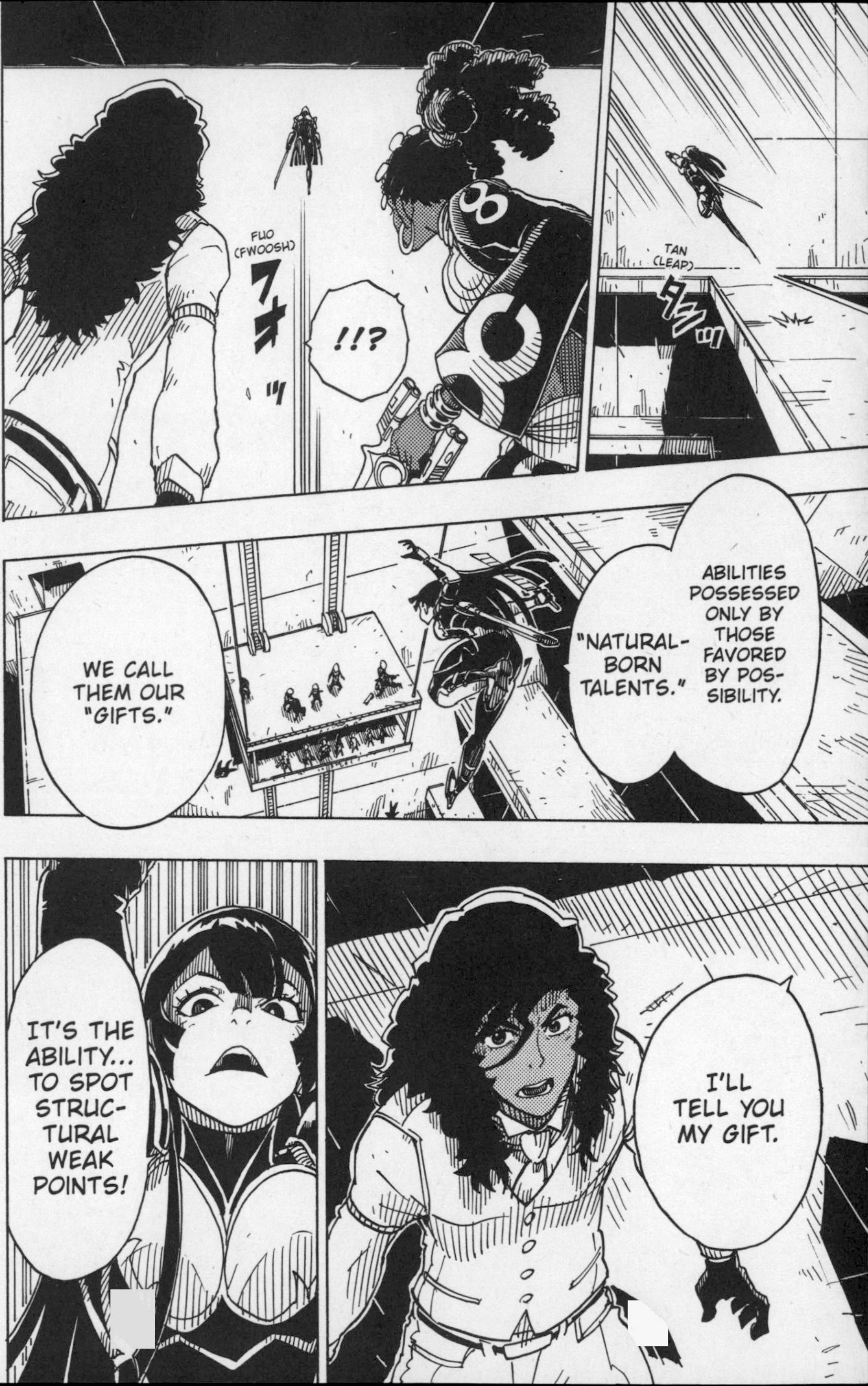
TAN (LEAP)
タンッ
FUO (FWOOSH)
フォッ
!!?
ABILITIES POSSESSED ONLY BY THOSE FAVORED BY POS-SIBILITY.
"NATURAL-BORN TALENTS."
WE CALL THEM OUR "GIFTS."
I'LL TELL YOU MY GIFT.
IT'S THE ABILITY... TO SPOT STRUC-TURAL WEAK POINTS!

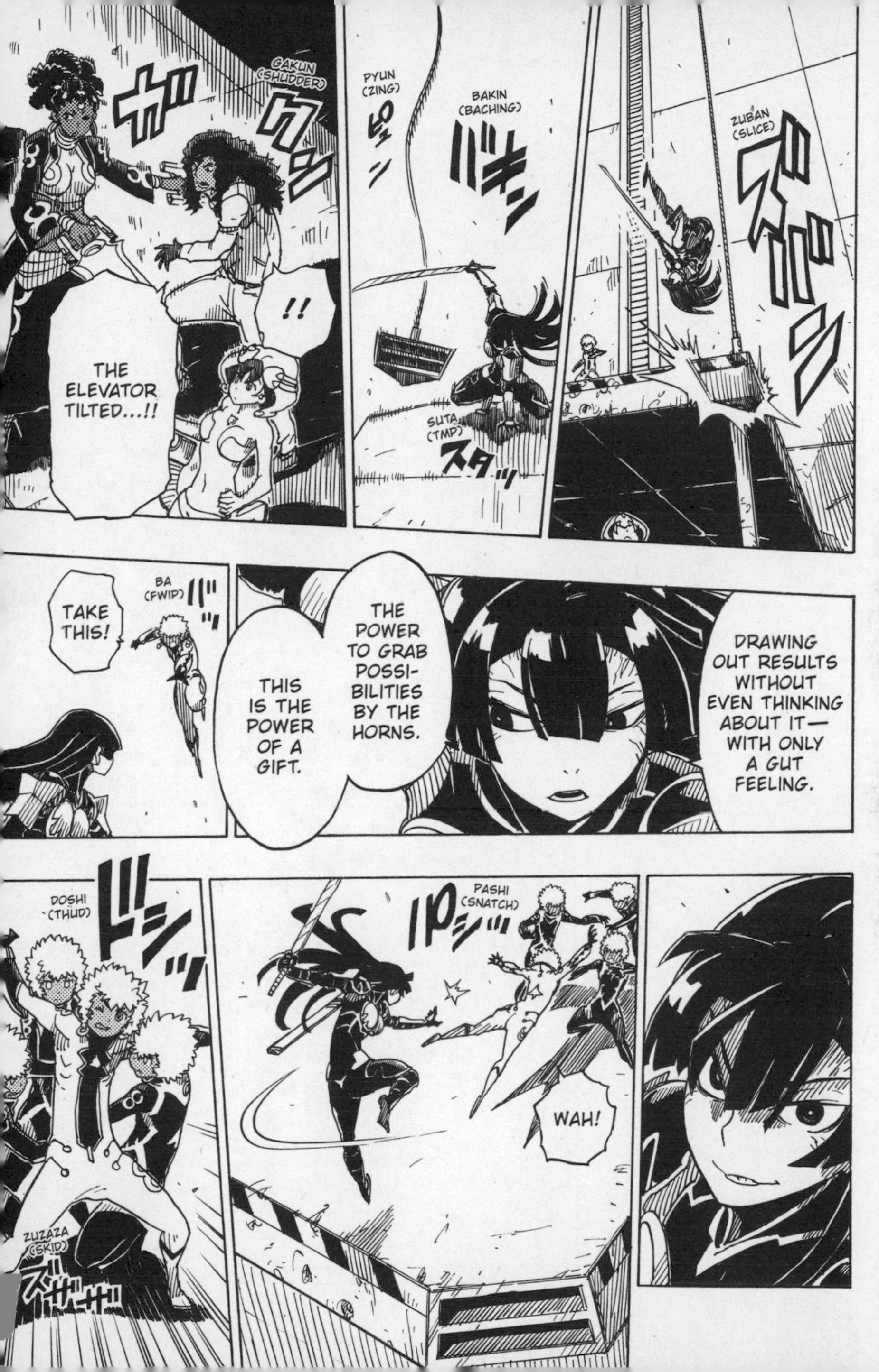
ZUBAN (SLICE)
PYUN (ZING)
BAKIN (BACHING)
SUTA (TMP)
GAKUN (SHUDDER)
!!
THE ELEVATOR TILTED...!!
DRAWING OUT RESULTS WITHOUT EVEN THINKING ABOUT IT— WITH ONLY A GUT FEELING.
THE POWER TO GRAB POSSI-BILITIES BY THE HORNS.
THIS IS THE POWER OF A GIFT.
BA (FWIP)
TAKE THIS!
PASHI (SNATCH)
WAH!
DOSHI (THUD)
ZUZAZA (SKID)

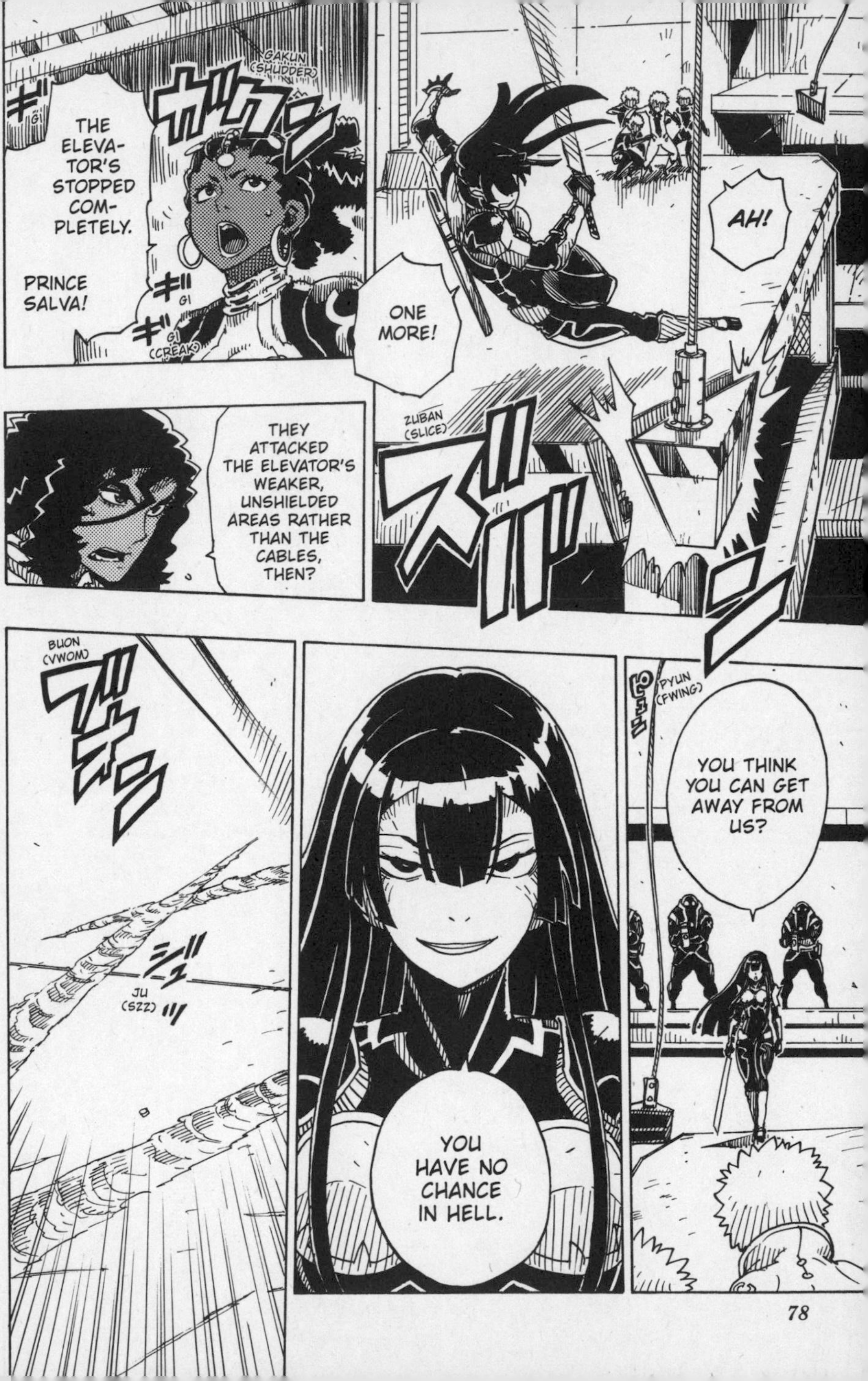
AH!
ONE MORE!
ZUBAN (SLICE)
GAKUN (SHUDDER)
GI
THE ELEVATOR'S STOPPED COMPLETELY.
PRINCE SALVA!
GI
GI (CREAK)
THEY ATTACKED THE ELEVATOR'S WEAKER, UNSHIELDED AREAS RATHER THAN THE CABLES, THEN?
PYUN (FWING)
YOU THINK YOU CAN GET AWAY FROM US?
YOU HAVE NO CHANCE IN HELL.
BUON (VWOM)
JU (SZZ)

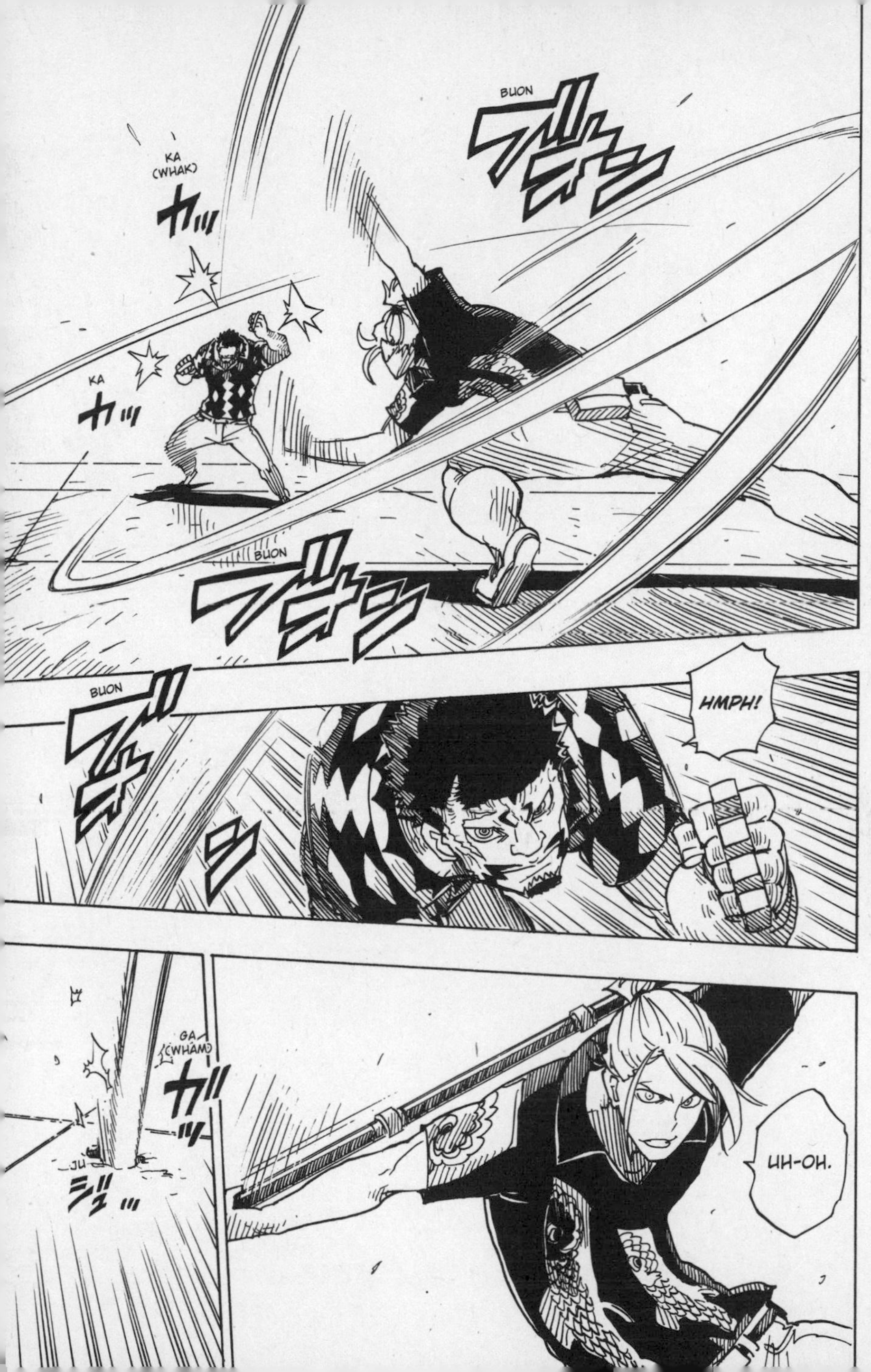

BUON
KA (WHAK)
KA
BUON
HMPH!
BUON
UH-OH.
GA (WHAM)
JU

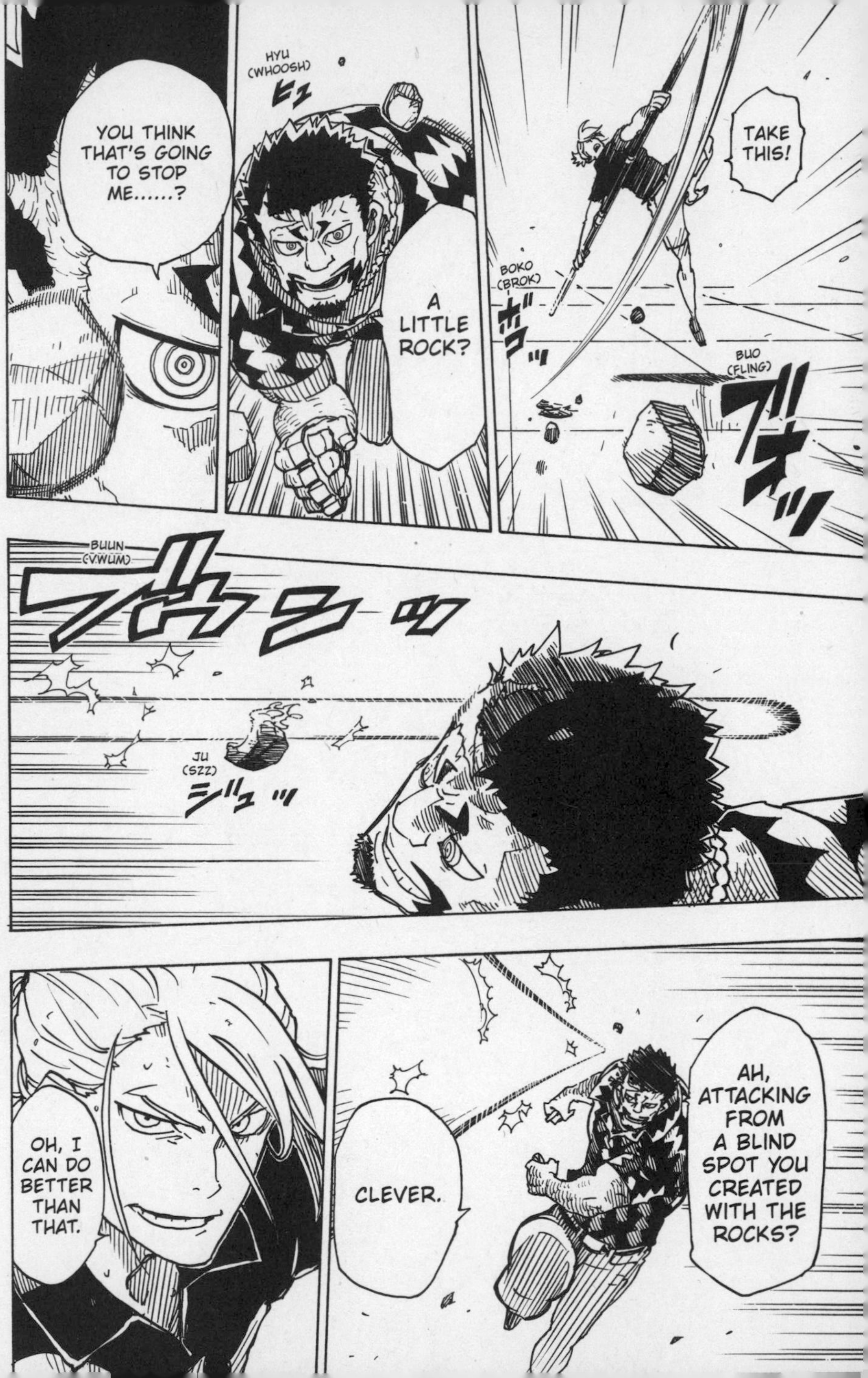
TAKE THIS!
BOKO (BROK)
ボコッ
BUO (FLING)
ブオッ
HYU (WHOOSH)
ヒュ
A LITTLE ROCK?
YOU THINK THAT'S GOING TO STOP ME......?
BUUN (V.WUM)
ブウンッ
JU (SZZ)
ジュッ
AH, ATTACKING FROM A BLIND SPOT YOU CREATED WITH THE ROCKS?
CLEVER.
OH, I CAN DO BETTER THAN THAT.

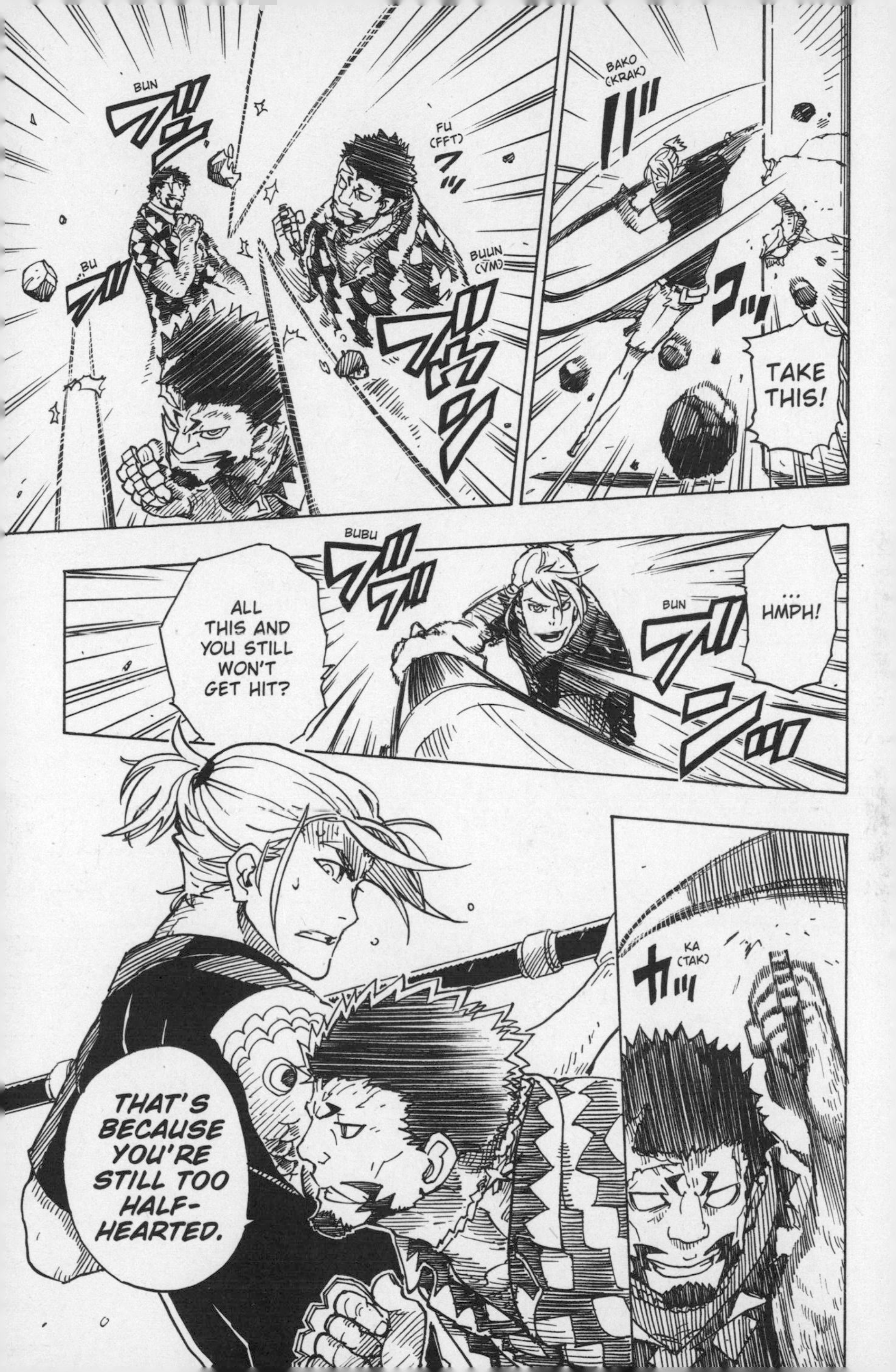
BAKO (KRAK)
TAKE THIS!
BUN
FU (FFT)
BUUN (VM)
BU
... HMPH!
BUN
BUBU
ALL THIS AND YOU STILL WON'T GET HIT?
KA (TAK)
THAT'S BECAUSE YOU'RE STILL TOO HALF-HEARTED.

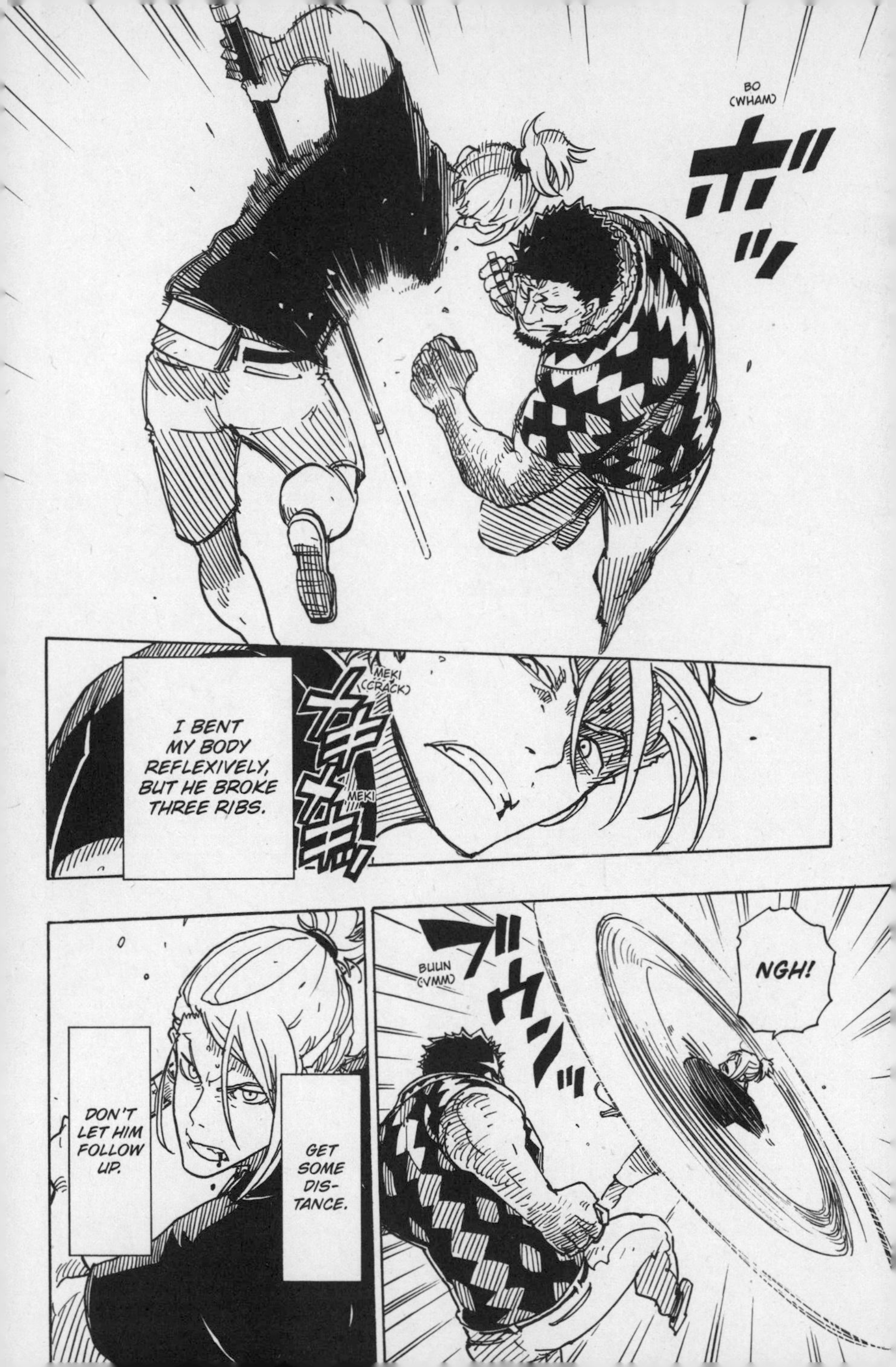

ボッ
BO (WHAM)
メキメキ
MEKI (CRACK)
MEKI
I BENT MY BODY REFLEXIVELY, BUT HE BROKE THREE RIBS.
NGH!
ブウンッ
BUUN (VMM)
GET SOME DIS-TANCE.
DON'T LET HIM FOLLOW UP.

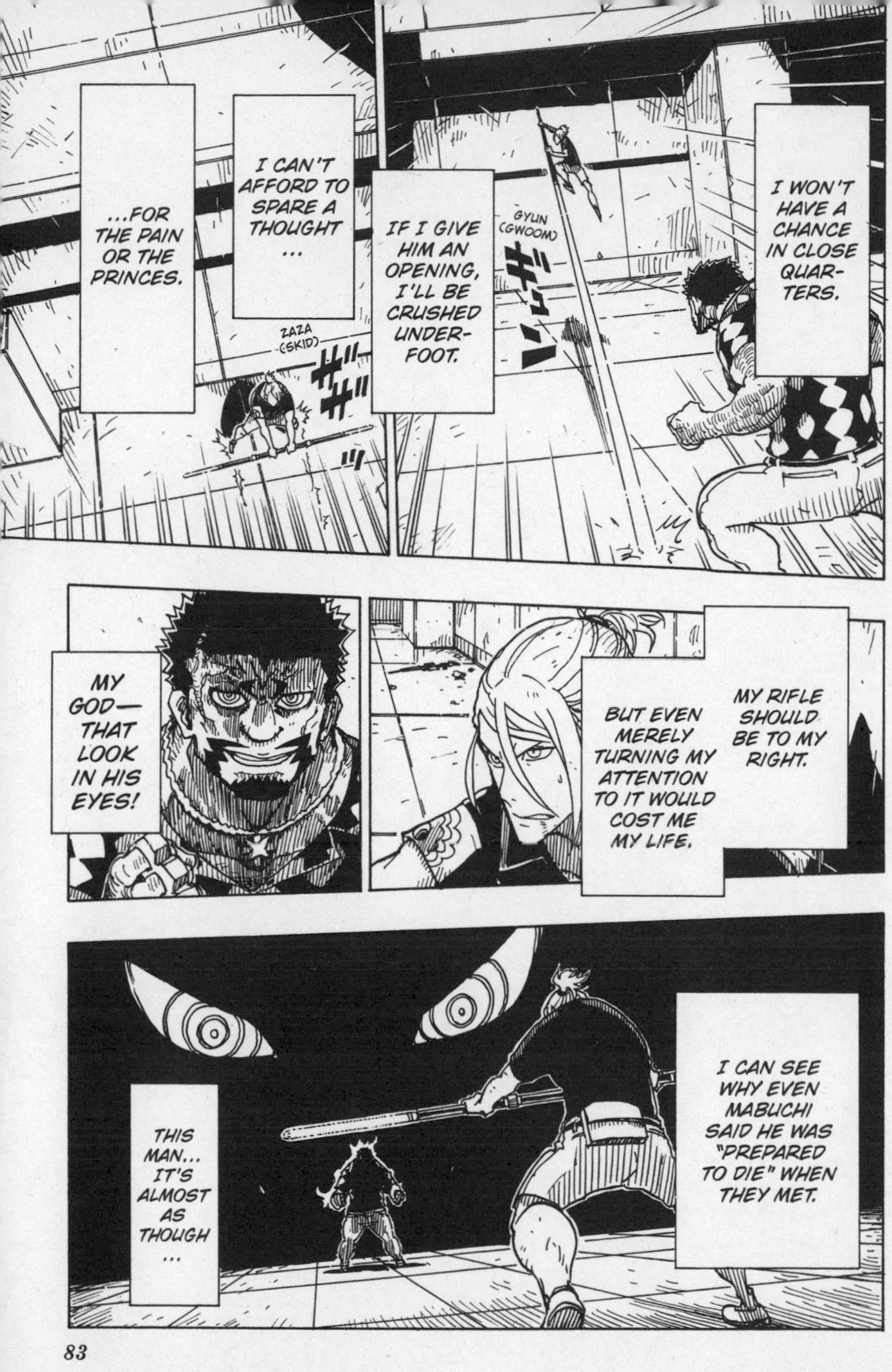
I WON'T HAVE A CHANCE IN CLOSE QUARTERS.
GYUN (GWOOM)
IF I GIVE HIM AN OPENING, I'LL BE CRUSHED UNDERFOOT.
I CAN'T AFFORD TO SPARE A THOUGHT ...
...FOR THE PAIN OR THE PRINCES.
ZAZA (SKID)
MY RIFLE SHOULD BE TO MY RIGHT.
BUT EVEN MERELY TURNING MY ATTENTION TO IT WOULD COST ME MY LIFE.
MY GOD—THAT LOOK IN HIS EYES!
I CAN SEE WHY EVEN MABUCHI SAID HE WAS "PREPARED TO DIE" WHEN THEY MET.
THIS MAN... IT'S ALMOST AS THOUGH ...

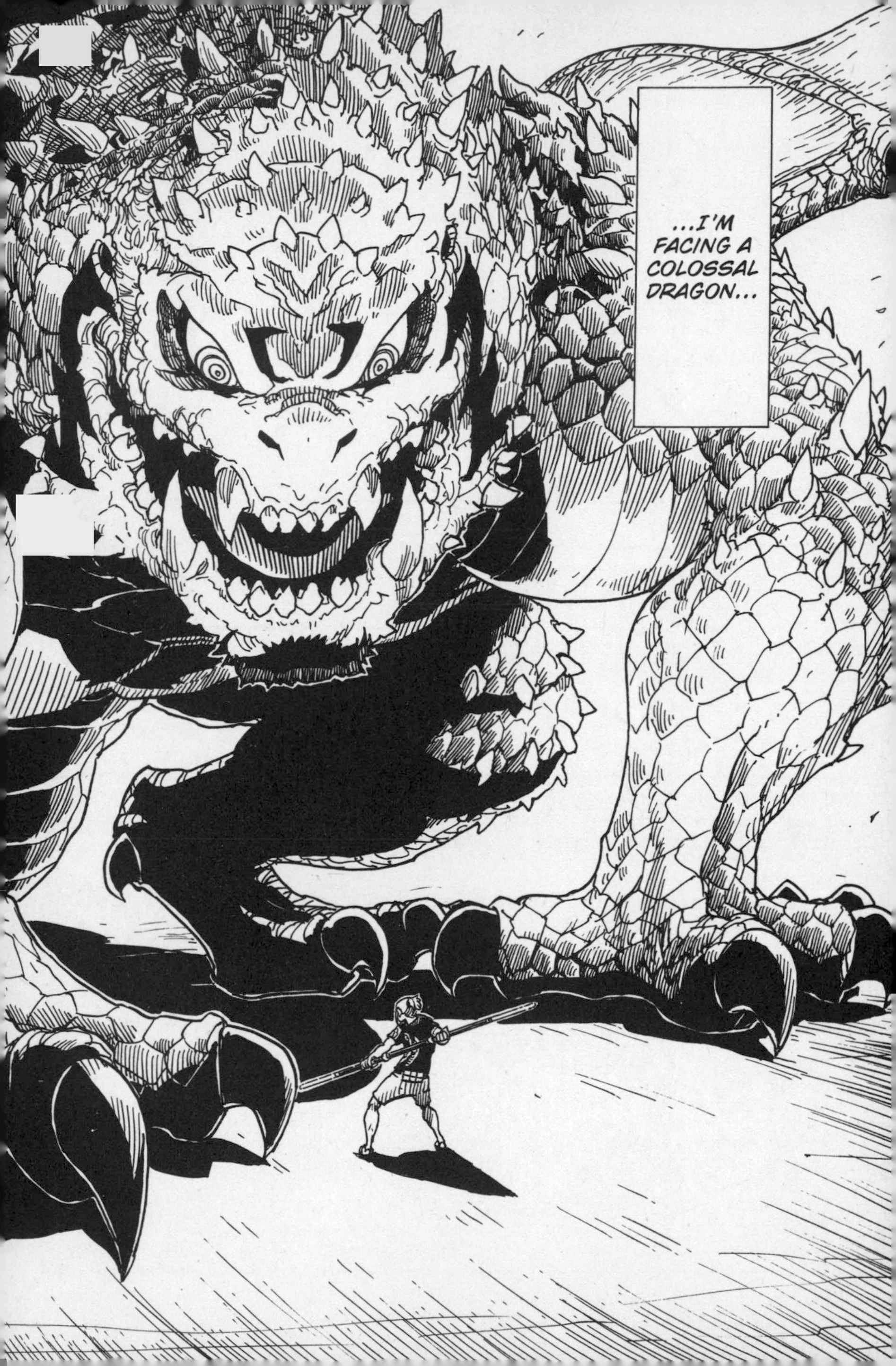
...I'M FACING A COLOSSAL DRAGON...

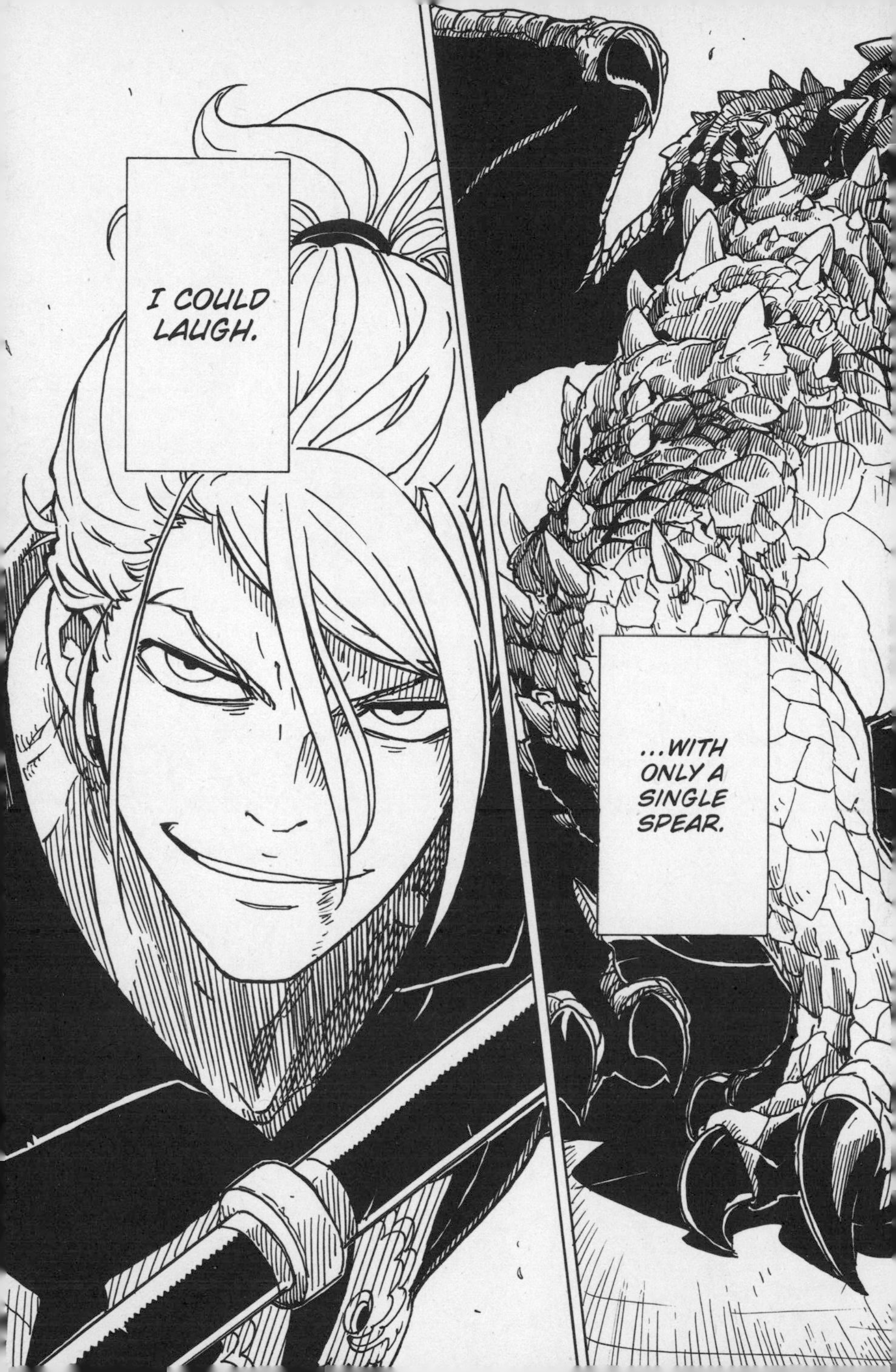
...WITH ONLY A SINGLE SPEAR.
I COULD LAUGH.

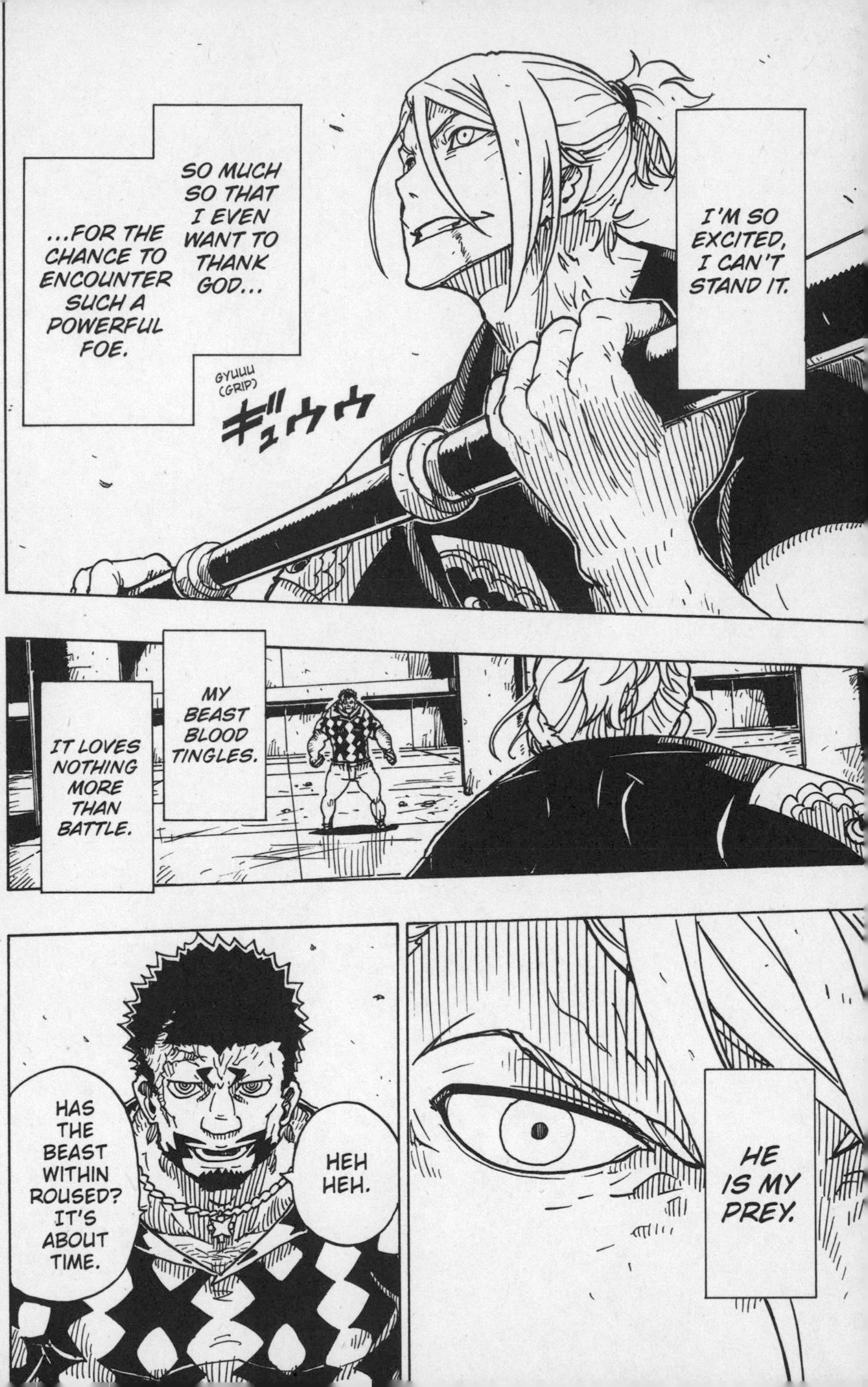
I'M SO EXCITED, I CAN'T STAND IT.
SO MUCH SO THAT I EVEN WANT TO THANK GOD...
...FOR THE CHANCE TO ENCOUNTER SUCH A POWERFUL FOE.
GYUUU (GRIP)
ギュウウ
MY BEAST BLOOD TINGLES.
IT LOVES NOTHING MORE THAN BATTLE.
HE IS MY PREY.
HEH HEH.
HAS THE BEAST WITHIN ROUSED? IT'S ABOUT TIME.

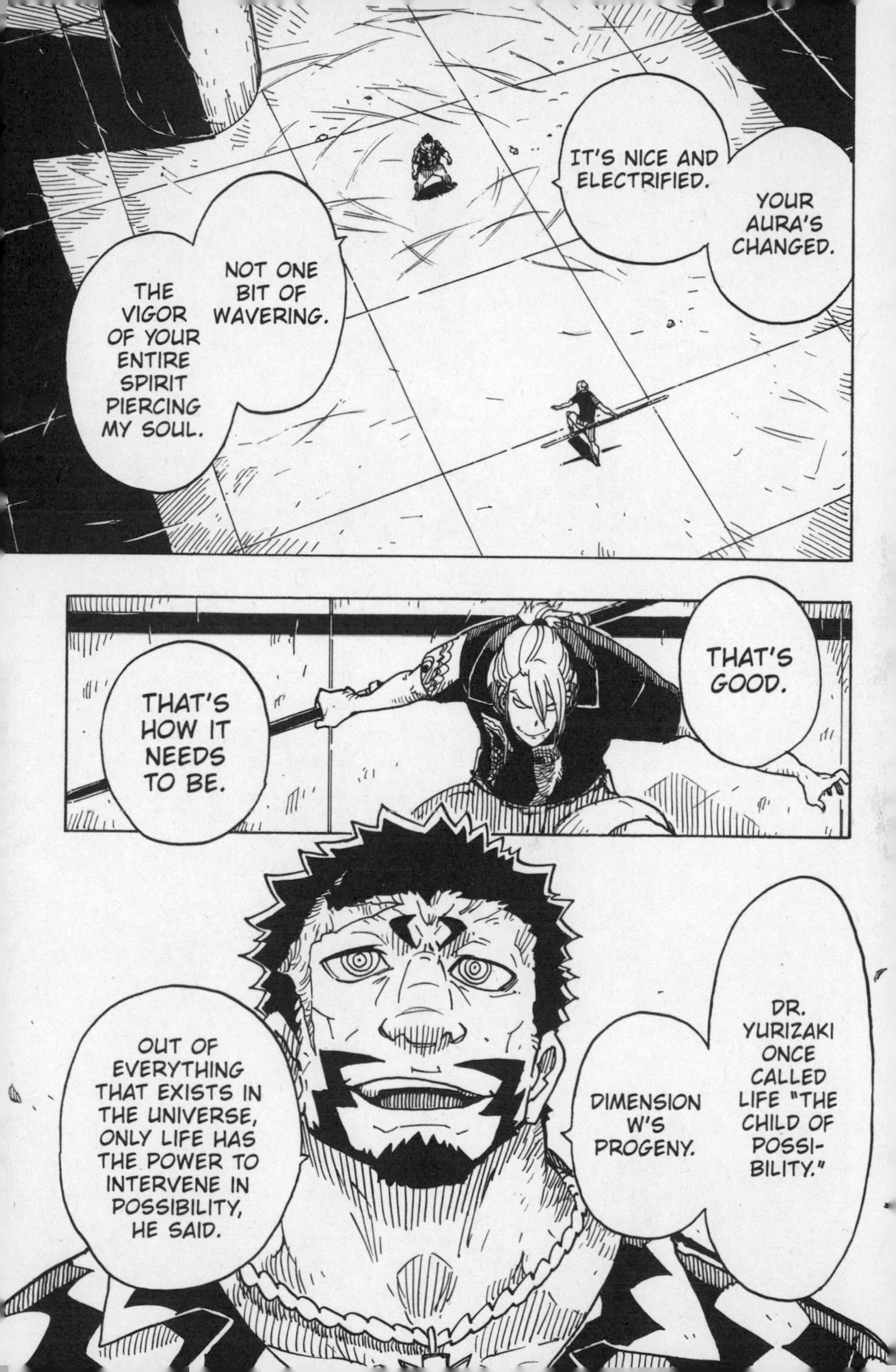
YOUR AURA'S CHANGED.
IT'S NICE AND ELECTRIFIED.
NOT ONE BIT OF WAVERING.
THE VIGOR OF YOUR ENTIRE SPIRIT PIERCING MY SOUL.
THAT'S GOOD.
THAT'S HOW IT NEEDS TO BE.
DR. YURIZAKI ONCE CALLED LIFE "THE CHILD OF POSSI-BILITY."
DIMENSION W'S PROGENY.
OUT OF EVERYTHING THAT EXISTS IN THE UNIVERSE, ONLY LIFE HAS THE POWER TO INTERVENE IN POSSIBILITY, HE SAID.

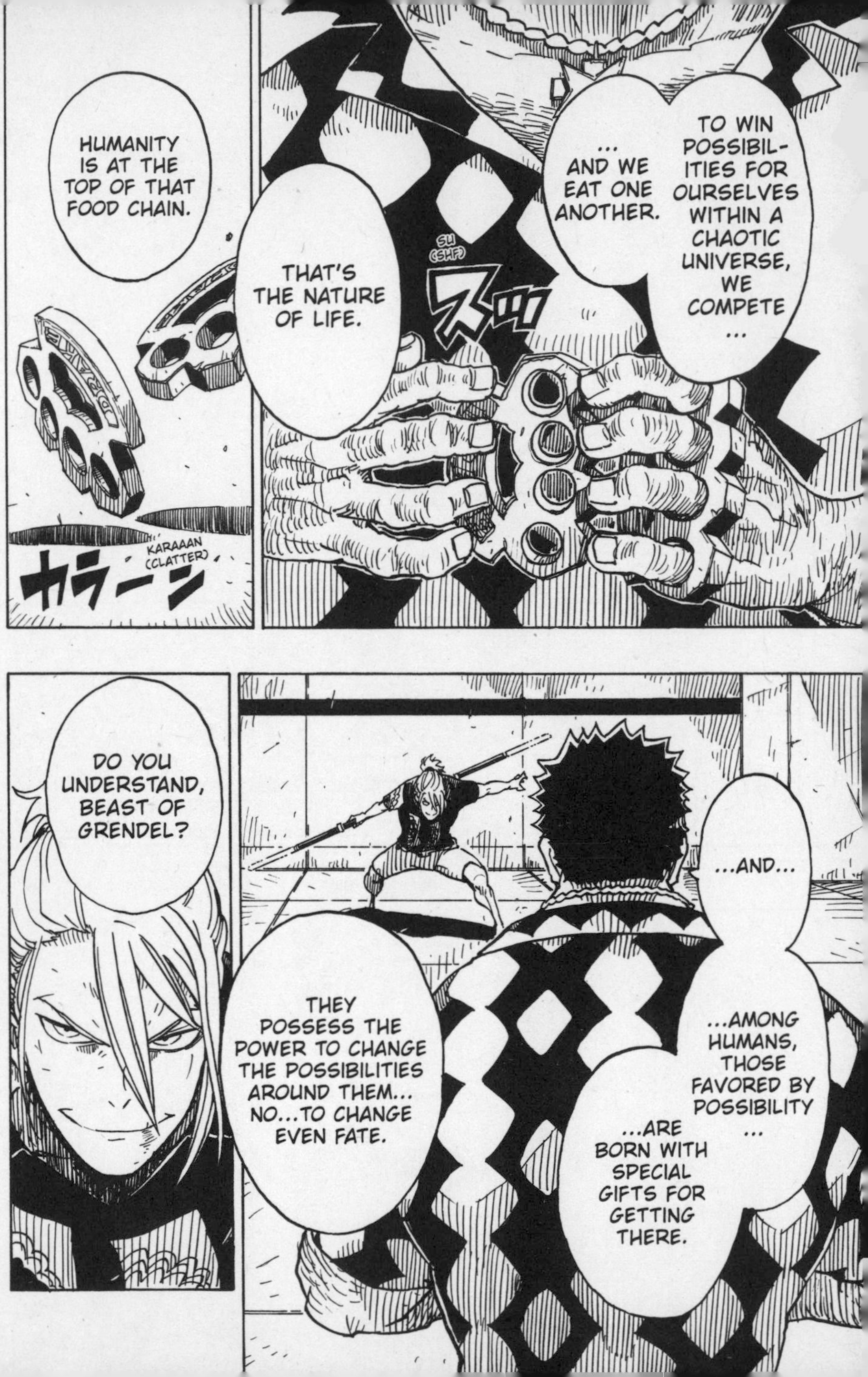
TO WIN POSSIBILITIES FOR OURSELVES WITHIN A CHAOTIC UNIVERSE, WE COMPETE ...
... AND WE EAT ONE ANOTHER.
SU (SHF)
THAT'S THE NATURE OF LIFE.
HUMANITY IS AT THE TOP OF THAT FOOD CHAIN.
KARAAAN (CLATTER)
...AND...
...AMONG HUMANS, THOSE FAVORED BY POSSIBILITY ...
...ARE BORN WITH SPECIAL GIFTS FOR GETTING THERE.
THEY POSSESS THE POWER TO CHANGE THE POSSIBILITIES AROUND THEM... NO...TO CHANGE EVEN FATE.
DO YOU UNDERSTAND, BEAST OF GRENDEL?

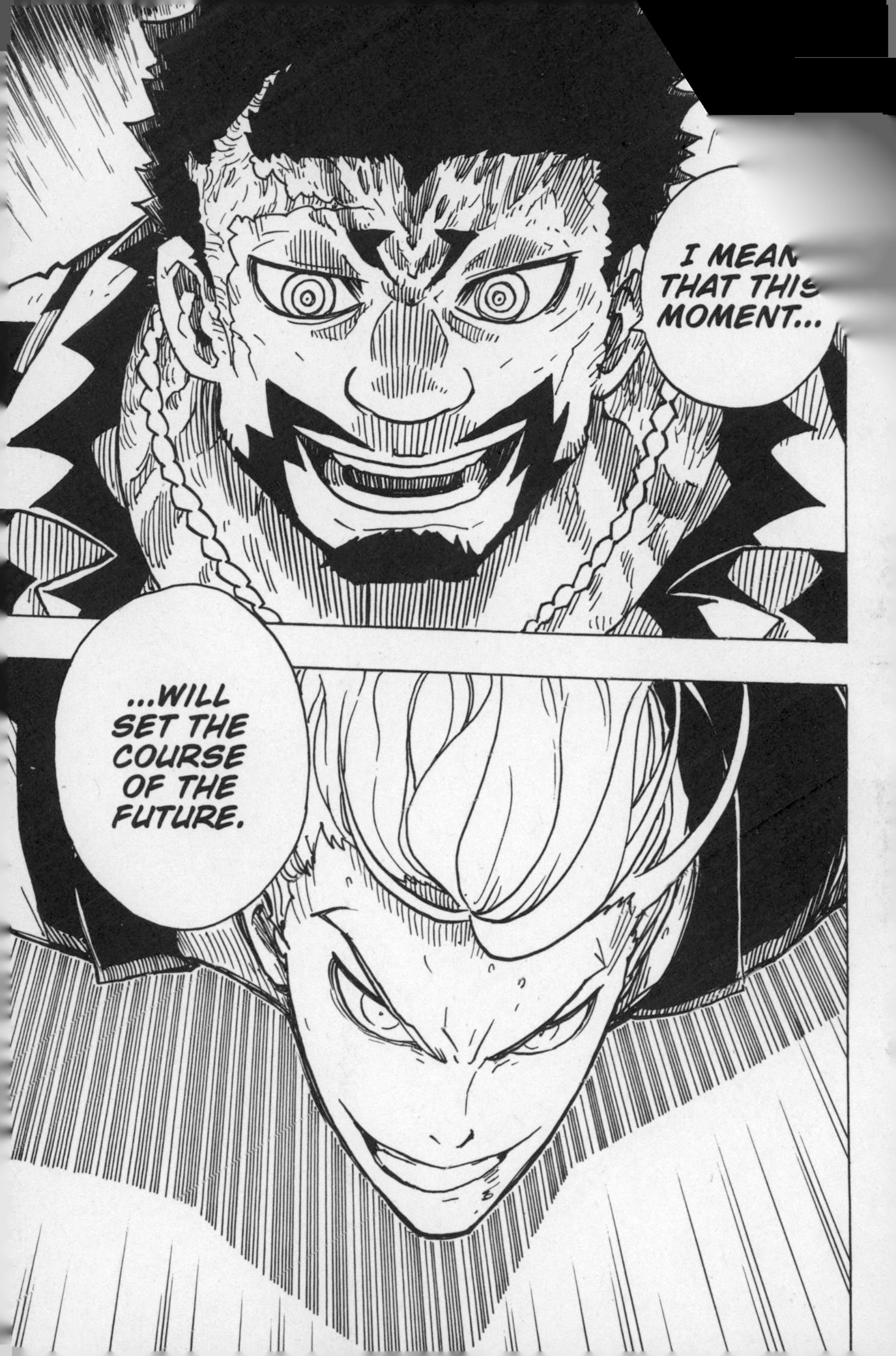
I MEAN THAT THIS MOMENT...
...WILL SET THE COURSE OF THE FUTURE.

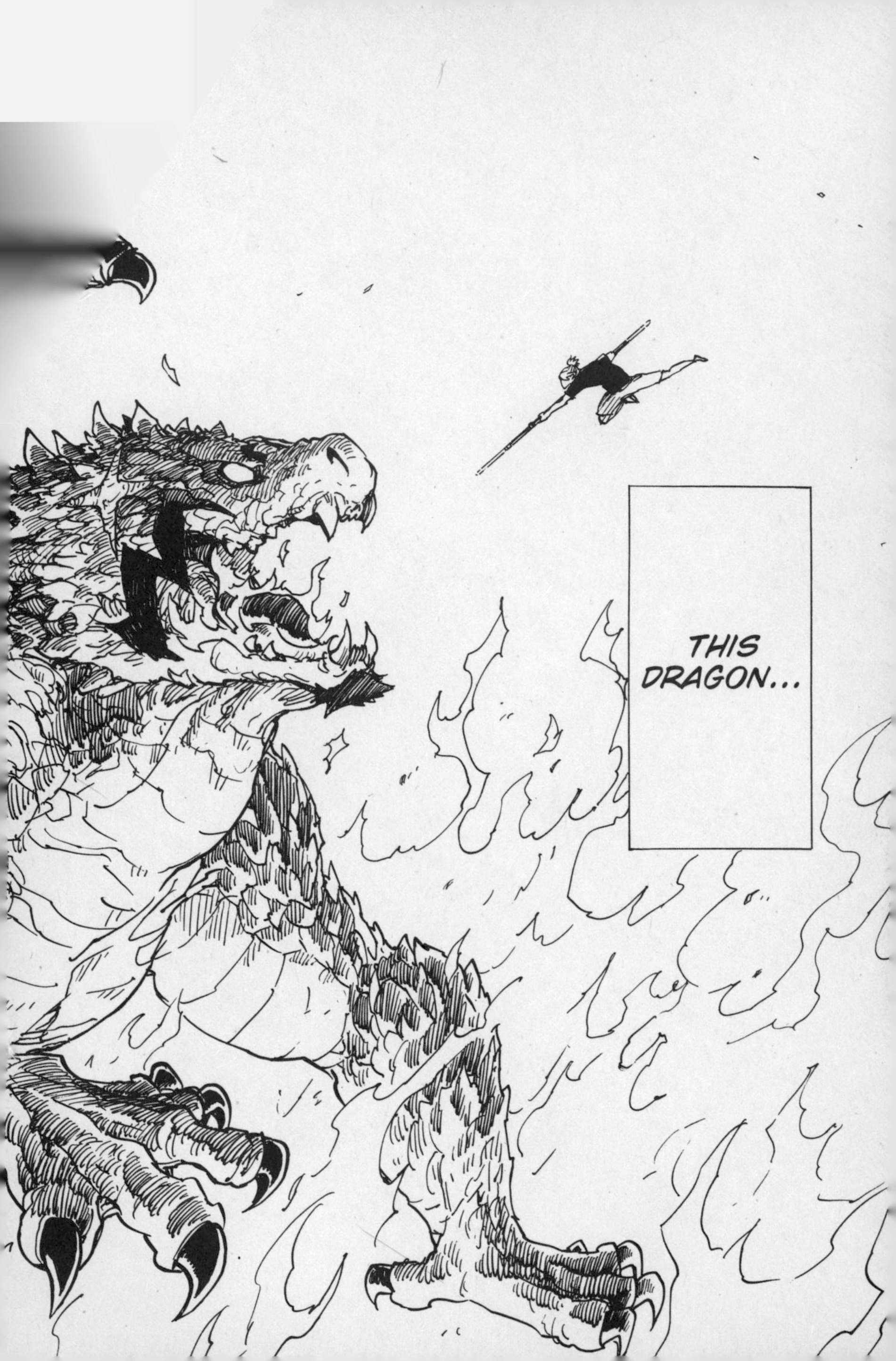
THIS DRAGON...

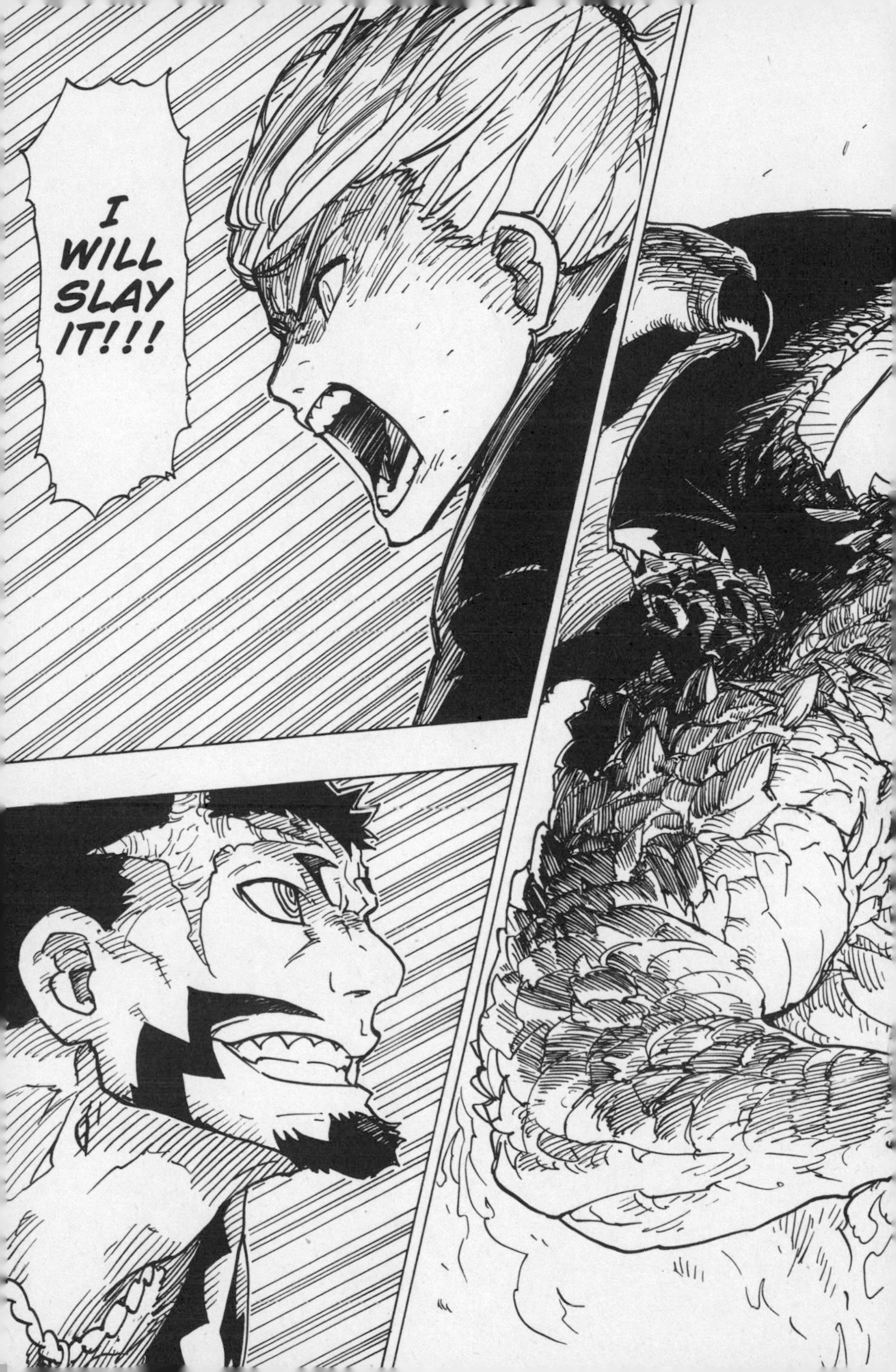
I WILL SLAY IT!!!

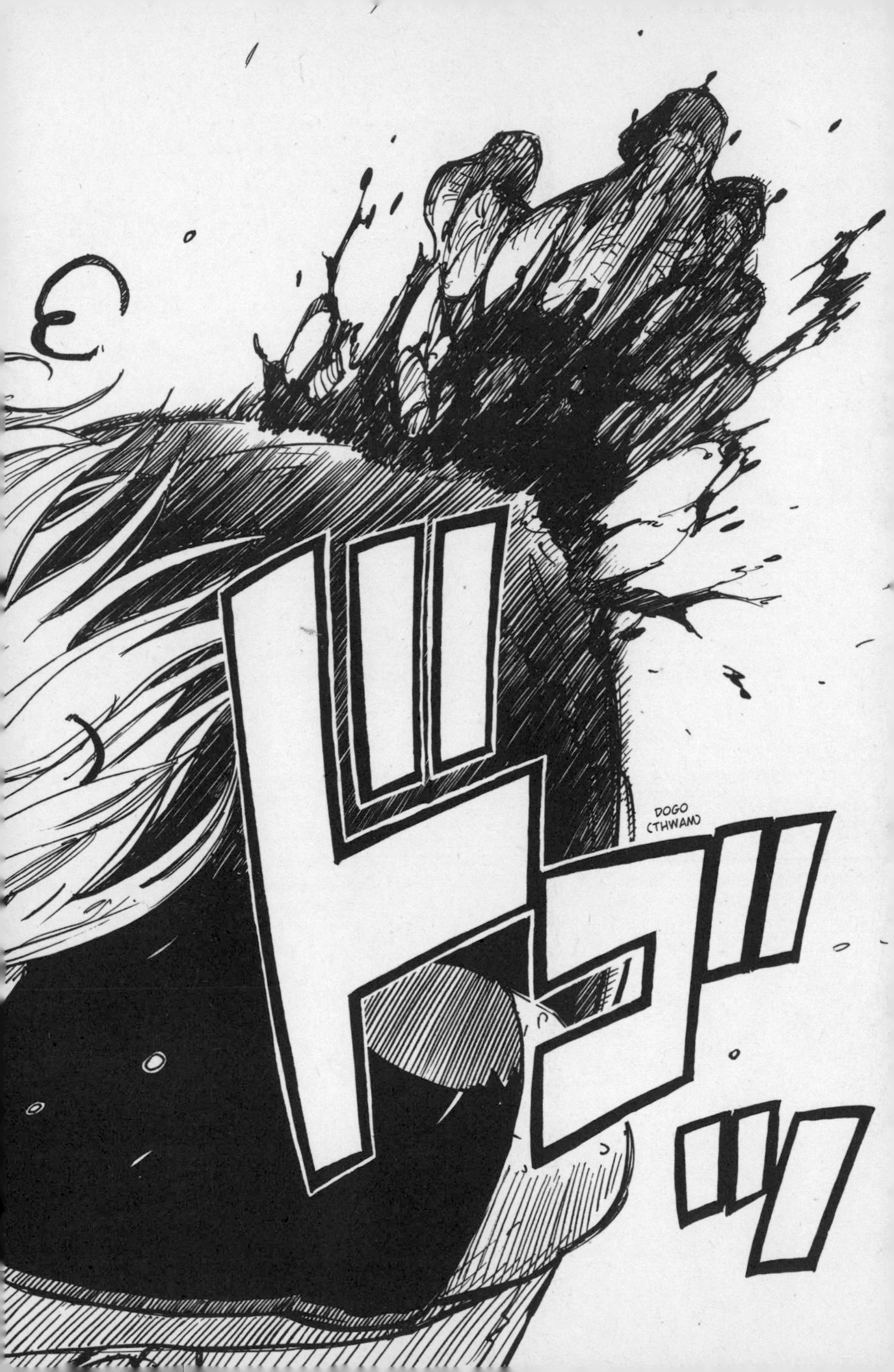
ドゴッ
DOGO
(THWAM)

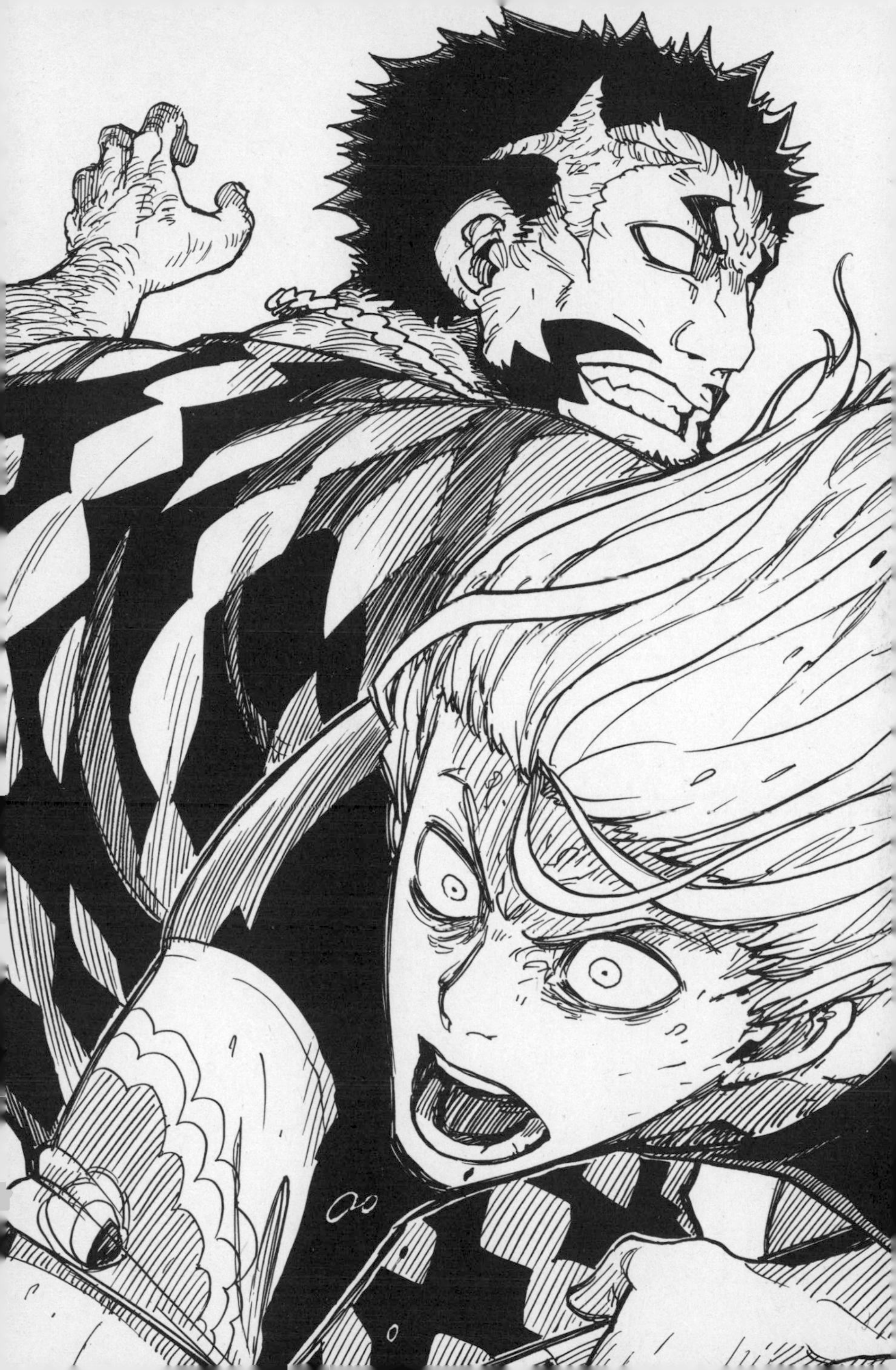

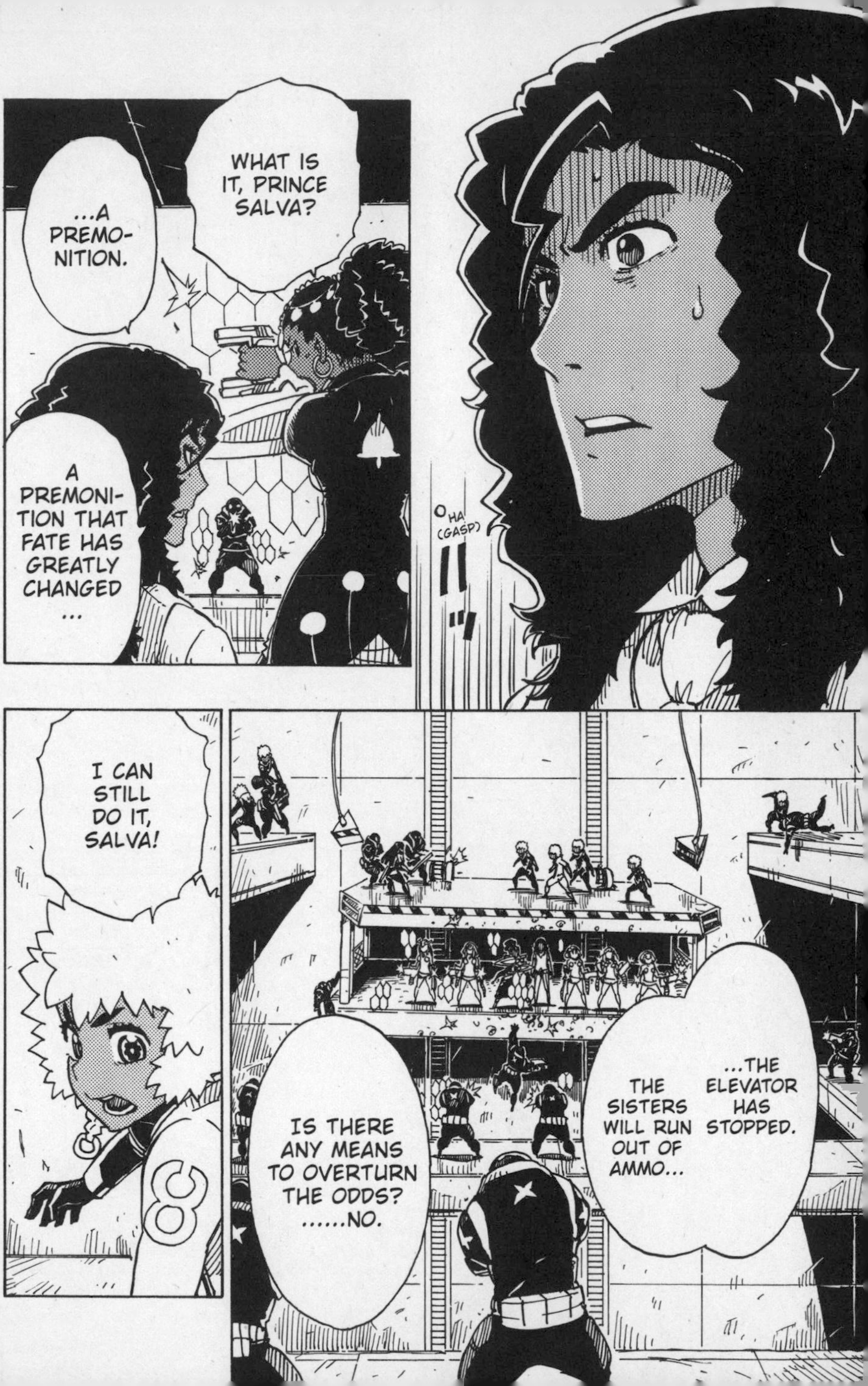
HA (GASP)
WHAT IS IT, PRINCE SALVA?
...A PREMO-NITION.
A PREMONI-TION THAT FATE HAS GREATLY CHANGED ...
...THE ELEVATOR HAS STOPPED.
THE SISTERS WILL RUN OUT OF AMMO...
IS THERE ANY MEANS TO OVERTURN THE ODDS? ......NO.
I CAN STILL DO IT, SALVA!

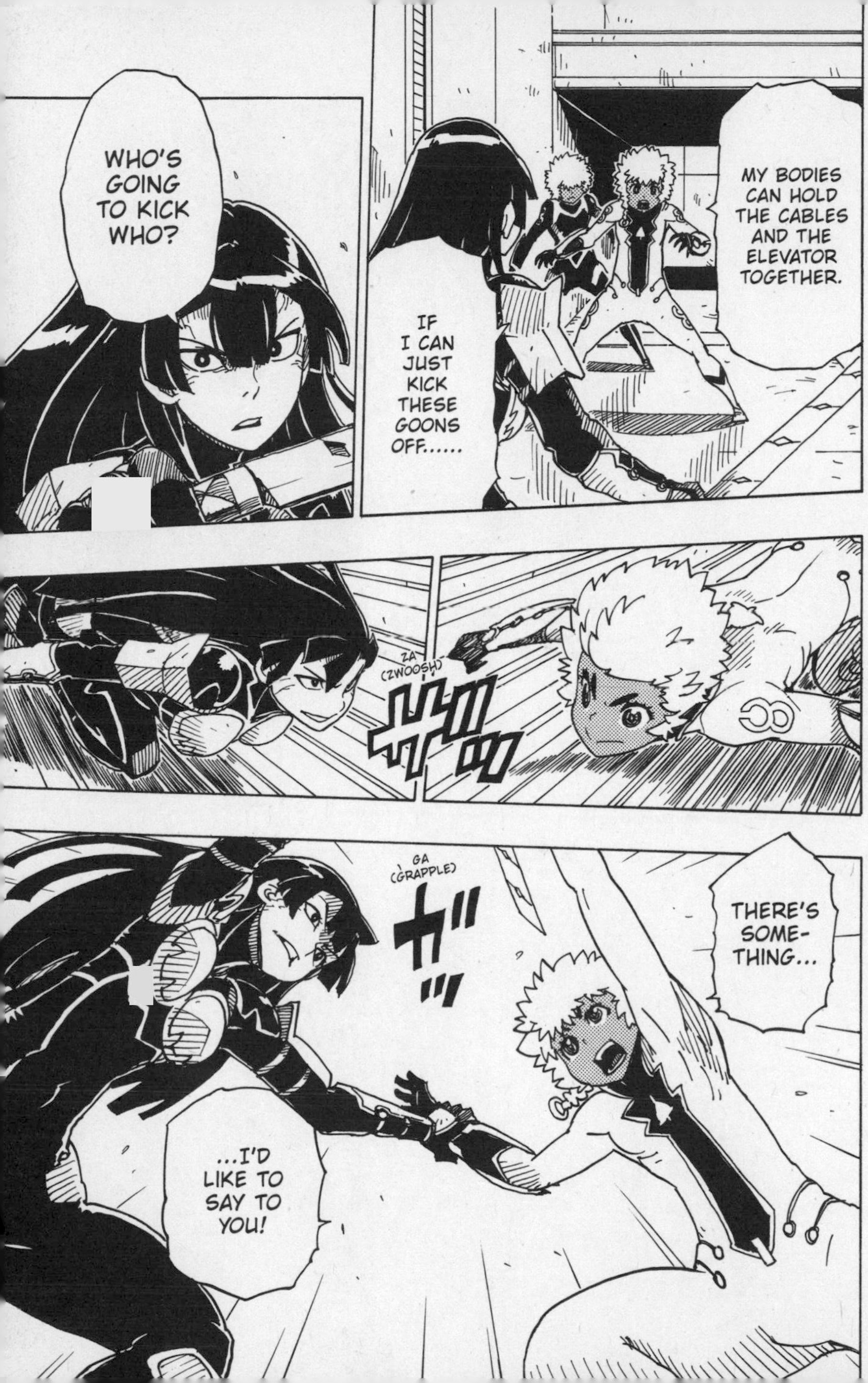
MY BODIES CAN HOLD THE CABLES AND THE ELEVATOR TOGETHER.
IF I CAN JUST KICK THESE GOONS OFF......
WHO'S GOING TO KICK WHO?
ZA (ZWOOSH)
GA (GRAPPLE)
THERE'S SOME-THING...
...I'D LIKE TO SAY TO YOU!

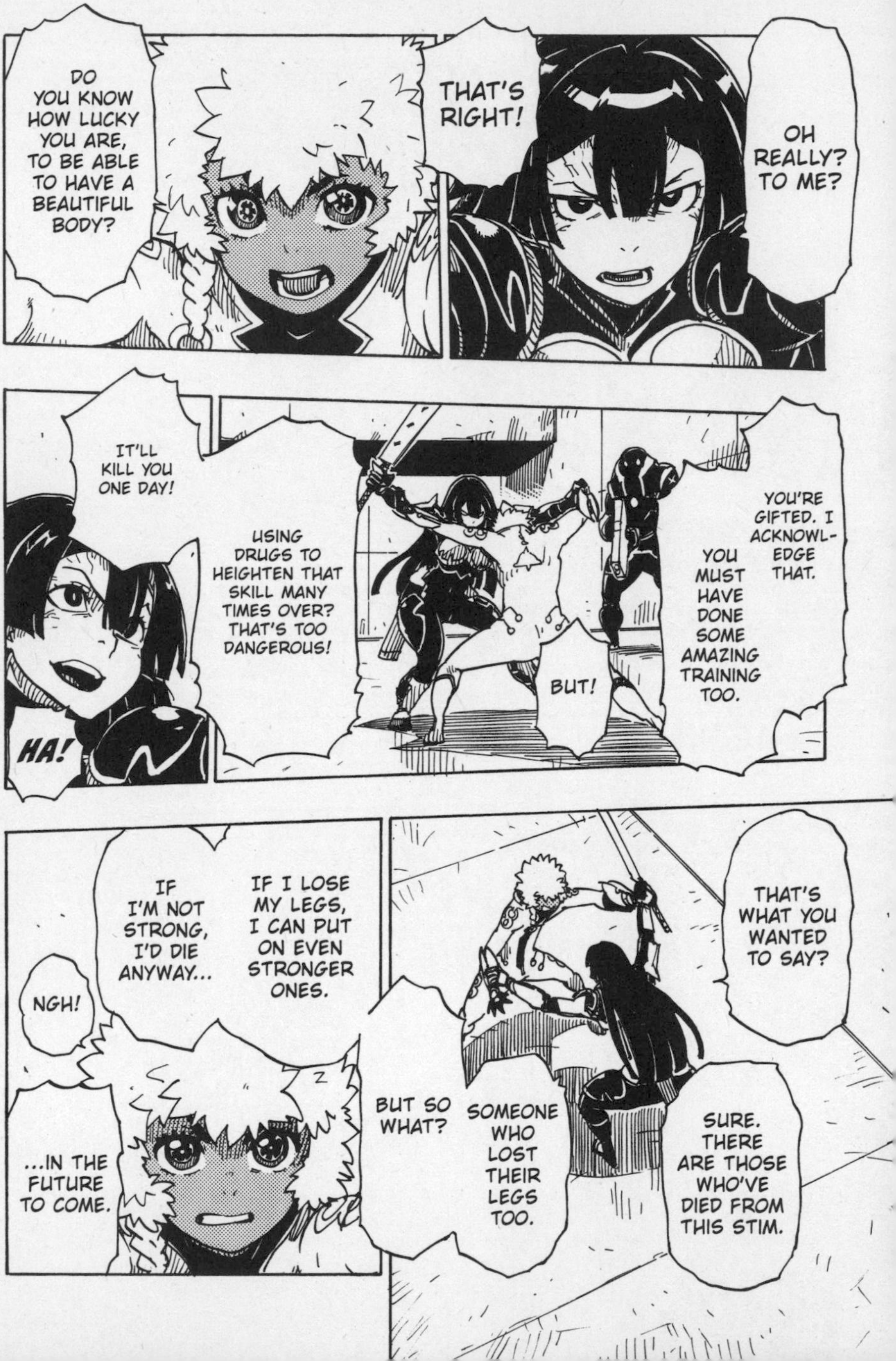
OH REALLY? TO ME?
THAT'S RIGHT!
DO YOU KNOW HOW LUCKY YOU ARE, TO BE ABLE TO HAVE A BEAUTIFUL BODY?
YOU'RE GIFTED. I ACKNOWL-EDGE THAT.
YOU MUST HAVE DONE SOME AMAZING TRAINING TOO.
BUT!
USING DRUGS TO HEIGHTEN THAT SKILL MANY TIMES OVER? THAT'S TOO DANGEROUS!
IT'LL KILL YOU ONE DAY!
HA!
THAT'S WHAT YOU WANTED TO SAY?
SURE. THERE ARE THOSE WHO'VE DIED FROM THIS STIM.
SOMEONE WHO LOST THEIR LEGS TOO.
BUT SO WHAT?
IF I LOSE MY LEGS, I CAN PUT ON EVEN STRONGER ONES.
IF I'M NOT STRONG, I'D DIE ANYWAY...
NGH!
...IN THE FUTURE TO COME.

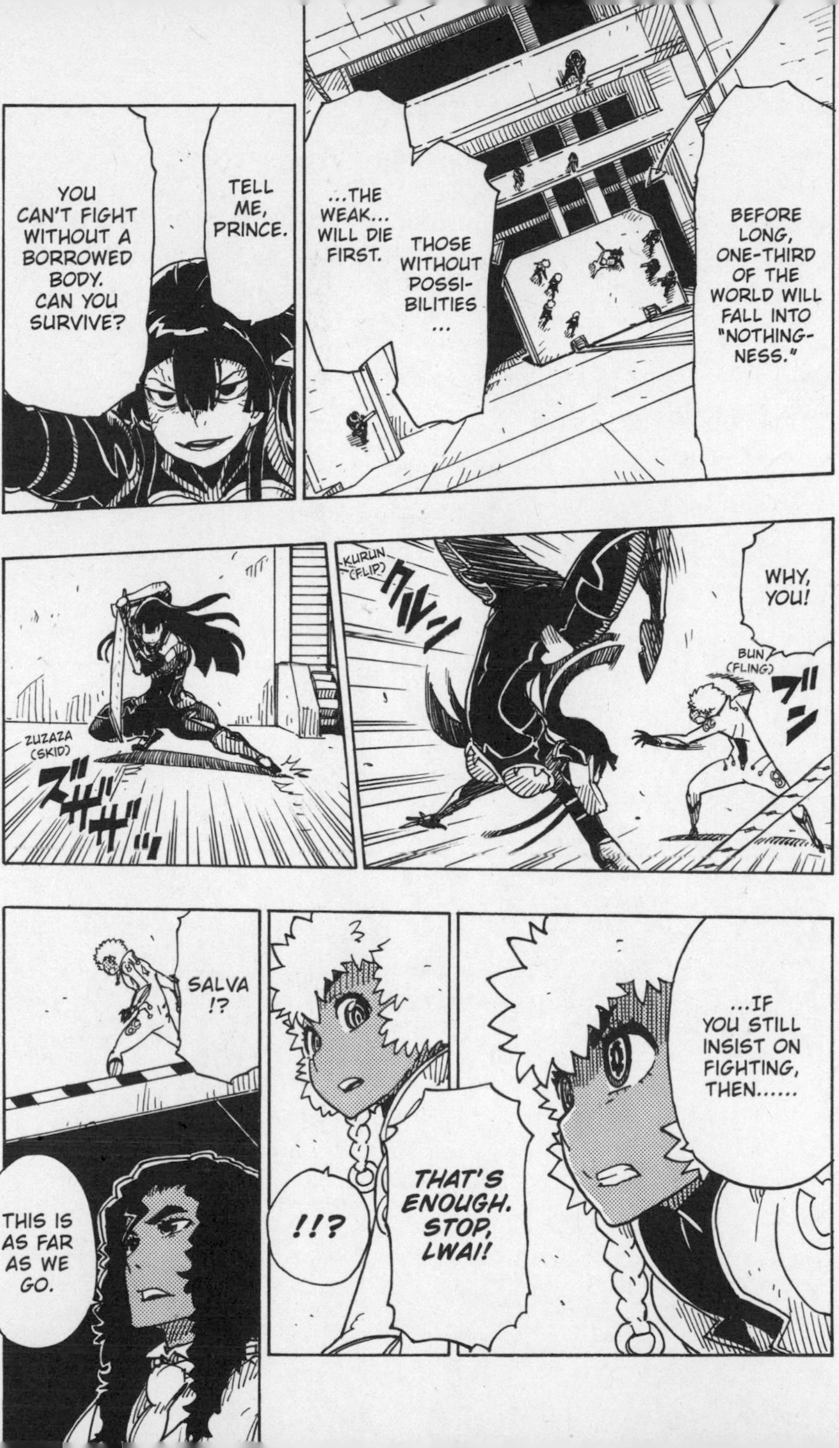
BEFORE LONG, ONE-THIRD OF THE WORLD WILL FALL INTO "NOTHINGNESS."
THOSE WITHOUT POSSIBILITIES ...
...THE WEAK... WILL DIE FIRST.
TELL ME, PRINCE.
YOU CAN'T FIGHT WITHOUT A BORROWED BODY. CAN YOU SURVIVE?
WHY, YOU!
BUN (FLING)
KURUN (FLIP)
ZUZAZA (SKID)
...IF YOU STILL INSIST ON FIGHTING, THEN......
THAT'S ENOUGH. STOP, LWAI!
!!?
SALVA !?
THIS IS AS FAR AS WE GO.

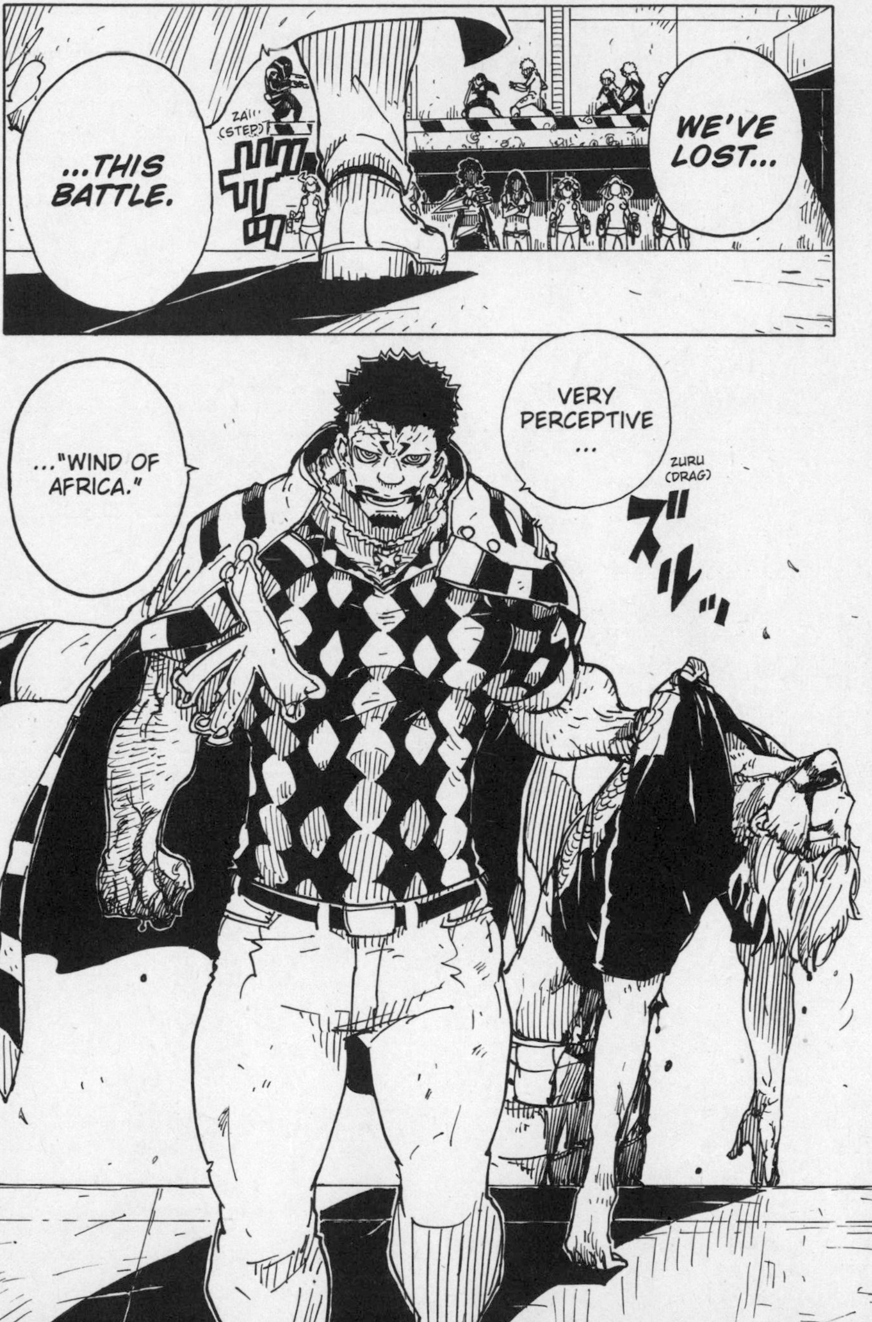
WE'VE LOST...
ZAI (STEP)
...THIS BATTLE.
VERY PERCEPTIVE ...
..."WIND OF AFRICA."
ZURU (DRAG)

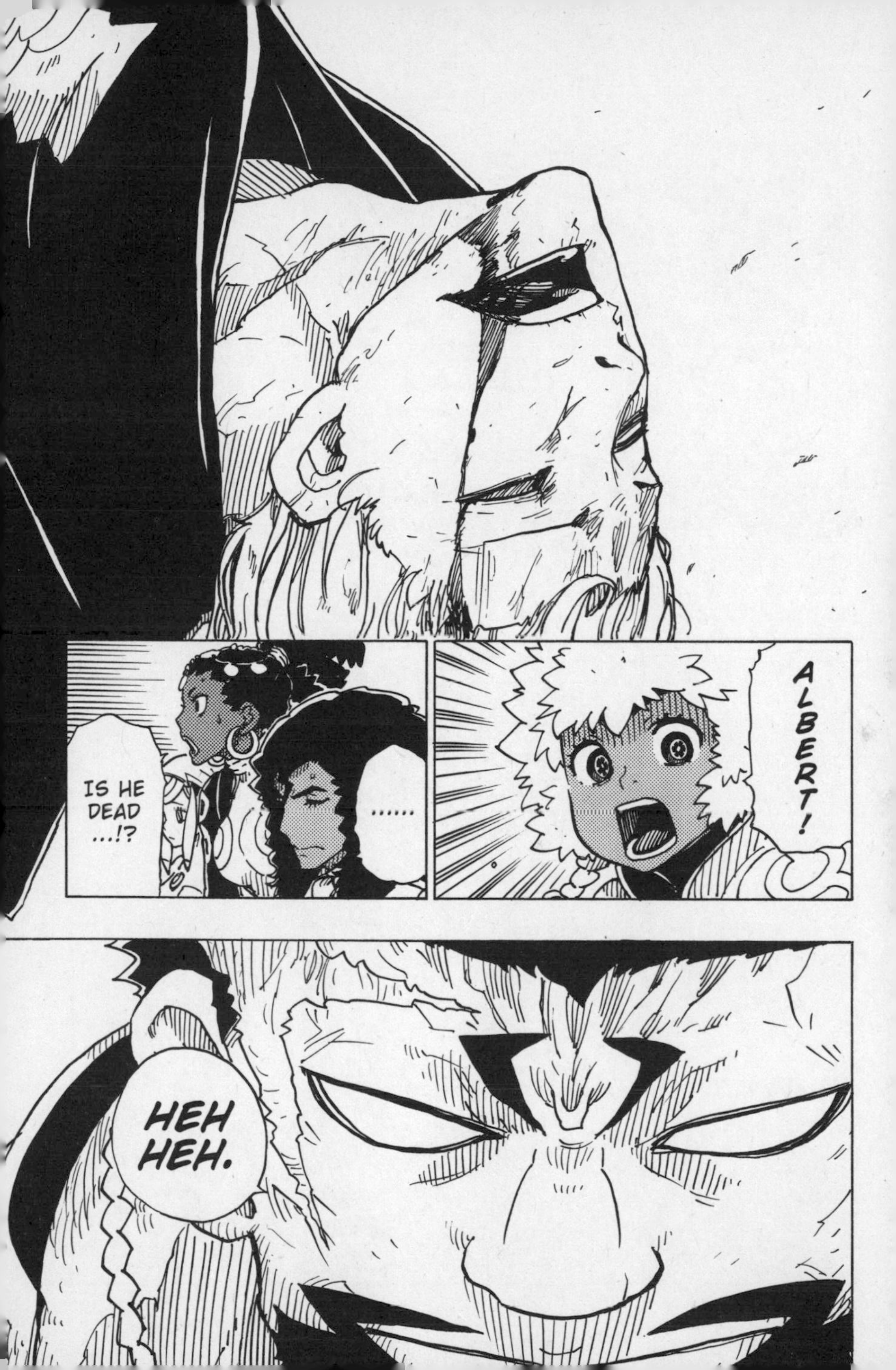

ALBERT!
......
IS HE DEAD ...!?
HEH HEH.

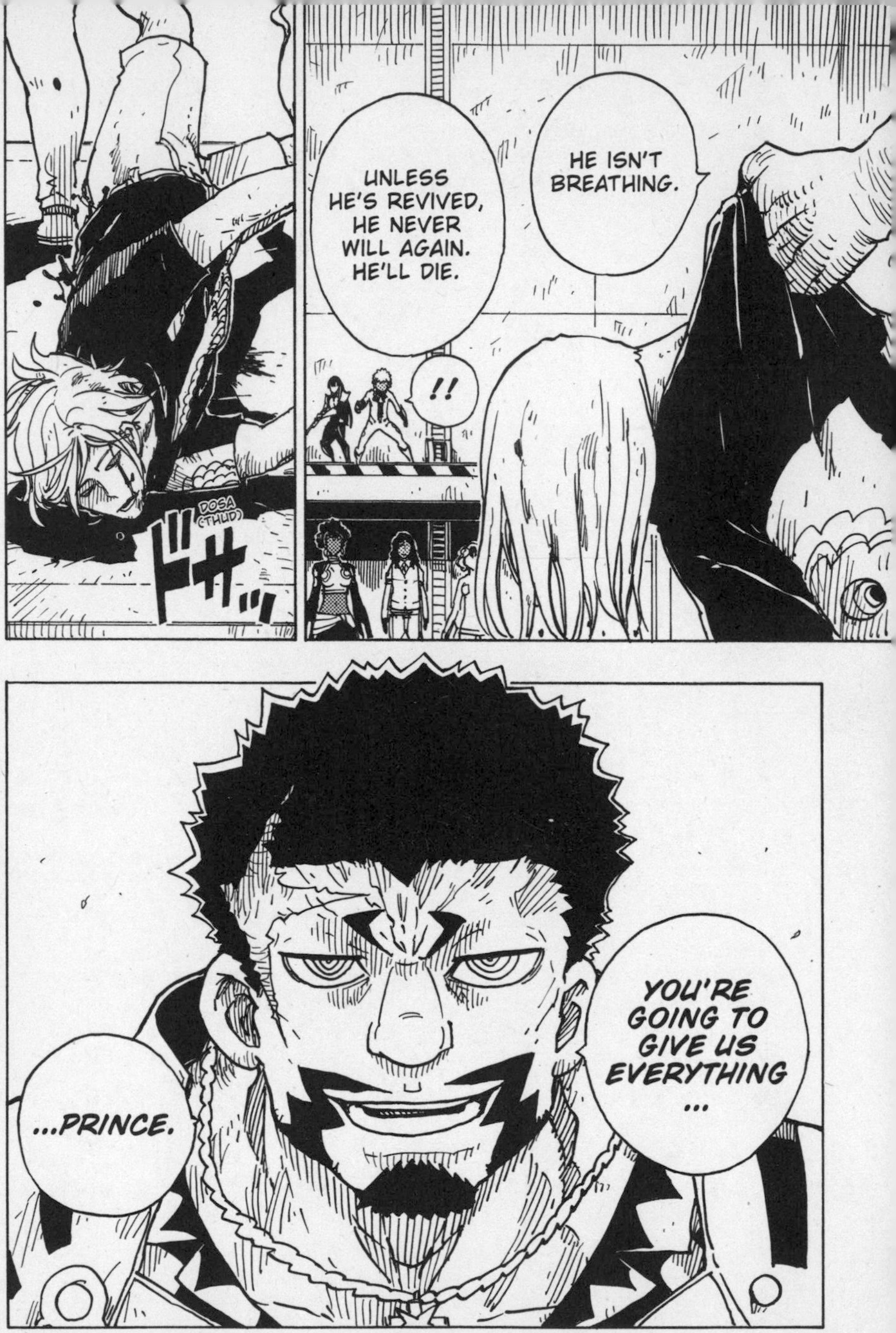
HE ISN'T BREATHING.
UNLESS HE'S REVIVED, HE NEVER WILL AGAIN. HE'LL DIE.
!!
DOSA (THUD)
ドサッ
YOU'RE GOING TO GIVE US EVERYTHING ...
...PRINCE.

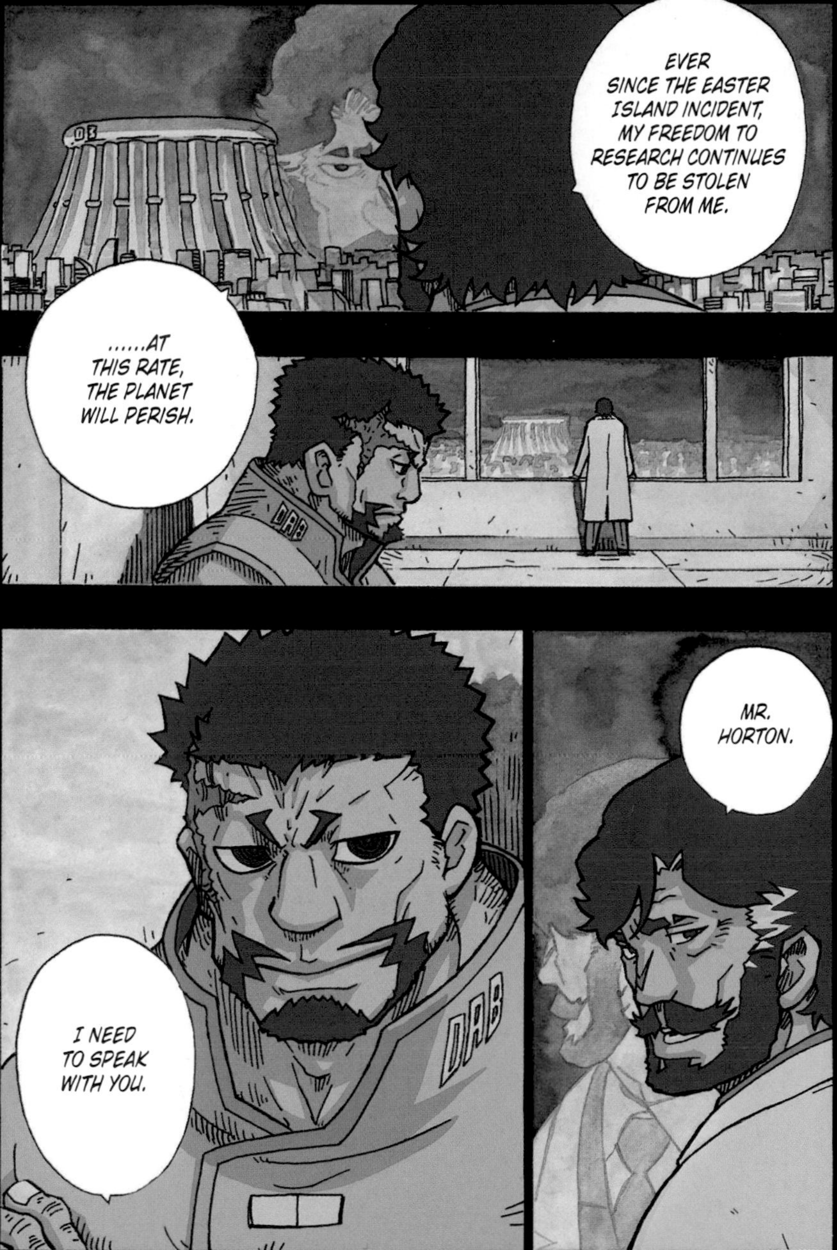
EVER SINCE THE EASTER ISLAND INCIDENT, MY FREEDOM TO RESEARCH CONTINUES TO BE STOLEN FROM ME.
......AT THIS RATE, THE PLANET WILL PERISH.
D.A.B
MR. HORTON.
I NEED TO SPEAK WITH YOU.
D.A.B

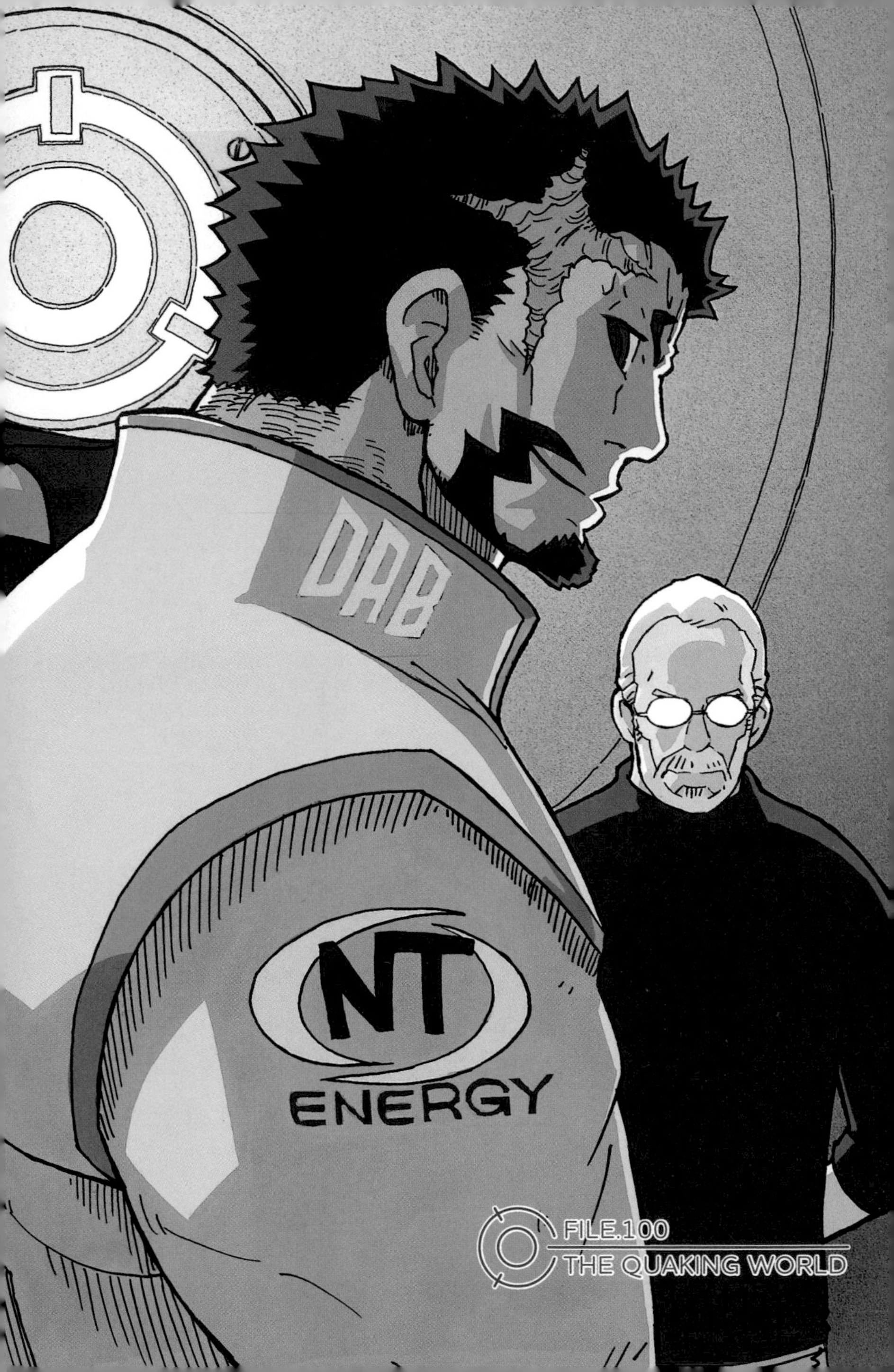
DAB
NT
ENERGY
FILE.100
THE QUAKING WORLD